*FM 3-09.21 (FM 6-20-1)

Field Manual
No. 3-09.21

Headquarters
Department of the Army
Washington, DC, 22 March 2001

Tactics, Techniques and Procedures for THE FIELD ARTILLERY BATTALION

Contents

	Page
PREFACE	viii
Chapter 1 **TASKS AND RESPONSIBILITIES**	1-1
Section I – Tasks and FA Organization for Combat	1-1
Tasks	1-1
FA Organization for Combat	1-1
Section II – Responsibilities of Key Personnel	1-9
Command Section	1-9
Battalion Operations Section	1-16
Battalion Intelligence Section	1-17
Battalion Fire Direction Center	1-18
Battalion Ammunition Officer	1-19
Fire Support Elements	1-19
Liaison Officer	1-19
Radar Section Leader	1-21

Distribution Restriction: Approved for public release. Distribution is unlimited.

*This publication supersedes FM 6-20-1, 25 November 1990.

FM 3-09.21 (FM 6-20-1)

Chapter 2	COMMAND POST OPERATIONS	2-1
	Section I – The FA Battalion Command Post	2-1
	CP Composition	2-2
	Section II – TOC Organization	2-5
	TOC Organization	2-5
	TOC Battle Staff Organization	2-7
	Section III – TOC Configurations	2-9
	Towed Cannon Battalion TOC Layout (Example)	2-9
	SP Cannon Battalion TOC Layout (Example)	2-10
	MLRS Battalion TOC Layout (Example)	2-11
	TOC Equipment	2-11
	Section IV – TOC Information Management	2-12
	Management of Tactical Information	2-12
	Information Management Tools	2-14
	Section V – CP Positioning and Movement	2-19
	CP Positioning Considerations	2-19
	Jump TOC Considerations	2-20
	CP Movement Techniques	2-21
	Section VI – Liaison Operations	2-23
	Liaison Organization	2-23
	Responsibilities	2-24
	Example LNO Checklist	2-26
	Example Outline of a LNO's Handbook/TSOP	2-28
Chapter 3	COMMAND and CONTROL	3-1
	Section I – General Communications Information	3-1
	Communications Responsibilities	3-4
	Battalion S6 Section Responsibilities	3-5
	Planning Considerations	3-6
	Section II – Command and Control Systems	3-9
	Army Battle Command Systems	3-9
	FA Tactical Data Systems	3-9
	Automation Considerations	3-10
	Section III – Radio Communications Systems	3-12
	Combat Net Radios	3-12
	FA Battalion Radio Nets	3-13
	Direct Support Mission	3-20
	Reinforcing Mission	3-22
	General Support Reinforcing Mission	3-23

	General Support Mission	3-24
Chapter 4	**THE FIELD ARTILLERY BATTALION PLANNING PROCESS**	**4-1**
	Section I – The Military Decision-Making Process	**4-1**
	Receive The Mission / Mission Analysis	4-3
	COA Development	4-13
	Courses of Action Analysis (Wargame)	4-16
	COA Comparison	4-18
	COA Approval	4-18
	FSP / FASP Production	4-18
	Summary	4-22
	Section II – FA Intelligence Preparation of the Battlefield	**4-25**
	Steps In FA IPB Process	4-25
	Section III – FA Battalion Rehearsals	**4-32**
	Rehearsal Principles	4-32
	Rehearsal Types	4-32
	Rehearsal Techniques	4-32
	Scripting the Rehearsal	4-33
	Conducting A Rehearsal	4-33
	Scheduling Rehearsals	4-34
	FA Battalion Rehearsals	4-36
Chapter 5	**DELIVER FIRES**	**5-1**
	Section I – Fire Mission Processing	**5-1**
	Fire Mission Requests	5-3
	Tactical Fire Direction	5-4
	Technical Fire Direction	5-7
	Massed Fires	5-8
	Continuity of Operations	5-8
	Section I – FA Fire Missions	**5-10**
	Improved Conventional Munitions (ICM)	5-10
	Illumination	5-11
	Smoke/White Phosphorous (WP)	5-12
	SCATMINE	5-17
	Copperhead	5-20
	Danger Close	5-22
	Section III – Counterfire	**5-24**
	Responsibilities	5-24
	Counterfire Considerations	5-26
	Radar Management	5-28

	Wargaming	5-31
	Rehearsing Counterfire	5-33
	Counterfire Drill	5-33
	Theater Missile Defense	5-34
	Section IV – Suppression of Enemy Air Defenses	5-36
	Considerations	5-37
	Section V – Meteorology	5-39
	Joint/Combined Met Considerations	5-39
	Basic Met Guidance	5-40
Chapter 6	**MOVEMENT AND POSITIONING CONSIDERATIONS**	6-1
	Section I – Terrain Management	6-1
	Position Coordination	6-2
	Movement Coordination	6-3
	Section II – Positioning	6-5
	Position Area Selection Considerations	6-5
	Types of Position Areas	6-5
	Occupation of Built-Up Areas	6-9
	Reconnaissance	6-10
	Section III – Movement	6-12
	Movement Techniques	6-12
	Movement Considerations	6-17
	Displacement Techniques	6-18
	Movement Control Measures	6-19
	Movement Planning	6-22
	Section IV – Survey	6-26
	Survey Planning Factors	6-27
	Section V – Deployment	6-29
	Deployment Readiness	6-29
	Deployment	6-30
Chapter 7	**COMBAT SERVICE SUPPORT**	7-1
	Section I – Organization and Functions	7-1
	Section Responsibilities	7-2
	FA Battalion CSS	7-4
	FA Battalion Trains	7-6
	Section II – Planning	7-14
	CSS Planning Process	7-14
	Planning for Changing Missions	7-16

	Special CSS Planning Considerations	7-16
	Section III – Logistical Support	7-18
	Supply	7-18
	Maintenance	7-30
	Field Services	7-33
	Section IV – Personnel and Health Services Support	7-35
	Personnel and Administrative Services	7-35
	Chaplain Activities	7-36
	Health Services Support	7-37
	Prisoners of War	7-39
	Section V – Reconstitution	7-41
	Reorganization	7-41
	Regeneration	7-41
	Weapon System Replacement Operations	7-41
Chapter 8	**FA OPERATIONS**	**8-1**
	Section I – Common FA Considerations	8-1
	Deploy/Conduct Maneuver	8-1
	Develop Intelligence	8-1
	Employ Fires	8-2
	Perform Logistics and CSS	8-2
	Exercise C2	8-3
	Protect the Force	8-3
	Section II – FA Support of Offensive Operations	8-4
	Basic FA Tasks in the Offense	8-4
	Forms of Maneuver	8-6
	Movement to Contact/Search and Attack	8-9
	Attacks	8-10
	Exploitation	8-12
	Pursuit	8-13
	Reserves	8-14
	Section III – FA Support of Defensive Operations	8-16
	Organization of the Defensive Battlefield	8-16
	Basic FA Tasks in the Defense	8-17
	Mobile Defense	8-20
	Area Defense	8-20
	Retrograde Operations	8-21
	Additional FA Considerations for Defensive Operations	8-21

Section IV – FA Support of Other Tactical Operations 8-23
Amphibious Operations 8-23
Air Assault Operations.. 8-25
Airborne Operations 8-26
Military Operations in Urban Terrain 8-28
Encircled Forces 8-31
Passage of Lines 8-32
Relief in Place 8-32
River Crossing Operations 8-33
Security Operations 8-34
Rear Area Operations 8-35
Linkup Operations 8-37
Breaching Operations 8-38
Artillery Raid Operations 8-38

Section V – FA Support of Stability Operations and Support Operations 8-42
Stability Operations 8-42
FA Support of Stability Operations 8-43
Support Operations 8-45
FA Support of Support Operations 8-46

Section VI – Climate and Terrain Considerations 8-48
Night Operations 8-48
Cold Weather Operations 8-50
Desert Operations 8-52
Jungle Operations 8-54
Mountain Operations 8-56

Appendix A **FIELD ARTILLERY SUPPORT PLAN** A-1

Section I – Field Artillery Support Plan Format A-1
FASP Outline A-1
Survey Tab to the FASP A-8
Automation Tab to the FASP A-8
Target Acquisition Tab to the FASP A-8
Artillery Intelligence Tab to the FASP A-8
Administrative-Logistics Tab to the FASP A-8
FA Support Matrix Tab to the FASP A-9

Section II – Example Field Artillery Support Plan A-11
FASP – Body (Example) A-12
Example Field Artillery Support Matrix (Tab) A-23
Example Positioning Overlay (Tab) A-24

	Example Target Acquisition Tab	A-25
	Example Radar Deployment Order (Enclosure to Tab)	A-28
	Example Capabilities Overlay (Enclosure to Tab)	A-29
	Example Survey Plan	A-30
Appendix B	**MANUAL TARGETING AND FIRE PLANNING**	B-1
	Section I – Manual Target Data Processing	B-1
	Recording Target Information	B-1
	Recording Targeting Information (Graphics)	B-3
	Battle Damage Assessment	B-6
	Purging Targets	B-6
	Section II – Manual Scheduling of Fires	B-8
	Planning Fires	B-8
	MLRS Fire Planning	B-18
Appendix C	**ENVIRONMENTAL AWARENESS**	C-1
	Section I – Army Environmental Awareness	C-1
	General Policy Statements	C-1
	Section II – FA Battalion Environmental Considerations	C-2
	Field Activities	C-2
	Munitions	C-3
	Hazardous Material and Hazardous Waste	C-3
	Maintenance	C-5
	Supply	C-6
	Spill Response	C-6
	Section III – Regulatory Requirements	C-8
	Laws and Regulations	C-8
	Regulatory Training Requirements	C-9
	Environmental Compliance Officer Responsibilities	C-10
	Section IV – Environmental Risk Management	C-11
	Environmental Risk Management	C-11
	The Five-Step Process	C-11
Glossary		Glossary-1
Bibliography		Bibliography-1
Index		Index-1

Preface

This field manual (FM) provides tactics, techniques, and procedures (TTP) for the commander and staff in field artillery (FA) battalions. It is intended as a general "how to" manual to assist in force standardization with sufficient flexibility to adapt to local conditions as reflected in unit tactical standing operating procedures (TSOP).

The publication sets forth doctrine pertaining to organization, command and control (C2), operations, and TTP for the FA battalions. It establishes responsibilities and general duties of key personnel by focusing on how an FA battalion supports the full spectrum of military operations.

It keys the battalion commander and staff to areas that must receive training emphasis in order to provide effective FA support. The specifics of how to train are outlined in soldiers' manuals and Army training and evaluation program (ARTEP) mission training plans (MTPs).

This manual applies to United States (US) Army and US Marine Corps (USMC) FA battalions assigned to the active, reserve, and National Guard (NG) forces. Unit organizations described in this publication reflect, in general overview, the L/A/F-series Department of the Army (DA) tables of organization and equipment (TOEs). Full consideration is given to recent and planned force structure changes and emerging technological opportunities – as of the date of publication.

The publication broadly describes how the FA battalion operates to support the combined arms team using available Field Artillery Tactical Data Systems (FATDS), and other automated C2 systems.

This FM addresses combat operations in support of both heavy and light maneuver forces, as well as stability operations and support operations and FA (support) operations in special environments. It is not a stand-alone document; but should be used in conjunction with maneuver and other FA doctrinal manuals.

The manual focuses on FA battalions performing the missions of direct support (DS) or general support (GS) to maneuver forces, as well as FA units providing reinforcing (R) or general support reinforcing (GSR) fires to other FA units in support of force operations.

This publication implements all applicable North Atlantic Treaty Organization (NATO) standardization agreements (STANAGs) (see the bibliography for a complete listing).

The proponent for this manual is the Commandant, US Army Field Artillery School. Submit changes for improving this publication on DA Form 2028 (Recommended Changes to Publications and Blank Forms). Please key your comments and recommendations to the page, paragraph, and line numbers to which they apply. If DA Form 2028 is not available, a letter is acceptable. Provide reasons for your comments to ensure complete understanding and proper evaluation.

Unless this publication states otherwise, masculine nouns or pronouns do not exclusively pertain to men.

Chapter 1

Tasks and Responsibilities

This chapter provides an overview of the tasks and responsibilities for a FA battalion. Section I discusses the basic tasks for a FA battalion and FA organization for combat. Section II outlines the responsibilities of key battalion personnel. This manual focuses on those TTP that are common to most FA battalions. For information unique to a specific type of FA battalion or battery, the reader should also refer to FM 6-50, *Tactics, Techniques, and Procedures for the Field Artillery Cannon Battery*; FM 6-60, *Tactics, Techniques, and Procedures for Multiple Launch Rocket System (MLRS) Operations*; and FM 3-09.6, *Tactics, Techniques, and Procedures for M109A6 Howitzer (Paladin) Operations*.

SECTION I – TASKS AND FA ORGANIZATION FOR COMBAT

TASKS

1-01. In combat, the FA battalion provides indirect fire support (FS) to maneuver forces on the battlefield. To do this, it must perform six basic tasks:
- Deploy/Conduct Maneuver
- Develop Intelligence
- Employ Fires
- Perform Combat Service Support (CSS) and Sustainment
- Exercise C2
- Protect the Force

1-02. These six tasks form a starting point in identifying all of the responsibilities that a FA battalion has as part of a combined arms force. Units receive additional responsibilities during the organization for combat process.

FA ORGANIZATION FOR COMBAT

1-03. A FA battalion's basic C2 guidelines and responsibilities are established by its organization for combat. FA organization for combat is a two-step process involving the establishment of a command relationship and the assignment of a FA tactical mission. While FA organization for combat is usually a division or corps level process, FA battalion commanders and staffs should have a thorough knowledge of the principles of the process, and most especially, the implications for the battalion of the various command relationships and FA tactical missions.

1-04. This section provides an overview on FA organization for combat from a FA battalion perspective. Detailed information on organizing FA for combat is contained in FM 6-20-2, *Tactics, Techniques, and Procedures for Corps Artillery, Division Artillery, and Field Artillery Brigade Operations*.

COMMAND RELATIONSHIPS

1-05. The first step in organizing FA for combat is the establishment of a command relationship with a senior headquarters (HQ). This relationship is normally established with a FA HQ, such as a division artillery (DIVARTY), corps artillery (Corps Arty), or FA brigade. However, it can be established with a maneuver HQ. C2 ensures that FA contributes total, responsive FS that adequately supports the mission. The most common C2 relationships between a FA battalion and another unit are: organic, assigned, attached, or operational control (OPCON).

Organic

1-06. This relationship is the most permanent type of C2 relationship between an element and a military organization. Normally, this is done at the Department of Defense (DOD) or DA level and is shown in the unit TOE or modified TOE (MTOE). An example is a Firefinder radar (AN/TPQ-36) section organic to a 105 millimeter (mm) cannon battalion in an infantry division.

Assigned

1-07. This relationship places units or personnel in an organization on a relatively permanent basis. The gaining organization controls, administers, and provides logistical support to the assigned unit or personnel. Assignment is normally a DOD or DA level action done as part of the strategic tailoring process. An example is an FA battalion assigned to a division.

Attached

1-08. Attachment temporarily places units or personnel under the C2 of another organization. Subject to limitations imposed by the attachment order, the commander of the gaining unit receiving the attachment exercises the same degree of C2 over the attached unit as he does over organic units. The parent unit, however, retains the responsibility for transfer and promotion of personnel. The attachment order should clearly state the administrative and support responsibilities of the gaining unit to the attached unit. Attachment is frequently used as part of the tactical tailoring process at corps and below. An example is a corps FA battalion attached to a division (normally with subsequent attachment, by the division commander, to the DIVARTY).

Operational Control

1-09. OPCON is the authority delegated to a commander to direct forces assigned so that he may:
- Accomplish specific missions or tasks usually limited by function, time, or location.
- Deploy units concerned.

- Retain or assign tactical control of those units.

1-10. OPCON does not, of itself, include administrative or logistical control or responsibility. Normally, OPCON is not a command relationship given to FA units. FA tactical missions perform the same function yet more precisely define the relationship with the supported command.

Joint and NATO Considerations

1-11. If the FA battalion is operating as part of a joint (multi-service) or combined (multi-national) operation, battalion commanders may encounter several other command relationship terms: combatant command (COCOM), operational command (OPCOM), tactical control (TACON), and support. Detailed information on these command relationship terms can be found in FM 101-5-1, *Operational Terms and Graphics; Joint Publication (JP) 1-02, DOD Dictionary of Military and Associated Terms*; JP 3-0, *Doctrine for Joint Operations;* and JP 0-2, *Unified Action Armed Forces (UNAAF)*.

1-12. Commanders also need to understand that some of the command relationship terms used have slightly different definitions within NATO than within DOD. As an example, in NATO, OPCON does not include authority to assign separate employment of components of the units concerned. (The NATO definition of OPCON more closely represents the DOD definition of TACON.) During joint and combined operations, FA battalion commanders should verify the definitions of operational terms through review of applicable publications or with inquiries to higher HQ.

FA TACTICAL MISSIONS

1-13. Once command relationships are established, the force commander assigns the FA tactical missions. He bases his assignments on the advice of the force artillery commander, who is the FS coordinator (FSCOORD) for the force. (For details on the duties and responsibilities of the FSCOORD, refer to FM 6-20, *Doctrine for Fire Support*; FM 6-20-30, *Tactics, Techniques, and Procedures for Fire Support for Division Operations*; FM 6-20-40, *Tactics, Techniques, and Procedures for Brigade Operations*; and FM 6-71, *Tactics, Techniques, and Procedures for Fire Support for the Combined Arms Commander.*)

1-14. An assigned FA tactical mission may be one of four standard FA tactical missions or a nonstandard FA tactical mission. The four standard FA tactical missions are DS, R, GSR, and GS. Nonstandard FA tactical missions are developed when none of these standard missions sufficiently addresses FA tactical requirements and/or responsibilities.

1-15. A FA tactical mission describes in detail the support responsibilities of a FA unit. The mission also clearly defines the relationship of the FA unit with a maneuver unit or another FA unit. It does not affect the organizational structure or the command relationships that result from that structure. Each standard FA tactical mission contains several inherent responsibilities (see Table 1-1). Nonstandard FA tactical missions usually address changes that are needed in these responsibilities or additional responsibilities not addressed by the standard missions.

Table 1-1. Inherent Responsibilities of Standard FA Tactical Missions

AN FA UNIT WITH A MISSION OF	DIRECT SUPPORT	REINFORCING	GENERAL SUPPORT REINFORCING	GENERAL SUPPORT
Answers calls for fire in priority from -	1. Supported unit 2. Own observers[1] 3. Force FA HQ	1. Reinforced FA 2. Own observers[1] 3. Force FA HQ	1. Force FA HQ 2. Reinforced unit[1] 3. Own observers[1]	1. Force FA HQ 2. Own observers[1]
Has as its zone of fire -	Zone of action of supported unit	Zone of fire of reinforced FA unit	Zone of action of supported unit to include zone of fire of reinforced FA unit	Zone of action of supported unit
Furnishes FS personnel[2] -	Provides temporary replacements for casualty losses as required	No requirement	No requirement	No requirement
Furnishes liaison to -	No requirement	Reinforced FA unit HQ	Reinforced FA unit HQ	No requirement
Establishes communication With -	Company FS officers and supported maneuver unit HQ	Reinforced FA unit HQ	Reinforced FA unit HQ	No requirement
Is positioned by-	DS FA unit commander or as ordered by force FA HQ	Reinforced FA unit or as ordered by force FA HQ	Force FA HQ or reinforced FA unit if approved by force FA HQ	Force FA HQ
Has its fires planned by -	Develops own fire plan	Reinforced FA unit HQ	Force FA HQ	Force FA HQ

[1] Includes all target acquisition (TA) means not deployed with supported unit (radar, aerial observers, survey parties, and so on).
[2] A FS element (FSE) for each maneuver brigade, battalion, or cavalry (cav) squadron and one FS team (FIST) with each maneuver company or ground cavalry troop are trained and deployed by the FA unit authorized these assets. USMC artillery battalions, upon deployment, provide forward observer (FO) teams to each company-sized maneuver unit. After deployment, FISTs, and FSEs remain with the supported maneuver unit throughout the conflict.

Direct Support

1-16. The DS mission is used to provide responsive FA fires to a particular maneuver unit. A FA battalion operating in DS of a maneuver unit is primarily concerned with the FA support needs of only that maneuver unit. The DS battalion commander is the FSCOORD for the supported maneuver force. Fires are planned and coordinated with the maneuver unit and the DS battalion commander positions his units where they can best support the scheme of maneuver. Because of this, a DS FA battalion's planning process and operations are significantly integrated with their counterparts in the supported maneuver unit. To best achieve the required coordination and training, the same FA battalion should habitually support the same maneuver force. DS is the most decentralized standard FA tactical mission.

Reinforcing

1-17. Commanders use the reinforcing mission to add weight (fires) to a specific area or maneuver unit by designating one or more FA units to augment the fires of another FA unit. A FA battalion will generally reinforce a FA battalion (or possibly a FA brigade) that has a DS mission. A reinforcing FA battalion can reinforce only one FA unit, but a reinforced battalion can be reinforced by more than one FA unit.

General Support

1-18. A FA battalion assigned the mission of GS supports the maneuver force as a whole and remains under the immediate control of the force artillery HQ. This mission ensures artillery is immediately responsive to the needs of the maneuver force commander. Like the DS mission, the GS mission establishes a relationship between a FA unit and a maneuver unit. It is the most centralized of the standard FA tactical missions.

General Support Reinforcing

1-19. The GSR mission requires the FA battalion to furnish FA fires for the maneuver force as a whole and to reinforce the fires of another FA battalion as a second priority. A GSR battalion remains under the control of the force FA HQ. The GSR mission gives the maneuver force commander the flexibility to respond to a variety of tactical situations.

Nonstandard FA Tactical Missions

1-20. If an unusual tactical situation exists, or none of the standard FA tactical missions accurately convey the maneuver commander's guidance for fires, he assigns a nonstandard FA tactical mission to the FA unit. A nonstandard FA tactical mission may amplify, limit, or change one or more of the seven inherent responsibilities, or it may spell out contingencies not covered by those responsibilities. If the revision is so complex that the standard FA mission is no longer recognizable, a nonstandard mission statement will address each of the seven inherent responsibilities.

1-21. Units sometimes use a nonstandard mission when there are not sufficient FA assets to cover all the contingencies or if a FA battalion is assigned more than one functional mission. It is also a means by which the commander can tailor his FA assets in anticipation of future operations. A nonstandard mission may involve limitations or guidance concerning ammunition, positioning, or other critical factors.

EXAMPLES OF NONSTANDARD FA TACTICAL MISSIONS

1-50 FA (155SP, M109A6): GSR 1-20 FA; do not exceed 50 percent of CSR in support of 1-20 FA.

1-89 FA (MLRS, M270A1): GS; provide liaison officer to DIVARTY TOC.

SP = self-propelled, CSR = controlled supply rate, TOC = tactical operations center

---

On-Order (o/o) FA Tactical Missions

1-22. During the course of a major operation, a FA battalion may change tactical missions. The assignment of an o/o FA tactical mission, in addition to its initial mission, gives the battalion advance notice of the future mission. This facilitates planning for and transition to the follow-on mission.

Positioning, ammunition requirements, and timing of the mission change are several of the key considerations for battalions that have an o/o mission. An o/o mission is usually stated in the maneuver operations order/FS plan (FSP) and/or the FA support plan (FASP).

EXAMPLES OF O/O FA TACTICAL MISSIONS

1-50 FA (155SP, M109A5): R 1-20 FA (do not exceed 25% CSR is support of 1-20 FA); o/o DS 3 Bde.

1-89 FA (155SP, M109A6): DS 1-23 Cav (division security force); after completing rearward passage, o/o GS 52 Infantry Div (Mechanized).

Div = division

Dedicated Battery

1-23. In special circumstances where immediately responsive fires are required, and/or the supported maneuver unit is operating independently or at an excessive distance from its parent unit, a dedicated battery can be established. "Dedicated battery" describes both a nonstandard tactical mission and informal support relationship whereby a battery-sized FA unit assumes responsibility for fulfilling a modified prioritized list of inherent responsibilities towards a battalion-sized maneuver unit. Establishing a dedicated battery is recommended by the FSCOORD and approved by the maneuver (normally brigade) commander.

1-24. A dedicated battery establishes communications with and responds to calls for fire from a specified maneuver force (usually a battalion task force) as its first priority (see Table 1-2). The battery will plot fires on the targets planned by the TF FSO. The artillery battalion will also plot these fires in case additional support is required. Close coordination between the supported maneuver unit and the dedicated battery is required. The battery commander must fully understand the maneuver battalion commander's intent and scheme of maneuver and should attend all maneuver rehearsals. Likely enemy locations and composition must be identified. Munitions for engaging the probable enemy targets must be identified. When not firing missions, the guns of the dedicated battery will be laid on the firing data for the next planned target identified by the maneuver unit. Subordinate unit leaders (company, platoon, and even squad) must understand the fire plan and be able to request and adjust fires. Intervention rules for FATDS systems will allow maximum responsiveness while providing safety from fratricide.

1-25. The circumstances and situations that call for the proper use of a dedicated battery are highly specific. A dedicated battery may be used to provide support to the lead battalion task force in a brigade or larger movement to contact when responsive vice massed fires is critical. The location of enemy forces is either unknown or suspect. The chance of unanticipated enemy fires (e.g. ambush) must be high. ROE must be very permissible. A dedicated battery is not the normal condition while providing fires to maneuver forces. The extensive use of dedicated batteries reduces the ability of the FA battalion to mass its fires on the targets that meet the brigade commander's intent and must be weighed against the capability to execute the other EFATs assigned. In order to permit continuous coverage for a moving battalion task force, the FA battalion may be forced to use several batteries. In this case, the remaining battalions of the brigade will have to rely on their organic mortars as their first choice for indirect fires against targets of opportunity.

Table 1-2. Inherent Responsibilities of a Dedicated Battery

ANSWERS CALLS FOR FIRE IN PRIORITY FROM:	HAS AS ITS ZONE OF FIRE:	FURNISHES FS PERSONNEL TO:	FURNISHES LIAISON TO:	ESTABLISHES COMMO WITH:	ESTABLISHES QUICK FIRE CHANNEL WITH:	IS POSITIONED BY:	HAS ITS FIRES PLANNED BY:
1. Supported Unit 2. Parent HQ	Zone of action of Supported Unit	BC as FSO if none in the supported unit	Supported Unit [1]	Supported Unit	Per Supported Unit Instructions	Supported Unit	Supported Unit [2]
1. Battery personnel (BC, XO, gunnery sergeant...) may perform liaison functions without being permanently positioned with the supported unit.							
2. Parent units may also plan fires for the dedicated battery (e.g. using multiple batteries or in preparation of a mission change back to parent unit control).							

FA Tactical Missions in Combined Operations

1-26. As stated, each of the standard FA tactical missions has specific inherent responsibilities. However, these tactical missions and responsibilities are not viewed the same by the armies of nations with which the US may operate. These differences must be identified and understood whenever FA battalions are involved in combined operations. A FA battalion commander may be required to operate in an environment covered by bilateral agreements. In this environment, the operation order (OPORD) will be his guide for bilateral operations. The US and its NATO allies have agreed to the terms of STANAG 2934, *Artillery Procedures,* with changes. When they are supporting allied troops or working with allied artillery, FA battalion commanders must know the responsibilities included in these agreements as viewed by other nations (see Table 1-3 for responsibilities in a NATO or Australia, Britain, Canada, America (ABCA) environment).

Table 1-3. Inherent Responsibilities of FA Tactical Missions - (NATO and ABCA)

INHERENT RESPONSIBILITIES OF FIELD ARTILLERY TACTICAL MISSIONS (NATO and ABCA)				
AN FA UNIT WITH A MISSION OF	DIRECT SUPPORT	REINFORCING	GENERAL SUPPORT REINFORCING	GENERAL SUPPORT
Answers calls for fire in priority from -	1. Directly supported formation/unit 2. Own observers 3. Force FA HQ[1]	1. Reinforced artillery unit 2. Own observers 3. Force FA HQ[1]	1. Force FA HQ[1] 2. Reinforced artillery unit 3. Own observers[3]	1. Force FA HQ[1] 2. Own observers
Has as its zone of fire -	Zone of action of the directly supported formation/unit[4]	Zone of fire of reinforced FA unit or zone prescribed	Zone of action of the supported formation/unit to include zone of fire of the reinforced FA unit	Zone of action of the supported formation/unit or zone prescribed
Furnishes FS personnel -	Each maneuver company of the directly supported formation/unit	Upon a request of reinforced FA unit[2]	Reinforced FA unit if approved by force FA HQ[1, 2, 3]	No inherent requirement
Establishes liaison with -	Directly supported formation or unit (battalion, regiment and brigade)	Reinforced FA unit	Reinforced FA unit	No inherent requirement
Establishes communication with-	The directly supported maneuver formation/unit	Reinforced FA unit	Reinforced FA unit	No inherent requirement
Weapons moved and deployed by -	DS FA unit commander or as ordered by force FA HQ[1]	Reinforced FA unit or ordered by force FA HQ[1]	Force FA HQ[1] or reinforced FA unit if approved by force FA HQ[1]	Force FA HQ[1]
Has its fires planned by -	Develops own fire plans in coordination with directly supported formation/unit	Reinforced FA unit	Force FA HQ[1] or as otherwise specified[3]	Force FA HQ[1]

[1] Force artillery HQ or higher authority HQ.
[2] Applies also to the provision of liaison officers (LNOs).
[3] Italy, in GSR, does not answer calls for fire from own observers, does not furnish FO, and has its fire planned by the HQ of the artillery-unit which receives the GSR.
[4] Netherlands FA in DS will not furnish FOs and/or FS officers (FSOs) since these elements are part of the maneuver units. United Kingdom (UK) artillery is not established (organized) to provide all maneuver companies of the directly supported unit/formation with a FO.

FM 3-09.21 (FM 6-20-1)

SECTION II – RESPONSIBILITIES OF KEY PERSONNEL

1-27. The activities of the FA battalion are supervised by a number of key personnel in addition to the battalion commander, the command sergeant major (CSM), and the executive officer (XO). These include primary staff officers such as the S1 (personnel officer), S2 (intelligence officer), S3 (operations officer), S4 (logistics officer), and S6 (communications and electronics staff officer [CESO]). The chaplain is a member of the personal staff.

1-28. Special staff officers include the fire direction officer (FDO), targeting officer, chemical officer, physician's assistant, battalion maintenance officer (BMO), battalion ammunition officer (BAO) (or support platoon leader [SPL]), and, in some battalions, the brigade and battalion FSOs and LNO.

1-29. The duties of each of these personnel are briefly discussed below. Additional information on battalion staff organization and the duties of staff personnel can be found in FM 101-5, *Staff Organization and Operations*.

COMMAND SECTION

BATTALION COMMANDER

1-30. The battalion commander, aided by the battalion staff and the battery commanders, controls all the tactical, logistical, administrative, and training activities of the battalion. He directs employment of the battalion in accordance with assigned missions, guidance from the force FA HQ, and in the DS role, the supported maneuver force. He works closely with the commanders of supported and supporting units to ensure that the battalion can accomplish its mission. Specific responsibilities include:

- Oversee the training of the entire battalion, with particular emphasis on those elements directly concerned with delivery of fires and FS.
- Continually assess the needs of the battalion in terms of its ability to sustain its internal operations and to support assigned missions.
- Establish clear and consistent standards and guidance for current and future operations. Ensure the battalion staff and battery commanders understand the battalion commander's intent.
- Establish policies to promote discipline and morale within the battalion.
- Provide for the administrative and logistical support of the battalion.
- In a DS mission, perform FSCOORD duties
  - Advise the supported maneuver commander on all FS matters.
  - Direct and supervise the planning and coordination of all FS assets supporting the maneuver unit, to include FSEs and FISTs.
  - Coordinate/control the operations and/or fires of R/GSR FA units.
  - Direct and supervise preparation of the FSP and the FASP as documents in support of the maneuver plan.
  - See FM 6-20-40 for additional discussion on the FSCOORD responsibilities of the DS FA battalion commander.

COMMAND SERGEANT MAJOR

1-31. The battalion CSM is the senior enlisted advisor to the commander. He is both a specialist and a generalist, as he must have technical competence as a field artilleryman while being broadly knowledgeable in all functional areas such as operations, administration, and logistics. The CSM best serves as an extension of the commander's eyes and as his primary troubleshooter. He works closely with each of the battalion staff sections and the firing battery leaders, frequently changing his area of focus based on the needs of the unit and the direction of the commander.

1-32. The CSM usually operates independently of but complementary to the commander, frequently at a critical location where the commander needs additional supervision, oversight, or observation. Because of this, the CSM requires his own vehicle, radio, and driver. The CSM's duties include:

- Assist the commander in maintaining effective communication with senior and subordinate leaders and staffs.
- Validate that the commander's directions and intent are being properly communicated through the leadership chain to the front line soldiers and that their feedback and concerns are reaching the commander.
- Advise the commander and staff on all matters pertaining to enlisted soldiers.
- Assist the S3 in planning, coordinating, and supervising collective and individual training to include certification requirements.
- Mentor unit first sergeants (1SGs) and noncommissioned officers (NCOs), supervise and direct NCO professional development, identify and develop future leaders from within the enlisted ranks.

EXECUTIVE OFFICER

1-33. As second in command and chief of staff, the XO must keep fully abreast of current and anticipated operations. He must be prepared to assume the duties of the commander when the need arises. He must position himself forward, traveling between the battalion command post (CP), the batteries, and the battalion trains area to perform his duties. Key duties in addition to those in FM 101-5, include:

- Direct, supervise, and coordinate all staff actions and operations, to include the battalion's military decision-making process (MDMP), especially production of the FASP, and, when applicable, battalion staff involvement in the FSP.
- Supervise and direct all CSS efforts within the battalion, to include development of the battalion's trains concept and CSS plan.
- Direct and supervise operations of the administration and logistics operations center (ALOC) and battalion support operations center (BSOC).
- Perform face-to-face contact with his counterparts on the maneuver, DIVARTY, Corps Arty, or FA brigade staff as required.
- Direct and supervise development of continuity of operations (CONOPS) plans for the CP, the various operations centers, and each staff section.

- Direct and supervise development of mutual support unit (MSU) operations, as necessary or as directed, with another FA unit.
- In the battalion commander's absence, enforce the commander's standards throughout the unit.

1-34. The battalion commander decides which function the XO will give his primary focus at any given time. This decision is based on the immediate requirements of the battalion and the overall tactical situation. Changing situations will require periodic changes in the XO's focus. The XO must recognize his primary function is to understand the battalion commander's intent and that he is normally the senior officer at the battalion responsible for executing that intent. When he is functioning primarily as second in command, one or more of the primary staff officers (often the S4) assumes a major portion of the functions of senior logistics coordinator. When the XO concerns himself primarily with the logistics support of the battalion, the S3 assumes a greater portion of the commander's duties in the battalion area.

S1 (PERSONNEL OFFICER)

1-35. The S1 plans, directs, and supervises the personnel, administrative, and health services for the battalion. He supervises the battalion personnel administration center (PAC) and serves as a shift leader in the ALOC or the BSOC. In addition to those listed in FM 101-5, the S1's duties include the following:

- Advise the commander and staff on all S1 areas, to include:
  - Strength accounting and replacement operations.
  - Casualty reporting.
  - Coordination of legal services.
  - Finance and postal services.
  - Administrative procedures and services.
  - Enemy prisoners of war (EPW) planning and coordination.
  - Health services.
  - Awards and evaluations.
  - Morale support activities.
- Recommend personnel priorities and employment of S1 assets that support the commander's intent and mission accomplishment.
- Prepare personnel/medical estimates and plans. In conjunction with the S4, prepare paragraph 4 of the FASP and the CSS plan/tab.
- In conjunction with the S4, establish and maintain the ALOC and BSOC. Supervise operations of the BSOC (if one is established – see Chapters 2 and 7 for additional ALOC/BSOC information).
- Ensure the S1 section and, when applicable, the BSOC establish and maintain situational awareness – of the general situation, FA battalion operations, and CSS, especially personnel/medical.
- Review the battalion's essential FA tasks (EFATs) for critical personnel, medical, and EPW requirements (e.g., personnel cross-leveling to achieve necessary strength, experience levels, or a particular skill in a battery or section).

S2 (INTELLIGENCE OFFICER)

1-36. The S2 performs a wide variety of tasks concerning intelligence, targeting, and force protection. In addition, he helps the S3 supervise the TOC operation. In addition to those listed in FM 101-5, the S2's duties include the following:

- Supervise the intelligence section.
- Develop artillery intelligence preparation of the battlefield (IPB) in conjunction with other staff elements and the senior FA HQ, with the supported maneuver S2 (DS units), and the S2 for any supporting/supported FA units.
- Develop enemy artillery order of battle and monitor tactics and techniques of enemy artillery, mortars, and TA assets.
- Predict artillery target locations and pass predicted locations to a fire control facility (FSE or fire direction center [FDC]), targeting cell, or weapon platform as appropriate.
- Provide survivability and mobility information to the battalion S3.
- In conjunction with the S6, assess the enemy's capability to interfere with signal communications and supervise the counterintelligence aspects of signal operations within the battalion.
- Recommend commander's critical information requirements (CCIR), especially priority intelligence requirements (PIR), related to the primary mission, tasks, and role of the battalion.
- Prepare intelligence estimates and portions of the FASP (the enemy situation portion (paragraph la) and the TA tab), with the assistance of the targeting officer and the radar section leader. This includes the radar deployment order (RDO) when applicable.
- In coordination with maneuver and FA S2s, as appropriate, organize and supervise an aggressive collection effort designed to answer PIR.
- Advise and assist the S3 in positioning, tasking, and supervising organic/attached TA assets, and coordinating survey for TA assets.
- Assist the S3 in managing the counterfire fight.
  - Develop and collect the intelligence and TA data necessary to support counterfire operations.
  - Recommend radar employment, positions, decision points for cueing and moving the radar, cueing schedules, and radar zones.
  - Template potential enemy locations, determine enemy-to-friendly FA force ratios, evaluate enemy FA/TA capabilities and tactics, and advise the FA battalion and maneuver commanders on the enemy indirect fire and counterfire threats.
  - Ensure IPB analysis includes evaluation of the role and capabilities of ground, air, and naval forces, and possibly even satellite/space-based assets in the enemy's counterfire program.
- Ensure all subordinate and supporting units are kept informed of the enemy situation.
- Coordinate the battalion ground and air defense plans.
- Advise the commander and staff on control of classified materials.
- Request and distribute maps (paper/digital), as required.

S3 (OPERATIONS OFFICER)

1-37. The S3 is responsible for training, planning, and execution of battalion operations. In addition to those listed in FM 101-5, S3 duties include:

- Advise the FA battalion commander in these specific areas:
  - FA organization for combat and FA attack guidance.
  - Identification and development of essential FS tasks (EFSTs) and EFATs.
  - Positioning and movement of firing/TA assets, CP, ALOC, BSOC.
  - The FA operations estimate, MDMP, and the FASP.
  - Employment of organic, attached, and reinforcing firing units.
  - Employment of organic or attached radars and other TA assets.
  - Employment of organic or attached survey assets.
  - CSS priorities, in coordination with the XO, S4, and S1.
  - Rehearsal supervision.
- Supervise and direct the operations and positioning of the TOC.
- Plan, coordinate, and control tactical movement, to include selection of positions, preparation of the tactical movement plan, and terrain management, for all elements under the battalion's control or direction.
- Supervise and direct preparation and dissemination of the FASP, orders, and directives.
- Plan, supervise, and direct battalion survey operations.
- Coordinate plans with higher, subordinate and adjacent FA units.
- Ensure databases and commander's guidances in automated C2 equipment are correct and properly coordinated within the battalion.
- In coordination with the S4 and BAO, plan and manage ammunition consumption, distribution, and resupply. Calculate ammunition requirements, basic loads, and required supply rates (RSRs)/CSRs.
- Integrate operations security (OPSEC) into the overall operations of the unit.
- Establish, in coordination with the S6, communications priorities.
- Direct and supervise the planning and execution of the FA battalion's participation in the counterfire fight.
  - Ensure counterfire plans meet the intent and guidance of the supported maneuver commander and of the FA battalion and force /higher FA commanders, as appropriate.
  - Ensure that priorities, mission routing, clearance of fires, and attack guidances for counterfire within the battalion's zone of fire are coordinated and understood by all members of the TOC and by the firing battery leaders.
  - In a DS role, maintain close coordination with the brigade FSE and force FA HQ to ensure that all of the battalion's counterfire responsibilities are coordinated and that higher and supported unit requirements do not conflict or overtax the FA battalion.

- Supervise radar management to ensure radar zone management, sector assignments, cueing, and positioning are properly incorporated into the decision support template (DST)/synchronization matrix and the TA tab to the FASP.
- Identify detailed counterfire responsibilities, to include specified and implied counterfire tasks, and assign counterfire responsibilities during the planning process.
- Ensure counterfire ammunition requirements are addressed in overall ammunition requirements. Evaluate assigned CSRs to determine the impact on counterfire responsibilities.
- With the S2 and FDO, evaluate force protection issues inherent in counterfire tasks and tactics.
- Coordinate meteorology (met) support for the battalion.

S4 (LOGISTICS OFFICER)

1-38. The S4 coordinates and manages logistical supply for the battalion. He supervises the battalion supply and ammunition sections, and serves as a shift leader in the ALOC. The S4's duties include the following:

- Advise the commander and staff on all S4 areas, to include:
  - CSS C2 – centralized versus decentralized CSS operations.
  - Battalion trains concept and positioning (see Chapter 7).
  - Ammunition estimates, distribution, and resupply operations.
  - Refueling operations.
  - Transportation requirements and main supply route (MSR) selection and operation.
  - Unit movements.
- Prepare logistics estimates and plans using logistics preparation of the battlefield (LPB) methodology (see Chapter 7). With the S1, prepare paragraph 4 of the FASP and the CSS plan/tab.
- Supervise, manage, and coordinate battalion supply and sustainment operations, to include ammunition and refueling.
- Distribution operations for all classes of supply except Class VIII (medical) within the battalion.
- Recommend logistics priorities and employment of S4 assets that support the commander's intent and mission accomplishment.
- With the S1, establish and maintain the ALOC and BSOC. Supervise operations of the ALOC.
- Ensure the S4 section and the ALOC establish and maintain situational awareness – of the general situation, FA operations, and CSS.
- Plan and coordinate administrative movements.
- Review the battalion's EFATs for critical logistical requirements (e.g., combat configured loads (CCLs) of ammunition, hot refuel).

S6 (COMMUNICATIONS AND ELECTRONICS STAFF OFFICER)

1-39. The S6 is responsible for communications and automation operations, management, and security. The S6 is a coordinating staff officer and is directly accountable to the XO. In addition to those listed in FM 101-5, S6 duties include the following:

- Advise the commander and staff on:
  - Selection of unit position areas (PAs), from a communications standpoint.
  - Communications and automation planning, operations, priorities, security, training, and rehearsals.
  - Electronic counter-counter measures (ECCM).
  - Communications and automation requirements associated with EFSTs and EFATs, e.g., unique communications and/or automation equipment, nets, database exchange, or procedures for sensor-to-shooter links or other critical communications.
- Plan, manage, and direct communications operations to include establishment of communications networks and systems and installation and maintenance of equipment.
  - Coordinate integration of battalion communications systems into those of a supported maneuver/FA unit and a FA HQ.
  - Coordinate with signal units for communications support.
  - Supervise operator and organizational maintenance of communication equipment.
  - Manage all frequency allocations and assignments.
- Manage and direct communications security (COMSEC). Direct and supervise the battalion COMSEC custodian who issues and accounts for COMSEC equipment, key lists, codes, ciphers, signal operating instructions (SOI), and authentication systems.
- Plan, manage, and direct automation systems administration, maintenance, and security.
  - Establish automation systems administration and security procedures for automation hardware and software.
  - Supervise and direct battalion local area networks (LANs) configuration and usage of battalion network capabilities.
- Prepare communications estimates and write the signal paragraph (paragraph 4a) of the FASP.
- Perform communications reconnaissance and survey to assist the S3 in positioning key elements of the battalion, to include retransmission (retrans) stations.

BATTALION CHAPLAIN

1-40. The chaplain serves the commander as the special/personal staff officer to plan, synchronize, coordinate, and provide personally delivered religious support within the commander's area of responsibility. He advises the commander on moral and ethical issues. He develops a religious support plan, conducts field services, and manages soldier welfare ministries. He provides counseling, as required, for all soldiers and helps maintain the morale and spiritual well being of all personnel. The chaplain is supported by a chaplain assistant who performs religious support duties and coordination for religious programs, worship, and crisis intervention.

BATTALION MAINTENANCE OFFICER

1-41. The BMO advises the commanders and the XO on maintenance procedures. He recommends maintenance procedures, priorities, and policies. He coordinates DS maintenance and manages and directs maintenance support teams. The BMO monitors and assists with battery level resupply of Class IX repair parts. He consolidates and forwards maintenance specific reports. The BMO operates from the ALOC.

BATTALION OPERATIONS SECTION

ASSISTANT S3

1-42. The assistant S3 supervises the activities of the operations section and manages the TOC operations in the absence of the S3. The assistant S3 constructs the FA support matrix (FASM) and the FA positioning overlay for the FASP. During execution, the assistant S3 may position himself near the operations situation map and status boards. He is responsible for maintaining current information on the status boards; supervising the upkeep of the operations map and overlay; verifying target plotting on the target overlay and advising the S3 of any targets that violate graphical FS coordinating measures (FSCMs) or maneuver control measures. His focus is on positioning and ranging targets established in the FSP, maintaining tube strength, and coordinating ammunition resupply. He positions and moves organic or attached radars in conjunction with the S2 and the targeting officer.

OPERATIONS NONCOMMISSIONED OFFICER

1-43. The operations NCO supervises the activities of all NCOs/enlisted soldiers in the TOC and assists the assistant S3 with operations functions. He performs and supervises net control duties for the battalion command net, maintains the staff journal and message log, and ensures the situation map/charts are current at all times. He also ensures the TOC complex is properly supplied and maintained.

BATTALION MASTER GUNNER

1-44. The battalion master gunner is the weapon system expert in the battalion. He should be the battalion's most knowledgeable soldier on the unit's primary weapon system (howitzer or MLRS launcher). He must be well versed on all aspects of the weapon (operation, maintenance, training, and record keeping) and where applicable, its supporting ammunition vehicle. The battalion master gunner's duties and responsibilities are as follows:

- Assist the S3 and CSM in managing the battalion's individual and crew training and certification program for 13B or 13M soldiers. This includes training and certification of officers and senior NCOs. Place special attention on the training and evaluation of howitzer/launcher section chiefs. Plan and conduct battalion certification events.
- Assist the S3 in management of the individual and crew training and certification program for all military occupational specialties (MOS).

- Assist the S3 in management of the battalion artillery safety program and coordinate these efforts with the battalion safety officer/NCO as part of the battalion's overall safety program.
- Assist the S3 and XO with maintaining maximum readiness and operational status in primary weapon systems. This includes crew training and maintenance issues for howitzers, launchers, and ammunition vehicles. Maintain close coordination with battalion and battery maintenance supervisors and with unit artillery mechanics.
- Assist the batteries with the management of their 13B or 13M training programs and with battery safety programs.
- Troubleshoot problems on the battalion's primary weapon system and ammunition vehicles. This is mainly in a support role to the gunnery sergeants in the firing batteries.
- Assist the S3 and S1 in maintaining the most current information and training packages on primary weapon systems and their supporting ammunition vehicles, to include FMs, technical manuals (TMs), bulletins, training circulars, training support packages, and all other possible pertinent information. The master gunner must frequently check official internet sites, professional publications, and other sources of information for current and emerging tactics, techniques, procedures, training, and safety information.
- Maintain a dialogue with master gunners in other battalions to ensure rapid identification of new issues noted by other units.
- Assist the S3 in rapid dissemination of all critical information concerning the battalion's primary weapon platform.

CHEMICAL OFFICER/NONCOMMISSIONED OFFICER

1-45. The chemical officer advises the commanders and staff on nuclear, biological, and chemical (NBC) defensive operations, contamination, and predicted enemy strikes. He also writes the NBC portion of the FASP; maintains current status of decontamination sites in the area of operations (AO) and mission-oriented protective posture (MOPP) requirements; and he processes all NBC reports.

BATTALION INTELLIGENCE SECTION

TARGETING OFFICER

1-46. In divisional DS cannon battalions, the targeting officer is in the maneuver brigade FSE and assists both the brigade FSO and the maneuver S2 with targeting. He also assists the DS FA battalion S2 as possible. The duties for a targeting officer in a DS unit are outlined in FM 6-20-40.

1-47. In divisional GS FA battalions and corps level FA battalions the targeting officer is in the intelligence section. In addition to his targeting duties, he functions as an assistant S2. His duties include the following:
- Assist the S2 and S3 in target production, processing, and administration and with external targeting coordination.
- Assist the S2 with order of battle development and IPB.

- Help the battalion S2 write the intelligence, TA, and surveillance portions of the FASP, to include the RDO when applicable.
- Help plan for and manage attached, organic, and OPCON TA assets.
- Assist the battalion S2 and S3 with development and execution of the FA TA and counterfire plans.
- Assist the S2 in identifying CCIR.
- Supervise the intelligence section in the absence of the S2.
- Perform officer in charge (OIC) shift duties for the S2 section.
- Conducts predictive battle damage assessments (BDA) and request BDA from external sources/higher HQ.

INTELLIGENCE SERGEANT

1-48. The intelligence sergeant assists the S2 in the planning, supervision, and execution of intelligence and targeting operations. The intelligence sergeant may be a shift leader for the section, especially if there is no targeting officer. In DS cannon battalions, the intelligence sergeant may perform many of the section's targeting functions. In Advanced Field Artillery Tactical Data Systems (AFATDS) units, the intelligence sergeant may also be a primary AFATDS operator.

BATTALION FIRE DIRECTION CENTER

FIRE DIRECTION OFFICER

1-49. The FDO supervises tactical and technical fire direction (FD) within the battalion. On the basis of guidance from the battalion commander and S3, the FSCOORD and/or FSO (DS units), reinforced FA unit FDO (R & GSR units), and force FA HQ, the FDO decides where and how the battalion and any reinforcing units will fire. Specific FDO duties include:

- Supervise the FD section.
- Assist the FSCOORD in developing the commander's criteria based on the supported maneuver commander's concept for FS. (FDOs in R/GSR/GS units provide input through the reinforced FA unit and/or force FA HQ.)
- Develop and supervise input of appropriate parameters into the AFATDS, Initial Fire Support Automation System (IFSAS), Fire Direction System (FDS), or Lightweight Tactical Fire Direction System (LTACFIRE). Coordination of these parameters with FSEs, reinforcing/reinforced FA units, and force FA HQ is critical. Coordination of digital communications and database elements may also be required with users of non-FA digital C2 systems.
- Analyze requested targets for attack by FA. Consider desired effects, method of fire, and types of ammunition needed.
- Ensure dissemination of fire plans and schedules of fires to subordinate and supporting unit FDCs and to FSEs occurs as appropriate.
- Coordinate with FSEs to process requests for other types of FS.
- Maintain the current target overlay.
- Keep FA elements informed of targets.

- Establish procedures and train personnel to accomplish tactical and technical FD in a degraded (manual/voice) mode.
- Establish procedures for interface between AFATDS, IFSAS, FDS, or LTACFIRE units, as well as any other digital system with which the FDC may be required to interface.

CHIEF FIRE CONTROL SERGEANT

1-50. He is the automated technical and tactical fire control expert in the battalion FDC. He is responsible for: establishing the tactical database in the battalion automated fire control system; monitoring the technical input and executions of fire plans and missions; advising the FDO on changes or updates to battlefield geometry and firing unit status; and cross-checking status boards with system data.

BATTALION AMMUNITION OFFICER

1-51. The BAO or SPL manages resupply of ammunition in the FA battalion. His primary duties include the following:
- Manage the use of the battalion's ammunition-carrying assets.
- Manage ammunition movement from the ammunition transfer point (ATP) to the combat trains area and then forward to the batteries.
- Maintain accountability of ammunition.
- Ensure ammunition basic loads delivered to the batteries contain the proper mix and quantities of ammunition.
- Perform mission analysis to verify ammunition handling capabilities can support current operations. Report shortcomings to the S3.
- Manage turn-in of residue and unexpended ammunition.

FIRE SUPPORT ELEMENTS

BRIGADE FIRE SUPPORT OFFICER

1-52. The FSCOORD cannot be at the brigade HQ constantly. Therefore, he has an assistant, the brigade FSO, to serve as a full-time liaison between the DS FA battalion and the maneuver brigade. The brigade FSO's duties and responsibilities are outlined in FM 6-20-40.

BATTALION FIRE SUPPORT OFFICER

1-53. The battalion FSO is the FSCOORD and principal FS advisor to the maneuver battalion commander. He is in charge of the battalion FSE and serves as the DS FA battalion commander's representative to the maneuver battalion commander. The battalion FSO's duties and responsibilities are outlined in FM 6-20-40.

LIAISON OFFICER

1-54. A LNO assists his FA battalion in accomplishing liaison with another FA unit or, when necessary, any other HQ with which the battalion requires liaison. Liaison is usually required as an inherent responsibility of a R or

GSR mission, but may also be used in any situation that requires extremely close coordination with another unit. A LNO is usually part of an organic liaison section, found in corps FA battalions and some divisional/GS battalions. However, when necessary, battalions without an organic liaison section sometimes create temporary liaison elements out of existing assets. A more detailed discussion of the liaison function is in Chapter 2.

1-55. Because the LNO represents his commander, he must have the commander's full confidence. He should be able to:
- Understand how his commander thinks and represent his position.
- Interpret his commander's messages.
- Convey his commander's vision, mission, and concept of operations and guidance.

1-56. The LNO's professional capabilities and personal characteristics must encourage confidence and cooperation with the commander and staff of the receiving unit. He must possess tact and:
- Be thoroughly knowledgeable of his unit's mission and its TTP; organization; capabilities; and communications equipment.
- Quickly become familiar with the receiving unit's organization, capabilities, mission, tactics, TSOP, and staff procedures. In the case of multinational forces, the LNO must also understand the receiving unit's doctrine and customs.
- Be familiar with the requirements for and the purpose of liaison; the liaison system, and its corresponding reports, reporting documents, and records; and the training of the liaison team.
- Observe the established channels of command and staff functions.

1-57. In addition to those listed in FM 101-5, the LNO's duties may include:
- Facilitate the exchange of situational awareness data between the two units – especially friendly and enemy FA information, fire plans, target lists, CSS information.
- Represent the reinforcing unit during the supported unit's MDMP and development of the FASP.
- Assist the S3 and S2 with the counterfire fight, and other missions that significantly involve the reinforcing unit.
- Assist the S2 with targeting and the rapid dissemination of targeting information to the reinforcing unit.
- Assist the S3s of both battalions in identifying EFATs and determining EFAT responsibilities for the reinforcing unit.
- Advise the S2 and S3 of CCIR and force protection support required by the reinforcing unit.
- Assist both units in development of MSU plans and CONOPS plans. Ensure MSU and CONOPS plans address the liaison function.
- Assist the staffs of both units in establishing and maintaining effective communication with their counterparts.

RADAR SECTION LEADER

1-58. In battalions that have an organic or attached radar section, the radar section leader is a key participant in the battalion's planning and operations. The radar section leader, assisted by the radar section chief, performs the day-to-day supervision of the radar section. He monitors and directs the training and performance of radar personnel and supervises operation, maintenance, and trouble shooting of radar equipment. He also:

- Advises the FA battalion commander and his staff on radar operations.
- Participates in developing radar employment plans and orders.
- Ensures the capabilities and limitations of the radar are considered.
- Selects radar positions that support the search sector requirements of planned zones, optimize TA, and facilitate movement.
- Identifies zone restrictions violated during planning and rehearsals.
- Coordinates, through the S3, positioning and security for the section.

Chapter 2

Command Post Operations

This chapter provides the FA battalion commander and his staff guidance for effective CP operations. It focuses on the main CP and the TOC, and discusses liaison operations. The chapter is organized into six sections. Section I provides an overview of the FA battalion CP. Section II discusses TOC organization and responsibilities. Section III provides examples and suggestions for TOC configurations. Section IV provides an overview of TOC information management. Section V covers CP positioning and movement. Section VI discusses liaison operations.

SECTION I – THE FA BATTALION COMMAND POST

2-01. C2 of a FA battalion is exercised through the establishment of a battalion CP and two to four operations centers. The TOC and the ALOC may both be part of the CP when all or most HQ and CSS elements are consolidated in one location. If the battalion establishes the trains separately, the ALOC will locate with the trains. If the battalion establishes dual trains, it may also establish a BSOC to control the field trains while the ALOC controls the combat trains. The ALOC and BSOC are discussed further in Chapter 7. The battalion may also form a tactical action center (TAC) to place C2 forward during high intensity, fast moving operations. The TAC would concentrate on the current battle, performing critical operations, FD, and intelligence tasks, while the TOC performed non-critical current tasks and planning and coordination functions. The TAC requires a vehicle that can keep up with the supported maneuver unit, two robust FATDS C2 systems (AFATDS or IFSAS) for operations and FD, and communications equipment noted in Chapter 3.

2-02. The primary C2 facility is the battalion CP. It is normally located where the battalion can best command and control all assets and influence FA and other FS systems in support of force operations. With the fielding of increasingly capable digital C2 systems, the battalion can establish limited CP operations at various locations, e.g., on the move operating out of one or two vehicles, at the unit trains, or at a FSE. Limited CP operations may consist of a temporary jump TOC (JTOC) used to facilitate movement of the TOC to a new location. Use of the JTOC is discussed further in Section V.

2-03. The battalion will also designate an alternate CP, which will assume control of battalion operations in the event the main CP becomes inoperable or loses communications. The alternate CP may be another FA battalion CP (especially likely with reinforced/reinforcing units), a firing battery, the brigade FSE, or the ALOC.

CP COMPOSITION

2-04. The make-up of the battalion CP will vary with the situation and the commander's concept of operations. Most of the elements that comprise the CP are in the headquarters, headquarters and service battery (HHSB) or in headquarters, headquarters battery (HHB) and service battery (SB). The CP may include elements from each primary staff section. However, it frequently is a small, operations oriented facility containing the following elements:

- Battalion command element.
- TOC.
- Communications support.
- Survey elements.

BATTALION COMMAND ELEMENT

2-05. The battalion command element consists of the battalion commander, assisted by the CSM, the XO, and their drivers. When they are in the CP, they frequently work out of the TOC where they can best monitor and control the battalion's operations. They may also have their own tent for personal use and as a place to work or conduct meetings away from the TOC.

2-06. The members of the command element are often away from the CP observing, directing, or otherwise influencing the action at critical places on the battlefield. The FA battalion commander positions himself where he can best fulfill all of his command responsibilities. This may be in the FA battalion CP, a trains location, a firing battery, or a key traffic or observation point. A DS battalion commander, as the FSCOORD, may at times be in the supported maneuver unit's HQ, a FSE, or with the supported maneuver commander at a critical location on the battlefield. A R FA battalion commander may position himself in the DS battalion CP, the maneuver brigade CP, or the R FA battalion CP. Commanders of GS/GSR battalions will locate based on guidance from the higher or force FA commander.

2-07. The battalion XO, CSM, S3 and, in divisional units, the brigade FSO provide critical C2 support which allows the battalion commander the flexibility to position himself wherever the situation dictates. In units equipped with the AFATDS, the FA battalion commander may have an automated C2 system in his vehicle that allows him to monitor digital traffic and aid in C2 of the battalion while he operates away from the CP.

2-08. The battalion XO may operate out of the ALOC instead of the CP, especially when focusing his efforts on the battalion's CSS operations. During periods of major planning actions, or when the commander and/or S3 may be out of the CP for extended periods, the XO will probably be in the TOC.

TACTICAL OPERATIONS CENTER

2-09. The TOC serves as the FA battalion's primary C2 hub (information management center), assisting the battalion commander in synchronizing FA fires in support of force operations. It is the location in the battalion where the majority of planning, staff coordination, plan execution, receiving/disseminating information, and monitoring of key events occurs. In order for the FA battalion to accomplish its assigned mission, the TOC (as a minimum) should be able to perform the following critical functions:

- Advise the battalion commander, and as appropriate, key FS personnel, on the FA organization for combat, FA positioning, allocation of ammunition, and FA attack guidance.
- Perform tactical FD – select FA units and ammunition to support fire mission requests in response to the maneuver commander's attack guidance and to ensure the desired effects are achieved.
- Plan FA operations – generate a FASP that outlines the concept of operations and responsibilities for the battalion and describes the FA battalion commander's plan for accomplishing assigned missions and responsibilities. In a DS battalion, the FASP must address the concept of employment and responsibilities of all FA supporting the maneuver force, and is prepared in coordination with the brigade FSE as part of the maneuver OPORD. The operations section, in coordination with the FSCOORD and the FSEs, ensures that the FA plan is synchronized with the maneuver force plan.
- Direct and execute current operations - control FA and TA assets that are organic, attached, or reinforcing the battalion. Move and position firing elements and orchestrate the delivery of effective fires in support of force operations.
- Monitor technical FD – provide technical assistance to battery FDCs/platoon operation centers (POCs).
- Maintain situational awareness of the overall combined arms operation to ensure the battalion provides timely, responsive support and rapidly adjusts to the changes encountered.
- Conduct information management operations, receiving, processing, and disseminating critical battlefield information in all formats.
- Plan and direct counterfire operations as directed by force FA HQ as part of force FA counterfire operations, in support of a maneuver force (DS mission), and as necessary for force protection.
- Conduct essential intelligence operations and tasks.
- Perform FA targeting – generally focused on counterfire or targets related to specific battalion missions (such as suppression of enemy air defenses [SEAD]). FA battalions with a DS mission will also be integrally involved in the total targeting process of the supported maneuver force.
- Plan and direct Class V operations in coordination with the S4 and BAO.
- Plan/direct survey operations to support the battalion's FA operations and any assigned external survey support taskings for radars, target area survey requirements, mortars, or TA/intelligence assets.
- Plan, direct, and conduct all communications operations, to include radio, wire, automation management, and signal security.
- Plan and direct NBC defensive operations within the battalion.
- Provide general direction and overwatch of administrative and logistics operations in coordination with the ALOC and the batteries.
- Perform MSU operations.

HHSB/HHB COMMANDER & FIRST SERGEANT

2-10. The HHSB/HHB commander and 1SG are responsible for the security and logistical support for all of the elements in the battery. Because elements of the HHSB/HHB are usually dispersed among both the battalion CP and the trains, the HHSB/HHB commander and 1SG must work closely with all staff officers and section leaders to ensure adequate support. Where applicable, the HHSB/HHB leadership team also monitors the status and administrative and logistical requirements of FS or liaison teams.

2-11. In a HHB/SB based battalion, the HHB leadership team can usually devote more attention to the security, support, and movement of the battalion CP as the SB leadership team supervises much of the battalion trains (e.g., the field trains). (Both leadership teams must coordinate their efforts as elements from both batteries may be dispersed between the CP and the trains.) The HHB leadership team may, at times, operate out of the CP with some supply, food service, and battery maintenance assets temporarily moved forward to service the CP. While positioning and movement of the CP are primarily an S3 responsibility, the HHB leadership team can provide assistance in reconnaissance, movement, and occupation.

2-12. Because the HHSB leadership team has a greater sphere of responsibilities, which includes support for the trains, the staff sections must take increased responsibility for the security and support of the CP (S3) and the trains (S1/S4). Also, the HHSB CSS assets normally operate out of the trains. Most support for the CP may be provided on a periodic or as needed basis; however, a maintenance contact team may support the CP on an extended basis if needed. The HHSB leadership team usually operates from the trains area, moving their operations to the CP only when necessary to better coordinate support.

2-13. The increased responsibilities of the HHSB commander and 1SG may increase the need for them to operate independently. At these times, the 1SG may need to use a vehicle from one of the HHSB sections.

CP COMMUNICATIONS SUPPORT

2-14. The S6, the S3, and the HHSB/HHB commander work together to ensure the CP has adequate communications support. This primarily includes assistance in the set up and maintenance of radio, wire, and digital communications/automation equipment and retrans capability. Since the S6 must also support the battalion's other operations centers and batteries, the communications element in the CP may consist of a contact team that travels with and gives priority to CP support. At times, the majority of the S6 section may operate within the CP. If the battalion is supplemented with additional communication assets to support special missions or circumstances, such as theater missile defense (TMD) or SEAD, these may also become part of the CP.

SURVEY ELEMENTS

2-15. The battalion survey sections may base their operations out of the CP in order to allow better C2 by the S3.

SECTION II – TOC ORGANIZATION

TOC ORGANIZATION

2-16. The FA battalion TOC consists of two major functional elements – the operations and intelligence (O&I) element (composed of the operations section and the intelligence section) and the battalion FDC. The O&I element manages both current and future operations and coordinates all aspects of FA support. It also performs the planning and operational functions, such as developing FA plans/orders, conducting "artillerized" IPB, developing artillery targets, tracking the status of subordinate units, and controlling unit movements.

2-17. The FDC performs tactical FD by processing calls for fire, determining the type and amount of ammunition required to achieve the desired effects, and transmitting fire orders to the firing battery FDCs or POCs. The battalion FDC also monitors technical FD within the battalion.

OPERATIONS SECTION

2-18. The responsibilities of the operations section are to:
- Plan/coordinate the positioning of key C2 and CSS elements and firing batteries/platoons supporting current and future operations.
- Plan/coordinate all battalion movements and assist the battery commanders with coordination of movements. This includes assignment of routes and PAs and their clearance through the supported unit.
- Maintain current operational status of all organic, attached, and reinforcing/reinforced units.
- Prepare and disseminate all operational reports.
- Maintain the friendly situational awareness and common operational picture.
  - Maintain the operations maps – manual and automated.
  - Maintain manual status charts, logs, reports, and equivalent automated databases and reports.
- Provide the FDC with the most updated operational data on battery and platoon positions, both current and planned. When applicable, ensure FSEs and/or reinforced/reinforcing FA units are receiving all necessary current and planned operational data.
- Coordinate survey requirements for the zone of responsibility with the force FA survey planning and control element (SPCE).
- Advise the FDC, FSE (if applicable), reinforcing/reinforced FA (as appropriate), and force FA HQ on scheduling of all preplanned fires.
- Prepare and disseminate the FASP. As appropriate, assist FSEs with development of the FSP (DS mission) and coordinate preparation of the FASP as part of the FSP.
- Monitor ammunition consumption and direct resupply for the battalion.
- Coordinate liaison with a reinforced FA unit and direct the efforts of liaison personnel provided to the reinforced unit.

- Inform other staff sections (S1, S4, combat trains and field trains) of the current status of the supported forces and any changes that will require changes in FA support.
- Supervise battalion NBC defensive operations.
- Plan, coordinate, and supervise OPSEC within the battalion. Coordinate OPSEC with the S2 and S6.
- Assume control of reinforcing/reinforced artillery battalions during MSU operations, if necessary.
- Coordinate communications requirements for the battalion.

INTELLIGENCE SECTION

2-19. The intelligence section is an integral part of the O&I section. The intelligence section provides the commander and S3 with intelligence information essential to the operation and survival of the battalion. Specific responsibilities of the intelligence section are:

- Prepare in-depth "artillerized" IPB products of the supported unit sector in coordination with the supported maneuver and/or higher FA HQ S2. The FA battalion IPB is not an independent product. It is an extension of the supported maneuver unit and/or higher FA HQ IPB, focused on specific artillery-related intelligence requirements. IPB production is a continuous process.
- Assist the S3 in PA selection to ensure that positions are in consonance with IPB insights and survivability requirements.
- Develop the TA tab to the FASP and the RDO for organic and attached radars. The RDO designates positions and establishes cueing procedures. Coordinate the use of all TA radars, organic, or attached, with the battalion S3. (For more detailed information see FM 6-121, *Tactics, Techniques, and Procedures for Field Artillery Target Acquisition*.)
- Develop targeting data based on the supported maneuver commander's high-payoff target list (HPTL), attack guidance matrix (AGM) and force FA HQ direction. Provide recommendations and input to the targeting team that develops the HPTL and AGM for the maneuver commander and/or the force FA HQ. (For detailed information on the targeting process, see FM 6-20-10, *Tactics, Techniques, and Procedures for The Targeting Process*.)
- Monitor enemy artillery tactics and techniques within the supported unit sector and report to higher HQ.
- Exchange combat information and intelligence with the supported maneuver unit, subordinate units, reinforcing/reinforced units, higher HQ, and adjacent units as appropriate.
- Coordinate with battery 1SGs to develop a ground and air defense plan for the battalion.
- Assist the S3 with planning, coordination, and conduct of OPSEC.
- Coordinate external battalion security requirements.

FIRE DIRECTION CENTER

2-20. The battalion FDC provides tactical fire planning and fire control through automated command and control systems with manual backup and communications equipment. Specific responsibilities are as follows:

- Monitor and operate in the battalion FD and FS coordination nets (voice and data).
- Schedule fire units for preplanned fires in coordination with the S3, brigade FSO (if applicable), reinforcing/reinforced FA (as appropriate), and force FA HQ.
- Review the maneuver commander's attack guidance and/or force FA HQ directives and ensure they are applied to all fire mission requests. Ensure all battalion elements have the proper guidances and attack criteria entered into digital systems for both current and planned operations. Where applicable, this includes all FSEs and requires close coordination with the brigade/regimental FSE.
- Execute preplanned fires as requested by force FA HQ, FSEs, observers, and reinforced units.
- Coordinate fire mission processing procedures (data and voice) with FSEs, force FA HQ, reinforced/reinforcing units, and targeting/intelligence assets as appropriate. This includes digital fire mission routing and AFATDS intervention rules.
- Respond to immediate fire requests in the priority established by the supported maneuver commander's attack criteria.
- Ensure the battalion meets the five requirements for accurate predicted fires:
  - Accurate target location and size.
  - Accurate firing unit locations.
  - Updated weapon and ammunition information.
  - Valid met information.
  - Accurate computational procedures.
- Determine registration requirements in coordination with the S3.
- Provide technical FD assistance to battery/platoon FDCs as required. Coordinate for technical FD in case of catastrophic loss of the technical FD capability of battery/platoon FDCs.
- Ensure that all fire missions comply with current FSCMs.
- Assist the S3 in monitoring ammunition expenditures. In cannon units this includes ammunition lot management. Recommend changes to attack criteria or other tactical FD guidances as necessary.
- Conduct MSU operations as required.
- Establish and practice standard procedures for FDC operations in a degraded mode.

TOC BATTLE STAFF ORGANIZATION

2-21. The activities of the TOC are supervised by the S3. For the S3 to manage the FA battle, the entire TOC must work as an orchestrated team under his direction. Usually, the S3 is not given a specific shift of duty because he is expected to be directing operations during critical times. Table 2-1 depicts a sample 24-hour TOC schedule of key personnel.

Table 2-1. Sample 24-Hour TOC Operations

DUTY POSITION	FIRST SHIFT	SECOND SHIFT
Operations/Duty Officer	S3	Assistant S3
Chemical Officer	NBC NCO	Chemical Officer
Operations NCO	Master Gunner	Operations SGT
Operations AFATDS Operator	Ops FATDS Specialist	Ops FATDS Specialist
Intelligence AFATDS Operator	Intelligence Analyst	Intel FATDS Specialist
Intelligence/Targeting Officer	S2	Intelligence Sergeant or Targeting Officer [1]
FDO	FDO	Ch Fire Control SGT
FDC AFATDS Operator	Fire Control SGT	FDC FATDS Specialist
CESO	S6	Signal Spt Sys Ch

[1] – In FA battalions with a DS mission the targeting officer will usually operate in the supported maneuver brigade or regiment FSE.
Ops = operations, Intel = intelligence, Ch = chief, Spt = support, Sys = system

2-22. The S3 positions himself in the TOC where he can see and hear critical information that will allow him to make sound tactical decisions based on the FA commander's guidance. In the event the S3 is not in the TOC, the assistant S3 or shift officer assumes the S3's responsibility of managing TOC operations.

2-23. Each section should maintain a shift log, documenting the major events, actions, and message traffic applicable to the section, as well as accomplishment of major shift responsibilities. The log serves as a record of the major events and as a tool to prepare for shift briefings.

2-24. Shifts should overlap by about an hour to allow proper handover of the battle. Also, shift changeover for each section may be staggered to improve continuity (e.g., operations at 1200, intelligence at 1400, and FDC at 1600). There should be, by TSOP, an established procedure where, approximately an hour before shift change, all maps, status boards, shift logs, and such are updated with the most current information, all filing and document destruction is accomplished, and general TOC housekeeping completed. Both manual and automated systems must be addressed. The oncoming shift should be given time to review maps, status boards, shift logs, and other applicable tools. The outgoing shift should provide a shift briefing that addresses, as a minimum, current operational status (FA and maneuver), TOC status (vehicles and equipment), and battalion, TOC, and section tasks. The S3, or section leaders, may establish a standard TSOP format for the shift change briefing.

SECTION III – TOC CONFIGURATIONS

2-25. The following figures provide examples of TOC configurations (external array and common area). They are provided only as examples and for use as guides to stimulate ideas for development of a functional TOC tailored to meet the needs of the unit.

2-26. The examples provided are for towed (T) cannon (Figure 2-1), SP cannon (Figure 2-2) and MLRS (Figure 2-3) battalion TOCs. However, any battalion can use any of the basic layouts (back-to-back, side-by-side) as a general guide in organizing a TOC. Figure 2-3 provides a more detailed example of the internal layout within a TOC to include the placement of C2 systems. The digital equipment shown in the figure can also be removed from the vehicles and set up in the track extensions when mobility and rapid displacement are not required. (Note – C2V is used generically for C2 vehicle)

TOWED CANNON BATTALION TOC LAYOUT (EXAMPLE)

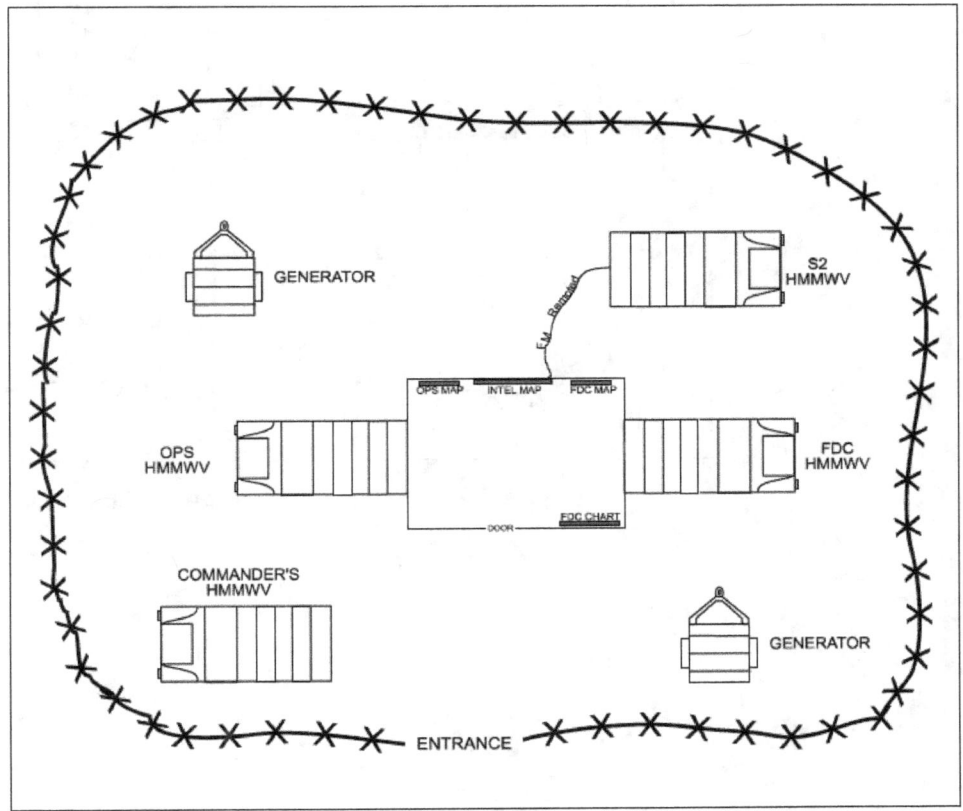

Figure 2-1. 105mm/155mm (T) Cannon Battalion TOC Array

FM 3-09.21 (FM 6-20-1)

SP CANNON BATTALION TOC LAYOUT (EXAMPLE)

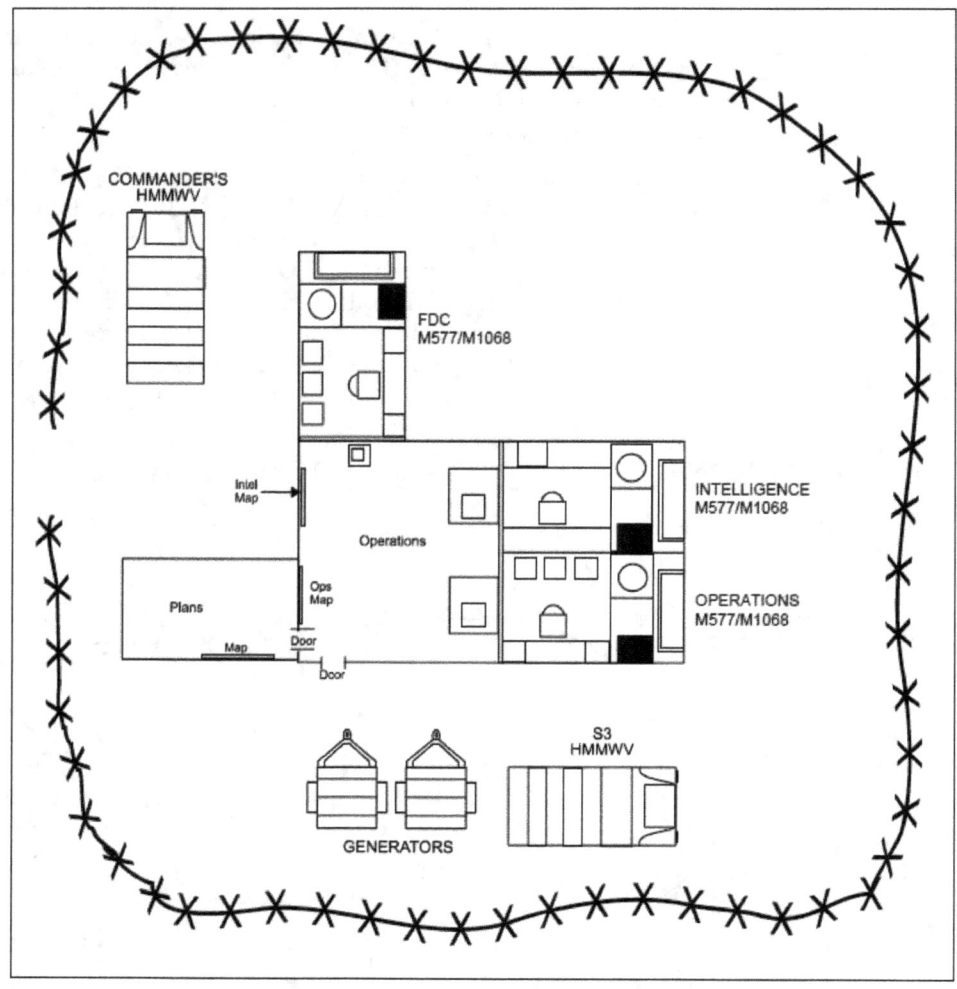

Figure 2-2. 155mm (SP) Cannon Battalion TOC Array

MLRS BATTALION TOC LAYOUT (EXAMPLE)

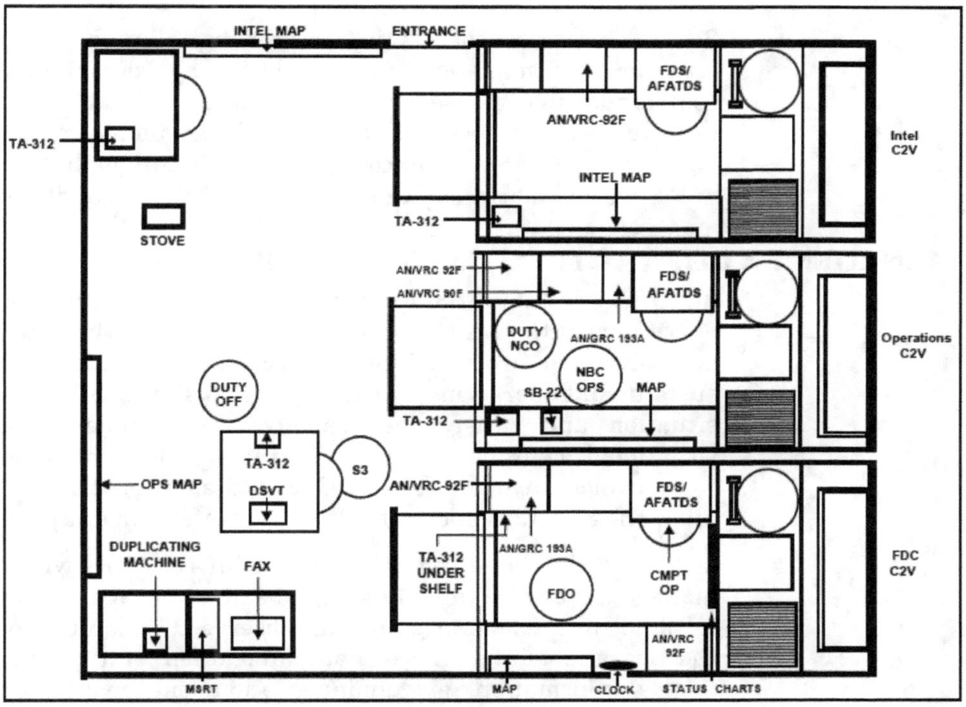

Figure 2-3. MLRS Battalion TOC – Side-by-Side Configuration

TOC EQUIPMENT

2-27. The following items are recommended (but not limited to) for use in the TOC common areas (extensions) to enhance mission execution:
- Tables/desks/chairs/clock/heaters (as required).
- TA-1035 telephones/remoted mobile subscriber radio telephone (MSRT).
- TA-312 telephones. Remotes for combat net radios (CNRs).
- Reproduction equipment and facsimile (fax) machine.
- Weapon and load bearing equipment (LBE) racks.
- Plans, intelligence, and operations map boards.
- Storage bins for overlays and maps.
- Status boards for tracking combat information.

2-28. The common area is the primary workspace for the key TOC members. During frequent or anticipated movement, much equipment will remain uploaded, with much work occurring inside the vehicles. If the TOC will remain in place for an extended time, most of the equipment can be moved or remoted to the common area. Space is a limitation and tentage may be needed to provide additional workspace. TOC leaders must consider weather, as some of the equipment may be sensitive to extreme temperature, humidity, dirt and dust, or other factors. As the common area is also more vulnerable to shrapnel and small-arms fire, the S3 should consider force protection measures in determining TOC setup.

SECTION IV – TOC INFORMATION MANAGEMENT

2-29. The process of C2 in the FA battalion is unique. Unlike the C2 structures of maneuver forces where the commander directs the forces commander-to-commander, the FA battalion S3 controls unit movements and executes artillery fires based on the FA battalion commander's guidance. The battalion commander still commands the battalion, but the S3 is the manager of FA assets and translates the vision of the commander into FA fires.

MANAGEMENT OF TACTICAL INFORMATION

2-30. The battalion S3 and the rest of the TOC staff control the day-to-day operations of the FA battalion. It is at the TOC where battlefield information is received and processed into FA tactical movement, delivery of FA fires, and sustainment operations. For the battalion staff to effectively track the tactical situation and satisfy the maneuver commander's concept of FA fires, situational awareness and battle tracking must be as accurate as possible. The physical layout of the TOC should support the flow of information and allow the S3 to direct the efforts of the staff in an efficient manner.

2-31. The S3 should position himself in the TOC where he can effectively manage his battle staff. He should be at a vantage point where he has access to radios and telephones and can observe the monitors of the C2 computers, the operations/intelligence maps, and other status charts. He can take in tactical information, give guidance, and avoid the common pitfall of becoming preoccupied with tasks better handled by subordinates.

2-32. The primary information pipelines in the TOC are its internal and external voice and digital nets. (See Chapter 3, for TOC net structures.) Normally, in a DS battalion, the two nets that give the S3 the clearest picture of current events on the battlefield are the maneuver brigade FS coordination and the maneuver command nets (voice). It is important to understand that the FA staff monitors these nets and does not normally transmit on them. To reduce confusion in the TOC, it is recommended these two nets be the only ones audible on remote devices in the operations (extension) area. The other voice nets should be monitored by headset or monitored from inside the appropriate staff vehicles. The S3 is kept informed of the majority of the traffic on the other nets (voice and data) by status charts updates, reviewing message forms, and computer printouts. Anything of significance that requires the S3's attention should be brought to him immediately. In a battalion providing reinforcing or GS fires, the communications requirements will differ, but the S3 will still focus on the nets that will provide him the tactical information to make sound, logical decisions.

2-33. The battalion FD nets, operations/fire net, and maneuver FS coordination net are the S3's principal conduits to understand where fires are planned and executed. These nets allow the TOC to execute its responsibility to review every mission and provide a secondary independent check to verify that no FSCMs are being violated and to reduce the chances of fratricide. Data and voice missions should be checked. The S3 observes where targets are in relation to the tactical situation to better understand the flow of the battle.

2-34. The O&I section must closely monitor the information received from all tactical information sources (voice, digital, fax) to verify critical data, identify potentially inaccurate information, and to resolve discrepancies between conflicting reports or data.

2-35. By monitoring the supported maneuver command net, the S3 can determine the tempo of the operation, anticipate where the focus of fires will be directed by the FSCOORD, and maintain the situation map(s). This allows the S3 to be proactive in positioning units and managing ammunition for effective tactical control of fires. If used, the net should be remoted to the S3's battle station.

2-36. The TOC passes tactical orders and information to the batteries and any supporting artillery over the battalion command net. This net can be remoted to the operations sergeant's post and monitored by a radio telephone operator with headset. The S3 receives the information passed on this net by monitoring the computer screens and status boards and by reviewing messages and reports used to update situation maps. Situation reports and updates of information with battalion combat and field trains should not be passed on this net. Routine administrative and logistical traffic should be sent on the battalion administrative/logistics net or mobile subscriber equipment (MSE) network.

2-37. The S2 monitors the supported maneuver O&I net. The focus of the traffic on this net is maneuver specific but the S2 can garner much information relevant to FA support requirements and operational/security considerations. The S2 section should monitor this with either a remote (with headset) or from inside the S2 vehicle. Routine traffic can be passed to the S3 on message forms. Critical traffic requiring the S3's attention may be monitored, from his battle station, on the S2's remote. FA battalions with a GSR/GS mission probably will not monitor this net, but the force FA HQ O&I net instead.

2-38. The DIVARTY/FA brigade command/fire network is the most immediate voice link the FA battalion has to access the force artillery counterfire system, request for additional fires, FS coordination, and C2 of subordinate units (particularly when out of the range of CNRs).

2-39. The MSE system gives the TOC a tremendous capability to coordinate actions and to verify or exchange critical information. It is ideal for routine traffic between the TOC, ALOC, FSEs, BSOC, force FA HQ, and supported force HQ. It is a superb tool for rapid land coordination with force FA HQ, supported brigade or battalion task forces for areas to move and position supporting FA units and assets.

2-40. On today's battlefield, an increasing amount of tactical information flows over the FA battalion's automated C2 equipment. The TOC constantly interfaces digitally with other units' primary C2 systems and with other digital devices/systems that generate, receive, or forward information. Automated battle management is a developing skill as system capabilities and unit tactics and techniques are rapidly evolving.

INFORMATION MANAGEMENT TOOLS

2-41. The capability of a TOC to function effectively is based on the staff's ability to manage information. This is not a simple task when considering the volume of traffic that is passed and captured in the TOC's battle command system (AFATDS, IFSAS, FDS, or LTACFIRE) and associated/stand-alone communications systems. It is very easy for units to experience information overload unless they have simple and effective methods in place to process information.

2-42. In the TOC, the staff may use graphical displays (e.g., map boards with overlays, status boards, and/or digital screens) to give the FA commander a complete situation report of the status of his unit, the supported maneuver unit, and/or the reinforcing/reinforced FA units. The displays should be informative enough to assist him in making tactical and administrative decisions, as well as aid in managing his FA assets. This will only happen if the staff has an effective system in place to visually display critical data.

AUTOMATED C2 EQUIPMENT

2-43. The S3 and all TOC officers and NCOs should understand the capabilities and limitations of their automated C2 equipment. They should understand what screen views are available and how those views can be changed to display desired data and to filter out undesired information that can clutter the screens. TOC leaders must quickly recognize bad or suspect data on the screens or automated reports as this data can be rapidly disseminated to numerous external and internal users.

2-44. Operators should be thoroughly trained in all aspects of the C2 systems they use. They should know how to enter, extract, and manipulate data, change screen views, and prepare/pull reports. They should also understand the significance of the data they are handling. This includes identifying critical graphics (such as a contaminated area), reports, and messages that must be brought to a leader's attention immediately. They should understand when to alert leaders to changes in key data such as ammunition levels. Leaders should ensure that C2 equipment operators are not merely keyboard operators but critical members of the warfighting team.

2-45. The TOC should have established procedures to maintain a manual backup capability. The TOC will quickly need accurate maps, overlays, charts, printed computer reports, and other manual records if automated systems fail. During peak periods, TOC leaders should monitor how well both automated and manual information tools are being maintained. They must ensure TOC personnel back up, print out, and post or record digital data so the TOC can immediately execute manual operations if necessary. TOC training should include drills in switching to degraded operations (in which one or more automated systems malfunction) and to a totally manual information management system in case of major automation failure.

MAP BOARDS

2-46. Standardized map boards should be established in accordance with force FA HQ and/or supported unit TSOP. This will facilitate standard map mounting procedures throughout the organization and allow overlays to be exchanged with minimum loss of accuracy.

OVERLAYS

2-47. Acetate overlays are constructed to conform to standardized map boards. All overlays should be the same size and edged with tape. The goal is to display graphics on an overlay, mount the overlay on various map boards, and maintain an acceptable degree of accuracy.

2-48. Units should establish a standard (TSOP) mounting and posting system for overlays. When an overlay is placed on a map board, the following information should be visible:
- Overlay description.
- OPORD, FASP, fragmentary order (FRAGO), number if applicable.
- Unit originating the overlay.
- Date-time group.
- Security classification (top and bottom).
- Grid-line tick marks for orientation (minimum of two).

STATUS BOARDS

2-49. The staff should track the current status of elements and other combat information on status boards (containing appropriate charts) that are neat and organized. Much of this information may exist in various automated formats in AFATDS or other C2 software. This information is automatically updated as the new information is input by TOC personnel or is digitally received from other elements. Manual status boards and information folders should be compared to the automated information formats/sources to facilitate maintenance and emergency transition to manual operations. However, the manual status boards should be designed to best organize/display required data in a TOC setting.

2-50. The TOC may position and maintain status boards along functional lines. For example, the S2's status board may contain a RDO, air defense status, survey section equipment status, MOPP level, or battalion defense diagram. The operations section status board(s) may contain all the call signs and frequencies, track combat strength and ammunition, FSCMs, observer locations, the FASM, or FS execution matrix (FSEM).

2-51. Within the TOC, the minimum information to be tracked includes:
- CCIR.
- Commander's intent (Immediate and two above).
- Missions two levels up and the battalion mission statement.
- The maneuver commander's concept of FS.
- EFSTs and EFATs.
- FASM/FSEM.
- Batteries'/platoons' primary, alternate, and supplementary locations.
- Howitzer/launcher status (crew and weapon system) and posture.
- Ammunition carrier strength.
- FS team-vehicle (FIST-V) status.

- FDC/POC status – to include personnel strength and status of automated FD systems.
- Ammunition count by type and platoon.
- Radar positions, zones (active and planned), and cueing schedule.
- Order planning timeline.
- NBC status.
- Priority of fires and current FSCMs.
- Call signs and frequencies.
- Air defense artillery (ADA) status.
- Personnel status.
- Task organization/FA organization for combat.
- Radiation exposure status.
- AGM and HPTL.
- Risk assessment.
- Friendly mortar locations.
- Main supply routes.
- Immediate-actions status.

SITUATION MAPS

2-52. There are normally three situation maps mounted on map boards in the TOC. They are plans, intelligence, and operations maps. Each has functions that may overlap. The plans map is used during the planning process and for future operations. The intelligence map is primarily used for IPB process, FA targeting, and current enemy situation. The operations map is the most widely used in the TOC to maintain the current friendly situation. The intelligence and operations maps should always complement each other.

2-53. The operations map should contain overlays depicting the current location of friendly maneuver forces, FISTs, FA units (and range fans), radars under battalion control, proposed PAs, FSCMs, and current fire plan(s).

2-54. Situation maps should be kept simple and manageable. Tactical information should be displayed on one of the following type overlays:
- Maneuver graphics overlay.
- FA position/movement overlay.
- The target overlay.

Maneuver Graphics Overlay

2-55. The supported maneuver TOC produces this overlay, which depicts the supported maneuver AO, objectives, battle positions, locations of boundaries, phase lines, other maneuver control measures, and airspace coordination graphics. Normally, the brigade FSO coordinates for a copy for the DS battalion TOC. The S3 uses this overlay in planning movements and clearing fires. As a minimum, the TOC disseminates copies to the firing batteries, survey section, organic/attached radars, combat and field trains, and R/GSR artillery TOC. The force FA HQ should provide graphics to GS battalions. Additionally, the brigade FSO will input the geometry into the automated tactical fire control system (for GS battalion, the DIVARTY, Corps Arty, or the FA brigade fire control element [FCE] provides the geometry).

2-56. Because it constitutes the frame of reference, the maneuver graphics overlay is the first overlay placed on the situation map boards during execution. On the operations map, the S3 uses it as a check to preclude fratricide and to gage the tempo of the battle in regard to the maneuver plan.

FA Position Area Overlay

2-57. The FA PA overlay is used for planning PAs for firing batteries, trains, the TOC, radar, reinforcing artillery units, and other force FA assets. It depicts all FA unit positions and range fans. Planning PAs is a continuous process that involves the close coordination between the DS TOC and the brigade TOC (for GSR/GS units, coordination is made with the DIVARTY or FA brigade TOC). The assistant S3, with help from the S2, normally prepares the overlay. PAs should be clearly identifiable on the overlay. Coordination is made with the brigade TOC, through the brigade FSO, for land clearance (also, force FA HQ is queried for position requirements for any GSR/GS assets). Copies of the overlay are distributed to the brigade FSO, firing batteries, organic/attached radar, combat and field trains, reinforcing artillery, and to the force FA HQ.

Target Overlay

2-58. As a planning tool, it supplements the target list worksheet or computer printout by graphically depicting all targets and the total fire plan for an operation. It is used in developing the PA overlay for ensuring batteries can be positioned to range targets. This is the top overlay on the situation map. Since the overlay supplements the printed target list and is subject to constant changes, it is not normally reproduced as part of any plan. The degree of precision needed for delivery of fires discourages its use for anything other than a tool for planning and graphic aid in execution.

2-59. As targets are fired, they should be colored red in accordance with FM 6-40. This graphically shows the S3 where fires are focused and assists him in anticipating future requirements.

Additional Overlays

2-60. There are other overlays that can be used to assist the S3 and TOC personnel in planning and executing the FASP. Most are only needed in special situations. The S3 decides the order in which they appear on the situation map. Some of these overlays may include:
- Obstacle overlay -- In addition to showing the location of planned and fired scatterable mines (SCATMINE) minefields, this overlay shows the location of existing and planned engineer obstacles. The S3 may use this overlay in planning PAs for firing preplanned SCATMINE, unit movements to avoid obstacles/choke points and establishing radar sensor zones to help protect forces. The S2 maintains this overlay.

- Event template with critical event matrix -- This overlay is developed by the S2 in the IPB process. It illustrates a timed-phased analysis of the enemy's course of action (COA). The event template is an overlay that may contain named areas of interest (NAIs), targeted areas of interest (TAIs), enemy timeline and order of battle, and DST or enemy critical events matrix. The overlay aids the FA staff in planning unit movements while providing continuous fires, ensuring the FASP will support maneuver operations and when used in conjunction with the FSEM, it assists in fine-tuning FA assets synchronization.
- NBC -- This overlay has two functions. The first is to show areas of NBC contamination in the AO. The second is to show the location of decontamination sites and routes to each. The overlay is generated and maintained by the battalion chemical officer/NCO.
- Communications capability -- If the terrain presents any unique communications profile limitations, the S6 would construct a site profile of the terrain in the AO. This assists the S3 in planning employment of retrans stations, displacement of units, and TOC site selection.
- Radar capability -- Radar capability overlays depict the locations/coverage of organic, attached or GS Firefinder radars. It is used to display all confirmed targets located by the radar(s) and control measures in the current zone of operations. This overlay is maintained by the S2.
- Logistics -- This overlay is generated by the S4 under the supervision of the battalion XO. It depicts all pertinent logistics facilities such as main supply routes, alternate supply routes, maintenance collection points, mortuary affairs collection points, and ATPs. The S1 and S4 representatives at both the combat and field trains maintain the logistics overlay. A copy is furnished to the TOC.

DIGITAL MAPS

2-61. Digital maps are increasingly valuable tools as C2 software versions are upgraded. AFATDS map controls allow the user considerable leeway in modifying the view and the data displayed. The S3, S2, and FDO should understand the map display capabilities of their AFATDS software and determine how to best set up and coordinate digital map displays within the TOC to maximize efficient use of the systems available. Different views may be needed for different situations. All AFATDS operators should be able to quickly display a digital map in the format needed. AFATDS training drills should include rehearsals in generating the map displays required by TOC leaders.

SECTION V – CP POSITIONING AND MOVEMENT

2-62. Movement and positioning of the battalion CP are controlled by the S3 based on the guidance and direction of the commander. The S3 is assisted by the S2, who provides mobility information concerning terrain, trafficability of roads, obstacles, minefields, and contaminated areas, and survivability information regarding ground, air, and NBC threat from enemy forces and information about the civilian populace in the area. The S6 provides guidance on communications factors. The HHSB/HHB leadership team and other members of the TOC may also assist with reconnaissance, security, and advance party operations. Clearance for the positions and movement routes must be coordinated with the maneuver force, a function that the FSEs assist with, especially in battalions with a DS/R mission.

CP POSITIONING CONSIDERATIONS

2-63. The S3 uses the IPB products in determining positions. The S3 usually plans primary, alternate, and possibly supplementary CP positions (see Chapter 6 for further discussion of these terms). The primary consideration for positioning the CP is its ability to accomplish its mission. He must also consider whether or not the CP will be collocated with other elements, such as the battalion trains or a supported maneuver unit CP. Several other factors must also be considered:

- The general movement of the forward line of own troops (FLOT), which may be forward, rearward, static, or erratic. In a sustained, rapidly advancing offensive operation, the CP may need to be positioned as far forward as feasible. During a rapidly withdrawing retrograde, the CP may be placed farther to the rear than normal. On a non-linear battlefield, the general ebb and flow of the fight and the disposition of forces is still a consideration, however, security considerations are increased as the situation maybe be less predictable than on a linear battlefield.
- Nature of the threat.
  - Counterfire threat. In response to a high counterfire threat the CP may be placed farther to the rear; outside the range of mortars and as many of the enemy's artillery systems as feasibly possible. Defilade/reverse slope positioning may provide increased protection, however, retrans of communications may be necessary.
  - Air/space threat. High air threat may place increased need for positioning the CP in heavily wooded or urban terrain that allows better camouflage. The CP may also be placed close to ADA that can provide coverage and away from anticipated or identified enemy air corridors. The use of wooded/urban terrain, coupled with camouflage and light discipline, are also critical to reducing vulnerability to air and satellite imagery.

- Ground threat. Consider positioning the CP with or near other friendly elements when there is a high risk from enemy penetrating forces or small force operations. When there is a threat of rapid penetration from an enemy attack or counterattack, position the CP off of the expected axis of advance, especially any high-speed avenues of approach, if possible. Increase the size of the CP by adding CSS elements or arranging infantry or military police (MP) support.
- Electronic warfare (EW) threat. To overcome jamming, position the CP closer to firing batteries or the retrans site. To reduce electronic locating vulnerability, position the CP in defilade/masked locations and use retrans. Also position the CP away from the maneuver CP and the FA trains to reduce the threat to them and to reduce the electronic signature. The CP should be kept small to present the smallest electronic signature.
- Communications factors such as digital and radio communication ranges and retrans capability must be considered. Communications is a function of the distances between units, the capabilities of the equipment, atmospheric conditions, and terrain.
- Terrain.
  - If canalizing terrain to the rear limits movement options, and the CP could be quickly cut off, consider positioning close to high-speed avenues needed for movement while considering potential exposure to threat penetrations.
  - Terrain that is extremely wet, rocky, or steep, and urban terrain may interfere with weapon platforms, grounding of equipment, tiedowns for extensions and shelters, and preparation of defensive positions.
  - Hilly or mountainous terrain provides survivability advantages, but may also interfere with communications for the CP.
- Friendly forces and missions.
  - When extensive coordination with the maneuver HQ is critical a DS battalion may position its CP close to the maneuver CP.
  - In a DS/R relationship, the CPs of the two FA battalions may be positioned laterally or in depth, depending on the deployment of the batteries and the concept for FS (in addition to the normal positioning considerations. C2 and survivability are critical considerations for DS and R units due to their generally closer proximity to the FLOT.
  - The CP of a GS/GSR unit is positioned to allow communication with the force FA HQ, its own elements, and when applicable, the reinforced unit. Communications, especially for corps FA units, is a critical consideration as GS/GSR units frequently communicate at more extended ranges than DS and R battalions.

JUMP TOC CONSIDERATIONS

2-64. To facilitate CONOPS during movement of the CP to a new location, the battalion may use a JTOC. This is a variation of movement by echelon in which a small portion of the TOC, and minimal security and support elements, will move to the new CP location in advance of the remainder of the CP. During the JTOC's movement, tactical fire control is maintained at the

CP/TOC (-), which also begins preparation for movement. Once the JTOC is in place it conducts a CONOPS exchange with the TOC (-) and establishes communications with subordinate, higher, and supported units before it assumes control of the battalion. The remainder of the CP then march orders and moves to the new CP location. Normal operations resume once the CP has been fully established.

2-65. Composition of the JTOC is limited to key equipment/personnel. As an example, a JTOC may consist of (but is not limited to) the following: high-mobility multipurpose wheeled vehicle (HMMWV), operations vehicle with extension, current status boards and situation maps, S2 or S3, assistant S3, TOC NCO, FDO/FDC NCO, S2 NCO, selected O&I and FDC personnel and other HHB or HHSB elements to provide support and security. However, the JTOC also could consist of about half of the CP. The size and composition of the JTOC will depend on the tactical situation and the S3's major concerns. A smaller JTOC may be preferred during periods of rapid advancement and frequent moves, while a larger JTOC would be desired if security is a major issue, and speed of movement is not critical. During a rapidly advancing offensive operation, the JTOC may be moving again shortly after the rest of the CP has closed and assumed control of the battalion.

2-66. The unit can use a version of the JTOC technique, basically a reversed sequence, during defensive operations when the battalion must move to the rear or laterally away from a penetration. The bulk of the CP would move first, while the JTOC remains in place controlling the battalion until a new CP is established. This allows C2 to remain close to the fight, while retaining the mobility to quickly move out at the last possible moment.

2-67. The battalion can also form a TAC to put the battalion commander and/or S3 closer to the action, near the maneuver commander, his CP, or a FSE. It is especially used during operations requiring frequent, fast moves where the main TOC would have trouble keeping pace with the supported maneuver unit. It would be the focal point for battalion C2 of the current fight, emphasizing operations, FD, and limited TA/intelligence functions. The main TOC would follow as possible and monitor the situation, prepared to assume control if necessary. It continues to conduct planning and other TOC functions in order to allow the TAC to concentrate on the current fight during a critical stage in the battle. The TAC will consist of only one or two vehicles that have the speed and maneuverability to keep up with the maneuver forces. It should have a more robust communications and FATDS capability than a JTOC as it may operate separate from the TOC for a longer period and must be fully capable of controlling the battalion's fires and directing all subordinate elements. The TAC technique is also useful when the commander wants to send a TOC element forward with a battery artillery raid.

CP MOVEMENT TECHNIQUES

2-68. CP movement is influenced by several factors: security, organization for combat, personnel strength, equipment status, availability of mutually supporting battalions, and tactical situation. The TOC may move as a single unit, in two or more echelons, or in several small elements. A major consideration in determining the TOC movement technique is the availability of a reinforcing, reinforced, or other mutually supporting battalion. If another battalion can temporarily assume the CP's functions, the commander and S3 have more options for moving the CP. Chapter 6 provides further discussion of movement techniques.

NO MUTUALLY SUPPORTING BATTALION

2-69. The CP may move by echelon and may utilize the JTOC concept more frequently when another FA unit is not available to temporarily assume control of the TOC's operations. If the battalion CP must move as a unit, the ALOC, a firing battery, or the brigade FSE (DS units) can assume portions of the C2 functions until the CP is reestablished. Rehearsal and clear TSOPs are needed to prevent confusion.

NO MUTUALLY SUPPORTING BATTALION - CATASTROPHIC LOSS

2-70. If the battalion TOC is not, or will not be operational and a JTOC cannot be established, the battalion commander may shift control to the brigade FSE, a designated battery/platoon operations center, or even force FA HQ. Another option is for the ALOC to assume all C2 functions except tactical and technical fire control, which would be performed by the brigade FSE, a firing battery, or force FA HQ. If this occurs, TOC staff still capable of performing their duties should collocate with and assist the temporary element in controlling the battalion until the TOC is capable of resuming control. Generally, the surviving elements of the CP will move rapidly as a unit to the new location (possibly the ALOC) and begin recovery, reorganization, and reconstitution as appropriate. As soon as possible, the TOC would assume control and normal CP operations would be restored.

MUTUALLY SUPPORTING BATTALION

2-71. When a reinforced, reinforcing, or other mutually supporting battalion is available and CP movements are required, MSU operations may be conducted to transfer tactical control to the other FA battalion TOC. The supported unit should ensure the supporting unit TOC has an updated status on all elements and digital/voice communications are established. Before reassuming control, the supported unit TOC should re-establish CONOPS with the supporting TOC and with all applicable elements.

FM 3-09.21 (FM 6-20-1)

SECTION VI – LIAISON OPERATIONS

2-72. One of the seven inherent responsibilities of a FA battalion assigned a R or a GSR tactical mission is to provide liaison to the unit being reinforced. However, the battalion commander may also direct liaison be established with another FA unit, a maneuver unit, or any other element when he identifies a need for close, effective coordination with that other unit or element. Liaison may even be necessary with non-military elements.

2-73. Liaison is the contact or intercommunication maintained between elements to ensure mutual understanding and unity of purpose and action. Liaison activities augment the commander's ability to synchronize and focus combat power. Liaison includes establishing and maintaining physical contact and communications. Liaison activities ensure the following:
- Mutual cooperation and understanding between commanders and staffs.
- Coordination on tactical matters to achieve mutual purpose, support, and action.
- Exact and precise understanding of implied or inferred coordination measures to achieve synchronized results.

2-74. Overall, liaison becomes another tool to help commanders overcome friction, gain assurance that supporting and supported commanders understand implicit coordination, and achieve synchronized results. Effective liaison enhances the commander's confidence in planning and in mission execution.

2-75. If the reinforced and reinforcing units are digitized, and both units maintain communications and situational understanding, the actual physical presence of a liaison team at the reinforced unit may not be required. If the two units choose to co-locate CPs or FDCs, the liaison requirement is met and no liaison is required.

2-76. When a corps FA battalion is assigned a tactical mission of GS, it will normally be positioned in the area of operation of a maneuver brigade. The FA battalion commander may consider sending one of his liaison teams to the maneuver brigade FSE. This team can help the battalion commander in tracking the maneuver situation and in keeping the maneuver commander informed of the location and status of a sizable friendly force that is in his area but not under his control.

2-77. When an Army FA battalion supports a US marine air-ground task force (MAGTF), it should establish liaison with the marine force. The marine controlling FA HQ will normally provide reciprocal liaison to the Army FA battalion.

LIAISON ORGANIZATION

2-78. Corps FA battalions have one or more organic liaison sections. Each liaison section consists of an officer, a sergeant, and one enlisted soldier. Equipment usually consists of a wheeled vehicle and a radio (AN/VRC-90F), a precision lightweight global positioning system (GPS) receiver (PLGR), and an AFATDS or IFSAS.

2-79. Divisional FA battalions do not have organic liaison teams since their requirement for liaison with the supported units is usually satisfied by the FSEs collocated with the maneuver force CPs. However, when divisional battalions are assigned a R or a GSR mission, they must provide for liaison if communications linkup is inadequate. If no means are available to establish full-time liaison, then periodic coordination between units may have to suffice. Additional information on liaison operations is in FM 101-5.

RESPONSIBILITIES

2-80. Both the supporting and the supported unit have responsibilities important to successful liaison. The supporting unit, which dispatches a liaison team, is frequently referred to as the sending unit. The supported unit, which receives the team, is called the receiving unit. The responsibilities of the sending and receiving units, the liaison section, and the LNO and sergeant are discussed below.

THE SENDING (REINFORCING) UNIT

2-81. Sending units are responsible for ensuring that liaison personnel are competent and thoroughly trained. The liaison personnel must:

- Remain up to date on current and future operations, be thoroughly briefed, and understand what information to pass to the receiving unit.
- Remain current with sending unit operations.
- Have the appropriate credentials for authenticating the liaison team to the receiving unit commander. This is especially critical if the team is being provided to an allied force.
- Have appropriate security clearances and courier orders.
- Have reliable transportation, communications, automation, and COMSEC equipment with appropriate codes. The sending unit must plan to replace equipment and COMSEC material, if necessary.
- Provide TSOPs to receiving units that outline liaison team missions, functions, procedures, and duties.
- Inform the receiving unit of the contents of any reports sent to the sending unit.
- Have weapons and ammunition for personal protection.
- Arrive at the receiving unit at the appointed place and time.

THE RECEIVING (REINFORCED) UNIT

2-82. The receiving unit is responsible for the following:

- Notifying the sending unit of the time, place, and point of contact for the liaison team.
- Briefing the arriving liaison team on the status of current operations and about the receiving unit.
- Providing the sending unit operational details, to include movement and logistic information, which impact on sending unit operations.

- Ensuring that liaison teams have access to the commander and key staff officers to communicate information critical to the sending unit.
- Providing communications and COMSEC equipment, if the liaison team operates in the receiving unit's radio nets and telephone system.
- Providing the following administrative support:
  - A copy of the receiving unit's TSOP.
  - Workspace, electrical power for automation equipment, and maintenance support, to include fuels and lubricants.
  - Life support facilities, rations, maps, small-arms ammunition, and Class II and Class IV supplies.
  - Medical support and physical security.

THE LIAISON SECTION

2-83. Specific liaison responsibilities for the section include the following:
- Exchange information on the tactical situation between the reinforcing/reinforced battalion CPs.
- Establish digital and voice communications as required for:
  - Exchanging orders, situation reports, and intelligence reports.
  - Passing fire missions.
  - Using quickfire nets, as required.
  - Passing unit locations, ammunition status, weapon strength, target lists, and fire plans between the two units.
  - Facilitating the rapid clearance of fires.
- Exchanging critical TSOP information.
- Coordinating the exchange of all digital information (communications settings and addresses, unit data, targeting information, technical and tactical fire control, and commander guidances.)

2-84. During the liaison tour, the LNO or team should also:
- Promote cooperation between the sending HQ and the receiving HQ.
- Proactively obtain information.
- Facilitate comprehension of the sending unit commander's intent.
- Help the sending unit's commander assess current and future operations.
- Remain informed of the sending unit's current situation and make that information available to the receiving unit's commander and staff.
- Expeditiously inform the sending unit of upcoming missions, tasks, and orders of the receiving unit.
- Inform the receiving unit's commander of the content of the reports it transmits to the sending unit.
- Keep a record of reports, listing everyone met (including the person's name, rank, duty position, and phone number) as well as primary operators and their phone numbers.

2-85. A checklist is provided on the following pages that may assist the LNO section in its preparations and operations. An example of an outline of an LNO's handbook or TSOP is also provided.

	**EXAMPLE LNO CHECKLIST**
	**PREPARATION FOR OPERATIONS**

	EQUIPMENT
	Personal field gear and equipment
	Night vision goggles
	GPS receiver
	Camouflage screening system
	Hex tent/stove/cots/water cans
	Fire control system (AFATDS or IFSAS)
	Communications Systems: - Radios/COMSEC devices - OE254 Antenna - AN/GRA-39 Remote - TA-312 Telephone - DR-8 (w/WD-1A/TT)
	TA-1035/U with MX-10891/G field wire
	Maps and overlay material
	Field table with chairs
	Office supplies and materials to include: - Pens/pencils/markers - Notepads and tablets - Rubbing alcohol/paper towels - DA Form 1594/fire mission logs
	INFORMATION
	TSOP/SOI/operations plan (OPLAN)/OPORD of parent unit
	TSOP/SOI/OPLAN/OPORD of supported unit
	Location and route to supported CP
	Intelligence update
	Current plans, orders, maps, overlays, and targeting information to include concept of operations, concept of fires, and commander's intent
	Unit locations/readiness and strength
	Land management coordinating agency (force HQ FSE)
	Logistical considerations and supporting agencies
	Current status of supported unit's mission
	References; field and technical manuals
	BEFORE DEPARTING THE SENDING UNIT
	Ensure you understand what the commander wants the receiving commander to know
	Arrange for a briefing from all staff elements concerning current and future operations
	Verify the receipt of and do you understand the tasks your staff has given you
	Obtain the correct maps, traces, overlays (including maneuver, engineer, and FS)

Figure 2-4. Example LNO Checklist

☐	Arrange for communications and cryptographic equipment, codes, and signal instructions; for their protection and security, and for their update or replacement, as necessary
☐	Arrange for the departure of the liaison party
☐	Complete route-reconnaissance and time-management plans so that you will arrive at the designated location on time
☐	Ensure you and your party know how you are to destroy the information you are carrying in an emergency, in transit, and at the receiving unit
☐	Ensure you have SOI, and that you and your party know the challenge and password
☐	Inform your HQ of when you will leave, the route you will take, when you will arrive, POC for linkup with receiving unit, when known, the estimated time and route of your return
☐	Pick up all correspondence designated for the receiving HQ
☐	Conduct a radio check (Ensure you have appropriate COMSEC equipment)
☐	Know the impending moves of your HQ and of the receiving HQ
☐	Bring the appropriate automation equipment or computers to support your operation
☐	Pack adequate supplies of Class I and III for use in transit
DURING THE LIAISON TOUR	
☐	Establish and maintain communication(s) with parent unit
☐	Notify your own HQ of your arrival
☐	Deliver all correspondence designated for the receiving HQ
☐	Visit staff elements, brief them on the situation of your unit, and collect information (maps, traces, overlays, etc.) from them
☐	Annotate on all overlays the security classification, title, map scale, grid intersection points, date-time group (DTG) information, DTG received, and from whom received
☐	Participate in supported unit's orders process, briefings, rehearsals and development of: - FSP/FSEM - FASP/FASM
☐	Advise on parent unit capabilities, requirements, limitations, and employment
☐	Visit and coordinate routinely with all supported unit staff elements
☐	Send parent unit updates on mission, locations, future operations, and commander's intent
☐	Organize sleep plan for 24-hour operations
☐	Ensure supported unit S3 is aware of your location at all times
☐	Accomplish mission without interfering with the supported unit's operations
☐	Facilitate information exchange
☐	Pick up all correspondence for your HQ when you left the receiving unit
☐	Inform the receiving HQ of when you would depart, what route you would take, and when you expect to arrive at the sending unit
AFTER RETURNING TO THE SENDING UNIT	
☐	Deliver all correspondence
☐	Brief the appropriate staff elements
☐	Prepare the necessary reports

Figure 2-4. Example LNO Checklist (Continued)

\multicolumn{2}{c}{EXAMPLE OUTLINE OF A LNO'S HANDBOOK / TSOP}	
1.	Table of contents, with the sending unit's proponency statement
2.	Purpose statement
3.	Introduction statement
4.	Definitions
5.	Scope statement
6.	Responsibilities and guidelines for conduct
7.	Actions before departing from the sending unit
8.	Actions on arriving at the receiving unit
9.	Actions during liaison operations at the receiving unit
10.	Actions before departing from the receiving unit
11.	Actions on arrival at the sending unit
12.	Sample questions
13.	Information requirements
14.	Required reports (from higher and sending units' TSOP)
15.	Packing list (administrative supplies and unit TSOP, field uniform, equipment)
	a. Credentials
	b. Forms (1) DA Forms 1594 (Daily Staff Journal or Duty Officer's Log) (2) Other blank form
	c. References
	d. Computers for information and data exchange
	e. Signal operating instructions extract
	f. Security code encryption device
	g. Communications equipment, including remote equipment
	h. Phone book
	i. List of commanders and staff officers
	j. Telephone calling (credit) card
	k. Movement table
	l. Administrative equipment (pens, paper, scissors, tape, hole punch, and so on)
	m. Map and chart equipment (pens, pins, protractor, straight edge, scale, distance counter, acetate, unit markers, and so on)
16.	Sending unit's command MTOE, unit status report (if appropriate because of the classification of the report)

Figure 2-5. Example Outline of a LNO's Handbook/TSOP

Chapter 3

Command and Control

The ability of the FA battalion to execute C2 communications with its higher HQ, subordinate elements, sustainment forces, and supported forces is perhaps the greatest factor in determining whether or not the unit will accomplish its mission. C2 must be considered as a critical factor in the planning and execution of any tactical operation. This chapter has three sections. Section I addresses general communications information. Section II discusses C2 systems. Section III covers radio communications.

SECTION I – GENERAL COMMUNICATIONS INFORMATION

3-01. Communication is a command responsibility, essential to efficient C2 of a FA battalion and to its ability to provide effective FS. The commander's communications plans should address all elements of his command, to include supported, reinforced, and adjacent units. To establish a responsive and dependable communications system, the FA battalion must overcome several limitations:

- The battalion relies heavily on radio communications, as the speed of battle may prohibit the efficient use of wire.
- The battalion is authorized a limited number of CNRs, area common-user systems (ACUS), and Army data distribution systems (ADDS) to support multiple requirements.
- The battalion monitors multiple radio networks while maintaining CONOPS during displacement.
- The battalion communicates over long distances to many diverse elements, such as FISTs, FSEs, reinforcing units, higher HQ, and supported maneuver force.
- The battalion relies increasingly on data communications, which have shorter range capabilities than voice communications on CNR.

3-02. Communications systems differ according to the various means of communication, the unit's mission and its MTOEs. The various communication systems have different capabilities and limitations, and thus should be employed so that they complement each other to provide flexibility and redundancy. Communications reliability can be greatly increased by planning for and using all means available. The primary communications systems used in a FA battalion are CNR, ACUS, ADDS, wire, messenger, and, to a lesser extent, visual and sound systems.

RADIO SYSTEMS

3-03. Radio communication plays a major role in the C2 of FA battalion operations. Radios transmit a variety of media (voice, data, fax), and FA battalions increasingly use radios for communication between computer systems. Section III addresses combat net radios in more detail.

AREA COMMON USER SYSTEM

3-04. The ACUS is a digital battlefield telecommunication system. The corps and below ACUS is the MSE.

3-05. MSE provides secure, automatic digitized voice, data, and fax communications to the user, whether static or mobile. It replaces the existing area common-user multichannel communications system and radio teletype in signal and FA units. It is an area communications system extended by mobile telephone. MSE can be used for digital data transmission; however, its primary purposes in FA battalions are for voice and fax communications. An MSE net functions similarly to a civilian telephone system. Subscribers are assigned individual telephone numbers that can be dialed directly. Text and graphics can be transmitted in hard copy via the fax capability of the system.

3-06. Division and corps signal units establish the MSE system by positioning signal nodes throughout the division and corps AO. They place extension nodes near maneuver brigade and DIVARTY CPs and throughout rear areas.

3-07. FA battalions access the MSE system either by wiring into the extension nodes at brigade or higher level or by using mobile radiotelephones through the signal nodes. The FA battle command systems at FA battalions and firing batteries are not normally connected to the MSE network for digital data traffic because of the limited number of available MSE circuits, equipment, and extreme distances to extension nodes.

3-08. The FA battalion can use three types of MSE equipment (Figure 3-1).
- The MSRT terminal, AN/VRC 97, is a mobile MSE telephone that links into the MSE network through one of the radio access units (RAUs) positioned throughout the AO by a signal unit. The RAU picks up the signal from the MSRT and switches it into the nearest signal node. The FA battalion has several MSRTs that are usually mounted in the vehicles of key personnel, and a few stand-alone installation kits that allow vehicular MSRTs to be dismounted for use in the TOC and trains. This is the most common method used in the battalion.
- The digital nonsecure voice telephone (DNVT), TA-1048/U, is the conventional telephone of the MSE system. It converts voice signals into digital signals and transmits the converted data. The DNVT must be wired into a junction box (J-1077), which is located near the unit and connected by cable to the small extension node (SEN). The user is responsible for laying the wire to the junction box. However, since the distances are usually too extreme to accomplish this, the use of DNVT is usually limited to situations where the FA battalion's elements are in close proximity to an extension node. Such as when the BSOC is collocated in the brigade support area (BSA).

- The lightweight digital facsimile (LDF), AN/UXC-10, when connected to the MSE network through a DNVT, digital secure voice terminal (DSVT) or MSRT, will allow the battalion to send and receive text and graphics in hard copy.

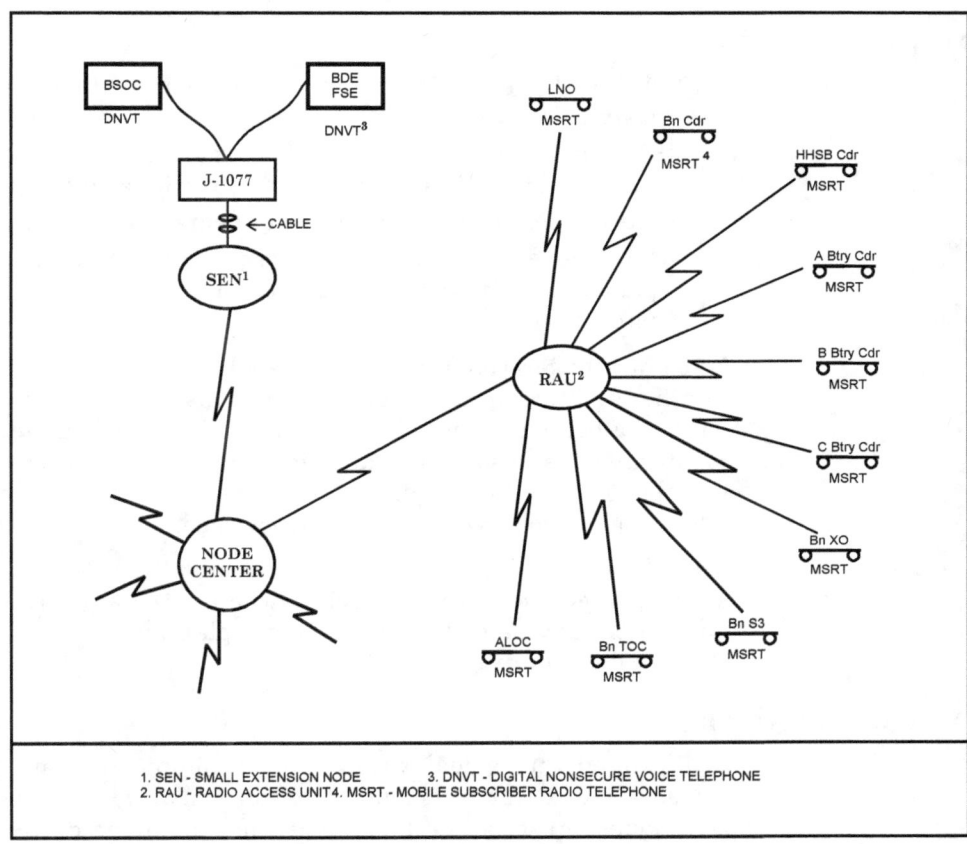

Figure 3-1. FA Battalion MSE NET

ARMY DATA DISTRIBUTION SYSTEM

3-09. ADDS is a C2 network that provides medium- and high-volume, real-time data communications to support the Army Battle Command System (ABCS). ADDS consists of Enhanced Position Location Reporting System (EPLRS) and the Joint Tactical Information Distribution System (JTIDS). It is deployed to provide data communications for those users that do not normally operate in or near CPs. CP-to-CP data traffic typically is exchanged over the ACUS. However, at the FA battalion, internal data distribution is primarily over secure frequency modulation (FM) radio, with EPLRS used mainly for its situational awareness information.

3-10. EPLRS passes targeting data, orders, situation reports, intelligence data, and messages between friendly units at the tactical level. It enhances situational awareness and aids in fratricide prevention by automatically tracking and identifying friendly units to other EPLRS equipped units. EPLRS interoperates with AFATDS. It provides secure, jam-resistant, near-real-time data communications, position location reporting, navigation, and identification services. EPLRS radios have do not voice capability.

3-11. JTIDS links Army ADA sensors and C2 elements and other services' air defense elements. This is a joint asset and not organic to FA battalions.

MESSENGER SYSTEMS

3-12. Although messenger systems are not used extensively, they are used in several situations:
- For delivery of overlays, packages, equipment, or other items or correspondence not suitable to radio or wire delivery.
- During periods of radio silence or degraded communications.
- For delivery of classified correspondence that must be discreetly or personally delivered to a commander, or that may require an immediate discussion and reply.

3-13. Messenger communications can be slow and unreliable during poor weather and terrain conditions. Security may be an issue due to enemy forces operating behind friendly lines, hostile citizens or bandits, or close proximity to front lines, especially during rapidly fluctuating battles. Most FA battalions do not have dedicated messenger vehicles, and may have difficulty allocating one for extended messenger usage.

3-14. Use of a short checklist in the unit TSOP can facilitate the rapid, efficient use of messenger services when necessary. Security, training, and navigational skills of the driver, route planning, leader briefings, and such should all be addressed.

VISUAL AND SOUND SYSTEMS

3-15. Sound and visual systems of communication are generally used at battery and lower echelons. Use of visual and sound communications techniques must be well planned and coordinated to prevent confusion, miscommunication, and deception from the enemy. Lights, mirror flashes, or sounds from adjacent or passing units can be mistaken as the designated cue or signal. Repeated use of a signal may result in duplication and deception by an observing enemy force. Fires can result from improper use of pyrotechnics.

3-16. The use of visual and sound communications methods should be addressed in unit TSOPs. Rehearsals should be conducted under realistic conditions to ensure that battlefield smoke, noise, distances, or intervening terrain do not interfere with the signals.

COMMUNICATIONS RESPONSIBILITIES

3-17. The commander is responsible for the adequacy and proper use of the communications systems within his command and for their efficient operation in the systems of the next higher command. The commander can delegate the authority to establish, maintain, control, and coordinate the battalion's various communications means to a subordinate The following paragraphs discuss general communications responsibilities.

ECHELONS OF COMMAND

3-18. The senior unit is responsible for establishing communications with its subordinate units, whether organic or attached. This responsibility is primarily one of planning and directing the establishment of the linking communications systems since assets belonging to either the senior HQ or the subordinate unit may be used.

TACTICAL MISSIONS

3-19. Each of the four standard tactical missions has an inherent communications responsibility.

Direct Support

3-20. An artillery unit with the mission of direct support must establish communications with the supported maneuver unit HQ (supporting-to-supported relationship).

Reinforcing

3-21. An artillery unit with the mission of reinforcing must establish communications with the reinforced artillery unit HQ (reinforcing-to-reinforced relationship).

General Support Reinforcing

3-22. An artillery unit with the mission of GSR must establish communications with the reinforced artillery unit HQ (reinforcing-to-reinforced relationship). The senior artillery HQ must establish communications with the GSR unit (senior-to-subordinate relationship).

General Support

3-23. An artillery unit with the mission of GS does not have an inherent responsibility for establishing external communications with any other unit. However, the senior artillery unit must establish communications with its subordinate GS artillery units (senior-to-subordinate relationship).

BATTLE AREA

3-24. Adjacent commands must maintain communications with each other to ensure coordination of the combat effort. When facing the FLOT (left-to-right relationship), the command on the left establishes communications with the command on its right.

JOINT MAINTENANCE

3-25. Regardless of which unit is responsible for establishing communications, all units served by the system must help restore any communications system outage.

BATTALION S6 SECTION RESPONSIBILITIES

3-26. The S6 section maintains the communications and automation systems, operates retrans stations, and installs wire systems for the FA battalion. The

S6 section is organized with a section HQ, an automation management section, and a radio section. In some battalions, the S6 section also has a wire section. The exact composition of the S6 section varies with each type of battalion.

3-27. All elements of the battalion evacuate communications equipment for repair through the S6 section. The maintenance communications mechanics in the section perform organizational maintenance on battalion HQ communications equipment. Mechanics also provide on-site organizational maintenance and assistance for the subordinate units of the battalion.

3-28. The automation management section provides assistance with the establishment, operation, and maintenance of the battalion's automation systems. This includes hardware, software, networks, and automation security. Their networking functions include management and maintenance of internal LANs and connection to external wide area networks (WANs).

3-29. The radio section establishes and maintains the FM retrans station as required. Dual retrans capability is essential to maintaining FM voice and data communications over extended distances.

PLANNING CONSIDERATIONS

PLANS

3-30. The communications plan is designed to fulfill the requirements of a tactical mission. Planners use communications responsibilities, communications requirements, and the unit MTOE (which provides the communications means) to produce a standardized system. To meet specific requirements, commanders may modify their systems based on mission, enemy, terrain and weather, troops, time available, and civil considerations (METT-TC). The S6 assists the S3 in developing the communications plan during the MDMP process.

Voice and Data Nets

3-31. FA battalions use a combination of voice and data radio nets, with the mix determined by the MTOE, operational status of assigned equipment, METT-TC, and the unit's digital training level. If digital data capability is lost by the battalion or by one or more of the batteries, the voice nets can quickly become overburdened. A FA battalion communications plan must include plans for converting some data nets to voice while continuing to support the remaining digital data stations and for reconverting to data nets as that capability is restored. It is extremely important to keep voice traffic off digital data nets and vice versa. A voice backup plan should be developed for various contingencies, and rehearsed frequently. Many of the details can be included in the unit TSOP.

Planning Ranges

3-32. Range capabilities vary with the method of communications, the type and model of equipment used, terrain, weather, and atmospheric conditions. Jamming also degrades communications range. Ranges of combat net radios are discussed in Section III. Since rehearsal on the actual terrain and under the exact conditions is often impossible, experience and thorough map reconnaissance are essential to proper estimation of communications ranges.

System Mixes

3-33. The factors of METT-TC have different effects on the communications means. The preferred communications setup is any system or mixture of systems that will communicate the information with the least exposure to enemy EW and not place total reliance on radio. A good communications plan maximizes the use of all available systems and backup plans to prevent over reliance on any one system. Much of a unit's basic communications planning can be addressed in the unit's TSOP.

Electronic Counter-Countermeasures

3-34. ECCM should be part of each battalion TSOP. They can improve OPSEC and preserve communications. ECCM techniques that have been found to be effective include the following:
- Require authentication on nonsecure nets if operating in the single channel mode of operation. Proper authentication procedures can eliminate intrusion and imitative deception.
- Do not mix plain and encrypted traffic on the same net. Doing so compromises the nature of the net, which makes interception and analysis easier for the enemy.
- Use secure equipment whenever possible. If the battalion is supporting a unit without secure capability, specify nets that will be unsecured and enforce secure discipline on all remaining nets.
- Limit transmissions to 5 seconds or less if operating in the single channel mode of operation. This makes interception and direction finding more difficult.
- Work through jamming if at all possible. Jumping nets should be a last resort. Remember that if jamming is bad enough to keep a unit from operating on a net, it may also keep many of the stations from receiving the signal to change frequencies. Anti-jam frequencies must be disseminated well in advance, so that subscriber stations can move to the alternate frequencies in sequence. Susceptibility to jamming is greatly reduced with frequency hopping CNRs.
- Use only authorized call signs from the automated net control device (ANCD) or SOI and change them on schedule.

OPERATIONS

3-35. Communications operations must take advantage of all techniques to facilitate mission accomplishment. Consider remoting transmitters, and using antenna multiplexers, directional antennas, and retrans.

Remoted Transmitters

3-36. Remoting transmitters allows for the separation of the RF emitter from the CP or other critical facilities. Also, remoting radios allows the transmitter to be sited for optimized communications while allowing the user to position in locations better suited to survivability. Remoting also minimizes on-site or mutual interference while dissipating and reducing electronic signature. For additional information concerning remoting, see FM 24-18, *Tactical Single-Channel Radio Communications Techniques*.

Retransmission

3-37. Battalions use retrans operations to extend the area of coverage of a specific radio net or to reduce the electronic signature of a position. By use of a retrans site, RF power output can be reduced at the CP or other location. Overall net ranges can be doubled by the effective use of retrans.

3-38. FM, very high frequency (VHF) transmission distances are restricted by terrain and obstacles. The siting of radio equipment is often critical. The following are helpful hints for using FM retrans:
- As a minimum, make a map reconnaissance of the AO. S6, S2, and S3 should discuss retrans operations during the planning phase.
- Analyze the terrain for optimum communications.
- Select primary and alternate locations for retrans. Consider accessibility, defense, and logistical support.
- Arrange the timetable for site occupation and net operation. Don't wait until the retrans vehicle is needed before sending it out.
- Ensure operators are well trained. They must be able to provide manual relay if they have equipment failures.
- Ensure users are aware of the tactical situation and how retrans works.
- If retransmitting digital data traffic, program additional key and/or delay time to allow radios to key up.

3-39. If using a forward entry device (FED), plan to use a nearby battery FDC, FIST, or FSO to relay messages. This capability is useful when direct communication with an element is not possible. Relay addressing should be established per TSOP or as identified in the appropriate SOI.

Antenna Multiplexers

3-40. Using antenna multiplexers reduces the number of ground plane antennas required to operate multiple radios. The time required to align and tune these devices is considerably less than the time required installing multiple antennas. However, multiplexers also have several disadvantages, to include reduced communications range and significantly increased bit error rate (BER) for data traffic (the BER will vary for different frequencies).

Directional Antennas

3-41. Directional antennas reduce electronic signature in two directions while extending the range of the radio along the long axis of the antenna. Directional antennas should only be used in single-channel mode not frequency-hopping mode.

SECTION II – COMMAND AND CONTROL SYSTEMS

ARMY BATTLE COMMAND SYSTEMS

3-42. ABCS is designed to provide the battle commander and his staff with a common operational picture, as well as all the information necessary to effectively plan, coordinate, control, and direct the battle. This includes the integration of battlefield functional area C2 systems (BFACS) that extend from corps to brigade, with some components at the battalion level, that interface with both higher and lower ABCS systems. The primary components of ABCS include:
- AFATDS.
- Maneuver control system (MCS).
- All source analysis system (ASAS).
- Air-missile defense planning and control system (AMDPCS).
- Combat service support control system (CSSCS).
- The Tactical Airspace Information System (TAIS).
- The Global Command and Control System-Army (GCCS-A).
- Force XXI Battle Command - Brigade and Below (FBCB2) system.

3-43. ABCS is interoperable with joint and multinational C2 systems at upper echelons, and it is vertically and horizontally integrated at the tactical and operational levels. For a more detailed discussion of ABCS refer to FM 100-34, *Command and Control*.

FA TACTICAL DATA SYSTEMS

3-44. The FATDS family of automation continues to grow with the fielding of newer, automation equipped weapon systems, new or upgraded handheld terminal units (HTUs), and improved hardware and software versions for all existing systems. While this section addresses only the primary FA C2 systems, the FATDS family currently consists of the following systems.
- Primary tactical C2 systems - AFATDS, IFSAS, LTACFIRE, FDS.
- Observer, and other systems – forward observer software, FEDs, HTUs.
- Weapon platform automation systems.
- Radars - AN/TPQ-36, 37, 46, and 47.
- Met systems
  - AN/TMQ-31 – meteorological data system (MDS).
  - AN/TMQ-38 – meteorological measuring set (MMS).

AFATDS

3-45. AFATDS is an integrated FS asset manager that operates as part of a networked tactical data processing system. It provides decision aids and an information system for the control, coordination, and synchronization of all types of FS means. It uses common hardware/software from the ATCCS program. AFATDS interfaces with the other four BFACS, via the common operating environment (COE), using a combination of either a limited set of messages or an ability to print data for distribution. The ST 6-3 series will provide detailed information concerning the interfaces and message exchange between AFATDS and the other systems.

3-46. AFATDS is also designed to interface across the battlespace with all existing and future FS systems, other ABCS BFACS, other services, allied forces (German Adler, United Kingdom Bates, French Atlas, & Italian SIR) and joint C2 systems.

3-47. AFATDS is composed of a common suite of hardware and software in varying configurations at different operational facilities (OPFACs) interconnected by tactical communications. Upgrades to both hardware and software occur periodically, and provide increased capability and performance. Because of this, the S3 and S6 must periodically verify the compatibility of their systems with those of the units with which they may operate.

3-48. AFATDS automates screening and filtering of potential targets and mission requests, to include target clearance and coordination in accordance with the maneuver commander's targeting guidance and attack criteria. Decision aids permit fully automated fire mission processing. For example, in contrast to IFSAS/FDS/LTACFIRE, AFATDS will prioritize fire missions based on target value analysis (TVA) and ensure that fire missions comply with FSCMs and unit zones of responsibility. It is also capable of deciding which type of FS asset should engage a particular target (for example, FA, mortars, attack helicopters, naval gunfire, or air) and recommending the best attack method for a given system (e.g., volleys, ammunition type, and firing unit). Although commanders can specify which missions to stop for review/coordination and can resort to voice execution, human intervention is not usually recommended. AFATDS was designed to plan and execute automatically for optimum efficiency.

INITIAL FIRE SUPPORT AUTOMATION SYSTEM

3-49. IFSAS is an interim tactical FD system that provides automated C2 capability to FA units until AFATDS is fully fielded. IFSAS consists of tactical FD software ported to lightweight computer units (LCUs). IFSAS can send and receive digital communication via radio and wire communications.

LTACFIRE

3-50. LTACFIRE is a compact and transportable C2 system for FA units in light divisions. It is similar to IFSAS.

FIRE DIRECTION SYSTEM (FDS)

3-51. The FDS performs tactical FD processing in MLRS units. The FDS receives processes, and transmits data on fire units, ammunition and targets. In addition, the FDS maintains data bases on fire units, munitions, and tactical fire plans/situations. FDS software runs on a LCU.

AUTOMATION CONSIDERATIONS

3-52. With the periodic upgrades in hardware and software, one of a battalion's greatest challenges is maintaining a high level of digital expertise.

FA battalions must regularly allocate time for digital data training, with some of that time focused on leader and collective training. Additional automation considerations include:

- Provide OPFAC focused operator training to leaders that are tactically knowledgeable, but weak on their automation systems. Leaders must be able to expertly operate the system if necessary, especially in smaller sections where personnel shortages have greater impact.
- Identify exceptional operators, and provide them training on the tactical and situational awareness functions of the section. Skilled operators should understand how to "fight" the system, not just enter and extract data.
- Identify the most skilled leaders (officer and NCO) and assign training and first line troubleshooting responsibilities. Clearly identify relationships and responsibilities of these "field" experts and the automation technicians in the S6 automation section.
- Establish guidelines in unit TSOPs that describe who is authorized to change databases and troubleshoot systems.
- Assign battalion level database management duties to someone, usually in the S3 section. This person assists the S3 and S6 in:
  - Developing the standard battalion database (startup and communications data and architecture, guidances, filters, etc.), and any variants necessary for particular wartime missions.
  - Establishing a database naming/numbering/dating system that helps ensure all battalion elements can clearly identify which database is in use, and when changes have been made.
  - Coordinating and disseminating battalion database requirements and changes with the senior FA HQ, subordinate elements, and when applicable, the supported maneuver force and any units with which the battalion may have a wartime or training relationship.
  - Coordinating the exchange and integration of databases with all other units during wartime operations and peacetime training.
- Maintain regular communication with other units in wartime missions and training. Identify hardware and software version and interface issues (use the ST 6-3 series). Seek out training opportunities with units that have different equipment (e.g., AFATDS-IFSAS).
- Develop a plan for short notice software-only and hardware/software upgrades. Identify key leaders that would help a new equipment training team or retrofit team in quickly upgrading the battalion to the newest equipment (which may occur prior to deployment or upon arrival in theater).
- Develop basic LAN management skills in key OPFACs (e.g., TOC, brigade FSE) to reduce the burden on the automation section. See FM 24-7, *Tactical Local Area Network (LAN) Management*, for detailed LAN information.
- Train on switching from data to voice operations and the reverse. Also practice digital CONOPS and MSU.
- Understand and monitor range limitations of digital data traffic. Establish plans for retrans or rerouting of digital data communications.

SECTION III – RADIO COMMUNICATIONS SYSTEMS

COMBAT NET RADIOS

3-53. The CNR is the primary means for FA C2, FD, and FS coordination, especially within a FA battalion and a maneuver brigade. The battalion uses CNRs for voice and data communications.

3-54. The single-channel ground and airborne radio system (SINCGARS) is the FA battalion's primary radio system. SINCGARS replaces the older series of radios as depicted in Table 3-1. Its main features are resistance to jamming through frequency hopping and increased capacity of 2,320 channels. SINCGARS is interoperable with AN/VRC 12 series radios only in the fixed frequency mode.

3-55. The S6, in conjunction with the S3, must perform frequency management and coordination to prevent frequency interference and to maximize communications capabilities.

Table 3-1. Radio Set Comparison

NOMENCLATURE	REPLACES	COMPONENTS (BASIC ISSUE ITEMS)				POWER OUTPUT
		RT	VEH ADAPT	DISMOUNT KIT[1]	PA	
Manpack AN/PRC-119	AN/PRC-25/77	1		1		LO, M, HI
Vehicular short-range AN/VRC-87	AN/VRC-53/64	1	1			LO, M, HI
Vehicular short-range dismount AN/VRC-88	AN/GRC-125/160	1	1	1		LO, M, HI
Vehicular long-range or vehicular short-range AN/VRC-89	AN/VRC-12/47	2	1		1	LO, M, HI, PA
Vehicular long-range AN/VRC-90	AN/VRC-43/46	1	1		1	LO, M, HI, PA
Vehicular long-range or vehicular short-range dismount AN/VRC-91	AN/GRC-160 plus AN/VRC-46	2	1	1	1	LO, M, HI, PA
Dual vehicular long-range AN/VRC-92	AN/VRC-45/49	2	1		2[2]	LO, M, HI, PA
1. Dismount kit includes manpack antenna, battery case/interconnecting box and handset. 2. Requires a power amplifier mount for second power amplifier. LEGEND: ADAPT = Adapter M = Medium VEH = Vehicle HI = High LO = Low RT = Receiver-Transmitter PA = Power Amplifier						

PLANNING RANGES

3-56. The FM radio planning ranges differ for voice and data communications. Although limited in range, SINCGARS range can be significantly extended with directional antennas, retrans stations, or relays. Planning ranges for SINCGARS and other radios are shown in Table 3-2. Planning ranges for data transmission are usually less than for voice transmission (1/2 to 2/3 the planning of voice). In the frequency-hopping mode, data transmission may be reduced as much as 50 percent, depending on the data rate set on the radio. The rule is the higher the data rate, the lower the planning range.

Table 3-2. Planning Range with WHIP Antenna

RADIO PLANNING RANGES				
RADIO	PWR (L)	PWR (M)	PWR (H)	PWR AMP
160 Series	0-8 km			
12 Series	0-8 km		0-40 km	
SINCGARS	0-400 meters	0-5 km	0-10 km	0-40 km
NOTE: The maximum range when transmitting digital data using a manpack radio on H power setting is 4 km.				

ANTENNAS

3-57. Long distances between transmitter and receiver, unfavorable terrain, and other conditions can cause poor communications or lack of communications. Units can often overcome this problem by the use of the right antenna. When the tactical situation allows, the battalion FDC, the BOCs, and POCs should use an extended-range antenna, the OE-254/GRC, or the OE-303/GRC to obtain the maximum planning range of their radios.

3-58. To obtain the maximum efficiency of an antenna, consider the following:
- An antenna site should not be located in or near obstacles such as tunnels, overpasses, or steel bridges because they can block or reflect signals.
- Trees with heavy foliage and dense underbrush can absorb signals and should be avoided if possible.
- Do not set up antennas near wire line poles and high-tension power lines. They can introduce interference and absorb part of the radio signals. This also constitutes a safety hazard.

SIGNAL OPERATING INSTRUCTIONS

3-59. In addition to the radios and antennas, radio communications relies increasingly on the battlefield electronic SOI system. The SOI system is a decentralized system for frequency management and the publication of unit level SOI. The electronic SOI is designed to provide more responsiveness to rapidly changing and highly mobile battlefield conditions. The system, which replaces the paper SOI, consists of a basic generation unit and an ANCD. Distribution channels are the same as those now used for the paper SOI.

FA BATTALION RADIO NETS

3-60. Radio communications systems are divided into separate groupings called nets. This division is based on the purposes for which the nets are used. A radio net is a channel, frequency, or sub-frequency with more than one subscriber for the purpose of transmitting information related to the mission requirements. Each net has a controlling station called the net control station (NCS). The net may be a "free" net, in which all stations are free to contact one another at any time, or a "directed" net, in which all stations must contact the NCS for permission to contact other subscribers.

Standard Radio Nets

3-61. The FA uses a set of standard radio nets for all of the standard tactical missions. This net standardization enables units to quickly and accurately interface with each other. Standard net structures and purposes should not be arbitrarily changed except to tailor them to a modified mission. Such modifications should be kept to a minimum. Standard net structures consist of the net titles, purposes, users, and equipment. Net structure information should be amplified in unit TSOPs.

NET TITLES / DESCRIPTIONS

3-62. Radio nets are usually titled and described in several ways:
- Controlling HQ (DIVARTY, battalion, battery, etc.).
- Purpose - command (Cmd), FD, intelligence.
- Communication system - MSE, frequency spectrum (high frequency [HF], VHF, ultrahigh frequency [UHF]), and/or modulation (FM, amplitude modulated [AM] or single sideband [SSB] a form of AM).
- Method of communication (voice [V], facsimile [fax], or data [D]).
- Internal/external.

3-63. For example, the battalion operations/fire (VHF-FM) (data) net is abbreviated as Bn Ops/F (VHF-FM) (D) net.

3-64. TSOPs should designate priorities for all battalion radio nets. This facilitates repairs, troubleshooting, retrans assignments, and anti-jamming efforts. Normal net priorities are FD, FS, C2, administration, and logistics nets. TSOP priorities for radio nets may need to be modified based on the communications situation and/or operational requirements.

FA BATTALION RADIO NET DESCRIPTIONS

3-65. FA battalions control and operate on many types of radio nets. Most FA battalions operate on approximately 12-17 primary internal and external nets, and may possibly monitor or operate on several additional external nets on an as required basis. Most FA battalions use two internal voice nets – (Bn Cmd and Bn Admin/Log). Usually, there are four or five internal digital data nets (Bn Ops/F, FD 1,2,3, and Bn TA/Intel). FA battalions that provide FS teams to maneuver units will also manage the FS nets. The brigade FSE operates on the maneuver brigade FS net. The battalion FSEs operate on the brigade FS net and on their own internal maneuver battalion FS net (the maneuver battalion mortar net may be used for this purpose in some units). The FA battalion FDC monitors the brigade FS net.

3-66. Most FA battalions will also operate on several external voice and data nets to their Force FA HQ. A unit's FA tactical mission may also require it to operate on maneuver unit nets and/or a reinforced FA battalion's nets.

3-67. All AFATDS-equipped units operate on both data and voice nets. To reduce the number of transmissions, voice nets should handle only traffic that cannot be transmitted digitally. Since voice traffic will overlay data transmissions, voice traffic on digital data nets should be limited to emergency situations.

3-68. A FA battalion CNR matrix is shown in Table 3-3. This matrix depicts what net(s) the unit should enter and at what level of communications based on the battalion's tactical mission (DS, R, GSR, or GS). Actual equipment, nets, and net titles may vary based on MTOEs, unit organizations, TSOPs, and other situational or unit factors.

Table 3-3. FA Battalion Combat Net Radio Matrix

NETS	MISSION			
	DS	R	GSR	GS
Internal				
Bn Cmd (VHF-FM) (V)	X	X	X	X
Bn Ops/F (VHF-FM) (D)	X	X	X	X
Bn FD 1 (VHF-FM) (D)	X	X	X	X
Bn FD 2 (VHF-FM) (D)	X	X	X	X
Bn FD 3 (VHF-FM) (D)	X	X	X	X
Bn TA/Intel (D)	X	A	A	A
Bn Admin/Log (VHF-FM) (V)	X	X	X	X
External				
Force FA Cmd (VHF-FM) (V)	X	X	X	X
Force FA Ops/F 1, 2, 3, (VHF-FM) (D or V)	X[1]	X[1]	X[1]	X[1]
Force FA Command Fire (CF) (MSE V-FAX)	X	X	X	X
Force FA TA/Intel (VHF-FM) (V or D)	X	X	X	X
Force FA Survey (VHF-FM) (V)	A	A	A	A
Force FA Admin/Log (VHF-FM) (V)	A	A	A	A
Supported Unit Admin/Log (VHF-FM) (V)	A	A	A	
Mvr Unit Ops/Intel (VHF-FM) (V)	X	X	X	X
Mvr Bde/Reg/Div/ or Corps FS (VHF-FM) (V)	X	X	X	X
Mvr Bn/Sqn FS (VHF-FM) (V) (3-4 nets)	X			
Mvr Bn Mortar FD (D)	X			
Reinforced Bn Cmd (V)		X	X	
Reinforced Bn Ops/F (VHF-FM) (D or V)		X	X	
Naval Gunfire (HF-AM) (V)	X			
Div FS (UHF-TACSAT) (D)	X	X	X	A
X = Full-time net subscriber, A = As required, D = Data, V = Voice, [1]=Ops/F 1, 2, or 3 as assigned Mvr = maneuver, Reg = regiment, Sqn = squadron, TACSAT = tactical satellite				

3-69. Tables 3-4, 3-5, 3-6, and 3-7 show subscribers and the internal and external radio nets for each tactical mission. The radio nets of the FA battalion must meet the requirements of the tactical mission assigned - DS, R, GSR, or GS. The organization of the FA battalions may differ.

3-70. Some battalions are organized with organic sections that provide FISTs, maneuver battalion FSEs, and maneuver brigade FSEs. Other battalions do not have these elements.

3-71. Apart from these differences in organization, the FD, operations, and intelligence sections are identical. This similarity forms the basis of the radio networks outlined in the preceding paragraphs and in the following tables.

FM 3-09.21 (FM 6-20-1)

Table 3-4. Direct Support Mission Radio Net Matrix

Element	INTERNAL NETS					EXTERNAL NETS												
	Bn Cmd (V)	Bn Ops/F (D)	Bn FD 1,2,3 (D)	Bn TA/Intel (D)	Bn Admin/Log (V)	Force FA Cmd (V)	Force FA Ops/F 1,2,3 (D)	Force FA CF (MSE V-FAX) (V/F/D)	Force FA TA/Intel (D)	Force FA Survey (V)	Force FA Admin/Log (V)	Mvr Bde Admin/Log (V)	Div FS (TACSAT) (D)	Mvr Bde FS (V)	Mvr Bn FS (V)	Mvr Bn Mortar FD (D)	Mvr Bde Ops/Intel (V)	Naval Gunfire (HF) (V)
Bn Cdr/FSCOORD	X		X[1]			X		X						X				
Bn XO	X				X			X			A	A						
S3	X							X						X				
S6	X				A						A	A						
Bn FDC	C	N	N	L			L							C				
Bn Ops	N	L		L	A	X	X[1]	X		A			X	X				X
Bn Intel/S2	C	L			N			X						C			X	
TAC Cmd Center	X	X	X	A	A	A	A[1]	X	A					X			A	
Survey Sections	X		X							A								
Radar (Atch /Org)	X		A[1]	X	A				X									
Retrans Team	X	X																
Btry Commanders	X		X[1]		A			X										
Btry Ops Center	X	X	X[1]											X				
Btry/Plt FDC	X	X	X[1]		A									X	A			
Btry Spt Plt Ldr[2]					X													
Mvr Bde FSE	X	X	X[1]		A	A[1]	X							X	N			X
Mvr Bde FSO	X	A	X[1]			A[1]								X				
Mvr Bn FSE		X	X[1]											X	N	X		X
Mvr Bn FSO			A[1]											A	X	X		
FIST HQ			X[1]											A	X	X		
Forward Observer			A[1]											A	A	X		
COLT/Striker			X[1]										X[3]	X	A	A	X	
ALOC/S4	X				N			X			A	A						
BSOC/S1	X				X			X			A	A						
UMCP					X							A						
BAO	X				X							A						
BMO					X							A						
Wrecker					X													
Recovery Vehicle					X													
Medical Officer					X							A						
Ambulance					X													
Unit Ministry Tm					X													

[1] – One of the 3 nets as directed by the NCS [2] – Where applicable [3] – COLT/Striker Plt HQ only
Atch = Attached, COLT = Combat observation/lasing team, Spt = support,
UMCP = Unit maintenance collection point
X = Full-time subscriber, A = As required, N = Net control station, L = LAN/Wire, C = Control unit/TOC Intercom

Table 3-5. Reinforcing Mission Radio Net Matrix

Element	INTERNAL NETS					EXTERNAL NETS										
	Bn Cmd (v)	Bn Ops/F (D)	Bn FD 1,2,3 (D)	Bn TA/Intel (D)	Bn Admin/Log (V)	Reinforced FA Cmd (V)	Force FA Cmd (V)	Reinforced Ops/F (D)	Force FA Ops/F 1,2,3 (D)	Force FA CF (MSE-V-FAX)(V/F/D)	Force FA TA/Intel (D)	Force FA Survey (V)	Force FA Admin/Log (V)	Sptd Unit Admin Log (V)	Mvr Bde FS (V)	Mvr Bde Ops/Intel (V)
Bn Cdr	X		X¹			X	A			X						
Bn XO	X				X					X			A	A		
S3	X									X						
S6	X				A								A	A		
Bn FDC	C	N	N	L				L	L						C	
Bn Ops	N	L		L	A	X	A	X	X¹	X		A			X	
Bn Intel/S2	C	L		N							X					A
TAC Cmd Center	X	X	X	A	A	X	A	X	X¹	X	A				A	A
Survey Sections	X			X								A				
Radar (Atch/Org)	X		A¹	X	A							A				
LNO Section	X	X								X						
Retrans Team	X	X														
Btry Cdrs	X		X¹		A					X						
Btry Ops Center	X	X	X¹		X										X	
Btry/Plt FDC	X	X	X¹		A										X	
Btry Spt Plt Ldr ²					X											
ALOC/S4	X				N					X			A	A		
BSOC/S1	X				X					X			A	A		
UMCP					X									A		
BAO	X				X									A		
BMO					X									A		
Wrecker					X											
Recovery Vehicle					X											
Medical Officer					X									A		
Ambulance					X											
Unit Ministry Tm					X											

¹ – One of the 3 nets as directed by the NCS ² – Where applicable
X = Full-time subscriber, A = As required, N = Net control station, L = LAN/Wire, C = Control unit/TOC Intercom

FM 3-09.21 (FM 6-20-1)

Table 3-6. General Support Reinforcing Mission Radio Net Matrix

Element	INTERNAL NETS					EXTERNAL NETS								
	Bn Cmd (V)	Bn Ops/F (D)	Bn FD 1,2,3 (D)	Bn TA/Intel (D)	Bn Admin/Log (V)	Reinforced FA Cmd (V)	Force FA Cmd (V)	Reinforced Ops/F (D)	Force FA Ops/1,2,3 (D)	Force FA CF (MSE-V-FAX) (V/F/D)	Force FA TA/Intel (D)	Force FA Survey (V)	Force FA Admin/Log (V)	Sptd Unit Admin Log (V)	Mvr Unit FS (V)	Mvr Unit Ops/Intel (V)
Bn Cdr	X		X[1]			X	X			X						
Bn XO	X				X					X			A	A		
S3	X									X						
S6	X				A								A	A		
Bn FDC	C	N	N	L				L	L						C	
Bn Ops	N	L		L	A	X	X	X	X[1]	X		A			X	
Bn Intel/S2	C	L		N							X					A
Tac Cmd Center	X	X	X	A	A	X	X	X	X[1]	X	A				A	A
Survey Sections	X			X								A				
Radar (Atch/ Org)	X		A[1]	X	A						X					
LNO Section	X	X								X						
Retrans Team	X	X														
Btry Cdrs	X		X[1]		A					X						
Btry Ops Center	X	X	X[1]		X										A	
Btry/Plt FDC	X	X	X[1]		A										A	
Btry Spt Plt Ldr [2]					X											
ALOC/S4	X				N					X			A	A		
BSOC/S1	X				X					X			A	A		
UMCP					X									A		
BAO	X				X									A		
BMO					X									A		
Wrecker					X											
Recovery Vehicle					X											
Medical Officer					X									A		
Ambulance					X											
Unit Ministry Tm					X											

[1] – One of the 3 nets as directed by the NCS   [2] – Where applicable
X = Full-time subscriber, A = As required, N = Net control station, L = LAN/Wire, C = Control unit/TOC Intercom

Table 3-7. General Support Mission Radio Net Matrix

Element	INTERNAL NETS					EXTERNAL NETS								
	Bn Cmd (V)	Bn Ops/F (D)	Bn FD 1,2,3 (D)	Bn TA/Intel (D)	Bn Admin/Log (V)	Force FA/FA Bde Cmd (V)	Force FA/FA Bde Ops/F 1,2,3 (D)	Force FA CF (MSE-V-FAX) (V/F/D)	Force FA TA/Intel (D)	Force FA Survey (V)	Force FA/FA Bde Admin/Log (V)	Sptd Unit Admin Log (V)	Mvr Div/Corps FS (V)	Mvr Div/Corps Ops/Intel (V)
Bn Cdr	X		X¹			X		X						
Bn XO	X				X			X			A	A		
S3	X							X						
S6	X										A	A		
Bn FDC	C	N	N	L			L						C	
Bn Ops	N	L		L	A	X	X¹	X		A			X	
Bn Intel/S2	C	L		N					X					A
Tac Cmd Center	X	X	X	A	A	X	X¹	X	A				A	A
Survey Sections	X		X							A				
Radar (Atch/Org)	X		A¹	X	A				X					
LNO Section	X	X												
Retrans Team	X	X												
Btry Cdrs	X		X¹		A	X								
Btry Ops Center	X	X	X¹	X									X	
Btry/Plt FDC	X	X	X¹	A									X	
Btry Spt Plt Ldr¹					X									
ALOC/S4	A				N			X			A	A		
BSOC/S1	A				X			X			A	A		
UMCP					X							A		
BAO					X							A		
BMO					X							A		
Wrecker					X									
Recovery Vehicle					X									
Medical Officer					X							A		
Ambulance					X									
Unit Ministry Tm					X									

¹ – One of the 3 nets as directed by the NCS   ² – Where applicable
X = Full-time subscriber, A = As required, N = Net control station, L = LAN/Wire, C = Control unit/TOC Intercom

DIRECT SUPPORT MISSION

3-72. Any FA battalion may be called upon to perform the DS mission, and several FA battalion TOEs are specifically designed to support heavy or light, maneuver brigades or regiments. While the types and quantities of communications equipment in a DS battalion will vary widely with the battalion structure, the radio nets (see Table 3-4) will generally follow the pattern outlined below.

INTERNAL NETS

3-73. The DS battalion normally operates on about six to seven internal nets. The DS Bn Cmd (VHF-FM) (voice) net is used for C2 and collection and dissemination of tactical information and intelligence. The DS battalion operations section is the NCS.

3-74. The Bn FD 1, 2, and 3 (VHF-FM) (data) nets are identical. They are used for tactical and technical FD from FOs through the DS battalion FDC to the controlling FDC. The FD nets (FD 1, FD 2, and FD 3) should be assigned according to the mission and the battalion's communications status, not necessarily one per battery. However, one technique frequently used under ideal communications, is to assign one firing battery per net, with the FOs, Strikers, FISTs, and Bn FSEs spread evenly across the three nets. This allows for quickfire linkages and for the direct exchange of message-to-observer traffic. The NCS for all three FD nets is the battalion FDC. One or more of the nets can be established as a voice nets if necessary.

3-75. The Bn Ops/F (VHF-FM) (data) net is used for FS planning and coordination between FA elements, for MSU operations and for tactical and technical FD to reinforcing artillery units. The NCS is the battalion FDC section. The Ops/F net may be established as a voice net during degraded operations.

3-76. The Bn TA/Intel (VHF-FM) (data) net is used for exchanging targeting, counterfire, survey, meteorological, and intelligence information within the battalion. These elements can include Firefinder radars, survey teams, and met teams. The NCS is either the Bn S2 section, or the Bn O&I section in light combined command posts.

3-77. The Bn Admin/Log (VHF-FM) (voice) net is used for coordinating all battalion administrative and logistical matters. The battalion ALOC is the NCS.

EXTERNAL NETS

3-78. The DS battalion may operate on several external nets (the actual number in part depends on availability of communications assets and unit SOP). Additional information on these external nets is in FM 6-20-2, FM 6-20-40, and FM 6-40, *Tactics, Techniques, and Procedures for Field Artillery Manual Gunnery*.

3-79. The Force FA Cmd (VHF-FM) (voice) net is used for C2, tactical operations, intelligence, and voice coordination with all artillery elements and units (organic, attached, and reinforcing). The force FA operations section is the NCS.

3-80. The Force FA Ops/F 1, 2, and 3 (VHF-FM) (data) nets are identical. They are used for tactical FD, FS planning and coordination, MSU operations, and met data. Normally, each of the DS battalions will be in one of the nets. Other artillery elements, such as the AN/TPQ-36 and AN/TPQ-37 radars, may be in one of these nets depending on the task organization. The FSEs at the division tactical CP and the division main CP, if not collocated with force FA CP, will also be in one of these nets. The force FA FCE is the NCS.

3-81. The Force FA CF (MSE) (V-FAX) network is a multipurpose area network. The battalion has voice, fax, and data (if necessary) access to the force FA HQ and other subscribers. It is used for C2 and FD coordination with units at greater-than-VHF ranges from the force FA HQ and in situations where hard copy message traffic is required.

3-82. The battalion S2 will operate on the Force FA TA/Intel (VHF-FM) (data) net, exchanging TA, counterfire, and intelligence information with the force FA S2. If the battalion controls a radar section, the section may also operate on the Force FA TA/Intel net.

3-83. If the DS battalion receives a reinforcing battalion, the reinforcing unit will normally be a subscriber on the DS unit's Ops/F net. However, the DS unit may sometimes enter the reinforcing Bn Ops/F (VHF-FM) (data) net if necessary. (This net is not displayed in the Table 3-4 matrix and must be resourced by LNO's from the reinforcing unit, or shifting radio assets within the reinforced unit.)

3-84. As required, the Bn operations and survey sections will operate on the Force FA Survey (VHF-FM) (voice) net (in units where it is still being used). This net, which is being phased out due to the reduction in PADS survey elements, provides for exchange of survey information with the force FA HQ. In most cases, the Force TA/Intel (D) Net has superceded this net.

3-85. As required, the Bn CSS staff, ASOC, and BSOC, operate on the Force FA Admin/Log (VHF-FM) (voice) net. This net is used to coordinate CSS operations and to exchange CSS information with the force FA HQ.

3-86. The supported Maneuver Unit Ops/Intel (VHF-FM) (voice) net is a maneuver net used for operational and intelligence traffic. The DS battalion S2 operates in this net to transmit and receive operational and intelligence information. This net is also used for cross-coordination between scouts and Strikers working forward in the brigade area, and their S2 sections. Non-FA observers, forward scouts for instance, may call for fire on this net. The maneuver unit S2 section is the NCS.

3-87. The supported Maneuver Unit FS (VHF-FM) (voice) nets are used for voice FS coordination and planning. They are also used to request and coordinate close air support (CAS) and naval surface fire support (NSFS) operations. Non-FA observers may call for fire in this net. The maneuver brigade/regiment FSE is the NCS for the Brigade/Regiment FS net. The DS battalion TOC operates in this net to provide immediate reaction to the maneuver commander's FS requirements. Each battalion/squadron FSE will also operate a battalion/squadron FS net, with the battalions/squadron FSE as the NCS. While the battalion TOC normally doesn't monitor these nets, the firing batteries or platoons may do so when close coordination and quickfire procedures are required.

3-88. The FS personnel supporting the maneuver battalion/squadron will also operate on the Maneuver Battalion/Squadron Mortar FD (VHF-FM) (data) net. This is used for data fire missions. The maneuver unit's mortar platoon is the NCS.

3-89. The supported unit Admin/Log (VHF-FM) (voice) net is used, as required, for coordination of administrative and logistical matters. The supported unit ALOC is the NCS.

3-90. The DS battalion TOC, brigade FSE, and COLT/Striker platoon HQ may also operate on the Division FS (TACSAT) (data) net. This net is used to coordinate fires and exchange FS data across extended ranges within the division area.

3-91. The battalion TOC, brigade FSE, and battalion FSE may also operate on a Naval Gunfire (HF) (voice) net. The unit uses this net to communicate with the ship(s) providing naval gunfire support.

REINFORCING MISSION

INTERNAL NETS

3-92. For a FA battalion assigned the R mission (see Table 3-5), the internal nets are the same as those required for the DS mission.

EXTERNAL NETS

3-93. External nets change to reflect the responsibility of reinforcing to reinforced. The battalion enters the Reinforced Bn Cmd (VHF-FM) (voice) net. The purpose is to be immediately responsive to the needs of the reinforced artillery unit. The battalion enters the Reinforced Bn Ops/F (VHF-FM) (data) net. The purpose is to receive tactical FD from the reinforced artillery unit.

3-94. The battalion CSS staff, BSOC, and ASOC may also, as required, enter the Reinforced FA unit's Admin/Log (VHF-FM) (voice) net, and/or the supported maneuver unit's Admin/Log net to coordinate CSS operations and exchange CSS information.

3-95. The battalion continues as a subscriber to the Force FA HQ CF (MSE) (V-FAX) network and, as required, the Force FA Ops/F 1, 2, or 3 net, Force FA TA/Intel net or Force FA Survey net, and Force FA Admin/Log net.

3-96. The battalion monitors the maneuver FS and Ops/Intel (VHF-FM) voice nets, as required.

MUTUAL SUPPORT UNIT

3-97. Mutual support between two battalions, normally a direct support and reinforcing battalion, means that the computer(s) of one provides tactical FD for the other when that unit must displace or has catastrophic equipment failure. The requirement for mutual support operations in situations of equipment failure has been minimized due to the increasing numbers and capabilities of automated C2 equipment in FA battalions. Internal continuity of operations procedures normally allow a battalion to retain tactical and technical control of its assets. However catastrophic equipment failure or hasty, survival TOC displacement may require reliance on MSU techniques.

3-98. When the reinforcing battalion must take control of the DS battalion firing batteries for tactical FD, it will operate on the DS battalion's three FD nets. When the DS battalion must provide tactical FD to the reinforcing battalion's firing batteries, it will do so on the reinforcing battalion's Ops/F net.

3-99. To establish the required digital link, the two battalions will use either the higher HQ Ops/F (1, 2 or 3) net or one of the two battalion's Ops/F nets to provide the computer-to-computer link necessary to properly exchange data.

3-100. These techniques could also be used between two GS/GSR battalions. In most cases the supporting battalion would assume control of the supported battalion on the supported battalion's Ops/F net. However, the criticality of an ongoing or planned mission involving the supported unit may require the supporting unit to assume control using one or more of the supported battalion's FD nets.

3-101. A well thought out alternate data communications plan and a solid FA technical rehearsal are crucial to successful mutual support unit operations.

GENERAL SUPPORT REINFORCING MISSION

INTERNAL NETS

3-102. A FA battalion may be assigned a GSR tactical mission (Table 3-6). The internal nets are the same as for the DS mission.

EXTERNAL NETS

3-103. External nets change to reflect the responsibility of reinforcing to reinforced. The battalion enters the Force FA Cmd (VHF-FM) (voice) net to continue to be responsive to Force FA HQ (GS).

3-104. The battalion enters the Force FA Ops/F 1, 2 or 3 (VHF-FM) (data) net to continue to be responsive to force FA HQ (GS). Through the force FA CF (MSE) (V-FAX) network, the battalion has access to the force FA HQ and other subscribers.

3-105. The battalion enters the Reinforced Bn Cmd (VHF-FM) (voice) net to be immediately responsive to the needs of the reinforced artillery unit. The battalion enters the Reinforced Bn Ops/F (VHF-FM) (data) net to receive tactical FD from the reinforced artillery unit.

3-106. The battalion monitors the Maneuver FS (VHF-FM) and supported unit or force FA Admin/Log nets as required.

3-107. If the battalion is part of an FA brigade, it may also operate on some of the FA brigade nets as required. The exact communications net requirements will depend on METT-TC and unit SOPs.

GENERAL SUPPORT MISSION

INTERNAL NETS

3-108. The FA battalion, with a GS mission, operates on three internal nets (and three as-required nets) (Table 3-7).

3-109. The Bn Cmd (VHF-FM) (voice) net serves the same purpose as that net for a battalion with a DS mission. It has similar subscribers. The Bn Admin/Log (VHF-FM) (voice) net serves the same purpose as the DS Bn Admin/Log (VHF-FM)(V) net and has similar subscribers. The battalion may also use a Bn TA/Intel (VHF-FM)(D) net similar to other battalions.

3-110. The Bn FD 1, 2, and 3 (VHF-FM) (data) nets are not normally all used simultaneously due to less traffic flow in the GS role. Initially one net may be used until the need arises to activate the other(s). Units must open and allocate additional FD nets (FD 2 and FD 3) as required.

EXTERNAL NETS

3-111. When GS to a maneuver force as a part of a FA brigade or DIVARTY, the battalion operates on four external nets and two as required nets.

3-112. The Force FA Cmd (VHF-FM) (voice) net is used for C2, tactical operations, intelligence, and voice coordination by all force FA elements. The force FA operations section is the NCS. Through the Force FA CF MSE (V-FAX) network, the battalion has access to the force FA HQ and other subscribers.

3-113. The Force FA Ops/F 1, 2, and 3 (VHF-FM) (data) nets are identical. They are used for tactical FD, FS coordination, TA, and met data. The force FA FCE is the NCS.

3-114. As required, the Force FA Admin/Log (VHF-FM) (voice) net is used for coordination of all administrative and logistical matters. The force FA ALOC is the NCS.

3-115. The battalion may monitor the Maneuver FS (VHF-FM) voice net.

3-116. If the battalion is part of a FA brigade, it may also, as required, operate on some of the FA brigade nets. The exact communications net requirements will depend on the METT-TC and unit SOPs.

GENERAL SUPPORT TO THE LIGHT INFANTRY DIVISION

3-117. When supporting a light infantry division, the FA battalion operates on three external nets and three as required nets:
- DIVARTY Cmd (VHF-FM) (voice) net.
- DIVARTY Ops/F 1, 2, 3 (VHF-FM) (data) net.
- DIVARTY CF (MSE) (V-FAX) network.
- As required, the Maneuver FS (VHF-FM) (voice) net.
- As required, the DIVARTY TA/Intel (VHF-FM) (voice or data) net.
- As required, the DIVARTY Admin/Log (VHF-FM) (voice) net.

Chapter 4

The Field Artillery Battalion Planning Process

This chapter provides an overview of the FA battalion planning process. Technological advancements in weapon lethality, TA, information management, and sensor-to-shooter links have required corresponding improvements in the speed and efficiency of the MDMP. This applies particularly to FA operations where reaction times are brief and crucial to overall mission success. FA battalion planning involves both the MDMP, which includes IPB, and the products of the planning process. These products include the FSP, the FASP, and the various orders used to disseminate instructions and information. This chapter is organized into three major sections: Section I covers the MDMP; Section II is an overview of FA IPB; and Section III addresses FA battalion rehearsals.

SECTION I – THE MILITARY DECISION-MAKING PROCESS

4-01. This section provides a general overview of the MDMP process in a situation with adequate planning time. The MDMP actions discussed throughout this section do not represent a "lock-step" process, but often overlap, occur simultaneously, or in a slightly different sequence. During time-constrained planning, planners may abbreviate and combine steps, but generally should not omit a step entirely. Also, the battalion commander will participate more directly in the process, receiving in-progress updates and providing immediate guidance and decisions (vice formal briefings).

4-02. The FA battalion commander and staff should use the MDMP methodology as a guide for the battalion's planning process. They must tailor the MDMP to fit the tactical situation and the battalion's FA tactical mission. In a battalion with a DS mission, they must integrate the battalion's planning process with the supported maneuver unit's planning process. This includes development of a FSP and its accompanying FASP as part of the maneuver unit's OPORD. Figure 4-1 is an example of parallel planning for a DS battalion. (See FM 101-5 for more information on the MDMP and FM 6-20-40 on integration of the DS FA battalion's MDMP with the maneuver MDMP.)

4-03. R, GSR, or GS FA battalions must also integrate and synchronize their planning processes with higher and/or supported maneuver and FA HQ planning. The extent of this integration varies with the situation. But often their MDMP may focus more on their battalion's execution of assigned tasks, and they usually do not prepare their FASP as an integral document to a maneuver OPORD/FSP.

FM 3-09.21 (FM 6-20-1)

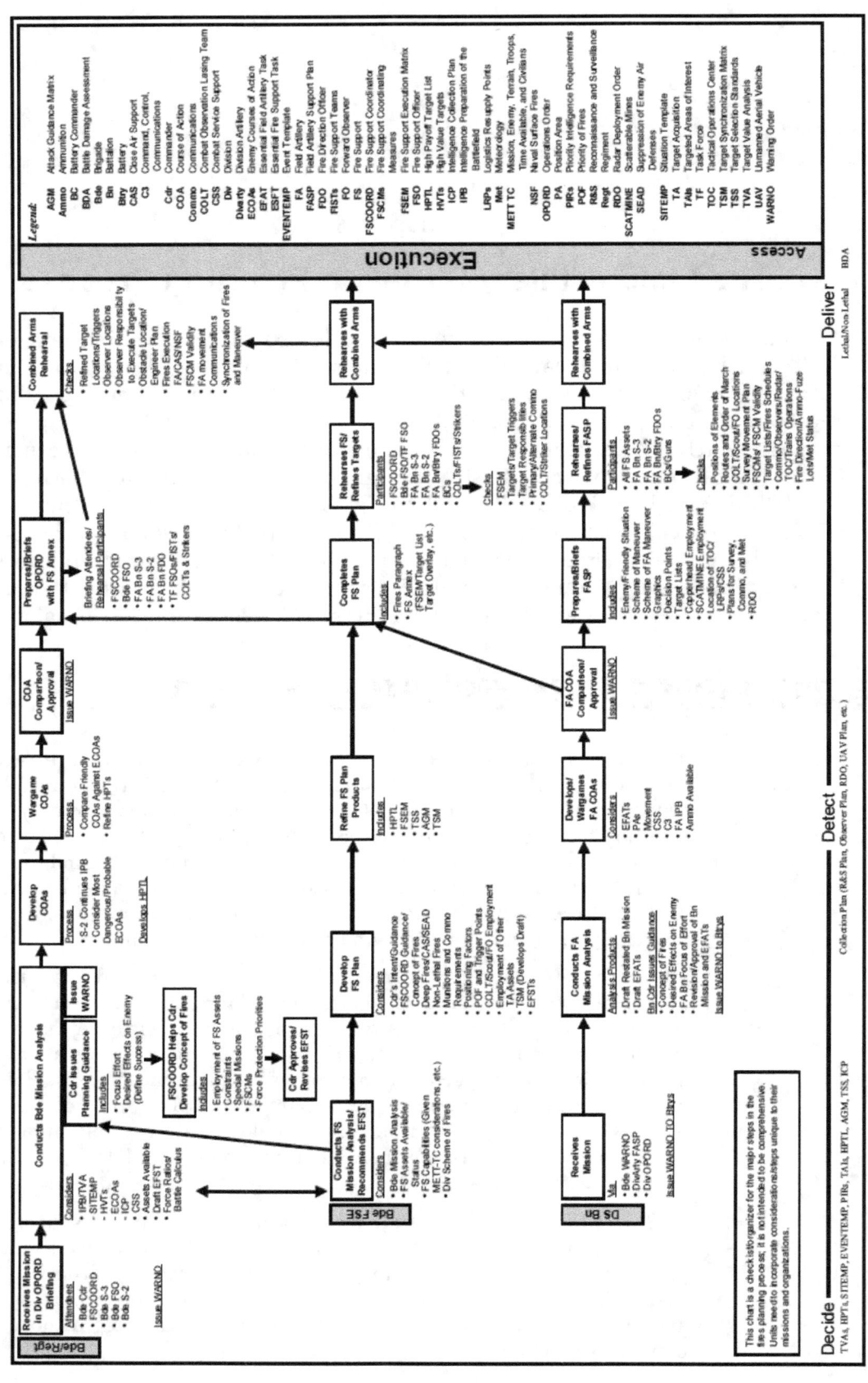

Figure 4-1. The Fires Planning Process

RECEIVE THE MISSION / MISSION ANALYSIS

4-04. MDMP and product development begin upon mission receipt or the identification of a pending mission or situation change. A FA battalion usually receives a mission alert via a series of verbal or written warning orders (WARNO) issued by a maneuver HQ, the FSCOORD, brigade FSO, force FA HQ, FA brigade HQ, or reinforced FA unit. As soon as the WARNO is received, the battalion S3 alerts the battle staff of the pending planning process. The XO, as chief of staff, has primary responsibility for supervision of the FA battalion's MDMP process, while the S3 has responsibility for preparation of the FASP, and the brigade FSO has responsibility for preparation of the FSP.

4-05. The commander and staff immediately initiate mission analysis with a quick review of the WARNO and begin preparing staff estimates by gathering information such as: status of all assigned, attached, and supporting units (to include FS sections, met, radar, and communication assets), CSS by class of supplies, and major equipment. This initial assessment should include rough estimates of survey and PA requirements, ammunition, fuel, and other critical items, especially requirements for external support (such as radar). Staff officers must "cross-talk" with respective counterparts in supported maneuver/FA units and higher FA HQ. The XO and key CSS planners (the S4 and/or S1) may move to the TOC to directly participate in the planning.

4-06. The commander, XO, and S3 conduct an initial assessment to optimize the available planning and rehearsal time while preserving time for batteries and supporting units to plan, rehearse, and prepare. Reverse planning is one method of timeline development. The battalion must synchronize its MDMP timeline with the maneuver and/or higher FA HQ timelines as closely as is possible at this stage.

4-07. The FA battalion commander may go to the maneuver or higher FA HQ to participate in their MDMP or receive a mission brief. Before departing, the commander should receive initial staff estimates and updates. He must thoroughly understand the battalion's current status, especially constraints and limitations, in order to accurately represent the battalion during maneuver/higher FA HQ planning. He should also issue his initial planning guidance to the staff. This guidance should focus the staff on mission specifics during mission analysis (e.g., CCIR, type of order to produce, critical tasks, rehearsal guidance, R&S, ammunition requirements, early movement/ positioning). (If the commander does not go to the supported/higher HQ, all this information must be passed into the supported/higher HQ MDMP by other means.) The battalion S3 then issues a WARNO to the batteries and supporting units to allow parallel planning to begin. This WARNO should include estimated times for issuance of the FASP and battalion and battery rehearsal schedules.

4-08. Upon returning, the commander or the S3 will conduct a quick mission brief to the staff while the operations NCO passes out copies of applicable documents. The commander issues new guidance as necessary and the staff provides the commander brief updates on their staff estimates. Timelines are revised, with emphasis on the FASP/FSP production and rehearsals. In DS units, FSP issues and brigade FSE-battalion TOC coordination may be discussed. Mission analysis and staff estimates continue in preparation for the key product – the mission analysis briefing. The following paragraphs discuss the various actions that occur during mission analysis.

ANALYZE THE HIGHER HQ ORDER

4-09. The FA battalion commander and his staff continue their analysis of higher HQ orders, ensuring they understand the maneuver or higher FA HQs mission and tasks, and the overall plan that they support. They identify the battalion's mission and tasks. The staff must also understand the missions assigned to other FA units, because this may impact how they are utilized during the battle. The FA commander usually obtains this understanding through direct discussion with the maneuver unit or higher FA HQ commander, and through active participation in the maneuver/higher FA planning process. The review of the order focuses on the commander's intent, concept of operations, areas of operation and interest, tasks, and potential issues involving constraints, restraints, limitations, and anticipated enemy actions that may necessitate special attention.

PLAN USE OF AVAILABLE TIME

4-10. Maximizing the time available is critical to the planning process. Some actions, such as FIST/COLT deployments or critical fire missions, may occur hours before the main H-hour for the operation. The commander and staff must continuously balance detailed planning against time available. The battalion S3 can maximize available planning time for the batteries and supporting units by sending additional WARNOs as planning develops to allow parallel planning, nested rehearsals and training, and completion of precombat checks (PCCs). In particular, WARNOs specify key details (time, place, types) for orders production, briefings, rehearsals, preparations, and actual operations. As more details become available, the S3 should refine the timeline, usually applying the one-third/two-third planning rule.

DETERMINE SPECIFIED, IMPLIED, AND ESSENTIAL TASKS

4-11. The FA battalion staff must identify all tasks the unit must accomplish to support the supported unit's mission. The staff extracts from all applicable orders and plans those tasks clearly identified (specified) as battalion responsibilities. The staff also reviews all orders and plans to identify those tasks that are not specified but are important to mission accomplishment (implied tasks). The staff then reviews SOPs and other applicable documents, and conducts a macro analysis of the battalion's role in the operation to identify any implied tasks that may be required. See FM 101-5 for additional information on tasks.

Specified Tasks

4-12. Specified tasks are those tasks clearly stated as requirements that the battalion must accomplish. Higher HQ orders, plans, or messages usually clearly state the specified tasks in the main order, annexes, and/or overlays. These may or may not be essential tasks critical to overall mission accomplishment. Some examples of specified tasks:
- Firing SCATMINE beyond the objective to slow retreat of enemy forces.
- Positioning COLTs to observe specified TAIs.
- CCIR that the supported maneuver or higher FA HQ tasked the battalion to answer.

Implied Tasks

4-13. Implied tasks are tasks are those that must be performed to accomplish a specified task, but which are not stated in the higher headquarters' order. Implied tasks are derived from a detailed analysis of the order, the enemy situation and courses of action, and the terrain. They do not include normal SOP-type activities. Examples of implied tasks are:
- Conducting an airmobile operation or artillery raid to position FA to range a particular target or target set.
- Providing a liaison team or FS team to support a nonstandard mission, organization, or situation.

Essential Tasks

4-14. Once the staff identifies all specified and implied tasks, they determine, in concert with the FSEs in DS units, which tasks are essential (EFSTs/EFATs) and identify relative task priorities based on maneuver/FA commander guidances. EFSTs are those FS tasks essential to the success of the maneuver operation. (e.g., Phase II fires disrupt and delay enemy second echelon maneuver brigades from H+1 to H+3 in order to deny access to our AO, vicinity Smithsville, until the brigade completes defensive preparations.) EFSTs are primarily applicable to DS units and are normally developed by the FSEs as part of the maneuver MDMP.

4-15. The FA battalion staff generally concentrates on EFATs - those FA specific tasks essential to support certain EFSTs and the maneuver operation. A primary source of EFATS is the "method" of an EFST that specifies the target is to be attacked by artillery. A fully developed EFAT addresses task, purpose, method, and effects. **Tasks** specify whether the target must be suppressed, neutralized, destroyed, screened, or obscured. The **Purpose** describes how the successful engagement of the target contributes to the maneuver commander's plan (taken from the EFST's purpose). The **Method** discusses how the FA battalion will achieve the task. The staff determines the method for each EFAT during COA development. **Effects** describe what the battalion must accomplish to successfully achieve the task.

4-16. An example of an EFAT supporting the previously described EFST might be "Provide interdiction fires (DPICM and SCATMINE) at chokepoints in engagement area (EA) Blue, between H+1 and H+2 to disrupt the enemy first brigade, cause 10% loss of vehicles, and delay it for 30-60 minutes". EFATs may also include:

- Firing smoke in support of a breaching operation.
- Destroying reconnaissance elements in a designated battle sector.
- Providing SEAD for an attack helicopter mission.
- Destroying dismounted infantry when they are most vulnerable (during dismount) or at a critical event (breach of a friendly obstacle).
- Conducting counterfire at a critical point in the battle to suppress enemy artillery.

Completed in detail, an EFAT may look like the following examples:
- EFAT 1 - Delay reinforcement by the 2nd echelon tank battalion (146th mechanized infantry brigade (MIBR)) for two to four hours.
  - Task: Emplace 400 X 400 and/or 200 X 800 medium density, short duration, remote antiarmor minefield.
  - Purpose: Delay or shape 2nd echelon tank battalion arrival into EAs Green or Hornet so that enemy echelons can be defeated sequentially.
  - Method: One battery per minefield; one survivability move after emplacement.
  - Effects: Enemy 2nd echelon tank battalion delayed and unable to assist lead mechanized and tank battalions before we complete their defeat in the EAs.
- EFAT 2 – Prevent or disrupt enemy attempts to breach friendly obstacles in EAs Green and Hornet during 146 MIBR attack.
  - Task: Attack enemy targets approaching or attempting to breach the friendly obstacles in EAs Green and Hornet.
  - Purpose: Prevent or disrupt enemy breaching attempts so that the 146 MIBR cannot penetrate friendly defenses before it is defeated.
  - Method: Battalion four rounds DPICM on company-sized (or larger) targets with repeat as necessary. Battery three rounds on smaller targets.
  - Effects: Friendly obstacles are not breached and 146 MIBR attack is defeated.

DEVELOP AN "ARTILLERIZED" IPB

4-17. A cornerstone to the MDMP is the IPB. If parallel planning is to occur, the maneuver unit/higher FA HQ S2 must provide the FA battalion with an accurate estimate of how the enemy plans to fight (i.e., an IPB). The FA battalion S2 must be proactive in obtaining as much information as possible, from the time the unit receives the first WARNO. (This is important as the S2 begins providing IPB information during the initial staff estimates discussed earlier.) A prioritized requirements list can facilitate this coordination and assist the maneuver/higher FA S2 in understanding the battalion's requirements. FSEs can also assist the battalion S2 in obtaining information.

4-18. The FA battalion S2 and staff must "artillerize" the IPB before other staff members can finalize their portion of the staff estimates. The artillery IPB process includes refinement of all provided IPB information and products (e.g., modified combined obstacle overlay (MCOO) and situation templates (SITEMPs)) to focus on enemy fires assets, enemy systems that pose a threat to the battalion (e.g., air, ground), and survivability/mobility issues. For example, the S2 must determine how the effects of climate and weather may impact achieved FA ranges and rates of fire (friendly and enemy) as well as the relative impact (Do the conditions favor either side?). The analysis must focus on the effects of the factors rather than just identification of raw data, as the staff uses the refined IPB in developing their staff estimates and FSP/FASP inputs. The S2 also further develops the FA battalion's PIR, and begins incorporating into R&S plans, the PIR that the maneuver/ higher FA HQ tasked the battalion to answer. Section II provides a step-by-step discussion of the FA IPB process.

4-19. The IPB products also support the FA battalion's participation in force targeting efforts. While targeting is a combined arms decide, detect, deliver and assess (D3A) effort, FA and FS personnel and agencies play integral roles in the process.

4-20. In developing the artillerized IPB, the FA battalion S2 must coordinate his work with the targeting personnel/cells in the appropriate maneuver and FA HQ. In a DS FA battalion the S2 works closely with the targeting officer in the brigade FSE, while in other FA battalions the targeting officer is part of the S2 section, directly assisting the S2 with IPB.

REVIEW AVAILABLE ASSETS

4-21. The staff translates raw facts and data into meaningful capabilities that allow the FA commander to clearly picture the battalion's ability to support the supported commander's intent. For example, 300 M825 smoke rounds may translate to five immediate smoke missions, three quick smoke missions and two average large smoke missions (by SOP standard planning factors). Time analysis is also critical, as the unit may have enough ammunition to fire the two large smoke missions, but not at the same time, or not in conjunction with other large fire missions.

4-22. This review includes assessment of the available assets, to include attachments, detachments, and supporting FA units as well as command relationships, and their implications for C2 and coordination. The staff should identify requirements for additional forces, external support, or changes in command relationships as early as possible.

4-23. The staff uses LPB methodology in preparing the CSS/logistic estimate. LPB is a continuous analysis of logistic factors affecting mission accomplishment. Emphasis is on how the status of CSS will impact on proposed COAs. Logistic planners use these estimates to recommend the best COA (that can be supported) and to develop plans to support the operations. Key concerns of battalion logistic planners are the status of Class III, IV, and V; and the operational status of FA weapons and FD equipment.

DETERMINE CONSTRAINTS

4-24. The staff determines any limitations that might influence task or mission accomplishment. These may be passed down from the supported maneuver or higher FA HQ, directed by the FA battalion commander, or identified by the battalion staff. In most battalions these will be listed in the FASP or its appendices. These limitations may consist of both restrictions and constraints as described below. While these are initially used for planning purposes and may change, the final restrictions and constraints will be published and disseminated in the FSP, FASP, or WARNOs as appropriate. The commander and staff may need to address some of the restrictions and constraints during risk assessment and COA development.

Restrictions

4-25. Restrictions are directive type limitations that prevent the unit from doing something that it may be capable of accomplishing. Examples of restrictions are:
- Restrictions on firing across or near international borders.
- Implementation of any type of restrictive fire measure.
- Restrictive minimum safe distance (MSD) guidance.
- Ammunition restrictions – e.g., prohibition against firing more than 40 percent of basic load during a reinforcing mission.

Constraints

4-26. Constraints are frequently resource, terrain, or weather limitations that prevent or hinder a unit's ability to accomplish tasks or missions. Examples of constraints include:
- A critical resource shortage – such as fuel or ammunition (the latter may due to a relatively low CSR).
- The number of operational howitzers or launchers in a unit.
- Weapon, communication, or automation equipment problems or personnel shortages that result in degraded operations.
- Terrain that limits positioning and movement of firing units.
- Fog or other conditions limiting use of laser-designators.
- The hours of daylight available to accomplish a task or operation that relies on daylight (or the reverse – darkness for night operations).

IDENTIFY CRITICAL FACTS AND ASSUMPTIONS

4-27. The staff determines critical facts and assumptions that can and will directly affect successful accomplishment of the mission. Some facts and assumptions will be contained in the maneuver or higher FA HQ orders, plans, or supporting documents. The staff verifies these and identifies others during mission analysis. The staff then lists all critical facts and assumptions for use during course of action development.

4-28. Facts are statements of known data concerning both the enemy and friendly situations. They include staff projections and assessments of tangible and intangible factors, such as, projection of Class V stockages and projections of forecasted replacement flow.

4-29. Assumptions are estimates that are developed when facts are not available. Assumptions must meet the tests of validity and necessity. An example of a valid assumption is "The enemy will use chemical weapons." If the enemy does use chemical weapons then the unit is prepared and can still accomplish the mission. Necessity defines whether or not the assumption is used in development of the plan. If the assumption is not necessary or appropriate, then it should not be considered. Assumptions are replaced with facts as soon as possible.

CONDUCT RISK ASSESSMENT

4-30. The commander and staff identify risk hazards and make an initial assessment of the risk level for each hazard (e.g., radiation exposure guidance, immediate action guidance [receiving counterfire], MOPP-level operations, radar cueing scheduling). The battalion S2 can provide input on enemy artillery vulnerabilities to optimize desired effects on the enemy, which could reduce friendly risk if engaged. The commander, with staff input, determines whether or not the level of risk is acceptable and provides guidance as necessary on actions to reduce the level of risk or advising higher HQ of the situation. Higher HQ may dictate degree of risk. (See FM 101-5 for additional guidance).

DETERMINE INITIAL COMMANDER'S CRITICAL INFORMATION REQUIREMENTS

4-31. CCIR identify information the commander needs to visualize the battlefield, make key decisions, and determine or validate COAs. CCIR are normally expressed as PIR (information about the enemy), essential elements of friendly information (EEFI) - information needed to protect friendly forces from the enemy's information gathering systems, and friendly forces information requirements (FFIR) - information about the capabilities of his or adjacent units. CCIR are often contained in the higher HQ orders or plans, and may be specified tasks requiring battalion action.

4-32. The battalion commander may expand the CCIR listed in higher HQ or supported unit's plan in order to accomplish his mission. The commander and staff begin identifying all information requirements (IR) and CCIR upon receipt of the WARNO so that the staff can quickly initiate actions and coordination as necessary. (The commander, based on staff recommendations, determines which IR are CCIR.)

4-33. Further identification and refinement occurs during mission analysis, especially the "artillerized" IPB and wargaming processes. The FA commander and staff should chose CCIR that parallel the supported commander's (and/or higher FA HQ) and drives decisions at decision points. CCIR should be limited to a reasonable number to avoid loss of focus and overburdening staffs and collection assets. See FM 34-8-2, *Intelligence Officer's Handbook*, for additional information on CCIR.

DETERMINE THE INITIAL RECONNAISSANCE PLAN

4-34. The S3 and S2 review the battalion's specified and implied R&S tasks that support higher HQ R&S plans. This includes any PIR or IR tasked to the battalion. Based on the refined IPB, PIR, and IR, the S3, S2, and the commander may identify gaps in the intelligence collection plan of the supported unit (and/or higher FA HQ). The S3 provides this information to the appropriate maneuver/FA HQ S3 (or FSE) for inclusion in the higher HQ's R&S plan. The S3 and S2 also identify R&S requirements necessary to support the FA battalion's force protection plans. The S3 and S2 develop a battalion R&S plan utilizing available collection assets (e.g., survey, ammunition sections, radars, firing units, FOs, FISTs, COLTs/Strikers, and

FSOs). Battalion R&S requirements that are beyond the battalion's resources are passed to the appropriate maneuver/FA HQ for coordination and inclusion into higher R&S plans.

WRITE THE RESTATED MISSION

4-35. The battalion S3 and staff prepare a proposed restated mission for the commander's approval or modification. It should provide precise terms defining who, what, when, where, and why. Of the five, the commander and staff must especially understand the what and why, as these aid them in anticipating and addressing the many changes that occur in fluid combat situations and in understanding the timing and effects issues.

4-36. The restated mission should be more than a general statement of the battalion's FA tactical mission "provide DS FA fires". It should highlight one or more critical aspects of that support or the commander's priorities. An example is "On D-day, H-hour, 1/12 FA provides DS fires to first brigade, to weaken enemy forward defenses (10 minute preparation); to support the main attack battalion (close support fires); and to suppress or destroy enemy FA HPTs during final assault (counterfire program/critical friendly zone (CFZ) Wings), in support of the attack to seize and hold Objective Tiger. O/O 1/12 FA provides GS fires (primarily reactive counterfire against enemy mortars and FA in call-for-fire zone (CFFZ) Halo) to 1st Division, for approximately two hours, to support exploitation beyond phase line Maple by 2nd brigade".

4-37. The restated mission should not become a long list of all EFATs (they belong in paragraph 3a, Concept of Operations). Anticipate identification of additional EFATs during COA development, wargaming, and rehearsal.

CONDUCT A MISSION ANALYSIS BRIEFING

4-38. The mission analysis briefing should not be a unit readiness briefing to the commander. The staff must know the status of the battalion and supporting units and brief relevant information as it applies to the situation. The staff should develop standardized charts to monitor and consolidate this type of data to assist the commander in obtaining a quick snapshot of his unit. Time permitting, the staff should brief the commander on its mission analysis using the following format:

- **XO** – Introduction, Purpose, and Agenda.
- **S2** – Abbreviated IBP.
  - Weather and its impact on FA operations.
  - Terrain - MCOO, mobility corridors, avenues of approach (AOA).
  - Evaluation of threat capabilities to impact on the FA battalion's operations.
  - SITEMPs (most probable and most dangerous).
  - Enemy assets and vulnerabilities.
  - Recommended CCIR – PIR, EEFI, FFIR.
- **S3** – Results of mission analysis.
  - Current combat power and situation of units.
  - Current and projected task organization.

- Mission and commander's intent - two levels up.
- Specified, implied, and essential tasks (EFATs and EFSTs).
- Limitations (constraints and restrictions).
- Recommended mission statement.
- Additional assets required.
- Requests for information (RFI).
- Results of risk analysis.
- **S4** – Logistic status.
  - Current status of Class I (water [W]), III, and V.
  - Current and projected maintenance status.
  - Critical shortages or concerns.
- **S1** – Personnel status.
  - Current and projected personnel status.
  - Medical status (assets available and major health issues).
  - Critical shortages.
- **S6** – Communications status.
  - Current and projected maintenance status.
  - Status of communications and automation systems (FM, MSE, WAN/LAN).
  - Critical shortages.
- **XO** – Timeline review, to include rehearsal schedule and time hack.
- **Commander** – FA commander's initial guidance.

APPROVE THE RESTATED MISSION

4-39. Immediately after the mission analysis briefing, the commander should approve a restated mission. This can be the staff's recommended restated mission, a modified version, or one that the commander has developed himself. Once approved, the restated mission becomes the battalion's mission.

DEVELOP THE INITIAL FA COMMANDER'S INTENT

4-40. After reviewing the mission analysis briefing and approving the restated mission, the commander finalizes his intent statement. The FA commander's intent is his personal expression (in broad terms) of:

- The critical tasks to be executed (e.g., counterfire, destroy dismounts, cover obstacles, attrit/disrupt first echelon).
- The purpose of the FA fires in support of the supported force (e.g., delay second echelon to allow attrition of first echelon, protect the force with counterfire to allow freedom of maneuver).
- The methods used by the FA battalion to assist the supported force in achieving the effects (e.g., initially position observers and firing units forward to delay lead elements with dual purpose, improved conventional munitions (DPICM) fires, destroy C2 elements with Copperhead fires, fire SCATMINE and smoke to delay and disrupt the second echelon).

- The effects or criteria for success (e.g., enemy unable to mass his direct and indirect fires against the brigade and we are in position to support the follow-on mission).

4-41. The FA commander's intent links his vision of the end state and the FA concept of operations (details of the "how to" written by the staff). It also provides linkage with the maneuver and higher FA HQ commanders' intent for fires.

ISSUE THE COMMANDER'S GUIDANCE

4-42. After the commander approves or issues the restated mission and states his intent, he must provide additional planning guidance to the staff. The intent of the commander's guidance is to establish guidelines and implant his vision of the operation into the minds of his staff to enable them to plan the FA operations consistent with his and the supported commander's (and/or higher FA HQ) intentions. When time is not significantly limited, this guidance can be general in nature, therefore, providing the staff maximum latitude. As time becomes more constrained, this guidance must be more specific and directive. Commander's guidance should address (but not be limited to) the following:

- Priority of EFATs, guidance on methods to accomplish each, and clarification on effects for each.
- COA development guidance – to include number of friendly FA COAs and enemy FS COAs to consider and decisive points (especially those where he expects fires to play a critical role).
- CSS priorities.
- Type of order to prepare.
- CCIR and RFI.
- Positioning priorities and deception guidance.
- Munitions mix (CCLs) and distribution.
- C2 and liaison arrangements.
- Radio retrans guidance.
- Survey and R&S priorities and guidance.
- Risk guidance.
- Timeline guidance.
- Rehearsal guidance. (See Section III for additional information.)

ISSUE A WARNING ORDER

4-43. Immediately after the commander gives his guidance, the S3 will send the batteries and supporting units a WARNO that contains, as a minimum:

- Intelligence update.
- The restated mission.
- AO and known mobility/countermobility information.
- The FA commander's intent, and that of the supported maneuver commander and the FA/maneuver commanders two levels up.
- Prioritized EFATs and any other key priorities.
- Timeline estimates – planning/rehearsal/execution.

- CCIR.
- Risk guidance and survivability guidance.
- Reconnaissance.
- Guidance on rehearsals.
- Precombat inspection (PCI)/PCC priorities.
- Other known details.

REVIEW FACTS AND ASSUMPTIONS

4-44. During the decision-making process, the commander and staff must periodically review all available facts and assumptions. New facts may alter requirements and analysis of the mission. Assumptions may have become facts or they may have become invalid. Whenever the facts or assumptions change, the commander and staff must assess the impact of these changes on the plan and make the necessary adjustments.

COA DEVELOPMENT

4-45. In a DS FA battalion, the FSCOORD and FS personnel participate in the maneuver unit COA development and FA fire planning is an integrated part of the maneuver MDMP. In all FA units, the staff analyzes possible FA COAs to determine the best COA to support the higher HQ mission. This effort often begins when the first WARNO is received. Each FA COA must be **feasible** (able to be accomplished with current or projected resources), **acceptable** (contains acceptable levels of risk), **suitable** (consistent with the commander's guidance and intent), **distinguishable** (if more then one), and **complete** (answers who, what, when, where, why, and how).

- **Who** - The type of unit supported.
- **What** - The type of operation supported and EFATs for the battalion.
- **When** - The time action will begin or must be completed by (e.g., on-order, D-day, H-hour, or specific DTG for artillery FS activities).
- **Where** - The assigned AO, such as PAs and routes, in the supported unit sector.
- **How** - The method the FA battalion will use to conduct or execute its EFATs in support of the operation.
- **Why** - The purpose of FA fires, and/or fires in general, in support of the mission.

4-46. The COAs that a FA battalion will develop and evaluate will address the various methods or options that the FA unit has to accomplish its mission and tasks. These may include different movement plans, tactical or technical FD controls (fire mission routing, sensor-to-shooter links, as examples), task allocations, positioning, logistics plans, or other aspects of FA operations. The FA battalion is not evaluating the maneuver or force FA HQ COAs, but rather its ability to support the operation. One technique for developing a FA COA includes:

- Review EFSTs and supporting EFATs.
- Task subordinate units (who, what, when, where, why – and how, if time constrained).
- Determine command post and trains configuration.

- Address fundamentals of the battlefield operating systems (BOS) (for CSS, it could be the tenets of CSS; for FA, it could be the five requirements for accurate, predicted fire).
- Task organic sections (usually part of the headquarters element). Again, indicate the who, what, where, when, and why.
- Graphically and/or verbally explain the COA, ensuring every specified and implied task is accounted for.

ANALYZE RELATIVE COMBAT POWER, FACTS, AND ASSUMPTIONS

4-47. First, the S2 focuses on artillery ratios to help determine what assets are needed to accomplish EFATs. By analyzing FA ratios and determining and comparing each force's FA strength and weakness as function of combat power, the staff can gain some insight into friendly FA capabilities in support of the operation. The analysis can also reveal what FA operation may be possible from both a friendly and an enemy perspective and FA vulnerabilities (friendly and enemy). (The FS estimate conducted by the FSE or supported unit should be the start point or extension for this analysis. The FA S2 must also understand the overall relative combat power assessment prepared by supported and higher HQ.)

GENERATE OPTIONS

4-48. Based on this analysis and the FA commander's guidance, the staff generates options for FA COA development in support of the mission. Brainstorming is the preferred technique for generating options. Once the staff has explored various concepts, they should examine each to determine if it satisfies COA selection criteria.

ARRAY INITIAL FORCES

4-49. The S3 and S2 should integrate the SITEMP into the COA development. The S3 overlays the SITEMP (see Section II for information on SITEMP) on the operations map and deconflicts positioning of firing units, critical nodes, and radar positions given the impending situation. The S3 ensures that PAs are not on enemy AOAs, regimental objectives, or other conflicting areas. It is very difficult to position out of range of the threat's artillery so the S3 should consider positioning units in areas that will cause artillery delivery problems for the enemy's artillery systems (e.g., sight to crest, intervening crest, and traverse limit problems). The staff conducts this process to eliminate PAs that do not meet the above criteria. Given the remaining PAs, the S3 can now narrow the focus of FA COAs to support the mission.

DEVELOP THE SCHEME OF MANEUVER (MOVEMENT PLANS)

4-50. The S3 section posts the MCOO on the operations map underneath the operations graphics overlay. The O&I section plots the HPTs or critical target areas (areas where the supported commander plans to engage HPTs, TAIs, chokepoints, NAIs, trigger points, etc.) by phase based on the HPTL, fire plans, templates, etc. The BAO and/or FDC provides the S3 with ammunition information (types and quantities of propellants, projectiles, rockets, missiles) for the upcoming mission. With this information the S3 and BAO determine which munitions mix is available in the greatest amounts. The S3 uses the range of the greatest percentage of propellant/shell (rocket/missile) mix available to the battalion to determine the planning range. This process avoids a common pitfall--using the wrong planning range to choose PAs. This information, passed through FSO channels, also provides the maneuver commander with the predominant range capability of his FS systems.

4-51. Using the correct planning range, the S3 draws range fans starting from the HPTs or critical target areas back to the proposed PAs. All PAs on the MCOO that are inside these range fans are identified as optimal PAs to engage HPTs or critical target areas. PAs outside of the range fans are identified as less than optimal. Units in less than optimal PAs will be required to expend propellants and munitions that are in short supply (e.g., rocket assisted projectiles [RAP]) to range the target area. During this process the FDO refines the optimal ranges given the conditions of accurate predicted fires. The FDO must ensure he addresses issues of powder temperature, gun above or below target, high angle fire requirements, and met data.

4-52. Once the S3 identifies the optimal PAs for each target area, by phase, he copies them onto the operations overlay and gives the MCOO back to the S2. There are times when the S3 must use less than optimal PAs and he does so understanding the constraints of those PAs. The FDO looks at each PA and identifies any technical fire delivery issues (e.g., site to crest, intervening crest, traverse limits) that must be resolved. When any of these issues are identified, the FDO should shoot a "dry" mission in the computer using data from the PA to determine if the identified concerns are valid. If the S3 directs occupation of any of these PAs, the FDO addresses these identified issues with the battery FDC during the battalion FA technical rehearsal.

4-53. The S3 (and brigade FSO) should perform a quality control check of the FA/FS scheme of maneuver to ensure it addresses:
- Battery/TOC/CSS movement plans, at least into primary positions.
- Alternate and supplementary positions.
- Azimuths of fire and planning range fans.
- EFST/EFAT requirements and key subordinate tasks.
- R&S requirements (radar support and coverage areas).
- Survey, met, engineer, and ADA support.
- C2 and CSS plans.
- Priorities of support.

EXAMINE C2 CONSIDERATIONS

4-54. The S3 examines C2 considerations that will influence support to the supported unit (e.g., FSCMs, radar zones, retrans stations, establishment of quickfire channel).

PREPARE COA STATEMENTS AND SKETCHES

4-55. The S3 prepares a COA statement and supporting sketch (containing PAs, movement plan, FSCMs, planning range fans, radar coverage, listing of EFATs, etc.) for each possible FA COA. Together, the statement and sketch should cover who, what, when, where, how, why, and any significant risks. At this point, the S3 should have well defined EFATs, each containing a specific task, its purpose, method of accomplishment, and task effects (desired results).

BRIEF COMMANDER AND REFINE COA

4-56. After the COAs have been developed, they are briefed to the commander for review. After the briefings the commander gives any additional guidance. If he rejects all COAs, the staff must begin again. If he accepts one or more of the COAs, they begin the wargaming process. The COA briefing may include:
- Update intelligence.
- Possible enemy employment of FA assets (SITEMP).
- The restated mission.
- The supported commander's intent for FS/FA.
- The COA statement and sketch.
- The rationale for each COA.

COURSES OF ACTION ANALYSIS (WARGAME)

4-57. COA analysis is wargaming the COA(s). It is a critical step that ensures the development of a fully integrated and synchronized support plan. In DS FA units, the FSCOORD/FSOs will participate in the supported unit's wargaming process. The steps of the wargame process are:
- Gather the tools, materials, data, and draft event template.
- List all friendly forces (display FA units by platoons or batteries).
- List assumptions, to include higher HQ.
- List EFSTs/EFATs and known decision points.
- Determine evaluation criteria to measure the relative effectiveness and efficiency (e.g., list EFSTs/EFATs, their purpose, method used to accomplish the tasks, and desired effects).
- Select the wargame method and a recording technique (see FM 101-5).
- Wargame the battle with emphasis on FA fires (use the procedures in the paragraphs below).

WARGAMING

4-58. Wargaming the COAs is critical to ensure the battalion can provide effective fires in support of the mission. The wargaming process is as follows:

Create a DST

4-59. Create a DST that relates the details of the event template to decision points that are of significance to the battalion. (A maneuver unit/higher FA HQ DST may assist the FA battalion, especially DS units.) This is accomplished by overlaying the event template on the operations graphic to depict time phase lines (TPLs) on the battlefield (see Section II for additional information on event template/TPLs refinement). The S3 then lists the EFATs for the battalion. These may be battalion mass missions, special munitions missions, unit movements, reconnaissance, or survey emplacement. The DST does not dictate decisions to the S3, but rather identifies critical events and threat activities relative to time and location

Wargame Each EFAT

4-60. Wargame each EFAT in order. The S2 discusses timing of the battle off his TPLs, the S3 addresses how the EFAT accomplishes the EFSTs, and the FDO briefs mission execution times (time of flight, shift times, first round to last). The wargame sessions may cover the entire operation or a particular phase.

Wargame the Fire Plan(s)

4-61. Wargame the fire plan(s) to determine if they are executable. The S2 describes what the enemy is doing and their rate of march, the S3 adds the type of target, the FA impact area (front, center, or rear of formation) and the number of rounds and volleys required. The FDO then states whether or not the battalion is laid on the target, who will fire the mission, shift time required, time of flight, and total time to execute the mission. It is critical that honest times, based on the unit's current level of training and not standard times from MTP manuals, are used. Given this information and using TPLs, place a decision point (star) on the operations graphic that represents the last time on the battlefield, when the enemy reaches this point, the FA can achieve its greatest effects. Two points are worth emphasizing:

- First, decision points established by the FA battalion in the forward battle area should correspond to the trigger points of the supported unit that is watching the decision point, unless the FA battalion has organic assets observing the area. For DS FA units, the decision points may be the same as those of the supported maneuver unit, or they may be decision points unique to the FA battalion.
- Second, as the S2 identifies threat forces at or near the decision points he alerts the S3 and FDO, who ensure the FA battalion is prepared to fire any missions tied to the decision points. FSOs should know the mission execution times of all supporting battalions.

Determine Other FA Decision Points

4-62. Use the FA battalion DST to determine decision points for critical FA events such as unit movements, special munitions missions, radar cueing, CSS operations, etc. In the same manner as described above, the S3 and the staff wargame the battle. They determine where to place decision points that will trigger specific critical events. For example, the S3 could establish a decision point to cue the radar to observe a breaching operation when lead elements of the breach force report their location at a certain point.

Display Decision Points on Operations Overlay

4-63. Graphically depict each decision point on the operations overlay. This will assist in focusing the staff on critical events that must occur during the battle. Time permitting, the staff may develop a FASM (see Appendix A for example) that addresses by unit, each task they are required to execute (usually created after the commander's decision on COA selection).

COA COMPARISON

4-64. After analyzing each COA, the S3 evaluates how each COA will meet certain predetermined criteria. The criteria should be fairly explicit, quantifiable, and unique to the situation. Initially evaluate each COA against the criteria, not each other, to prevent bias. Clearly identify the criteria standards prior to the comparison. (e.g., If the COAs require 2, 3, and 6 moves respectively are they rated 1, 2, and 3 or 1, 1, and 3?) The comparison ultimately leads to a staff recommendation of one COA to the commander. Table 4-1 is an example of a COA comparison matrix.

Table 4-1. COA Comparison Matrix (Example)

CRITERIA	WEIGHT	COA 1	COA 2	COA 3
Accomplishment of EFATs, especially #1,2, & 5	4	1 = (4)	3 = (12)	2 = (8)
Logistical resupply – Class V & III	3	2 = (6)	3 = (9)	1 = (3)
FA maneuver – Min of 2 Btrys available - Ph I & IV	3	2 = (6)	1 = (3)	3 = (9)
C2 – especially during EFATs #1, 2 & 5	3	1 = (3)	3 = (9)	2 = (6)
Counterfire operations – during Phases I & IV	2	3 = (6)	2 = (4)	1 = (2)
Simplicity – fewest moves	3	1 = (3)	2 = (6)	3 = (9)
Survey operations – requirements for hasty survey	1	1 = (1)	2 = (2)	3 = (3)
Met operations – distance and time validity	1	2 = (2)	1 = (1)	3 = (3)
Force protection – exposure to ground attack	3	1 = (3)	3 = (9)	2 = (6)
Future operations – tubes, critical ammo, PAs	2	3 = (6)	2 = (4)	1 = (2)
Numerical Total Weighted Total 1 (lower) = better		17 (40)	22 (59)	21 (51)

COA APPROVAL

4-65. The commander may agree with the recommendation, modify it, or select another. Once the commander makes his selection, the staff immediately issues a WARNO with essential information so batteries and supporting units can refine their plans.

FSP / FASP PRODUCTION

4-66. Based on the commander's selected COA and final guidance, the units finalize schedules of fires and prepare the FSPs and FASPs as addressed below. Once approved by the commander(s), the FSP and/or FASP are disseminated, rehearsed, and executed. Section III addresses rehearsals in more detail.

SCHEDULING FIRES

4-67. The FA fire planning process is a cooperative effort involving close coordination between personnel in FSEs and FA TOCs. The FA battalion S3 usually directs the final stages of the process and the preparation of approved FA fire plans and schedules as he has the most current and anticipated status of the firing units. The final approving authority is usually the supported maneuver commander or FSCOORD, or in some cases, the FA commander responsible for a specific FA mission.

4-68. In a DS/R FA battalion scenario, the FSEs, on the basis of the maneuver commander's guidance for fires, plan and tentatively schedule targets to be fired by the FA units. Ultimately, the DS FA battalion S3, working with the brigade FSO and the reinforcing unit S3 (when applicable), refines all of the requested fires into one or more FA fire plans. The fire plan(s) includes all on-call and scheduled individual targets, groups, series, programs, preparations, counterpreparations, and/or other targets or schedules of fires that must be fired at a specific time or event and/or in a predetermined time pattern. Each fire plan may support a particular plan, phase, event, or a specific FA task.

4-69. Fire planning and scheduling for GSR/GS units may primarily be done by the higher FA HQ as part of the overall fire planning effort. GSR/GS units may receive completed fire plans and schedules assigning their responsibilities. However, they may also be given targeting data and specific missions or tasks, and required to develop their own fire plans and schedules. An example would be a GS FA battalion given the mission to fire a SEAD program in a designated zone as part of a deep attack helicopter operation. The FA brigade HQ may give the battalion the mission and general guidance. The battalion then conducts the target development and coordination with the aviation brigade or attack helicopter battalion FSE to prepare the program and establish a trigger or method of fire control.

4-70. Appendix B addresses specific scheduling techniques, considerations, and definitions of scheduling terms. While the appendix primarily addresses manual targeting and fire planning, much of the information is also applicable to fire planning in general and must be read to fully understand automated fire planning.

FIRE SUPPORT PLAN

4-71. The FSP, developed in the FSE, outlines the integration and synchronization of all FS assets into the scheme of maneuver. A simple FSP may consist of only the fires portion of the concept of operations subparagraph in the maneuver OPORD and the FS subparagraph (See Figure 4-2). The FS subparagraph includes a section for each FS agency involved in the operation. The appropriate FS representatives (air force, naval, etc.) prepare their input.

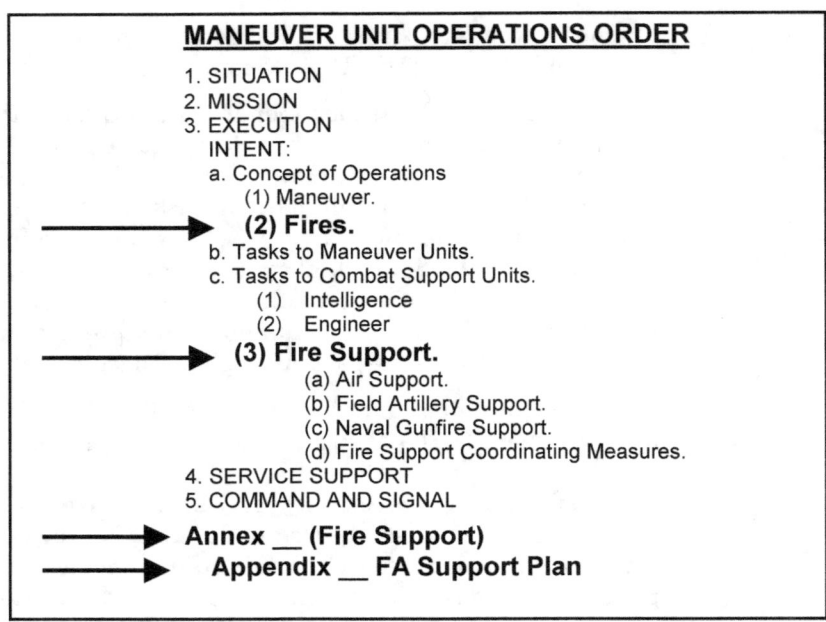

Figure 4-2. Elements of a Fire Support Plan

4-72. If the FSP requires amplification that is too extensive for the FS subparagraph, the FSE publishes a FS annex to the maneuver OPORD. The combined information in the fires/FS subparagraphs, FS annex, and any FS related enclosures or appendices then constitute the FSP. The FSP may include a FASP as an appendix to the FS annex. For detailed information on the FSP refer to FM 6-20-30, FM 6-20-40, or FM 6-71.

FIELD ARTILLERY SUPPORT PLAN

4-73. The FASP is a tactical plan for employing all organic, assigned, attached, and supporting FA assets. It disseminates the maneuver/FA commander's guidance, assigns responsibilities for FA tasks (such as EFATs), and outlines the commander's concepts for FA fires, movement, C2, TA, CSS, and force protection. The FASP is one of the products of the battalion's MDMP. A FA battalion prepares one of two basic types of FASPs depending on its FA tactical mission.

DS BATTALION FASP

4-74. A DS FA battalion prepares a comprehensive FASP that covers the employment of **all** FA assets in support of a maneuver operation, to include reinforcing units, attached radars, or other FA assets. The battalion develops the FASP as part of the larger combined arms MDMP process. The FASP is based primarily on the supported maneuver and FA battalion commanders' guidance and intent for fires, the scheme of maneuver, the concept for fires, and higher HQ OPORDs, FSPs, FASPs, and guidance. The DS battalion FASP usually becomes an appendix to the FS annex in the maneuver OPLAN/OPORD. Thus the DS battalion is integrally involved in development of both EFSTs and EFATs.

4-75. The DS FA commander, as both the FSCOORD and the force FA commander, must ensure that the FSO and the FA battalion S3 closely coordinate preparation of the FSP and the FASP. The FA battalion S2 coordinates IPB, TA, and targeting with the targeting officer in the FSE and with the maneuver S2. The S6, S1, and S4 also coordinate key aspects of their functional areas with their maneuver staff counterparts, and the brigade FSE as appropriate. The commander and staff of a reinforcing FA unit will also participate closely in the FASP development.

R/GSR/GS BATTALION FASP

4-76. A FA battalion with a R mission may develop a joint FASP with the DS battalion or develop an independent FASP, in a parallel process synchronized with the DS battalion's MDMP. A FA battalion with a GSR, or GS mission usually develops its own FASP in a parallel process coordinated with the MDMP of the supported FA unit or higher FA HQ. This type of FASP generally addresses only battalion unique requirements and directives not covered in the FASP of the supported or higher FA HQ or unit SOP. It also provides the FA commander's concept, intent, and guidance for execution of the battalion's mission. It is not published as part of a maneuver OPORD.

4-77. R, GSR, or GS FA battalion may not need to publish a full FASP. If the reinforced or higher FA HQ FASP is detailed enough, a R, GSR, or GS battalion may issue only a FRAGO that provides the limited additional information needed. This is possible when the commander and staff of a R, GSR, or GS unit directly participate in the preparation of the FASP prepared by a DS battalion, FA brigade, DIVARTY, or Corps Arty.

FASP PREPARATION AND DISSEMINATION

4-78. The FA battalion S3 and the operations section have primary responsibility for preparation and dissemination of the FASP. All staff sections provide/prepare their input as outlined in unit SOP. The XO ensures staff coordination and quality control, and encourages cross-talk between internal and external staff elements during the process.

4-79. A FA battalion can use any of several formats to include: a formal, five-paragraph field order format, a FASM, FRAGOs, or oral orders, depending on time available. Newer C2 systems, such as AFATDS and MCS, allow automated preparation and dissemination of the FASP. See Appendix A for information on FASP content and a description of the FASM.

4-80. The FA battalion disseminates copies of the FASP to all subordinate and reinforcing FA units, any attached or supporting elements, and force FA HQ. The unit may supplement the FASP with verbal updates or FRAGOs detailing changes, additions, etc.

SUMMARY

4-81. The following table provides an overview of the FA battalion MDMP.

Table 4-2. FA BN Planning Process

MDMP STEP	INPUTS	ACTIONS	OUTPUTS
Receipt of Mission	• Higher HQ WARNO or OPORD, FSP, FASP. • All available/updated internal & external data.	• Evaluate higher HQ information – mission/task/guidance focus. • Initiate staff estimates FS, FA Ops, Intel/TA, C2, & CSS & data collection. • Identify draft CCIR. • Conduct time analysis.	• Initial EFST/EFAT list. • Initial staff estimates & briefs to FA Bn Cdr. • Draft CCIR/RFI. • Initial timeline for MDMP & rehearsals. • Initial Cdr guidance • WARNO.

Mission Analysis	• Higher HQ (Mvr/FA) OPORD, FSP, FASP
	• Facts from higher, lower, supported, supporting, & adjacent elements (to include FSEs).
	• IPB Products (MCOO, SITEMPs).
	• CCIR.
	• Enemy COA from S2.
	• HVTs by phase or critical event.
	• Outputs from previous step.
	• Internal/external replies to CCIR/RFI.
		• Understand 2 higher maneuver orders/FSPs & FASPs.
		• Identify specified & implied tasks.
		• Identify CCIR.
		• Organize and analyze facts.
		• Translate facts & status of FS/FA/TA assets into capabilities, limitations & constraints.
		• Analyze effects of IPB on FS/FA/TA.
		• Develop draft EFSTs &/or EFATS.
		• Refine staff estimates FS, FA Ops, Intel/TA, C2, CSS.
		• Initiate TVA.
		• Identify potential wargaming & rehearsal aids (models, tables, maps, sketches, & audio/visual [AV] equipment).
		• Refine rehearsal plan (Timelines, C2 & FATDS/database requirements).
		• Develop mission analysis brief.
			• Updated staff estimates.
			  - Facts & Assumptions.
			  - Constraints & restrictions.
			  - Critical shortage lists.
			  - Artillerized IPB products (MCOO, SITEMPs, enemy COAs).
			  - CCIR, RFI
			• Restated mission.
			• Specified & implied tasks.
			• Approved EFSTs &/or EFATs.
			• Cdr's guidance and intent.
			• Mission analysis brief.
			• Initial movement, C2, CSS, fires (fire control and schedules), & R&S plans/concepts.
			• Updated timelines.
			• WARNO.

COA Development	• See outputs from previous step.
	• Higher HQ updates (Mvr/FA).
	• Internal/external replies to CCIR/RFI.
		• Develop FA Bn COAs in synchronization with Mvr/higher FA COAs.
		• Identify FS &/or FA decision points & firing unit/FC options.
		• Determine where to find and attack EFST/EFAT formations.
		• Identify HPTs in those formations.
		• Quantify the effects for EFSTs/EFATs.
		• Plan D3A methods for EFSTs &/or EFATs, to include triggers.
		• Integrate triggers with Mvr/higher FA COA.
		• Allocate assets to acquire & attack.
		• Develop draft targeting & fire plans products.
		• Identify FA/TA PAs, routes, movement & timing options.
		• Identify FA trains/CSS options (FA ammo distribution & resupply options).
		• Use battle calculus to test feasibility.
		• Refine R&S plan.
			• For each COA developed:
			  - COA statement & sketch
			  - Concept of fires
			  - Draft FSEM/FASM
			  - Draft target lists/overlay
			  - Draft/modified TSM
			  - Changes/differences in FS/FA guidances, TSS, IPs, fire order standards.
			  - Basic schedule of fires requirements.
			  - R&S plan differences.
			• Refined MCOO & SITEMP.
			• Wargaming aids (charts, sketches, overlays, handouts, models, AV requirements).

Table 4-2. FA BN Planning Process (Continued)

MDMP STEP	INPUTS	ACTIONS	OUTPUTS
COA Analysis and COA Comparison	• See outputs from previous step.	• Targeting decisions: finalize HPTL & TSM. • Wargame the FA Bn COA & FASP(s) vs. enemy COAs. • Wargame the brigade COA & integrated FSP(s) vs. enemy COAs (DS units). • Modify/refine inputs as required. • Test & refine FSP &/or FASP. • Finalize staff estimates FS, FA Ops, C2, Intel/TA, CSS. • Finalize/coordinate draft target lists & schedules of fire. • Refine/finalize CCIR. • Prepare/modify draft FASP/FSP.	• COA decision matrix • Refined MCOO & SITEMP. • Detailed task organization. • Refined staff estimates. • Refined risk estimate. • Refined CCIR & RFI. Final Drafts: • Fires paragraph. • FSP/annex (DS units): FSEM Target list/overlay TSM or modified TSM (HPTL, AGM, TSS)* • FASP: FASM Fires schedules RDO & R&S plan
COA Approval	• See outputs from previous step.	• Conduct Mvr Bde/FA Bn approval briefing. • FSCOORD/FSO presents analysis to Mvr Cdr as part of staff. • FA Bn XO/S3 presents analysis to FA Bn Cdr as part of staff. • FSP/FASP briefed as part of each COA. • Mvr Bde/FA Bn Cdrs direct changes and approve COAs as appropriate.	• Approved/modified FA Bn COAs (& Mvr/FS COAs for DS units). • Cdr/XO issues OPORD, FSP, FASP guidance (format, coordination, addressees, timelines) • FA staff/FS back briefs. • Issue final rehearsal guidance/information. • Issue WARNO as required.
Orders Production	• See outputs from previous step.	• Finalize staff and other inputs/products. • Gather all inputs, prepare and quality check final FA/FS products. • Verify receipt & understanding. • Gather & evaluate lower/higher feedback & rehearsal results. • Recommend post-production changes and updates as necessary based on rehearsal results, feedback, and METT-TC changes to the Cdr for decisions. • Prepare modified products, WARNOs &/or FRAGOs to reflect changes & Cdr decisions.	• Issue OPORD/OPLAN, FSP, FASP. • Disseminate post-production changes & updates via WARNOs/FRAGOs.

* An example of a combined HPTL/AGM/TSS/Collection Plan is provided in Figure 4-3. This is only an example of one format that can be used to display HPTL, AGM, and TSS information.

FM 3-09.21 (FM 6-20-1)

HPTL/AGM/TSS/Collection Plan

Phase: **II**   High Payoff Targets   DTG: _____

Priority	1	2	3	4		Remarks
Target Description	ADA Assets	Enemy Artillery	C3	RSTA Assets		
Remarks	SA 6/8 SA 9/60 ZSU-23-4	2S5/7 BM 21/22 SCUD/Frog	BDE CPs DIV CPs Signal Assets	Long Track/FlatFace Cymbeline Div Recon		
Weapon / Attack System — 155mm	1. 50m **3** 2. SEC 3. S 4. 30 min	1. 100m **3** 2. BTRY 3. S 4. 10 min	1. 200m **4** 2. Co 3. S 4. 120 min	1. 50m **2** 2. SEC 3. S 4. 60 min		
MLRS	1. 200m **2** 2. SEC 3. S 4. 30 min	1. 200m **2** 2. BTRY 3. S 4. 10 min	1. 200m **3** 2. Co 3. S 4. 120 min	1. 200m **3** 2. SEC 3. S 4. 60 min		
ATACMS	1. 500m **2** 2. SEC 3. S 4. 30 min	1. 500m **6** 2. BTRY 3. S 4. 10 min	1. 200m **3** 2. C0 3. S 4. 120 min	1. 200m **6** 2. SEC 3. S 4. 60 min		
ATK Helo	1. 500m **5** 2. SEC 3. S/M 4. 90 min	1. 500m **1** 2. SEC 3. S/M 4. 60 min	1. 200m **5** 2. Co 3. S/M 4. 120 min	1. 500m **1** 2. SEC 3. S 4. 60 min		
CAS	1. 500m **6** 2. SEC 3. S/M 4. 30 min	1. 50m **5** 2. SPLL 3. S/M 4. 60 min	1. 200m **2** 2. Co 3. S/M 4. 120 min	1. 500m **5** 2. SEC 3. S/M 4. 90 min		
AI	1. 500m **1** 2. SEC 3. S/M 4. 30 min	1. 500m **3** 2. SPLL 3. S/M 4. 60 min	1. 200m **2** 2. Co 3. S/M 4. 120 min	1. 500m **1** 2. SEC 3. S/M 4. 90 min		
EW	1. 5K **4** 2. SEC 3. S 4. 30 min	1. 5K **4** 2. BTRY 3. S 4. 60 min	1. 5K **1** 2. Co 3. S 4. 120 min	1. 5K **4** 2. SEC 3. S 4. 60 min		
Trigger Sensor	1. Quickfix Guardrail 2. OH58D 3. TUAV	1. Q36/37 2. LRSD 3. JSTAR	1. LRSD 2. Quickfix Guardrail 3. JSTAR	1. JSTAR 2. CAS/AI 3. GSRs		
When	I/P	I/A	A	I/P		
Damage	D	N	S	N		
BDA Required	Y	Y	N	Y		

REFERENCES: ☐ Priority of Attack: 1. TLE=Max, 2. TGT Size=Min.
3. Target Activity=Stationary(S)/Moving(M), 4. Valid Acquisition Time
WHEN: I=Immediate A=As Acquired P=Planned, DAMAGE: S=Suppress N=Neutralize D=Destroy, BDA Required: Y/N

Figure 4-3. HPTL/AGM/TSS/Collection Plan

SECTION II – FA INTELLIGENCE PREPARATION OF THE BATTLEFIELD

4-82. This section discusses how to conduct an FA IPB and to incorporate it into the battalion's MDMP. The S2 must expand the supported maneuver unit and/or higher FA HQ IPB products, particularly the threat data, to focus on survivability and mobility issues for the FA battalion. The S2 must answer, "How can the threat and terrain affect my FA unit?" FM 34-130, *Intelligence Preparation of the Battlefield*, contains detailed IPB information.

4-83. The FA battalion S2's order of battle studies must focus on:
- Threat Maneuver Force Doctrine
  - Enemy task organization to include signature items (e.g., equipment that uniquely identifies the type of enemy force or the main effort).
  - Numbers and capabilities of vehicles by type (e.g., light vs. heavy, amphibious, gasoline vs. diesel, caliber/range).
  - Formations used.
  - Movement rates: Day, night, MBA, pre-battle, battle, etc.
  - Depth and width of the brigade (or regiment), battalion, and company (battery) in both offense and defense.
  - The threat SOF or specialized threat forces present to the FA battalion and rear area operations.
  - Threat air assets (fixed/rotary-wing), doctrine, capabilities, and vulnerabilities.
- Threat Artillery Doctrine and Capabilities
  - Weapon types and the number of tubes per battalion.
  - Capabilities of each system: Ammunition, ranges, rates of fire.
  - Dispositions: Deployment considerations, distances between firing units and specific artillery groupings.
  - Counterfire capability: Radars, ranges, typical locations, time from acquisition of incoming rounds to time counterfire mission is fired.
  - Enemy EW and reconnaissance threat to friendly counterfire radars: Detection capability, jamming capability.
  - Types of fire by maneuver phase: What type of indirect fires will the enemy conduct during each maneuver phase?
- Threat Air Defense Artillery Doctrine
  - Numbers and capabilities by echelon.
  - Disposition: Deployment on the battlefield.
  - Air phases of support.

STEPS IN FA IPB PROCESS

DEFINE THE BATTLEFIELD ENVIRONMENT

4-84. The battlefield environment, to include the AO and area of interest (AOI), is normally provided to the FA battalion S2 by either the supported maneuver unit or the higher FA HQ. The S2, together with the commander and S3, reviews the identified AO and AOI to determine if changes should be recommended based on the battalion's mission. As an example, if enemy FA can range the supported maneuver zone or the FA battalion from just beyond the maneuver/higher FA AOI, the FA battalion commander want to request an expansion of the AOI to include those enemy indirect fire assets that pose a significant threat. The AO and AOI, as defined by the commander, focus the S2's efforts, R&S, and RDO development.

DESCRIBE THE BATTLEFIELD EFFECTS

4-85. This step includes weather analysis; MCOO; observation, cover, and concealment; AOAs, obstacles, and key terrain; and FA specific considerations. The supported unit or higher FA HQ normally provides the products that describe the battlefield effects. The FA battalion S2 must refine all products to accurately reflect the battalion's AO and AOI.

4-86. The defining product in this step is the MCOO (Figure 4-4). It is a graphic depiction of an in-depth study of the battlefield area incorporating terrain and weather. Refinement of the MCOO must:

- Analyze terrain from an FA perspective.
- Determine intervisibility lines.
- Identify avenues of approach and potential PAs.
- Identify key and decisive terrain.

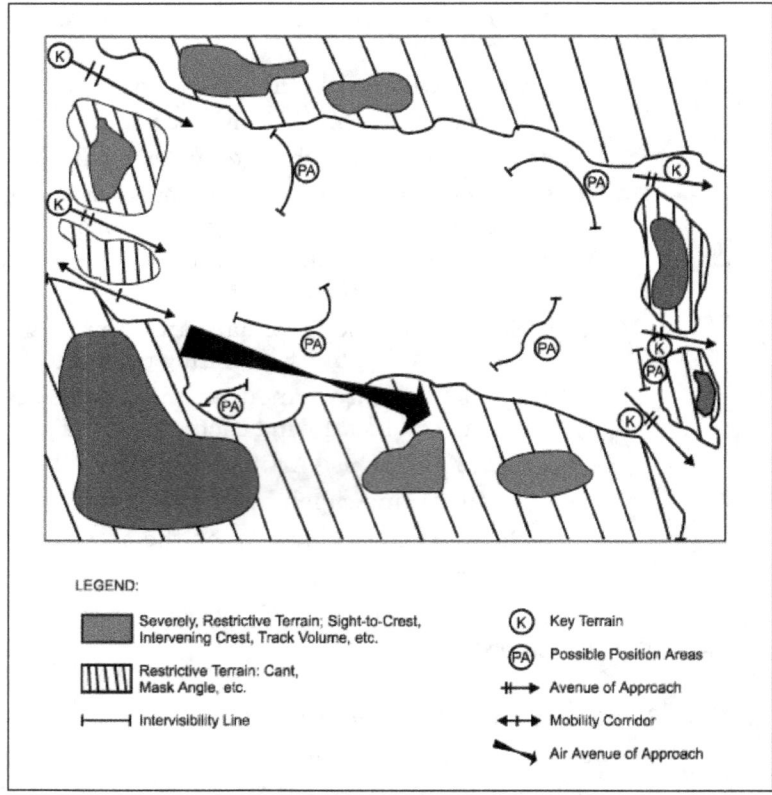

Figure 4-4. Modified Combined Obstacle Overlay

Analyze Terrain

4-87. Identify terrain that may cause firing problems. The FA definitions for different types of terrain are:
- **SEVERELY RESTRICTED** (green crosshatch marks) - causes extreme difficulty for weapon emplacement and firing.
- **RESTRICTED** (green single-hatch marks) - hinders emplacement and firing to a lesser degree and probably requires a detailed reconnaissance effort to locate suitable positions.
- **UNRESTRICTED** - is suitable for unit positioning.

4-88. To determine SEVERELY RESTRICTED, RESTRICTED and UNRESTRICTED areas, the FA battalion S2 analyzes:
- Elevation.
- Slope.
- Soil composition.
- Mobility problems.

Determine Intervisibility Lines

4-89. The second step is to graphically depict the areas that deny intervisibility between opposing forces on the same overlay. Draw intervisibility lines where the terrain dictates. An intervisibility line is an area on the battlefield that opposing forces cannot observe beyond. Some examples include ridgelines, wadi systems, finger off a ridge, forested areas, etc. Intervisibility lines are particularly important when looking for PAs that are hidden from enemy AOAs. Following a map reconnaissance, the S2 can coordinate with the maneuver brigade or higher FA HQ for use of their stereoscope and satellite photography to further analyze the terrain. Most brigade level S2s are issued a computer assisted terrain analysis model called "Terra-Base," which is helpful in determining intervisibility lines.

Identify Avenues of Approach

4-90. The third step is to identify and graphically depict air and ground AOAs on the MCOO overlay. Use the standard symbols in FM 34-130. Refine the higher or supported HQ IPB products that usually depict brigade and division-sized AOAs. Depict regiment and battalion sized AOAs that can affect the positioning plan.

4-91. Depict all enemy platoon and above size mobility corridors that can affect the battalion's AO. Focus this effort down to enemy platoon level because of the threat an enemy platoon poses to artillery units. An enemy tank platoon can easily destroy a firing unit. If the MCOO becomes too busy and unreadable with platoon-sized mobility corridors--only identify company-level mobility corridors. Finally, combine two or more mobility corridors into their appropriate battalion and regimental AOAs.

4-92. During this process the S2 must carry the higher-level unit's AOAs throughout the FA battalion's AO. The maneuver brigade usually stops its depiction of enemy AOAs at the brigade battle positions as they are not concerned about platoon- or company-sized units.

4-93. During the COA development process, the S3 should position units away from identified enemy mobility corridors and AOAs. If the situation dictates that units must be positioned on enemy air or ground AOAs, then the S2 should brief the affected commanders on the specific threat to his location. This provides the battery commander with critical information to consider during his own COA development.

Identify Key and Decisive Terrain

4-94. The fourth step is to identify and highlight key and decisive terrain using standard symbols. This information is graphically displayed on the MCOO overlay. During COA development, the S3 will avoid positioning batteries in these areas because they are where the close-in fight will likely take place.

Identify Potential Position Areas

4-95. This step is a key reason for performing the first four steps. The S2 evaluates the AO and templates all possible battery-sized PAs given the constraints of terrain identified in Steps 1-4. See the appropriate battery-level FM for friendly PA dimensions. Enemy PA dimensions will vary based on the type of weapon and tactics used. This templating of PAs is maintained for use during current and future operations. The S2 provides a product that assists the S3 in choosing appropriate battery PAs during COA development. This is most important during operations when the staff has limited planning time.

EVALUATE THE THREAT

4-96. Analyze threat templates that accurately portray how enemy forces normally execute their operations and how they react to current conditions. Determine which enemy capabilities may significantly affect or be targeted against friendly FA operations.

4-97. Use doctrinal templates (which show how enemy doctrine dictates their tactical approach without terrain and weather constraints) to assist in providing answers to important FA questions: What are the HVTs for the enemy forces? What phases of FS will the enemy use based on friendly maneuver force actions? To which areas can the enemy FA and mortars range with conventional and rocket-assisted projectiles? Where will enemy FA, mortar units, electronic intelligence, and counterfire acquisition assets reposition? At what point will the enemy firing units need to resupply? How are they being resupplied? What is the enemy threat in friendly rear areas? (These questions are examples only.)

EVALUATE THREAT COAs

4-98. Concurrent with the development of friendly FA COAs by the battalion staff, the S2 analyzes the SITEMP (which is a doctrinal template adjusted for terrain and weather) and event template (which identifies and analyzes significant battlefield events and activities that provide indications of enemy COA). This is his next step in preparing for the COA analysis and comparison.

4-99. The S2 will usually receive the maneuver brigade or higher FA SITEMPs. Normally, the SITEMPs do not address all the concerns of the FA battalion. The S2 should refine them to focus on specific FA issues--including enemy indirect fire systems and units down to the battery level. As a minimum, the S2 must refine two SITEMPs: first is the most probable threat COA; second is the most dangerous threat COA.

Refinement of the SITEMP

4-100. The refinement of the SITEMP involves the following steps.
- Analyze the enemy's mission (Usually provided by the supported maneuver unit or higher FA HQ).
- Locate enemy artillery and mortars (to battery/firing element level for FA and to tube level for FA and mortars in small scale contingencies).
- Analyze threat maneuver forces.
- Analyze threat AOAs and objectives.
- Analyze threat NBC strikes and capabilities.
- Analyze terrain for possible airborne and air assault insertion sites, terrorist or special forces type safe havens or assembly/staging areas, or small element indirect fire areas (use NAIs to focus R&S efforts).

Event Template

4-101. The event template graphically depicts the events and timing of the upcoming battle. The template helps the S2 gauge the pace and tempo of the operation and identify potential targets by type, number, location, and time. The essential element in developing the event template is to have graphics that tie an enemy event to a location and that show trigger events to assist in synchronizing fires. At a minimum, the S2 should develop the event template for the enemy's most probable course of action and possibly most dangerous COA.

4-102. The brigade or higher FA HQ S2 will normally provide the FA battalion with the event template. This template focuses on the brigade/division/corps fight and the FA battalion S2 must refine it to focus on specific FS/FA issues. The primary problem the S2 faces is in the time increments used by the maneuver forces. The S2 may need to use smaller time increments (e.g., minutes vice hours) to facilitate FA planning. The steps in refining the event template for FA use are:

4-103. **Named Areas of Interest.** Copy all applicable NAIs onto the battalion event template. This includes any FA battalion specific NAIs necessary to prevent the battalion from being surprised by enemy actions such as a rear area airborne insertion, partisan activity, attack along an unexpected flank, etc. NAIs assist the FA battalion TOC in monitoring the progress of the battle, executing tasks, and anticipating battalion requirements. The S2 uses NAIs specific to the FA battalion in developing and executing the FA battalion's requirements for the R&S plan. Firing units, survey teams, ammunition convoys, and logistical elements may monitor some NAIs during the execution of their primary missions. External coverage must be coordinated if coverage of a battalion specific NAI is beyond the battalion's capabilities.

4-104. **Time Phase Lines.** The S2 develops TPLs that clearly depict the pace of the battle through all phases of the fight. The artillery's success or failure is determined in terms of minutes and seconds, so the S2 must focus TPLs in these terms. Increments of 5- to 15-minutes work best (e.g., 10, 20, 30).

4-105. There are two types of TPLs: friendly offensive operations (blue lines) and threat offensive operations (red lines). Thus, if friendly units are conducting a defense, the S2 uses red TPLs to time the enemy offense. If friendly forces plan a counterattack, the S2 uses blue TPLs.

4-106. **Radar Zones.** The S2 incorporates proposed radar zones onto the event template. FSOs and the battalion staff will generate proposed operations and areas requiring coverage by radar zones. Based on the capability of the radar or the number of zones allocated by the force artillery HQ, the battalion staff finalizes the number, type, location, cueing assets, and/or time for all approved radar zones.

4-107. The TPLs on the event template assist the S2 in determining a proactive cueing schedule covering critical events such as friendly breaching operations or an enemy artillery fire plan by phase. TPLs also assist in determining triggers to implement or cancel preplanned radar zones. An example of an event template is at Figure 4-5.

IPB Refinement

4-108. The process doesn't end when the S2 has produced the IPB products. IPB refinement is an ongoing process. The FA battalion S2 uses his knowledge of the AO and AOI in conjunction with intelligence feeds from all sources to update the IPB products and advise the commander and S3 on changes to the threat COA and on impacts for the battalion.

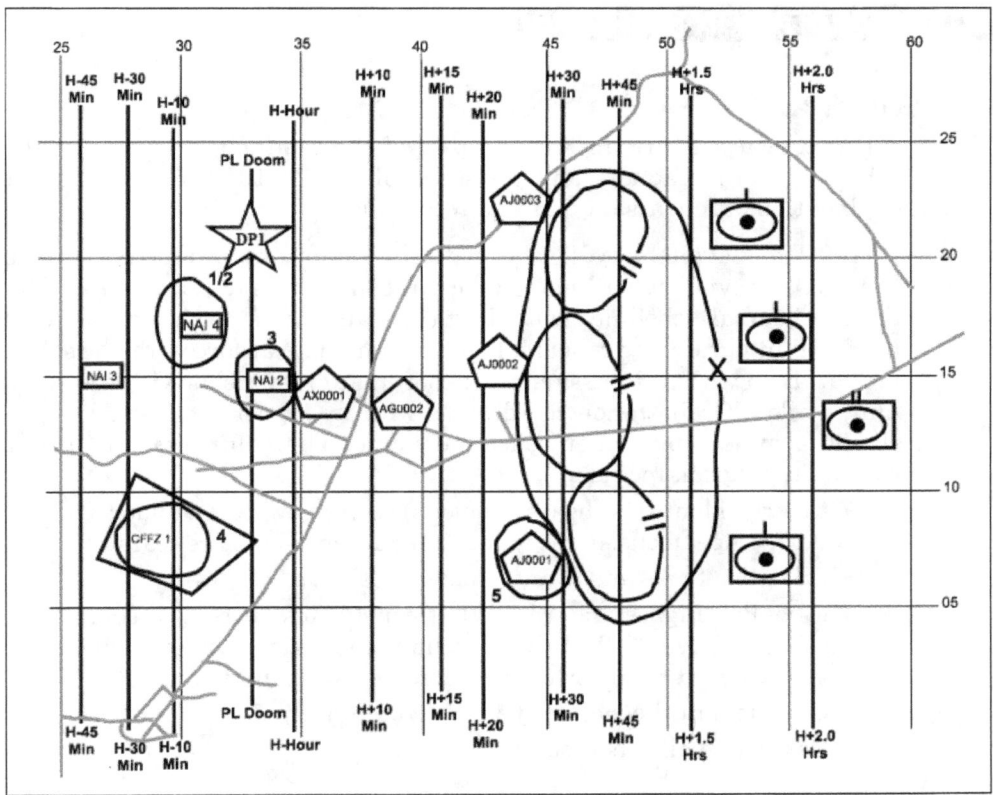

No	PIR/IR/ EFST/DP	Enemy Event	Target No NAI/TAI	Latest Time Information of Value	Friendly Decision Points	Actions/Reports Required
1	Fire SCATMINE @ Bde Obstacle	Enemy CRP at NAI 4, MRR 45 min from Bde obstacle	AG0002, NAI 3	H-5	DP1	Alert FSCOORD, S3, FDO, Bde FSO; send PERINTREP to battalion
2	Will enemy use chemical on BP?	Enemy Phase II/III fires on BP.	NAI 4	H		Alert FSCOORD, FSOs; check RDO; warn CHEMO and battalion
3	Mass the battalion on lead MIBN.	Lead MIBN @ PL Boom (10 min from target area)	AX0001, NAI 5	H-10		Alert FSCOORD, S3, FDO, Bde FSO; send out PERINTREP
4	Mass the battalion on the enemy's BRAG	Beginning of Phase II fires (CRPs within visual range of BP)	CRP @ NAI 4	H-15		CFFZ 1 in effect? Who is available to mass? Can DIVARTY help?
5	When will the firing batteries be in jeopardy from enemy direct fire?	1st echelon MIBN begin to breach the southern comp BP (45 min warn)	TF FPF, AJ0001	H+20		Alert the FSCOORD, S3, battery commanders; send out PERINTREP

LEGEND:
BP = Battle Position
CFFZ = Call for Fire Zone
CHEMO = Chemical Officer
CRP = Combat Reconnaissance Patrol
DP = Decision Point
IR = Information Requirement
MIBN = Motorized Infantry Battalion
MIBR = Motorized Infantry Brigade
NAI = Named Area of Interest
PERINTREPS = Periodic Intelligence Reports
PIR = Priority Intelligence Requirement
PL = Phase Line
BRAG = Brigade Artillery Group
TAI = Targeted Area of Interest
TF FPF = Task Force Final Protective Fires

Figure 4-5. Enemy Critical Events Matrix on the Event Template

SECTION III – FA BATTALION REHEARSALS

REHEARSAL PRINCIPLES

4-109. Rehearsals are an integral part of the planning process. An effective rehearsal both practices and tests the plan. FM 101-5 contains a detailed explanation of rehearsal types and techniques.

4-110. Time availability is the critical element in conducting rehearsals. WARNOs provide subordinates enough lead time and details to synchronize their rehearsal schedules with battalion and higher rehearsals. A DS FA battalion integrates its rehearsals into the maneuver force's rehearsal plan. A FA battalion with a R mission must coordinate rehearsals with the reinforced unit, while a GS battalion coordinates with its higher FA HQ. All rehearsals should complement higher rehearsal plans. The principles for an effective rehearsal program include:

- Clearly identify rehearsal objectives (review commander guidance on type, scope, focus, and commander's intent for the rehearsal).
- Prioritize tasks and events (focus on EFSTs, EFATs).
- Establish high standards (What constitutes successful completion of a rehearsal event? Will the unit limit repetitions to retraining to correct substandard tasks or to also reinforce successful training?).
- Conduct multi-echelon, synchronized rehearsals.
- Determine all rehearsal participants.

REHEARSAL TYPES

4-111. Each of the five types of rehearsals described in FM 101-5 achieves a specific result and has a specific place in the MDMP time line.

- Confirmation brief.
- Backbrief.
- Combined arms rehearsal (CAR).
- Support Rehearsals.
- Battle drill or SOP rehearsal.

REHEARSAL TECHNIQUES

4-112. FM 101-5 identifies six primary rehearsal techniques that differ in the level of detail, time, resourcing, and operational security.

- Full dress.
- Reduced force.
- Terrain model.
- Map.
- Sketch map.
- Radio.

SCRIPTING THE REHEARSAL

4-113. Use of a script keeps the rehearsal on track and serves as the checklist to ensure the rehearsal addresses all battlefield functions and all critical issues. A script has four parts:

- **Agenda** – Use the FSEM, FASM, FASP, RDO, and other tools as appropriate to drive the rehearsal and to keep it focused.
- **Response Sequence** – Establish a logical sequence for player response to rehearsal events (e.g., by BOS, front-to rear, left-to-right). Disseminate the sequence prior to the rehearsal to all participants.
- **Unit Actions Checklist** – Describe friendly and enemy actions succinctly yet in enough detail that critical items aren't forgotten or assumed. Use established formats or checklists.
- **Sequence Of Events** – Provide advance notice of the rehearsal format.

CONDUCTING A REHEARSAL

BEFORE THE REHEARSAL

4-114. The unit should accomplish the following prior to the rehearsal:

- Determine objectives, standards, and scope of the rehearsal; the rehearsal type and technique; the participants; and the date, time, and place for the rehearsal. Coordinate rehearsal schedules.
- Disseminate rehearsal information. Include a list of personnel, equipment, information, and/or materials they need to bring.
- Prepare rehearsal support items: models, maps, sketches, overlays, and copies of key documents (e.g., OPORDs, matrices, or handouts).
- Review the agenda, identify decision points, branches, and repetition requirements.
- Validate time required with time available and modify as necessary.
- Coordinate adequate representation of elements that cannot attend.
- View and prepare the rehearsal site as appropriate.

DURING THE REHEARSAL

4-115. The following paragraphs provide a generic sequence of events.

- Step 1. **Review Ground Rules**. Participants, sequences, times.
- Step 2. **Deploy Enemy Elements**. Briefly describe key factors.
- Step 3. **Deploy Friendly Elements**. Briefly describe key factors.
- Step 4. **Initiate Action Sequence**. Enact friendly and enemy events.
- Step 5. **Identify Decision Points**. Both friendly and enemy.
- Step 6. **Identify End State**. For the COA or branch.
- Step 7. **Recock**. Repeat for all decision points, branches, COAs.
- Step 8. **Rehearsal Review** – Identify and resolve outstanding issues.

4-116. The staff ensures all changes, coordination, and new requirements resulting from the rehearsal are clearly understood by all participants and documented by the recorder. All changes are considered verbal FRAGOs until the staff publishes the written changes.

AFTER THE REHEARSAL

4-117. The staff must translate modifications identified during rehearsals into verbal and/or written changes to previously published plans, orders, and even SOPs. Post rehearsal actions may include the following:
- Revise the FSP, FASP, schedules of fires, pre-planned and on-call target lists, RDO, EFSTs, and EFATs.
- Notify key personnel not in attendance of the results of the rehearsal and all changes or issues.
- Disseminate a verbal or written FRAGO and supporting documents as necessary to document and disseminate the changes.
- Coordinate changes with supporting/supported elements.
- If time is too short to properly incorporate all target changes, designate new targets as on-call targets.
- When time becomes available, conduct an internal/staff AAR to identify changes necessary to the rehearsal process and SOP.

SCHEDULING REHEARSALS

4-118. The FA battalion must coordinate and synchronize its rehearsal schedule with higher FA HQ and maneuver force rehearsals. Units can conduct rehearsals in a top-down or bottom-up approach. The latter method better prepares subordinates for the higher HQ' rehearsals. The nested rehearsal technique facilitates rehearsal planning and conduct of rehearsals.

THE NESTED REHEARSAL

4-119. The nested rehearsal technique integrates mission or task specific rehearsals and makes maximum effective use of time by initiating the preparation/rehearsal process immediately upon receipt of the first WARNO. The goals of the nested rehearsal are to:
- Ensure all types and echelons of rehearsals are prioritized.
- Ensure all rehearsals are fully time-resourced.
- Ensure leader involvement in subordinate rehearsal processes.
- Provide command-driven, bottom-up refinement of all plans.
- Prevent procrastination of rehearsal processes.

4-120. Before implementing the nested rehearsal concept:
- Identify mission/task specific PCCs and PCIs.
- Revise the battalion battle book to include detailed battery through section level rehearsals and drills.

4-121. Standardization of battle drills ensures all leaders will understand what type of rehearsals and standards are expected at critical phases of the planning process. Several key principals guide the nested concept:
- Higher rehearsals occur last in the timeline.
- Lowest level drills occur first and as soon as possible.
- All orders and rehearsal DTGs are directed by the higher HQ.
- Stagger same-echelon rehearsals to facilitate leader supervision.
- Leaders and key personnel attend all subordinate echelon CARs.

EXAMPLE NESTED REHEARSAL

4-122. This section uses the maneuver brigade and DS FA battalion as an example in describing the nested rehearsal process.

Phase One - WARNOs

4-123. Initial WARNOs go out giving all units broad mission/task guidance and tentative OPORD and rehearsal timelines. The FA battalion receives the brigade WARNO and issues its WARNO which provides:
- The nature of the mission.
- Approximate DTG of the brigade OPORD and the battalion FASP.
- The tentative DTGs of the brigade FS & combined arms rehearsals, FA battalion support rehearsals, and battery rehearsals.

4-124. Battery commanders review the battalion WARNO and issue guidance concerning battery, platoon, and section rehearsals and anticipated EFATs. Platoon and section leaders review the commander's guidance and begin developing their rehearsal plans.

Phase Two – Planning/Preparation

4-125. The brigade and battalion develop and wargame their plans, and assemble the detailed information for OPORDs, FSPs, and the FASP. As the MDMP progresses, subsequent WARNOs provide more detailed information on missions, tasks, EFSTs, and EFATs. Rehearsal times may also change, which can cause a ripple effect in all rehearsal time lines. Synchronization of all higher, parallel and subordinate rehearsal schedules is a major task for leaders at all levels.

4-126. Units should issue as much detailed information as possible before section and platoon rehearsals begin. The most critical information includes the type of tasks, the conditions under which they must be performed (e.g., night, MOPP4, digital versus voice, AFATDS/IFSAS/FDS interface), and any changes from SOP.

Phase Three - Rehearsals

4-127. The rehearsal process begins with section and platoon PCCs, drills, and rehearsals. Battery leadership should attend these when possible. <u>These lower level rehearsals may begin even before the FASP is published.</u>

4-128. Lower rehearsals complement and build toward higher rehearsals. Units may modify plans based on feedback from lower level rehearsals. Staggering battery rehearsals can facilitate battalion observation. Additional section through battery level rehearsals can occur when the battery is not conducting its formal rehearsal. However, units must balance rehearsal time with planning and preparation time.

4-129. An example battalion rehearsal timeline is shown in Table 4-3. Actual times and sequences will vary based on the situation.

Table 4-3. Example Rehearsal Schedule

FA BATTALION TIMELINE	REHEARSAL ACTIONS
1900	Bde issues WARNO with rehearsal guidance/schedules. FA Bn initiates staff estimates.
2000	FA Bn issues WARNO with Bn rehearsal guidance/schedules.
2030	Battery commanders receive WARNO and issue alerts and rehearsal guidance.
2100	FA Bn staff finalizes mission analysis and prepares briefing.
0000	FA Bn staff briefs mission analysis and continues COA development.
0300	COA development brief.
0500	FA Bn issues second WARNO with FASP time. FA Bn begins wargaming.
0600	Platoons and sections begin drills. Times established by battery commanders.
0800	FA Bn begins production of FASP (including rehearsal plan). FA Bn issues third WARNO with mission-specific rehearsal information.
0900	FA Bn issues/briefs FASP. FA Bn disseminates final EFATs, movement, targeting, and fire control information.
0930	FA Bn Cdr receives confirmation briefs from battery commanders & staff.
1100	Bde, Bn FSEs, FISTS, & COLTs/Strikers begin drills.
1100	C Btry rehearsal begins - EFAT 1& 4. - Bn Cdr attends, receives backbrief.
1100	ALOC – CSS support map rehearsal begins. - Bn XO attends.
1200	B Btry rehearsal begins - EFAT 2 & 4. - Bn CSM Bn S3 attends.
1200	CP/TOC – Drill/SOP rehearsal as necessary. - Bn Cdr, XO, or S3 attends.
1300	A Btry rehearsal begins - EFAT 3. - Bn Cdr, XO, or CSM attends.
1330	Remaining battery commander & staff backbriefs to FA Bn Cdr begin.
1500	FA Bn integrated FS/tactical/technical support rehearsal begins.
1700	Mvr Bde FS rehearsal begins. - FA Bn Cdr participates at FA Bn TOC or Bde FSE.
1900	Mvr Bde combined arms rehearsal begins. FA Bn Cdr participates at FA Bn TOC or Bde FSE.
2100	Additional FS/FA rehearsal(s) as needed. Goal = Improve/reinforce rehearsed tasks and/or rehearse new tasks identified during previous rehearsals.

FA BATTALION REHEARSALS

4-130. The following information provides broad guidance and possible techniques. Timeframes mentioned are rough estimates based on lessons learned feedback from units, publications, and other published documents. Actual rehearsal techniques, schedules, and time frames will vary depending on the situation and unit SOPs.

CONFIRMATION BRIEFS AND BACKBRIEFS

4-131. FA commanders and staff leaders give and receive confirmation briefs and backbriefs. Since confirmation briefs often occur immediately after the briefing or issuing of the OPORD, commanders and staff should prepare in advance. If time is limited, the FA battalion commander may have the XO and S3 take some of the briefings from subordinate leaders. A supported maneuver force may also use this disseminated briefing technique, however the DS commander should try to give his briefing to the maneuver commander whenever possible.

COMBINED ARMS REHEARSALS

4-132. FA battalion participation in CARs will occur more frequently, and will be more extensive for FA battalions with a DS or R mission. Divisional GSR or GS FA battalions may participate, to a lesser extent, in division CARs. FA battalions at corps level may have little involvement in corps CARs, but may participate extensively in corps artillery or FA brigade rehearsals. (Note: The following discussions are oriented toward DS/R battalions and the CAR process. In most cases, use of "CAR" can be replaced with "higher FA HQ rehearsal" and the information will be just as applicable for GS/GSR units.)

4-133. The maneuver or higher FA HQ commander, the type of rehearsal, and the technique will determine the extent of the FA battalion's involvement in a CAR. As a minimum, a FA battalion's FS personnel and the FA battalion TOC will participate in CARs.

4-134. When time is limited, the FA battalion may integrate some of its support rehearsals into the CAR. However, this should not interfere with the CAR. The battalion should rehearse critical tasks prior to the CAR.

SUPPORT REHEARSALS

Fire Support Rehearsals

4-135. **Purpose.** FS rehearsals verify synchronization of the FSP with the scheme of maneuver. They focus on the execution of EFSTs and the FSEM, the effectiveness of FSCMs, and the timing and synchronization of all FS efforts. FS rehearsals are most applicable to DS FA battalions.

4-136. **Types.** Two possible types of FS rehearsals are:
- A maneuver brigade FS rehearsal involves the brigade staff and all other elements involved in the FS process. It rehearses all EFSTs, or when time is limited, the ones designated by the maneuver commander. This rehearsal can be used prior to the CAR, as a preparation tool, or after the CAR, to reinforce previous rehearsals, or to address weaknesses or changes identified during the CAR.
- A small-scale rehearsal involving only the FA FS personnel in FSEs, FISTs, COLTs/Strikers and possibly the FA battalion TOC. It focuses on the functioning of the FS chain. Units use these rehearsals to prepare for other rehearsals, to reinforce training, or when limited time is available.

4-137. **Agenda.** Use the FSEM and DST, focusing on critical EFSTs. Normally prior to rehearsal, the DS battalion FDO, or force FA HQ, will announce a consolidated target list. For each target or EFST in the FSEM, address location, trigger point, engagement criteria, primary/backup observer and communications methods, clearance of fires, method of engagement, and attack guidance. CARs are excellent opportunities to identify terrain and route management issues. Ensure the DS battalion S3 presents FA movement plans and out-of-action cycles for DS and R units as appropriate. Rehearse radar target handoff and counterfire, having the radar section leader insert one or two acquisitions per phase of the rehearsal. Inserting unplanned counterfire requirements and close support requests into the rehearsal at key points in the FSEM is necessary to evaluate priorities of fire and possible FS related decision points.

4-138. The sequence should usually mirror that of the CAR, following all necessary branches and decision points. However, the FSCOORD or BDE FSO may determine the specific sequence.

FA Tactical Rehearsals

4-139. **Purpose.** Tactical rehearsals ensure the FASP properly plans and synchronizes FA tactical fire control, movement, and key CSS operations.

4-140. FA tactical rehearsals focus on:
- The tactical execution of EFATs, the FASM, and schedules of fires – primary and backup methods (shooter focus).
- Tactical fire control and mission routing procedures.
- Clearance of fires requirements and procedures.
- Commander's attack criteria and priority of fires considerations.
- The effectiveness of FA movement and positioning plans, primary and alternate, for firing, C2, and CSS elements.
- Targeting, counterfire, and SEAD operations.
- Mutual support/continuity operations.
- Communications requirements – use and positioning of retrans equipment, use of voice versus digital.
- Survey requirements.
- The timing and synchronization of all FA efforts with each other and with the maneuver operations.

4-141. **Types.** Methods for conducting FA tactical rehearsals include:
- A robust, detailed rehearsal involving all elements involved in the tactical fire control process – FA battalion TOC, firing batteries, brigade/battalion FSEs, radars, key CSS personnel, and reinforcing units. It would address the full range of tactical issues and extend down to platoon and possibly section level.
- A leader-focused rehearsal may involve only the FA TOC, the brigade FSE, firing battery C2, and radar. The rehearsal may focus on the highest priority EFATs or FASM events or on particular aspects of tactical operations, such as fire missions and movement.

4-142. **Agenda.** Use the FASM, focusing on critical EFATs. The S3 should also review the maneuver DST, the FSEM, EFSTs, and consolidated target list for any critical events with FA applicability that may not be reflected on the FASM. For each target or EFAT in the FASM, address location, trigger point, engagement criteria, primary/backup observer and communications methods, clearance of fires, method of engagement, and attack guidance. The battalion S3 should present FA movement plans and out-of-action cycles for all FA units as appropriate. If time permits, rehearse radar, survey, and counterfire contingencies that require evaluation of alternate plans or methods.

4-143. The sequence may mirror the CAR, or higher FA HQ rehearsal, or the battalion commander or S3 may determine the sequence.

FA Technical Rehearsals

4-144. **Purpose.** FA technical rehearsals are used to ensure that the FASP properly addresses FA technical FD and to exercise the technical FD process. FA technical rehearsals focus on:

- The technical execution of EFATs and the FASM – sensor-to-shooter links and primary and backup methods (FDC focus). Rehearsal of backups includes evaluation of reactions to catastrophic loss of an FDC (battalion or battery) and loss of digital or voice capability.
- Integration of tactical and technical fire control processes and computation of firing solutions, to include the communication and interaction between FS, FD and firing elements.
- Identification of technical FD issues – high angle fire, MSD, target/munition/range/FSCM conflicts.
- Digital database verification – Setup, communications, positions, FSCMs, target and attack guidances, mission routing and intervention points, target list, and scheduling data.
- Digital CONOPS – minor and catastrophic.
- Digital interface requirements – AFATDS-IFSAS/FDS, AFATDS version differences, and any other digital systems.
- Integration of voice and digital operations, to include backup plans.

4-145. **Types.** FA technical rehearsals can include the following:

- A robust, detailed digital rehearsal designed to exercise the entire FA digital communications system, verify databases, and ensure interoperability of different digital systems. This rehearsal verifies that all nodes can effectively communicate, all message formats can be passed, and fire mission routing will execute as required.
- (**AFATDS NOTE:** In AFATDS, a unit cannot rehearse a plan digitally until it is implemented into the Current Situation. Before each phase can be rehearsed, it must be implemented by all AFATDS OPFACs involved in the rehearsal.)
- A rehearsal focused on technical FD, to include the FS/Ops/FDC mission routing/handoff process. While FS personnel may be involved, the focus is on the exchange of fire mission data and timing issues rather than the tactical decision-making process.
- A FDC rehearsal from the battalion FDC down to firing sections.

4-146. **Agenda.** The agenda and sequence will vary dependent on the focus. In a technical rehearsal with a FD focus, the FASM and EFATs may be the key reference. For rehearsals focused on digital operations, the unit may use a combination of the FASM and a digital rehearsal SOP. The latter would identify the major digital communications events to be rehearsed and the database elements to be verified.

4-147. **Digital considerations.** Units must consider the potential dangers inherent in automatic data distribution during digital rehearsals, and take safeguards to separate the rehearsal and "real world" events. As an example, digital missions initiated during a rehearsal may automatically generate artillery target intelligence (ATI) messages or mission fired reports (MFR) messages to external OPFACs that are not participating in the rehearsal.

FM 3-09.21 (FM 6-20-1)

Also, movement of unit icons in AFATDS during the rehearsal may generate unit updates to external OPFACs. (In order to process rehearsal targets in AFATDS, firing units must be able to range their respective targets).

4-148. These external OPFACs will be unable to differentiate between "real" and "rehearsal" information, unless they have been notified of the rehearsals and have been clearly briefed on how to identify rehearsal traffic from real data. Because of this, units should consider modifying their digital communications settings to prevent external dissemination of rehearsal data. Units must ensure that all elements reset required settings after the rehearsal is over.

4-149. At the same time, units must be prepared to quickly restore "real world" settings and databases and return to the current battle. Units must keep rehearsal fire missions distinctly separate from live missions. The S3 should postpone rehearsals when a "real world" fire mission needs to be processed. The commander may need to terminate the rehearsal to prevent database corruption and confusion.

FA CSS Rehearsals

4-150. **Purpose.** CSS rehearsals verify and reinforce FA CSS planning and synchronization, and ensure that the FASP and FASM address essential CSS tasks. FA CSS rehearsals address:
- The CSS required to support execution of EFATs and the FASM – primary and backup methods.
- Positioning and movement of the battalion trains – Synchronization with FASM and higher/subordinate CSS locations and operations.
- Ammunition distribution, positioning, expenditure, and resupply.
- Maintenance and recovery operations – when, where, how.
- Refueling and resupply requirements – when, where, how.
- Medical treatment and evacuation procedures.
- EPW procedures.

4-151. **Types.** FA battalion CSS rehearsals may include:
- A robust rehearsal involving the TOC, ALOC, BSOC, CSS leaders, firing batteries, reinforcing units, and possibly the brigade FSE.
- A limited rehearsal conducted in the ALOC, by the XO, and involving primarily leaders from the CSS sections.

4-152. **Agenda.** Useful guides include a CSS rehearsal checklist and the FASM; however, the agenda may vary dependent on the rehearsal's focus.

Integrated Rehearsals

4-153. Units may integrate FS and FA tactical, technical, and CSS rehearsals to maximize use of limited time. The commander will determine the amount of focus placed on each major area. As a minimum, integrated rehearsals usually:
- Verify EFSTs/EFATs planning, to include:
  - Each HPT, its number, location, purpose, and priority.
  - Primary and alternate triggers, observers, and sensors.

- The unit that will deliver fires.
- Attack guidance – shell-fuze combination, number of volleys, and units to fire.
- Method of engagement is specified – time on target (TOT), at my command (AMC), when ready.
- Time-space relationship between unit response time, duration of fires, and scheme of maneuver.

- Rehearse the mission thread from the observer/sensor to the firing unit for each EFST/EFAT. Validate the following:
  - Primary and backup sensor-to-shooter communication links are coordinated - supported unit, observers (ground/air), FSEs, FDCs, firing sections, radars, intelligence assets.
  - Correct solution of the FS system.
  - Attack methods (shell, fuze, unit).
  - The use of intervention points in automated FS systems.
  - Correct function of mission routing information.
  - Coordination and deconfliction of targets, if required.

- Identify key FA actions that support each phase, to include:
  - Movement requirements, especially the trigger events that initiate moves and their relationship with the EFSTs and EFATs. Discuss survivability move criteria.
  - Verification of time-space relationships between EFATs and FA movements to ensure units are in position to mass during critical periods and verifies the terrain management plan.
  - Logistic requirements, especially critical CSS tasks.

- Verify FSCMs and coordination requirements for critical targets.
- Review who has priority of fires during each phase.
- Verify the digital database.

Chapter 5

Deliver Fires

This chapter focuses on execution - the delivery of fires. The chapter has five sections. Section I covers the fire mission process, including tactical and technical FD, massed fires, and continuity of operations. Section II discusses various types of special fire missions. Section III provides information on counterfire, to include support for theater missile defense. Section IV discusses FA support for SEAD operations. Section V provides general information on FA meteorological operations.

SECTION I – FIRE MISSION PROCESSING

5-01. FA functions directly associated with the delivery of fires are encompassed in the fire mission process. The delivery of FA fires depends on:
- Accurately locating an appropriate target (TA process).
- Initiating a call for fire into the FS system (the fire request).
- Analyzing the fire mission to determine the proper method of attack (tactical FD in FSEs, force FA HQs, and battalion and battery FDCs).
- Converting the call for fire into gun data (technical FD in battery/platoon FDCs and on newer weapon systems like Paladin and MLRS).
- Delivering the required ordnance on the target to meet the needs of the supported commander (deliver fires).
- Determine and report BDA.

5-02. Whether this process is done manually or through an automated system the process is the same. Automating fire control does not change what we do but how we do it. The basic fire mission flow is shown in the DS example in Figure 5-1.

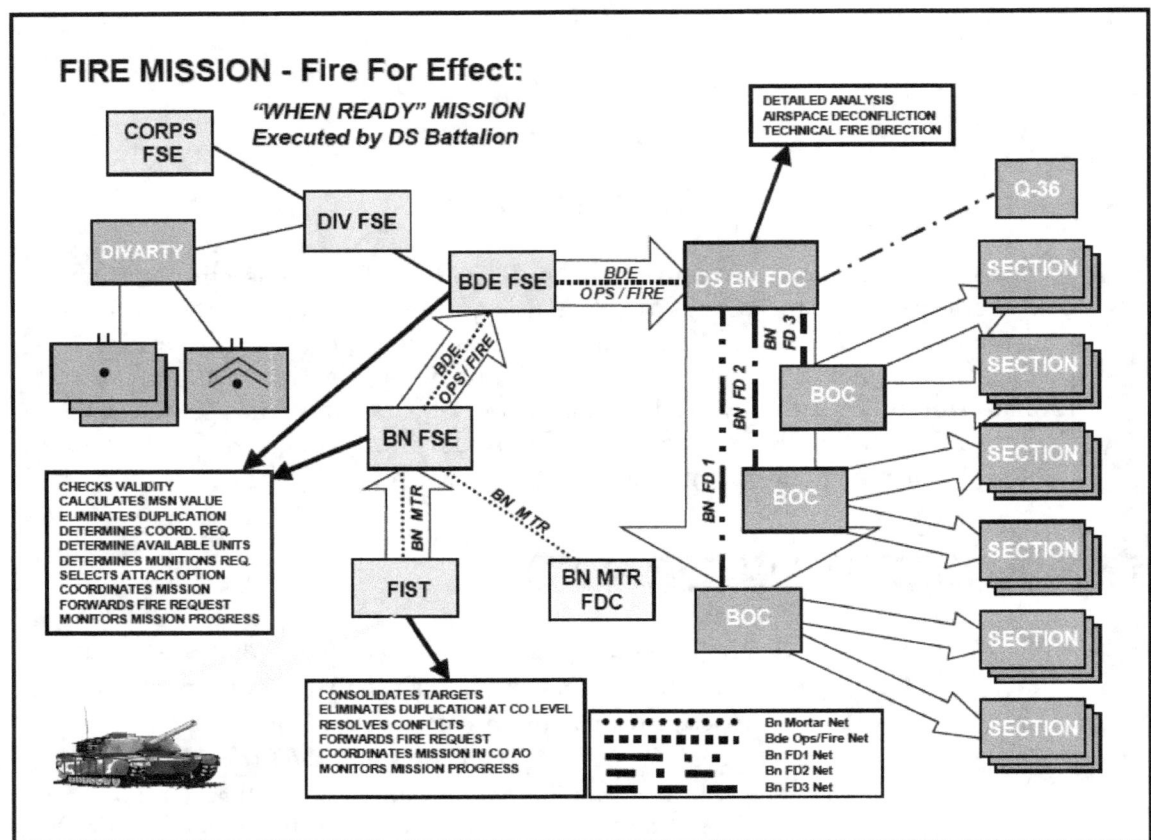

Figure 5-1. Fire Mission Flow (DS Example)

5-03. To expedite fires, the unit can coordinate the use of various quickfire linkages, designed to facilitate rapid fire mission execution, while achieving desired control. For example, in Figure 5-2, a quickfire channel could be established from a FIST, through the Bn FSE, and then directly to the Bn FDC. Or for even faster response and more decentralized control, the FIST may send the mission directly to the BOC or POC that will execute the mission. This is often used for priority targets and FPFs. Quickfire channels can be used for any observer or sensor, such as the radar shown in the figure. Any FSE or FA CP that is normally in the fire mission flow, but is bypassed during quickfire operations, should receive a notification of each fire mission through message of interest processing. While the example is of a DS FA battalion, the technique can be used to expedite fires to any FA unit.

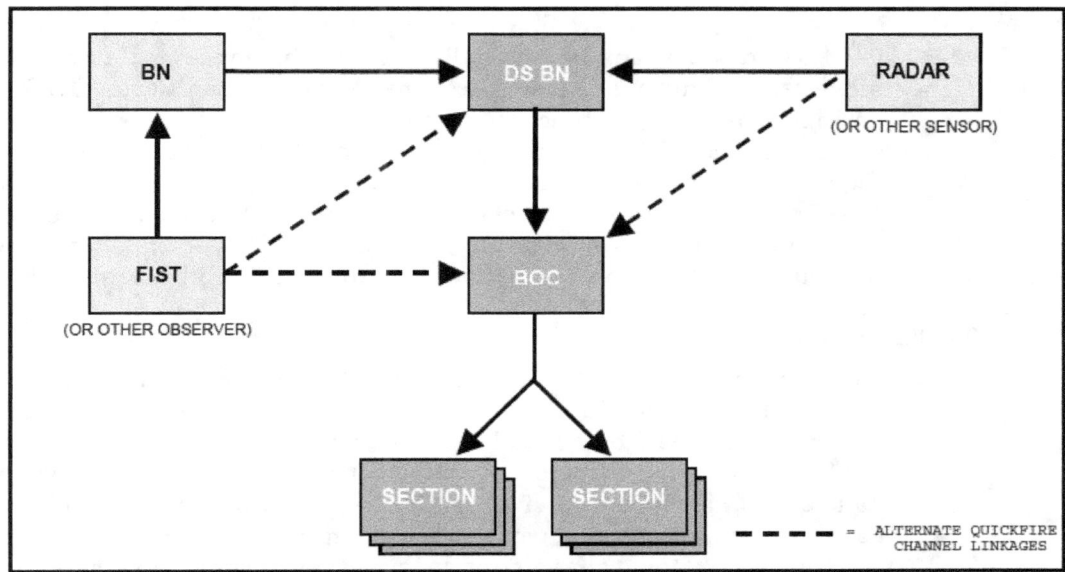

Figure 5-2. Quickfire Channel Example

FIRE MISSION REQUESTS

5-04. Units plan and execute FA fires digitally, as much as possible. However, FA battalions may receive planned and non-planned missions from a wide variety of sources, in both voice and digital formats. They may have been generated at lower or higher echelon maneuver, FS, or FA elements. They may have been routed through several elements in the FS/FA system or arrived in a battalion or battery FDC directly from the requestor.

DIGITAL

5-05. Digital fire missions may be received from FA and non-FA digital systems. Procedures and capabilities may vary depending on which digital systems are interfacing with one another. FA battalion commanders face two major challenges in the digital arena:

- Maintaining technical expertise in a rapidly changing hardware/software environment. Each new/upgraded device and software version brings new capabilities, procedures, problems, and workarounds.
- Finding digital training opportunities involving digital equipment that the unit does not possess (e.g., AFATDS to IFSAS communications).

5-06. Training opportunities should be aggressively sought out. Digital, FA technical support rehearsals should thoroughly address digital interface issues and possibilities. Whenever possible, critical digital fire missions should be rehearsed along the entire sensor-to-shooter link, under the same digital conditions anticipated for the actual operation (extended communications distances, surge digital traffic capacity, degraded operations, alternate routes). For DS battalions this involves significant coordination responsibilities for both FS and FA digital operations.

VOICE

5-07. Use of voice may be especially effective for unplanned, immediate fire requests, or during adverse communications conditions. FDCs must anticipate the circumstances and the types of voice missions they may encounter. The tactical solution and effects on the target should be essentially the same regardless of whether the mission was processed voice or digital. Missions involving FS personnel, radars, and other FA elements are usually easy to handle. However, missions from non-FA personnel may require innovative solutions to coordination, communication, and clearance of fire.

UNTRAINED OBSERVERS

5-08. Occasionally the FA battalion may need to process fire missions from untrained observers. Often these are critical requests where the requestor is under fire. This is a battle drill that needs to be practiced. Specific members of the battalion and firing battery FDCs should be identified as the primary handlers of untrained observer missions. These personnel should possess good communications skills, patience combined with a sense of urgency, and the ability to remain calm in stressful situations. These individuals should be identified during training and given the opportunity to practice untrained observer missions during major training exercises. FM 6-40 contains a detailed explanation of untrained observer procedures.

TACTICAL FIRE DIRECTION

5-09. The battalion FDC performs the tactical FD functions. It is the process that results in a fire order. A fire order is the FDO's decision, under supervision of the S3, on whether and how to attack a target. The FDO considers the following:
- Location of the target. Is it cleared to fire? Is it within range? Can the target be attacked?
- Nature of the target. How large is it? What is its degree of protection?
- Ammunition available. What do the batteries have on hand to fire?
- Firing units available. Who is in range and ready to fire?
- Maneuver commander's guidance and/or TSOP. What do we want to do to the target?
- Request for fire. What did the observer ask for? Can the battalion give it to him? Should the battalion give it to him?
- Munitions effects. Given the ammunition available, nature of the target and commander's guidance, how should the target be attacked?
- Tactical situation. When should the battalion fire? Are special instructions required?

5-10. The objectives of tactical FD are as follows:
- Provide continuous accurate and responsive FS under all conditions.
- Maintain the flexibility to engage all targets types over wide frontages.
- Mass the fires of all available units quickly.
- Engage a number and variety of targets simultaneously.

CENTRALIZED CONTROL

5-11. Centralized tactical fire control may be used when there are few firing units, when ammunition is low, during critical operations where the commander needs to carefully control operations, or when restrictive rules of engagement are in place. Under maximum centralized control, all fire requests go through the brigade FSE and FA battalion FDC. Also, AFATDS intervention point rules and commander's guidances are restrictive. Most missions are stopped for review at each OPFAC (as a minimum at the brigade FSE and battalion FDC), with only pre-designated critical missions flowing automatically through the fire control system.

DECENTRALIZED CONTROL

5-12. Decentralized tactical fire control (TFC) is used when maximum responsiveness and speed of execution is necessary. Some degree of decentralized control may be used even when resources are scarce if the maneuver commander (with input from his FSCOORD) determines the risks inherent in reduced control are warranted.

5-13. Decentralized control involves the use of sensor-to-shooter linkages and quickfire channels that may bypass some or all of the normal intervening OPFACs. Another method is to modify the AFATDS intervention rules and commander's guidances so that most missions flow through intervening OPFACs without stopping.

5-14. With decentralized control, FA battalion commanders and S3s must more closely monitor ammunition expenditures and the number of rounds fired from current positions. The potential for ammunition shortages and forced survival moves may increase under decentralized control procedures.

QUICKFIRE CHANNELS

5-15. When significantly responsive fires are necessary, a quickfire channel may be established. This may be a voice or digital link. The quickfire channel can be established as a direct link between the sensor (observer) and the shooter, or it may have one or more intervening C2 elements that evaluate and or relay traffic. Quickfire channels can be established using existing nets, with the only changes being in the actual routing or reporting of information. Establishment of quickfire channels may also involve the use of alternate nets or communications methods.

5-16. Quickfire channels are sometimes used in the following instances:
- Counterfire – to link a radar and a firing unit.
- SEAD/TMD – to link an EW/intelligence asset or an aircraft with a firing unit.
- Immediate suppression – to link a FO/COLT/Striker or other observer with a designated firing unit.
- Deep operations – to link scarce, time blocked EW and intelligence assets such as UAVs with firing units to find and immediately attack specific targets or target types.

5-17. Quickfire channel situations may involve supplementing the FA battalion with special communications equipment or coordinating nonstandard digital communications protocols. The S6 plays a critical role in identifying and evaluating EFATs involving quickfire channels. Wargaming and rehearsals require detailed analysis, as testing of the communications links may not be possible until during or immediately prior to the event. Requesting lessons learned information from other units that performed similar operations can prove extremely beneficial in identifying potential problems that can not otherwise be caught during planning and rehearsal.

AUTOMATED TACTICAL FIRE DIRECTION

5-18. The delivery of FA fires is significantly enhanced through the use of AFATDS, IFSAS, FDS, and LTACFIRE. These automation systems digitally link the FA battalion with its force FA HQ and adjacent, subordinate, reinforced, and supported units. The systems automate tactical FD and planning functions. AFATDS, IFSAS, FDS, and LTACFIRE can process and disseminate the following:

- Conventional fire plans.
- Target information.
- Fire missions generated from incoming target intelligence (tactical FD).
- FSCMs and other forms of battlefield geometry.
- Ammunition and fire unit data.
- Messages of interest to other OPFACs.
- Met and survey data.
- OPLANs/OPORDs, FS estimates, wargaming, graphics, and matrixes (AFATDS only).
- Movement control and logistics management (AFATDS only).

5-19. Although AFATDS, IFSAS, FDS, and LTACFIRE can perform all of the above functions, only tactical FD will be discussed in this segment.

5-20. AFATDS TFC program analyzes nominated targets, selects the method of attack, reviews available firing units and selects the optimal firing unit(s) for engagement. After analysis is completed and approved by the FDO (either through intervention or pre-established standards), the TFC program directs the delivery unit to attack the target.

5-21. The first step in providing for tactical FD involves establishing setup parameters in the computer. These parameters, entered prior to operations, consist of the tactical database and commander's criteria. Much of the general planning data is entered at maneuver brigade/DS FA battalion level or higher and disseminated downward, with some modification at each level. Unit locations, ammunition counts, and other data is input at lower levels and forwarded to higher HQ.

5-22. The tactical database consists of geometry, firing units, and ammunition and met information. The tactical database includes information from unit plans and orders such as the maneuver unit's zone, FSCMs, ammunition status, available firing units, firing unit locations, and atmospheric conditions.

5-23. The commander's criteria are simply the translation of the maneuver commander's concept for fires into system language. It includes information such as attack methods, priority zones, target types, shells, priority of selecting firing units, and exclusion of any firing units or shells/fuzes. The computer uses commander's criteria to produce a fire order. Therefore, this information must be kept current and accurate.

5-24. AFATDS, IFSAS, FDS, and LTACFIRE contain information from the joint munition effects manuals (JMEMs) concerning amount and type of ammunition and the optimum number of units to fire for a particular target. The information enables the computer to select the best ammunition for a particular target. If the commander wants to reserve a certain ammunition for future use or to vary the JMEMs data, that guidance should be converted into commander's criteria and entered into the computer (FSE assisted by FDC). Once they have been established, the computer implements the criteria without delay in mission processing. Moreover, commander's criteria may be overridden manually anytime an urgent situation warrants it.

5-25. It is essential that the FDO, in concert with higher FA HQ and the brigade FSO (if applicable), continually assesses and adjusts the commander's criteria based on his guidance for the different phases of the operation. Changes in the tactical situation may make assumptions and guidance that were valid earlier inadequate or even dangerously wrong. If anticipated ammunition fails to arrive, firing units are lost, or if new threat units or equipment arrive in the supported unit's sector, the parameters in the computers must be adjusted. In a manual environment, this process is no less important, but it is much less easily overlooked. The FDO must aggressively seek new guidance from the FSCOORD (or battalion commander), brigade FSO, and S3 and adjust the commander's criteria to reflect current reality.

5-26. In the automated tactical FD process, AFATDS, IFSAS, FDS, and LTACFIRE automatically prepare a request for additional fires whenever the unit cannot provide the volume of fire specified by the commander's criteria. The unit sends the request to the force FA HQ and/or appropriate FSE.

TECHNICAL FIRE DIRECTION

5-27. Technical FD is the process of converting weapon and ammunition characteristics (muzzle velocities, propellant temperature, and projectile weight), weapon and target locations, and met information into firing data. Weapon sections use the results of this process for firing.

5-28. Technical FD is an increasingly decentralized process. Most technical fire computation is done in the battery or platoon FDC, and transmitted to the firing section, or it is done on the weapon system itself. As newer weapon systems are fielded, the latter method will predominate, and battery and platoon FDCs will increasingly assume a backup role.

5-29. The technical FD capability will be incorporated into future versions of AFATDS, but currently is done within BCS, FDS, or the onboard automation system of the newer individual weapon systems (Paladin, Crusader, MLRS, and high mobility artillery rocket system (HIMARS) at the time of this publishing).

5-30. Manual technical FD procedures are also maintained within cannon FDCs in case of catastrophic loss of automation capability.

MASSED FIRES

5-31. Massing all available fires enables the artillery to inflict maximum damage on the enemy with a minimum expenditure of ammunition. It reduces the vulnerability of the firing unit to the enemy's TA capabilities. Failure to mass fires may give the enemy time to react and seek protection. A clear understanding of the maneuver commander's guidance for FS and an accurate commander's criteria input into the AFATDS, IFSAS, FDS, or LTACFIRE are key to determine how much FA is enough. Every mission received must be evaluated, in the light of the commander's criteria, and sufficient massed fire should be employed to achieve effects required. If the FDO consults the JMEMs or accepts computer generated gunnery solutions, he will discover that most targets worth engaging should be engaged with volleys from two or more batteries or battalions. Suppression can be achieved, but the desired effects are achieved on few, if any, of them.

5-32. A FA battalion should maintain the maximum feasible degree of centralized control over the firing systems. There will very likely be many more calls for fire than assets available to fire them and still achieve the effects specified by the commander. The maneuver commander or his FSCOORD must be the one to decide which missions are critical to the success of the unit and which missions will not be executed or will be delayed. Commander's criteria are critical in managing the fires of the battalion. If good commander's criteria are developed and accurately entered into the automated systems, the computer can assume much of the burden of sorting the missions as they are received and assign them the appropriate priority.

5-33. One of the best techniques available to the FDO for massing fires is the use of TOT. Also, the FDO can effectively mass fire for effect on mobile targets through use of AMC in his fire order. With these techniques the element of surprise is not lost since the delivery of fires is controlled. Survivability of firing units is enhanced, because mass fire techniques require fewer rounds to achieve the desired effects and because massed fires temporarily saturate enemy TA devices. These two techniques for massing fires, when properly applied against appropriate targets, can result in maximized effects for the amount of ammunition used.

5-34. The key to massing fires effectively when more than one battery is to be fired for effect is the efficient use of voice to execute digital fire order(s). By using voice to execute the order(s), the battalion FDO can ensure that targets are engaged with the required number of firing units in a synchronized manner. Unit TSOPs should address the procedures for both digital and voice fire orders.

CONTINUITY OF OPERATIONS

5-35. AFATDS, IFSAS, FDS, and LTACFIRE equipped units have at least two or three central processing units (CPUs) in the battalion TOC. This redundancy has significantly reduced the need for complex and carefully orchestrated MSU operations. Once the systems are initialized and the data sharing paths established according to the operation, the computers will automatically, without human intervention, update all other systems with which a particular station is sharing information. A loss of any single computer or group of computers in AFATDS, IFSAS, FDS, and LTACFIRE will not have a catastrophic impact. CONOPS functions are built into the software for rapid reaction to the loss of an operational element. The CPU at brigade FSE has the capability to serve as a backup system for the battalion if planned.

5-36. In addition to CONOPS, manual means will remain an effective backup to catastrophic loss of automated capability. The TOC should thoroughly plan and rehearse transfer to manual backup operations. A battalion FDO can establish manual operations more easily if the following tools are on hand:

- A current fire order standard. Issuing a correct fire order will greatly reduce confusion and errors.
- Written attack guidance. The JMEMs and graphical munition effectiveness tables (GMETs) are too cumbersome to be useful in a fluid tactical situation.
- A current ammunition count for the firing units. In cannon units, this includes projectiles, propellants, and fuzes by lot.
- A current situation map. As a minimum, the following information must be clearly and accurately displayed:
  - Maneuver boundaries.
  - Firing unit locations.
  - FSCMs.
  - The FLOT.
  - Observer locations.
- Range fans or the range-deflection protractor (Graphical Training Aid [GTA] 6-5-1) for checking ranges.

SECTION II – FA FIRE MISSIONS

5-37. This section provides general information and guidance concerning FA fire missions that may require special consideration by a FA battalion. Additional information about these missions, from the perspective of the observer, FDC, or FSE can be found in FM 6-30, FM 6-40, and FM 6-20-40.

IMPROVED CONVENTIONAL MUNITIONS (ICM)

5-38. ICM munitions are delivered by 105mm and 155mm howitzers and by MLRS (rockets and missiles). There are three types of ICM:

- **Antipersonnel (APICM).** APICM is a cannon ICM most effective against unwarned, exposed personnel. When the submunitions hit the ground, the grenade is hurled upward 4 to 6 feet and then detonates.
- **Antipersonnel, Antimaterial (APAM).** APAM is a missile ICM most effective against unwarned, exposed personnel and light material targets. It is a fragmentary grenade that explodes on impact.
- **Dual-purpose (DPICM).** DPICM, delivered by cannons and MLRS, is most effective against lightly armored vehicles and other materials. It is also effective against personnel. DPICM submunitions explode on impact, using both a shaped charge and fragmentation to achieve its effects.

CONSIDERATIONS

Dud Rates

5-39. Anytime ICM is fired, between one and three percent of the submunitions fail to detonate. About 50% of these duds will be armed. These dud rates may increase in adverse weather and terrain conditions. This hazard must be considered in development of the maneuver commander's guidances and in planning and firing missions. In AFATDS units, consideration of this hazard and the maneuver commander's guidance should be reflected in the AFATDS guidances and/or the FSCMs established by the FSE/FSCOORD. During periods of extensive ICM use, safety warnings about duds may need to be reissued within both military and civilian channels.

Weather and Terrain

5-40. Generally, ICM should not be fired into forests, mountainous areas (slope greater than 60%), or extremely rocky or uneven terrain. Deep snow or surface water, soft sand, and marshy terrain can also decrease the effectiveness of ICM and increase the dud rate. High winds may adversely affect the dispersal pattern, as well as the effectiveness and dud rate.

Height of Burst

5-41. Height of burst (HOB) is normally not a major factor for ICM, but it can sometimes vary and affect the dispersal pattern and dud rate. HOB can be adjusted for cannon ICM but not MLRS ICM. FM 6-30 and FM 6-40 provide observer and gunnery information on cannon ICM HOB adjustment. If frequent HOB problems occur (too low or too high), the FDO or S3 should

Danger Close

5-42. Caution should be used when firing ICM in danger close situations as an ICM round, rocket, or missile has a relatively large dispersal pattern and strong winds can affect the submunitions. A single round, rocket, or missile may be fired initially to verify targeting data and weather impact. Subsequent adjustments should be made with the entire firing unit. The observer should make corrections from the near edge of the effects pattern.

ILLUMINATION

5-43. Illuminating projectiles are available for 105mm and 155mm howitzers. They are used to illuminate a designated area, to aid in adjusting FA fires at night, for marking locations, or to orient friendly forces. They can also be used to mark targets (by air or ground burst) for air attack, or to "wash out" enemy passive night-sight systems when used at ground level. Depending on the caliber, an illumination shell can provide light for up to 2 minutes and can light an area up to 1,000 meters in diameter.

5-44. The amount of illumination ammunition required for a particular mission depends on the observer-target (OT) distance, the visibility, and the size, width, and depth of the area to be lit. The FDC and the observer must coordinate selection of the proper illumination pattern and controlled rate of fire to maximize illumination effectiveness with minimal ammunition expenditure.

5-45. Illumination is conducted by using one of the following techniques:
- The **one-gun** illumination pattern is used when effective illumination can be achieved by firing one round at a time.
- The **two-gun** illumination can be fired in range-spread or lateral-spread patterns. This is commonly used for aerial observers.
- The **four-gun** illumination pattern illuminates a large area. Four rounds burst at the same time in both lateral and range spread patterns.

5-46. Illumination missions may be fired as illumination only missions or as coordinated illumination missions. In the latter, firing of the illumination is coordinated with the firing of high explosive (HE), DPICM, or other attack munitions so that the observer can see the effectiveness and adjust fire as necessary.

CONSIDERATIONS

5-47. Except in unusual situations, the majority of a unit's illumination missions may be relatively close to the FLOT, involving shorter ranges and lower propellant charges. Using the lowest propellant charge possible also reduces damage to the round's parachute. The S3 should factor this into ammunition estimates and ensure the S4, BAO, and firing batteries understand the ammunition plan.

5-48. Identify EFATs involving illumination early in the MDMP. This facilitates the preparation of CCLs of ammunition and delivery of CCLs at the proper time and place (e.g., illumination package Bravo, not-later-than (NLT) 1900 hrs, to battery A's supplementary position.) See Chapter 7 for additional discussion of CCLs.

5-49. Illumination missions may be lengthy missions, increasing the firing unit's vulnerability to enemy acquisition and attack. The S3 should consider directing platoons to fire illumination missions from supplementary positions as much as possible. If a high counterfire threat exists, the S3 should monitor lengthy missions and consider shifting the illumination to a backup unit or terminating the mission if it is low priority (with maneuver/higher FA concurrence). Wargaming during the MDMP can assist the S3 in identifying the best solution.

5-50. Coordinated illumination missions may involve several weapon systems and firing units, and without proper planning can tie up assets for relatively extended periods. During the MDMP, the S3 should evaluate EFATs requiring coordinated illumination missions to determine their potential impact on the overall fire plan, and the priorities of the fires potentially ongoing at that time.

5-51. Illumination can interfere with friendly night vision devices and expose friendly troops to enemy observation. S3s and FDOs must ensure that all firing restrictions are understood and properly disseminated and that all FSCMs and commander's guidances are correctly entered into both manual and automated fire control systems.

5-52. On a non-linear battlefield there may be more frequent safety/FSCM conflicts involving illumination as the canister continues on after the illumination package is ejected. Increased use of high angle fire may be necessary and selection of firing units may require more detailed planning.

SMOKE/WHITE PHOSPHOROUS (WP)

5-53. Smoke can significantly reduce the enemy's effectiveness both in the daytime and at night. Combined with other suppressive fires, it gives more opportunities for maneuver forces to deploy and aircraft to attack frontline targets. The effective delivery of smoke by the FA at the critical time and place helps the combined arms team accomplish its mission. (See Table 5-1 for smoke capabilities and effects.)

SMOKE MUNITIONS

5-54. Smoke munitions are available for both 105mm and 155mm cannon systems. There are three types of smoke projectiles used for FA delivered smoke. Each has different characteristics and capabilities that must be considered in their employment. The various smoke projectiles are often used in combination to more quickly and effectively deliver the required smoke coverage in the time required and for the conditions on the battlefield:

- **Hexachloroethane (HC).** HC projectiles, available for 105mm and 155mm howitzers, are used for screening, obscuration, spotting, and signaling. The projectile is not designed to cause casualties. The round expels smoke canisters that emit smoke for a period of 40 to 90 seconds.

- **Burster-type WP.** WP projectiles are available for 105mm and 155mm howitzers. They can be fired with point-detonating (PD) or MTSQ fuzes. Normally, shell WP is employed for its incendiary effect. It is also used for screening, spotting, and signaling purposes.
- **M825 WP.** The M825 WP projectile is a FA-delivered 155mm base-ejection projectile designed to produce a smoke screen on the ground for a duration of 5 to 15 minutes. The projectile contains 116 WP-saturated felt wedges that fall to the ground in an elliptical pattern. Each wedge then becomes a point or source of smoke. These burning wedges can also present a potential obstacle or hazard to friendly soldiers passing through the smoked area. FS planners must consider this when planning smoke operations.

EMPLOYMENT TECHNIQUES

5-55. Smoke is used for obscuration, screening, deception, and signaling.
- **Obscuring Smoke.** A smoke screen placed directly on or near the enemy with the primary purpose of suppressing observers and minimizing their vision.
  - To defeat flash ranging and restrict enemy counterfire programs.
  - To obscure enemy observation points (OPs) and reduce the accuracy of enemy observed fires.
  - To obscure enemy direct fire weapons, including wire-guided missiles, to reduce their effectiveness up to 90 percent.
  - To obscure enemy lasers to reduce their effectiveness.
  - To instill apprehension and increase enemy patrolling.
  - To slow enemy vehicles to blackout speeds.
  - To increase command and control problems by preventing effective visual signals and increasing radio traffic.
  - To defeat night observation devices and reduce the capability of most infrared (IR) devices.
  - To increase effectiveness of obstacles.
- **Screening Smoke.** A smoke curtain used on the battlefield between enemy observation points and friendly units to mask maneuvers.
  - **Deceptive Screens.** Smoke draws fire. Deceptive screens cause the enemy to disperse his fires and expend his ammunition.
  - **Flank Screens.** Smoke may be used to screen exposed flanks.
  - **Areas Forward of the Objective.** Smoke helps maneuver units consolidate on objectives unhindered by enemy ground observers.
  - **River-Crossing Operations.** Screening the primary crossing site denies the enemy information. Deceptive screens deceive the enemy as to the exact location of the main crossing.
  - **Obstacle Breaching.** Denies the enemy the ability to observe the breaching unit and to place accurate fires on that unit.
- **Deception Smoke.** A smoke curtain used to deceive and confuse the enemy as to the nature of friendly operations.
- **Signaling Smoke.** Smoke used to orient or signal friendly forces.

Table 5-1. FA Smoke Capabilities and Effects

DELIVERY SYSTEM	TYPE ROUND	NOMEN-CLATURE	FUZE	TIME TO BUILD EFFECTIVE SMOKE	AVERAGE BURNING TIME	AVERAGE OBSCURATION LENGTH PER ROUND (METERS) WIND DIRECTION	
						CROSS	HEAD OR TAIL
155mm Howitzer	WP	M110A2	M557 or M739	½ minute	1 to 1 ½ minutes	150	50
	Smoke	M116B1	M501A1	1 to 1 ½ minutes	4 minutes	350	75
	Improved Smoke	M825	M557 or M739	½ minutes	7 minutes	350	100-200
105mm Howitzer	WP	M60A1	M557 or M739	½ minute	1 to 1 ½ minutes	75	50
	Smoke	M84B1	M501A1	1 to 1 ½ minutes	3 minutes	250	50

DELIVERY TECHNIQUES

5-56. There are two types of delivery techniques used to employ FA smoke: immediate, and quick smoke.

5-57. **Immediate Smoke.** Immediate smoke is used to quickly obscure point or small area targets of 150 meters or less, for short durations. It is frequently used in a suppressive role against targets of opportunity, either by itself, or in conjunction with immediate suppression HE or ICM. The HE/ICM provides immediate suppression while the smoke extends the suppression over a wider area and a longer period. Immediate smoke is also used for planned, on-call fires against known or suspected enemy locations.

5-58. Immediate smoke missions normally are fire for effect (FFE) missions fired by one platoon, and are designed to provide obscuration for approximately 1-5 minutes. The initial volley may be fired with shell WP, fuze quick, or a mix of shell WP and shell HC in order to obtain rapid effects (within 30 seconds of impact). If additional volleys are fired, all howitzers should fire HC smoke. When firing the M825 smoke round, all howitzers should fire the M825 projectile for the initial and subsequent volleys. Unit TSOP should dictate the number of volleys and which howitzers will fire WP and which will fire HC smoke, if applicable. If immediate smoke is required for longer than 5 minutes, the requestor should notify the FDC during planning, or early in the fire mission. Because of potential target location error and changing environmental factors, the FA battalion S3 and FDO should always anticipate and plan for at least one correction, even for planned immediate smoke missions.

5-59. **Quick Smoke.** Quick smoke is used to quickly provide obscuration, screening, deception, or signaling smoke over a small to moderate area (100 to 600 meters) for approximately 5-15 minutes. (Environmental factors may extend quick smoke effects over a 1,500 meter area.) It may be fired as a planned target or target of opportunity. However, smoke screens larger than 250 meters in length should be preplanned due to ammunition constraints and the possible need to segment the target. Quick smoke missions usually involve the fires of one or two firing batteries. A "standard" quick smoke mission is frequently used in TSOPs or in FASPs to facilitate planning and ammunition coordination. Deviations from the standard must then be identified early in the planning process or request for fire.

5-60. Quick smoke requests may be processed as adjust-fire or FFE missions. Accurate and effective FFE smoke is sometimes difficult to achieve due to surface winds and other environmental factors. The S3 and FDO should consider this during planning, and coordinate with the requestor to determine procedures for ineffective or inaccurate FFE smoke missions (switch to adjust fire procedures or repeat the FFE with an adjustment).

5-61. Obscuration, screening, or deception smoke over a relatively large area (600 – 1,500 meters) or for an extended period of time (greater than 15 minutes is usually fired as a planned mission as the ammunition, firing unit, and coordination requirements can be significant. To expedite emplacement of larger smoke screens, the FDC may direct multiple quick smoke missions. The S3, S4, and BAO must carefully evaluate EFATs involving large smoke missions to determine the impact on overall ammunition capability.

CONSIDERATIONS

Adjust Fire Missions

5-62. Adjust fire mission techniques vary dependent on the type of mission and ammunition. The following techniques apply only to standard adjust fire smoke missions as immediate smoke missions are FFE missions.

- **Shell Smoke (HC).** HE is used in adjustment until a 200-meter bracket is split. The observer then requests shell smoke. One smoke round is fired, and any necessary corrections (to include HOB) are made until the smoke is accurately located. Then FFE is requested. A subsequent adjustment may be necessary for maximum effectiveness.
- **Improved Smoke (M825).** The M825 does not need HOB adjustment. As a result, a 200-meter bracket is not split and FFE is started after a 200-meter bracket is achieved.
- **Burster-type WP.** HE projectiles are used during the full adjustment with WP fired when FFE is requested.

Available Means

5-63. For a FSO this entails analyzing all available sources, such as FA, mortars, and chemical unit smoke generating sections. FA battalion S3s must evaluate which firing unit(s) and what type of ammunition are best capable of supporting each FA smoke EFAT. MDMP wargaming and rehearsals must include careful evaluation of smoke EFATs and alternate smoke plans to ensure that the proper quantities and types of smoke ammunition are in the right places at the right times. In DS FA units, the S3 and FSO coordinate the integration of FA and mortar smoke capabilities. Mortars can back up a FA smoke EFAT, or the FA unit can back up the mortars. The FA S3 must also understand that based on the conditions and the size of the screen, two or more platoons or batteries may be required to effectively fire the mission.

Ammunition and Timing

5-64. Smoke EFATs must be carefully evaluated for ammunition and timing requirements. Basic loads usually include minimal smoke ammunition to support a few immediate or quick smoke missions. Projectile type, fuze, and, for 155mm, propellant requirements must be considered. Ammunition to support larger smoke requirements should be positioned near or delivered to the shooter relatively close to the time it will be needed. Backup plans must be considered, especially when smoke is a constrained resource. Timing is critical as firing too early or late can have adverse effects for the requesting unit, and can result in wasted ammunition.

5-65. FA battalion commanders and S3s must ensure that the supported maneuver commander and FSO or senior FA HQ thoroughly understand the FA battalion's smoke capabilities, and that planning for smoke does not exceed available resources. At times, the S3 may need to direct redistribution of smoke ammunitions to correct for imbalances or changing circumstances, such as loss due to hostile fire or accident. The S3 must quickly calculate the impact on smoke EFATs to determine the actions and notifications required.

Firing Unit Information Requirements

5-66. For the FDC to provide an effective smoke screen, the FDO needs to obtain additional information not normally provided for other missions. From the observer, the FDO needs the following:
- The center grid of the smoke screen.
- The length (size) of the smoke screen.
- The screen time (duration), in minutes.
- The maneuver target direction. The direction from the point at which the maneuver element will be most susceptible to enemy observation to the target.
- Wind direction in reference to the maneuver target line. The observer must let the FDC know if the wind is head, tail, left cross, or right cross in relation to the maneuver target line.

5-67. From the met station (or from currently available met data), the FDO will need to know the relative humidity for line 00 of the latest met message.

5-68. The FDO relies on a series of tables to determine the number of rounds to fire to establish and maintain the smoke screen for the desired duration requested. Until the necessary information is received, the FDO cannot properly calculate the number of rounds required. For planned missions, the FDO must analyze how potential changes in conditions may impact on firing requirements. If the number of aimpoints, rounds, or guns exceeds unit capabilities, the FDO will notify the S3 per unit TSOP.

Environmental Factors

5-69. Environmental factors impact significantly on the effectiveness of smoke. Atmospheric stability, wind direction, and wind speed are the major factors influencing the effectiveness of smoke. Whenever significant changes in weather conditions are expected, the S3 and FDO should determine the potential impact on smoke EFATs, such as higher ammunition requirements.

5-70. **Wind.** High winds can reduce the effectiveness of smoke. Wind speeds ranging from 4 to 14 knots are best for the production of smoke screens. The observer is the normal source of wind data for the target area.

5-71. **Temperature.** A rise in temperature may increase the rate of 70, causing smoke to dissipate more rapidly and lose effectiveness.

5-72. **Humidity and Precipitation.** High humidity and precipitation may enhance the effectiveness of smoke.

5-73. **Terrain.** Smoke seeks low spots. In built-up areas smoke may be effective for longer periods when trapped between buildings where strong winds are not prevalent. Smoke may cause fires in dry vegetation or in built-up areas. Smoke is normally not effective in deep mud, water, snow, or in mountains or other steeply sloped areas.

5-74. **Night.** Smoke is also effective at night. Atmospheric conditions at night may produce different effects on smoke than experienced during day.

SCATMINE

5-75. FA SCATMINE, which is currently limited to 155mm howitzers, gives the maneuver commander an all-weather capability to quickly emplace minefields. The two types of FA-delivered SCATMINE are:
- **Area denial artillery munitions (ADAM).** ADAM is an antipersonnel mine activated by deployed trip lines. ADAM are often used in conjunction with remote anti-armor mine system (RAAMS) to hinder the clearing of a RAAMS minefield by dismounted troops. ADAM may also be used alone against personnel and unarmored targets.
- **RAAMS.** RAAMS are used to create antiarmor or antivehicle obstacles. A percentage of the RAAMS have an antidisturbance device to hinder mine-clearing operations. RAMMS are most effective when used in conjunction with ADAM.

5-76. Both the ADAM and RAAMS have a self-destruct (SD) capability that destroys the mine if it has not been detonated within a certain period of time. Both the ADAM and RAAMS come in two SD versions – long (48 hours) and short (4 hours).

5-77. The corps commander has the authority to employ SCATMINE. He may delegate this authority for specific operations or limited periods as follows:
- Long duration down to maneuver brigade.
- Short duration down to maneuver battalion.

EMPLOYMENT

5-78. There are four basic uses of FA-delivered SCATMINE:
- To create an obstacle.
- To reinforce an existing obstacle.
- To deny use of an area.
- To interdict or disrupt enemy operations.

Create an Obstacle

5-79. FA-delivered SCATMINE enables the maneuver commander to quickly create an antipersonnel, antivehicle, antiarmor, or multi-purpose obstacle. ADAM can be fired by itself to create an obstacle effective against personnel and light vehicles. RAAMS can be used to create an antiarmor obstacle, however, ADAM are usually used in conjunction with RAAMS to prevent easy clearing of the obstacle. A combination ADAM/RAAMS minefield creates a multi-purpose obstacle that obstructs personnel, vehicles, and equipment.

5-80. Like any obstacle, SCATMINE is best used at a choke point covered by effective indirect and direct fire. The principles of obstacle coverage apply even more strongly to SCATMINE because:
- The mines are surface-laid and visible.
- FA-delivered minefield tend to be small and of low density (because of ammunition constraints).
- They are easily bypassed and/or breached. An undisturbed enemy can work through a SCATMINE minefield relatively quickly.

Reinforce an Obstacle

5-81. ADAM and RAAMS can be used in combination or individually to reinforce other antipersonnel, antivehicle, and antiarmor obstacles emplaced by engineers or maneuver forces. ADAM can strengthen antipersonnel obstacles such as concertina wire, or disrupt beaching of antiarmor obstacles like abatis and trenches. This is especially useful when time or unit resources limit the size or effectiveness of an engineer or maneuver force obstacle. The SCATMINE may be fired in soon after the primary obstacle has been completed, or it may be scheduled as a planned mission to be fired at a specific time or on-call based on an event or other triggering factor. SCATMINE can also refresh or strengthen obstacles that have been weakened, breached, or are otherwise ineffective in obstructing the enemy.

Area Denial

5-82. SCATMINE can be emplaced on key terrain or facilities to deny the enemy use of the area. This may be critical high ground, a potential landing area, or other location that can not be effectively controlled by other means. As with obstacles, area denial minefields have little or only short-term effectiveness unless covered by direct or indirect fires.

Interdiction/Disruption

5-83. SCATMINE can be used by itself, or with other munitions (from any FS system) to interdict movement and disrupt enemy operations. It can be effective in the following situations:
- River crossing sites, airmobile landing zones, or beachheads.
- Large multi-column convoys in restricted terrain.
- Concentrated vehicle and/or troop formations (at critical times or locations – such as dismounting mechanized infantry).
- Counterfire – artillery firing locations.

- SEAD – EAD sites (most effective when synchronized with air operations).
- Logistics facilities – ammunition and POL sites, railyards, tactical air or helicopter landing zones.

5-84. For interdiction and disruption, SCATMINE is most effective when used in conjunction with other munitions. The other munitions cause damage, injuries, fires, disorientation, and fear. This creates hasty movement, forces armored elements to button up, and hinders clearing operations.

5-85. For counterfire and SEAD, fire DPICM first, then smoke (optional), followed by SCATMINE. The smoke will obstruct vision and may initially force an increased MOPP posture further degrading vision. This makes it difficult for the enemy to see and clear the SCATMINE, which disrupts the enemy's ability to reorganize, reconstitute, and move. The SCATMINE causes additional injury and damage and continues to interfere with operations after the firing has ended. SCATMINE by itself may not be very effective for counterfire or SEAD as the enemy may be able to remain in place and continue firing with little disruption, especially in SP units.

5-86. Because interdiction/disruption minefields are often not observed or covered with direct fire, they are more effective when synchronized as part of a larger operation. As an example, used for SEAD, SCATMINE would be most effective immediately prior to or during an air operation in the area. SCATMINE at an enemy river crossing site would be most effective just as the enemy was trying to establish the site or use it for a major operation.

SCATMINE MISSIONS

5-87. FA SCATMINE minefields consist of two general types:
- **Planned minefields.** A planned target, on the target list. Planned minefields are normally less than 600 meters wide, but may be as large as necessary to achieve the effects desired. They also:
  - Are emplaced as scheduled or on-call targets.
  - Require extensive coordination between maneuver, engineer, and FS/FA personnel.
  - Require extensive logistical support.
  - Use primarily long SD mines.
  - Allow safety zones to be computed before firing.
- **Target of opportunity minefields.** Are emplaced as a result of an immediate call for fire request on an unplanned target. They:
  - Are a standard minefield based on unit TSOP (For example - 400x400 meters, high angle, medium density, two aimpoints).
  - Consist of a combination of 24 RAAMS and 6 ADAM projectiles (these numbers may change depending on the threat and the commander's guidance).
  - Use only short SD mines (carried as part of the basic load).
  - The safety zone, based on a single aimpoint, is computed immediately after the minefield is fired.

SCATMINE CONSIDERATIONS

5-88. Battery minefield angle (BMA), range, and target size all impact the fire order requirements for effective SCATMINE delivery. Because SCATMINE missions can be lengthy missions to fire (10-30 minutes), the S3 must consider the time the unit will be unavailable to fire other missions and the increased vulnerability of the unit to enemy acquisition and counterfire. The S3 should consider force protection measures, such as using additional howitzers to decrease the time, firing the mission from an alternate (possibly hardened) position, or directing a survival move after mission completion.

Safety Considerations

5-89. Firing SCATMINE close to friendly troops is potentially hazardous, as SCATMINE is an area weapon that can be affected by high winds. If the center of the minefield is less than 700 meters from the nearest friendly position, the unit should follow danger close procedures as the edges of the minefield could easily fall within normal danger close distance (600 meters). Planned danger close SCATMINE minefields should be adjusted in with HE or ICM whenever possible.

5-90. A safety zone should be computed for each SCATMINE minefield. The controlling FSE is generally responsible for determining safety zones. However, the actual data may be computed by the firing FA FDC or by the FSE. See FM 6-40 for specific techniques.

Recording and Reporting the Minefield

5-91. The SCATMINE delivery unit's FDC is responsible for initiating the scatterable minefield report, first by radio and later by hard copy. The FDC submits the report through the FSE to the engineer, generally with an information copy through FA channels. See FM 6-40 for more information.

COPPERHEAD

5-92. Copperhead is a 155mm cannon-launched guided projectile with a shaped warhead and a laser seeker. When fired at moving or stationary hard targets, Copperhead homes in on laser energy reflected from the target during the final 20 seconds (approximately) of its trajectory. The ground laser operator may use a G/VLLD, a laser target designator (LTD), or modular universal laser equipment (MULE). Airborne systems with lasers include the AH-64, OH-58D, and unmanned aerial vehicles.

CONSIDERATIONS

5-93. Much of the responsibility for planning and executing Copperhead missions rests with the FSEs and observers. However, the FA battalion S3 and battalion and battery FDOs must thoroughly understand the process in order to better support the mission, to anticipate changes, and to identify effective workarounds or troubleshooting techniques when problems arise.

Planning

5-94. Copperhead targets can be engaged as planned targets or targets of opportunity, however, planned targets are preferred. Planned targets fall into two categories: priority and on-call.

- For priority targets, data are precomputed and set on the guns, and the Copperhead round is laid in its loading tray. Unless otherwise specified on the target list, two Copperhead rounds are prepared in advance for each Copperhead priority target.
- On-call targets are processed the same as priority targets, except the guns are not laid on firing data until after receipt of the mission. On-call target procedures for Copperhead are the same as those for conventional on-call missions.

5-95. **NOTE**: FDC personnel must ensure that at least two howitzers and two Copperhead rounds are prepared for any mission. This action increases firing unit responsiveness if a round or howitzer malfunctions. The criteria in Table 5-2 are used for all Copperhead missions.

Table 5-2. Copperhead Criteria

TARGET STRENGTH (Observer Entry)	ROUNDS SPECIFIED (FDC ENTRY)	NUMBER OF HOWITZERS
1[1]	2	2
2	2	2
3	3	2
4	4	2
5	5	2
6[2]	6	2

[1] If a single target element is important enough to warrant firing Copperhead, the observer should request 2 rounds and "By round, AMC." This reduces response time in case of a target miss and prevents wasting the second round if the first succeeds in destroying the target. An optimum of one round per target is used as a planning factor.

[2] No more than six rounds will be prepared for any given mission.

Control Procedures

5-96. If the number of rounds to be fired is not specified in the call for fire, the FDC will fire the number of rounds specified for that target on the Copperhead target list. If the number of rounds is not specified on the target list, the FDC will fire one round at the target and direct the howitzer(s) to prepare, but DO NOT LOAD, a second round. The message-to-observer (MTO) will reflect 1 round.

5-97. When the observer requests AMC, the Copperhead rounds will be fired at intervals of at least 30 seconds when the observer gives the initial command to fire. When BY ROUND, AMC is requested, the observer will control the firing of each Copperhead round. The observer must understand this and act accordingly so as not to waste rounds.

Pulse Repetition Frequency (PRF) Code Set

5-98. The three-digit PRF code set on the Copperhead round must match the PRF code set on the observer's designator. The FDC should have a list of all observer PRF codes by call sign, from which it selects the proper PRF code for the observer lasing the mission. The PRF code is then sent to the howitzers in the fire commands and is placed on the Copperhead round. The observer verifies the PRF code announced in the MTO. Early identification and coordination of PRF codes is a key FDO/FSO responsibility.

DANGER CLOSE

5-99. The term "danger close" is used when friendly troops are within a prescribed distance of the intended impact of munitions, specifically 600 meters for cannon FA and 2,000 meters for MLRS. This is simply a warning and not a restriction to both the maneuver commander and the FDC to take proper precautions. Risk-estimate distances are used in danger close situations to determine whether or not to fire. Risk-estimate distances are defined as the distance in meters from the intended center of impact at which a specific degree of risk and vulnerability will not be exceeded. Risk estimate distances are for combat use and are not minimum safe distances for peacetime training.

5-100. The risk-estimate casualty criterion is the 5-minute assault criterion for a prone soldier in winter clothing and helmet. The probability of incapacitation (PI) means that a soldier is physically unable to function in an assault within a 5-minute period after an attack. The 0.1 percent PI value can be interpreted as being less than or equal to one chance in a thousand. The ground commander must accept risk when targets are inside 0.1 percent PI.

Table 5-3. Risk-Estimate Distances

Item/System	Description	Risk Estimate Distances (Meters)					
		10% PI			0.1% PI		
		1/3	2/3	Max Rg	1/3	2/3	Max Rg
M102/M119	105mm Howitzer	85	85	90	175	200	275
M109/M198	155mm Howitzer	100	100	125	200	280	450
M109/M198	155mm DPICM	150	180	200	280	300	475
M270A1	MLRS	2 km	2 km	2 km	2 km	2 km	2 km
M270A1	ATACMS	5 km	5 km	5 km	5 km	5 km	5 km

CONSIDERATIONS

5-101. Normally the observer will include danger close notification in his call for fire. However, untrained, or non-FA observers may not provide this alert. In the latter case, an FSE or FDC should notice the danger close situation during mission checks. AFATDS currently does not provide automatic danger close alerts, but may have this capability in future versions. In relatively static situations, various automated FSCMs, such as RFAs, can sometimes be used to provide increased warning of danger close situations.

5-102. In danger close missions the situation, type of ammunition being fired, the number of rounds, method of fire, observer-target-gun (OTG) angle, weather, and terrain conditions all must be considered to ensure safe firing. HC smoke or illumination rounds do not present as much danger as HE or ICM rounds. Likewise, a battery or battalion fire-for-effect mission carries more risk than an adjust fire mission. Leaders should closely monitor danger close missions to ensure extra caution is applied, any required TSOP guidelines are followed, and commander's risk guidances are not violated.

5-103. FSOs and FDOs should quickly assess the experience of the observers and firing elements whenever possible. FSOs, FIST chiefs, and battery commanders can often answer these queries. In the case of an inexperienced observer, the FDC may need to guide the observer's decisions and give recommendations. If a firing section is inexperienced or undermanned, the platoon leader or sergeant may want to directly observe the firing.

5-104. If the FSE/FIST and FDC can anticipate the danger close situation (such as a FPF), they should discuss the possibility of adjusting in the fires before they are required. If the weather changes significantly over time, the FDC will need to update firing data for a new met and the FDC may coordinate a check round with the observer to verify accuracies.

5-105. Weather and terrain can impact certain munitions such as ICM, smoke, illumination, and variable time (VT) fuzes. High winds can blow ICM bomblets and illumination rounds off course. Some munitions such as smoke, illumination, and WP present a potential fire hazard that may be critical in danger close situations. Dry, grassy terrain, spilled fuel, damaged vehicles loaded with ammunition, wooden structures all present potential hazards.

5-106. Mountainous and urban terrain complicate danger close missions as steep slopes make observer adjustment more difficult to estimate, and crests or buildings can interfere with firing, stopping rounds or causing VT fuzes to function early. High angle fire can alleviate problems with crests or buildings, but may have greater dispersion (probable error). Rocky terrain and hard surfaces present increased risk of ricochets, especially with flat trajectories.

5-107. The OTG angle is a factor because range dispersion of artillery fires is generally greater than lateral dispersion. Consequently there is less risk when the firing trajectory runs parallel to the forward edge of the friendly troops than when it is perpendicular to them.

5-108. Whenever possible, the most accurate weapon system and shell/fuze/charge combination should be used for danger close situations. Ground burst smoke or illumination can be used as marker to verify expected impact, observer, and target locations.

SECTION III – COUNTERFIRE

5-109. The counterfire battle is not a separate battle, but one aspect of the overall combined arms fight. As such it must be properly integrated and synchronized with all elements of the maneuver commander's battle plan. Successful counterfire operations will complement all aspects of the combined arms battle.

5-110. Effective counterfire includes the destruction or neutralization of enemy weapons (to include EW weapons such as jammers), counterfire TA systems (such as radars and EW systems), supporting C2 and communications, transportation, and logistics sites. However, the critical aspect in counterfire operations is information management, which involves two key areas: intelligence/TA and information processing. Friendly and enemy intelligence and TA assets compete to find the various parts of each others indirect fire system, analyze the information, decide the most effective method to attack, and disseminate orders to shooters, jammers and other attack assets. Accuracy (of information and fires), speed, and effectiveness all combine to determine the outcome of the counterfire battle. FM 6-121, *Field Artillery Target Acquisition*, provides thorough tactics, techniques, and procedures for FA TA assets.

RESPONSIBILITIES

5-111. The maneuver commander at brigade and higher levels has overall responsibility for the planning and conduct of counterfire operations as part of the overall combined arms battle plan. In a FA battalion the key counterfire personnel are the FA battalion commander, S2, S3, targeting officer, and where applicable the brigade FSO, radar section leader, and LNO (from a reinforcing battalion, if available). The maneuver commander receives input and recommendations from his FSCOORD, FSO, maneuver S3 and S2, other staff officers involved in counterfire operations. He issues decisions and guidance as necessary to direct counterfire efforts, to ensure effective coordination occurs, and to ensure that counterfire is synchronized with all other battlefield operations. While DS FA battalions receive this guidance through direct involvement with the supported maneuver units, R, GS, and GSR units frequently receive this counterfire guidance through the supported or higher FA HQ.

5-112. The FA battalion commander has overall responsibility for the FA battalion's execution of counterfire responsibilities. In a DS battalion, the FA battalion commander, as the FSCOORD, advises the maneuver commander on the integration of counterfire into combined arms operations, the priority of counterfire within the overall operation, and basic counterfire priorities.

5-113. A FA battalion's counterfire responsibilities will vary dependent on the echelon, tactical mission, and guidance from the maneuver and senior FA commanders. A DS FA battalion may have full responsibility for planning and executing a counterfire plan in support of a maneuver force, while a GS FA battalion's responsibilities may be limited to planning and executing its participation in a larger counterfire plan developed by a FA brigade, DIVARTY, or Corps Arty. Acquired counterfire targets may be fired by the battalion or forwarded through FA or FS channels for attack by other FA or even non-FA assets.

5-114. A major part of counterfire is a FA battalion's counterbattery efforts. The S3, based on the commander's guidance, considers counterbattery force protection measures in all phases of operations, from placement selection, to movement, and firing. He directs measures to decrease the battalion's vulnerability to detection and minimize exposure to enemy fires. He and the S2 attempt to locate and destroy enemy mortars and artillery that pose the greatest threat before they can attack. Reactive counterbattery drills are executed to quickly counter enemy artillery and mortars before they can inflict significant damage on the battalion.

DS/R BATTALIONS

5-115. A DS battalion supporting ground forces usually manages the counterfire battle within the maneuver zone of responsibility. Much or most of this responsibility may be given to a reinforcing unit. At this echelon, the DS battalion commander, as the FSCOORD, is responsible for directing the planning and execution of counterfire operations for the supported maneuver force. This includes:

- Supporting the maneuver commander's force protection priorities, normally stated in terms of assets, functions, and/or positions that are critical to the unit's mission, and when they are critical.
- Development, dissemination, and management of intelligence and order of battle information on the enemy's indirect fire system. This concerns all systems in the maneuver unit's zone of responsibility, as well as any outside the zone that can impact the maneuver unit's mission. This includes:
  - Indirect fire weapon systems – mortars, cannons, rocket, and missile launchers.
  - TA assets – observers, radars, sound/flash systems, and electronic intelligence.
  - C2 elements relevant to counterfire operations.
  - Enemy indirect fire tactics.
  - Enemy counterfire tactics – to include use of lethal and nonlethal ground and air forces against friendly FA.
- Advising the maneuver commander in establishment of attack guidance for counterfire targets.
- Coordination of the maneuver unit's counterfire operations with higher echelon counterfire operations.
- Integration of counterfire into the maneuver plan in a complementary manner that helps enable specific maneuver operations.
- Achieving indirect fire superiority within the maneuver zone.

GS/GSR BATTALIONS

5-116. GS and GSR units are usually not responsible for development of the counterfire battle plan as the force FA HQ or an FA brigade HQ normally will plan counterfire. Much of the counterfire intelligence and order of battle information will be collected, analyzed, and disseminated from these higher echelons. However, radars and other TA or intelligence assets may be attached to, or reporting to GS/GSR units. The GS/GSR FA battalion commander must understand his unit's responsibilities as a role player in the larger counterfire fight, and ensure efficient execution of assigned counterfire tasks. At division level, a GS/GSR battalion may be given significant responsibilities for actual execution of the counterfire fight.

COUNTERFIRE CONSIDERATIONS

TYPES OF COUNTERFIRE

5-117. Counterfire can be proactive or reactive. Corps is generally responsible for proactive, deep counterfire planning and operations. They establish overall priorities and allocate resources that direct or influence lower level counterfire operations. However, the basic principles of proactive and reactive counterfire are applicable even at the DS battalion.

Proactive Counterfire

5-118. Proactive counterfire involves the aggressive use of all available intelligence, TA, and attack assets to quickly find and destroy as much of the enemy's indirect fire assets as possible; preferably before they have a chance to fire or to effect the outcome of the battle.

5-119. Counterfire PIR are identified and prioritized by the maneuver commander based on advice from his staff, FSCOORD, and FSO. Intelligence and TA assets are then tasked to acquire the needed information. Attack assets are aligned against identified and anticipated targets, and general counterfire missions. Intelligence, TA, and attack requirements beyond the unit's capabilities are forwarded to higher HQ for support.

5-120. The force FA HQ (possibly a DS battalion) works closely with the supported maneuver unit to develop and coordinate procedures to receive, analyze, process, and disseminate the acquired information. This involves the establishment of commander's guidances and priorities and of communications channels. Quickfire channels may be used to facilitate the attack of critical counterfire targets or to weight the counterfire battle in a specific area of the battlefield or a particular phase of a battle. Targets may be attacked immediately or developed into preparations and counterfire programs synchronized with maneuver and air operations to gain a synergistic battlefield effect.

5-121. Proactive counterfire involves the aggressive use of non-FA attack systems to include:
- Aircraft - fixed and rotary-wing. Planned missions may be increased and air assets may be encouraged to aggressively seek indirect fire targets of opportunity whenever possible.
- Ground force operations. This may involve quick, moderately deep penetrations oriented on destroying or encircling specific enemy artillery forces, or small, focused, special forces type attacks.

- EW attacks. Proactive jamming and other EW attacks are frequently best used in conjunction with other attack methods, especially major combined arms team attacks as they do not have an attrition effect comparable to other attack methods.
- The use of free fire areas (FFAs), especially where counterfire planners have found, or expect to find, concentrations of enemy indirect fire systems.

5-122. Proactive counterfire frequently involves the dedication of additional indirect fire assets, such as mortars, FA, and naval gunfire to the counterfire effort. This support may be focused during a specified time frame to better allow the synchronization of all assets supporting the counterfire battle. Frequently one or more FA battalions may be given a reinforcing mission with the specific purpose of concentrating on proactive counterfire in a designated maneuver brigade zone. A DS battalion may even briefly receive reinforcement, or priority of fires from an entire FA brigade in order to proactively prosecute counterfire long enough to influence a battle.

5-123. Major, proactive counterfire efforts are especially effective in providing force protection to the combined arms force, enabling major maneuver operations, and in reducing the enemy's ability and will to fight. Because proactive counterfire can be resource intensive, it may be planned for a specific time during a battle. This may be immediately preceding a friendly offensive operation or at a culminating point where a friendly or enemy attack begins to stall. Proactive counterfire can also be used during lulls in the ground fight, when more assets may be available, to reduce enemy FA capability prior to the next major maneuver operation.

Reactive Counterfire

5-124. Reactive counterfire focuses on fires in response to enemy artillery or EW weapons that have begun firing, jamming, or otherwise impacting the overall battle or the counterfire fight. Reactive counterfire is not a passive activity. It requires careful analysis of anticipated and potential reactive counterfire requirements, and the planning and coordination to ensure that effective reactive counterfires are immediately available when and where they are needed.

5-125. In the defense, planning of reactive counterfire programs and counterpreparations is especially critical when an enemy attack is imminent. These programs are fired immediately, while FA and maneuver S2s attempt to identify the main effort and to determine how significantly the enemy has weighted his indirect fire assets in that area. Effective reactive counterfire involves the rapid reallocation, movement, and focus of counterfire assets to quickly counter and eliminate a possible enemy indirect fire advantage.

5-126. During offensive operations, reactive counterfire is essential in protecting attacking forces and in blunting the enemy's ability to use indirect fires to defeat the friendly force attack. Units may establish radar CFZs to provide increased force protection to key attack elements and to allow rapid reactive counterfire to be placed on any enemy indirect fire elements that threaten a protected friendly force. Planners may position CFFZs on locations where enemy FA is suspected but accurate targeting data has not been refined. Quickfire channels and preclearance of fires can be used in these circumstances to facilitate rapid reactive counterfire (and FSCMs such as FFAs). Speed is especially important in reactive counterfire as the enemy artillery or mortars must be destroyed or neutralized before they can do significant damage.

5-127. FA fires are a primary source of reactive counterfire due to the quick reaction time required. FA units may need to quickly move to forward supplementary positions specifically intended for use in attacking deep, reactive counterfire targets. These are often brief, intensive, shoot-and-scoot operations. If extended stays in these positions are necessary, hardening of the PAs should be planned.

AMMUNITION

5-128. Counterfire operations can require significant amounts of ammunition, especially DPICM and extended range munitions. Accurate IPB templating, and the use of counterfire CCLs of ammunition and standard counterfire fire orders can help the S3 and BAO can more accurately anticipate both expenditures and resupply requirements.

5-129. At maneuver brigade level, effective allocation of counterfire tasks is essential to efficient ammunition distribution when a reinforcing unit is involved. If the reinforcing unit is an MLRS unit (or a 155mm unit supporting a 105mm battalion), assigning the reinforcing unit a majority of the counterfire responsibility may allow the DS unit to carry additional ammunition to support the close battle. If both the DS and R unit are a similar caliber, the S3 has more flexibility in directing fire missions, however primary counterfire shooters should be identified to facilitate planning, ammunition management, and positioning. To range some counterfire targets, the designated firing units may need to be well forward with increased amounts of extended range ammunition.

5-130. MLRS is an especially effective counterfire weapon. However, ammunition reload times must be considered. During extensive counterfire operations, the S3, S4, and BAO must be extremely proactive in pushing CCLs forward to the launchers to keep reload times to a minimum.

RADAR MANAGEMENT

5-131. FA counterfire operations frequently involve the attachment or support of one or more counterfire radars. The following paragraphs provide information concerning radar management. FM 6-121 contains detailed information on radar operations and TA.

5-132. The S3, S2, and the radar section leader, in coordination with higher FA headquarters and FSEs of supported maneuver units, must work closely to ensure organic, attached, or assigned radars are effectively managed. In determining the positioning, movement, orientation, and cueing of radars the S3 and S2 must consider:

- Radar capabilities.
- Security.
- Communications.

- Position Considerations.
- Survey.
- Mission.

RADAR POSITIONING

5-133. The primary consideration in selecting a radar position is mission accomplishment. The secondary consideration is survivability. Radar position selection starts when the S2 and/or targeting officer conduct terrain analysis. They use the MCOO, Terrabase, Firefinder positioning analysis system, and the situational template developed and refined by the intelligence section. They conduct map reconnaissance and select several potential positions. After detailed analysis of these, they recommend primary, alternate and supplemental positions to the S3, who accepts, rejects, or modifies the positions. The staff should consider the following when positioning radars:

- Does the position support the commander's intent?
- Where are the enemy's indirect fire systems, or where will they most likely be?
- Where will the enemy focus his indirect fires?
- Can the radar acquire targets throughout the zone of the supported force?
- What are the EW, ground, and air threats to the radar?
- Does the position effectively maximize the radar's range capabilities while simultaneously minimizing the risk of enemy TA?
- Does the position offer a screening crest?
- What is the track volume and aspect angle?
- When applicable, are AN/TPQ-36 and AN/TPQ-37 radars positioned to complement each other?
- Does the position offer good communications with the FA battalion?
- Does the position consider future operations and movement?
- Where are the radar alternate positions? Supplemental positions?
- Are there positions to move forward or fall back to?
- Where are the positions of other friendly units?
- Is the radar on a high-speed avenue of approach that could potentially make it vulnerable to rapid advancement by the enemy?
- Where are possible sites for enemy chemical strikes or air assaults?
- Is the route clear of enemy, chemicals, and mines?
- What is the friendly scheme of maneuver?

5-134 When possible, the radar section leader or section chief should reconnoiter the sites and provide input to the S3. The S3 coordinates the radar's position(s) with the maneuver unit S3 via the FSE.

RADAR ZONE MANAGEMENT

5-135. Radar zone management involves the use of both sectors of search and various types of zones. The S3, S2, targeting officer, radar section leader, and the brigade, division, or corps FSE work together to ensure that sectors and zones adequately support the overall plan. This involves close coordination with their counterparts in R (or reinforced), GSR, and GS FA units and higher/lateral FA HQ.

Sectors Of Search

5-136. Sectors of search are areas on the battlefield where radars focus their TA capabilities. The S3 and S2/targeting officer determine sectors of search during the decide function of the targeting process, on the basis of a thorough IPB. They also make decisions concerning what targets should be acquired and attacked, where and when targets are likely to be found, and who can locate them. Doctrinal employment considerations, in conjunction with templates and intelligence produced in the IPB process, dictate the areas in which the radar should focus its searches. The location of friendly boundaries and FS coordinating measures may also affect the assignment of sectors of search. The area given to a specific radar as a sector of search may be affected by the positioning of a common sensor boundary (CSB).

Zones

5-137. Zones are a means of prioritizing radar sectors of search into areas of greater and lesser importance. Zones allow radar managers to orient on the maneuver commander's battlefield priorities. Four types of zones can be entered into a Firefinder radar computer. These are CFZs, CFFZs, artillery target intelligence zones (ATIZs), and censor zones (CZs). The firing unit locations the radar has developed as targets are displayed for transmission in the order of the priority of the zones in which targets are located. The zone priorities for location identification, from highest to lowest, are:

- Locations of weapons firing into a CFZ.
- Weapons firing from a CFFZ.
- Weapons firing from an ATIZ.

5-138. All other weapon firing locations are displayed after locations associated with these zones. All locations other than those associated with a CFZ or CFFZ are formatted by the radar computer as target reports in ATI;CDR format. If the radar has no zones loaded, then all locations are transmitted in the ATI;CDR format. The radar computer will not develop weapon locations that are within a censor zone. See FM 6-121 for additional information on radar zones.

RADAR MOVEMENT

5-139. The S2 or targeting officer moves the radar based on METT-TC and the radar's accumulated cueing times. Moving the radar at a critical time in the battle may cause the supported unit to take heavy losses. The radar should move when the enemy's FA is silenced or moving. The best way to anticipate the enemy FA movement is to force it to move with counterfire. When the radar moves, coverage must be coordinated with the force FA HQ.

5-140. During the wargaming process, the battalion S2 and S3 decide when they want to try to force the enemy's FA to move and when accumulated cueing time can cause radar detection. They include these events as decision points on the DST.

RADAR CUEING

5-141. The longer a radar radiates, the more susceptible it is to enemy acquisition. Cueing allows the radar to transmit intermittently, for relatively short periods in order to reduce vulnerability. Cueing should be event driven. The critical factor when planning radar cueing is responsiveness. It should allow for the radar to locate the enemy positions during initial volleys of fire, preferably the first rounds.

5-142. The S2 and/or targeting officer has basically two techniques for cueing: situational (proactive) and demand (reactive). While situational cueing in generally preferred, the S2 can use these separately or in combination.

5-143. **Situational cueing** can potentially be the most responsive. This method ties cueing to events and/or triggers that are determined during the IPB and planning processes. For example, during offensive operations an event or trigger may be a breaching or air assault operation. In a defensive or offensive operation, cueing may be tied to suspected enemy phases of fire depicted on the DST. Situational cueing also focuses the radar on the commander's intent and what is critical.

5-144. **Demand cueing** is the activation of a radar once the enemy has begun firing. For demand cueing to be effective cueing agents must be designated and a responsive communications system between the agents and radar established. Possible cueing agents may include COLTs, FISTs, OH-58Ds, scouts, FSOs, intelligence and electronic warfare (IEW) systems, or the S2.

5-145. The S2 and/or targeting officer in the controlling FA TOC will establish cueing guidance to include authorized agents, communications links and conditions under which the radar may be cued. The information will be published in the TA tab to the FA support plan. Specific cueing guidance must be established to fully exploit the radar's capabilities and still minimize or eliminate unnecessary radiation that may result in the radar being located by ELINT. An important part of cueing is the cueing schedule. The cueing schedule informs the radar on how long to radiate. FM 6-121 states: "Maximum continuous transmission time for Firefinder radars should never exceed 2 minutes when an EW threat exists." Some cueing guidelines used effectively by units at the National Training Center were as follows:
- If the ELINT threat is high, the radar should cue no more the 15 to 30 seconds "on" and 15 to 60 second "off," and
- During the enemy's most intense fires, the cueing time should increase to 30 to 45 second "on" and 5 to 15 seconds "off".

WARGAMING

5-146. The S2 and targeting officer plan, coordinate, and synchronize the counterfire fight during the wargaming process. They recommend CFFZs, decision points, and triggers for cueing and moving radars and for changing zones. They coordinate with the FSEs for supported force CFZs. The following should be considered when planning counterfire during wargaming:
- What is the counterfire unit? (Unit designated by the S3 on the FDO's recommendation, considering range, munition, and position.)
- What will happen if multiple acquisitions occur simultaneously?

- What is the standard fire order? (The FDO recommends a standard fire order for S3's approval, ensuring it meets the commander's guidance.)
- What are the decision points on when to move the radar? (Decision points are based on the phases of fire or accumulated cue time.)
- What are the decision points to change the radar zones? (The decision points are based on the phases of fire or maneuver unit's advance.)
- What are the decision points on when to start cueing?
- Are radar zones planned throughout the depth and width of the battlefield, anticipating enemy and friendly movement?
- When does the S3 want the enemy's artillery to move?
- Does the plan account for overwhelming success? For catastrophic failure?
- How many tubes must be destroyed to meet the commander's intent?
- Can the CFFZs be pre-cleared with the FSOs? Consider use of FSCMs such as FFAs and RFAs.)
- What are the decision points on massing the battalion on the enemy's artillery?
- What is the cueing schedule during the difference phases of fire?
- What is the methodology to track the destruction/force ratio of the enemy artillery?

5-147. There are several critical decision points in the wargaming process. One of the most important involves forcing the enemy's forward artillery to move, which allows the radar and the counterfire unit to move (without jeopardizing force protection). This may be accomplished by suppressive, neutralization or destruction fires. Another critical decision arises when target acquisitions occur simultaneously: the counterfire unit can become overwhelmed. Table 5-4 lists the options available when the radar receives multiple acquisitions.

Table 5-4. Multiple Target Acquisitions

Type Targets	Direct Support Unit With A Reinforcing Battalion	Direct Support Unit Without a Reinforcing Battalion
Multiple Targets in Range	• R Bn engages one target and passes other target to the DS Bn. • R Bn engages both targets simultaneously. • R Bn engages both targets sequentially.	• DS Bn engages both targets simultaneously. • DS Bn engages both targets sequentially. • DS Bn engages one target and passes the other target to force FA HQ/FSE for attack with other assets.
Multiple Targets in Range, but the DS Bn is Involved in Missions with a Higher Priority	• R Bn engages one target and passes the other target to the force FA HQ/FSE for attack with other assets.	• DS Bn passes the targets to the force FA HQ/FSE for attack with other assets.
Multiple Targets - Some Out of Range	• R Bn and DS Bn engage the target within range and pass the other target to force FA HQ/FSE for attack with other assets.	• DS Bn engages the target within range and passes the other target to the force FA HQ/FSE for attack with other assets.

REHEARSING COUNTERFIRE

5-148. Counterfire rehearsal synchronizes the counterfire fight with the scheme of maneuver and the sensor-to-shooter link. The S2 and/or targeting officer should rehearse the counterfire plan with the radar and intelligence sections. They should rehearse management of radar zones during different phases, using radio nets (digital and voice with cueing agents); decision points for movements and prepare to march order; times to be ready to radiate (cueing schedules); and reporting accumulated cueing.

COUNTERFIRE DRILL

5-149. The following paragraphs provide a scenario that describes possible TOC counterfire procedures. They focus on the interactions of the staff, which are most important in synchronizing the counterfire fight.

PLAN

5-150. During the MDMP and wargaming processes the maneuver and FA battalion staffs identified counterfire, targeting, and TA data, requirements, and responsibilities. The OPORD, FS annex, FASP appendix and TA tab provide all necessary information. All FA assets are in place, ready to support the mission. The battalion has an attached Firefinder radar.

ACQUIRE

5-151. As the battle begins, the radar acquires enemy artillery firing from a CFFZ. The radar section assigns a target number from its allocated block of numbers and immediately calls in the counterfire information grids (impact and origin).

DECIDE

5-152. The O&I section receives the radar fire mission digitally or by voice. The automated FD system operator or radio operator sounds off with "fire mission, radar" or a similar SOP phrase to alert the FDC. (For a basic radar acquisition (ATI:CDR) the operator would sound off with "radar acquisition" or a similar, by SOP, phrase and the information processed to determine what action was required.) Then he announces target number, origin and impact grids and time acquired to the S2 and assistant S3. The FDO immediately sends a fire mission to the battery(ies), with a fire order of "AMC" for MLRS, or "do not load" (DNL) for cannons. The assistant S3 and S2 plot the grids. The assistant S3 makes a quick map spot, determines if units are in range of the target and informs the S3. The S2 begins to verify his template and identify the type unit(s). The S3 requests clearance of fires through the FSE, if necessary. The FSE clears the fires (through maneuver channels) and the FDO cancels "DNL."

DELIVER

5-153. The FDO fires the mission and requests additional fires from the force FA HQ, if necessary. If attack criteria is achieved, the S3 directs end-of-mission (EOM) on that target. Alternative actions the S3 may direct are:

- **Handoff.** The battalion may be forced to handoff the mission to force FA HQ or FSE if it cannot service the mission.
- **End of Mission.** The S-3/FDO may have to direct EOM before the mission is fired because FSCMs or boundaries are violated and clearance cannot be granted in a timely manner, clearance of fires is denied, or there is a duplication of missions.

ASSESS

5-154. The O&I section coordinates with maneuver and force FA HQ to receive BDA. The S2 updates logs and revises enemy artillery positions based on origin grids, and revises enemy most likely COA based on impact grids. The targeting officer evaluates the S2's revised enemy artillery positions and recommends refinement to the radar zones (in coordination with targeting officers in higher/supporting headquarters). The S2 may also need to update the RDO, make cueing schedule changes, move the radar, and arrange for coverage during movement. The S3 may also need to relocate firing elements.

THEATER MISSILE DEFENSE (TMD)

5-155. TMD is a joint mission, accomplished by establishing an effective battle management/command, control, communications, computers, and intelligence (BM/C4I) system that permits the joint force commander to integrate and enhance the joint force's capabilities to:
- Destroy theater ballistic missiles (TBMs) in-flight (active defense).
- Reduce the vulnerability of friendly force and critical assets from the effects of theater missile attacks (passive defense).
- Destroy hostile theater missile capability by offensive actions against missile launchers; C4I; and logistics facilities; and other theater missile infrastructure (attack operations).

5-156. Army FA plays a key role in TMD attack operations by supporting TA operations and by executing deep fires to attack all elements of the hostile TBM system. This mission is primarily conducted by rocket/missile units under the control of corps, joint task force (JTF), or other echelon above corps commands. However, in smaller theaters or during deep, rapid maneuver penetrations, TBMs may periodically be within the ranges of cannon or rocket systems. Firefinder radar support for TMD, currently limited by range capabilities, will improve as newer, increasingly capable radars are fielded.

CONSIDERATIONS

5-157. FA participation in TMD attack operations is in essence a counterfire operation. However, sensor-to-shooter response times are especially critical in TMD operations as TBMs usually displace immediately after firing. Also, TMD sensor-to-shooter coordination is frequently more complex because of the number and type of TA/intelligence/communications assets involved, and the extreme distances between sensors, shooters, and C2.

5-158. FA weapons and TA systems supporting TMD operations are frequently in a dedicated role, making them unavailable for other support. TMD support may be part of a battalion's standard FA tactical mission (normally a unit in a GS role), or may be assigned as a non-standard mission. Because of the complexity of TMD support, FA battalion commanders must ensure that responsibilities are clearly defined as the responsibilities inherent in standard FA tactical missions may not be appropriate.

5-159. While TMD support is usually a higher echelon operation involving only a few FA units, all FA units need to understand the attack guidances involved if TBMs are acquired as targets of opportunity. TBMs are usually high value/high payoff targets, attacked immediately upon detection. However, FA battalion S2s should have a thorough knowledge of the enemy threat and recent intelligence on NBC considerations. S3s, FDOs, and FSOs (where applicable) should understand the command's attack criteria and ensure that digital attack guidances reflect current, accurate information

5-160. Airspace management is a critical issue in TMD operations. While this is usually coordinated through FS channels, FA battalion commanders must understand the issues and ensure that their units both provide accurate unit data and receive and post all fire control measures.

SECTION IV – SUPPRESSION OF ENEMY AIR DEFENSES

5-161. SEAD involves all activities to neutralize, destroy, or temporarily degrade surface-based enemy air defenses (EADs) by lethal and non-lethal means. Effective SEAD increases friendly aircraft survivability, enhances air operations, and facilitates rapid US air superiority. This in turn supports the ground maneuver and counterfire battles. Army SEAD operations are primarily designed to support operational and tactical plans by protecting air assets near the FLOT or during cross-FLOT operations. However, the increasing range of FA weapons has extended the FA's ability to support increasingly deeper air operations.

5-162. The bulk of the planning, targeting, and coordination for SEAD support is usually done in FSEs. Both ground force FSEs and aviation unit FSEs may be working together in planning and coordinating SEAD for an air operation in support of the ground force. Additional information on SEAD can be found in FM 6-20, FM 6-20-30, and FM 6-20-40.

5-163. FA battalions DS to ground or aviation units may be very involved in overall SEAD planning and coordination due to the battalion commander's FSCOORD responsibilities. This includes planning and executions of both EFSTs and EFATs. SEAD responsibilities for other FA battalions may be limited to executing SEAD related EFATs. However, there may be instances where a GS, GSR, or R FA battalion plays a major role in the overall SEAD for an operation. In this situation, the FA battalion commander (and/or the S3) may go to the planning HQ or FSE and actively participate in the detailed SEAD planning. GS, GSR, and R battalions should also consider the possibility of establishing temporary liaison with the aviation or ground force FSE during the planning and execution of critical SEAD missions.

5-164. FA battalion involvement in SEAD may include:
- Planning, conducting, or participating in SEAD programs designed to degrade and suppress EAD assets throughout the zone or to destroy, degrade, and suppress EAD within a specific area or corridor.
- Planning, executing, or participating in SEAD fire plans designed to support specific air operations.
- Providing immediate fires to rotary or fixed-wing aviation assets in support of an ongoing air operation.

5-165. A SEAD plan or program may involve several FA battalions, with divisional cannons and MLRS providing fires along ingress and egress routes while corps MLRS units fire deeper SEAD fires. Early identification of air routes and attack by fire (ABF) areas is crucial in focusing TA assets and intelligence templating efforts, in developing attack plans, and in coordinating air corridors and ACAs with FA positioning requirements.

5-166. One technique for localized SEAD for a deep attack is to prep the ABFs with FA fires before occupation by the attack helicopters. MLRS fires are well suited for this role and may prep all ABFs simultaneously. Time separation is critical to preventing fratricide and to allow the helicopters to occupy the ABFs unopposed. The unit should fire the ABF prep based on an H-hour with the last rounds impacting from one to ten minutes before the aircraft arrive in their ABFs. Terrain and weather conditions must be taken into account since large amounts of dust and debris may disrupt the aircraft's ability to begin locating and engaging targets in the engagement area.

5-167. FA fires can also be used to orient the attack aircraft to the engagement area. They should be fired as the aircraft are arriving in their ABFs and are establishing situational awareness. The EA prep serves two purposes. First, it suppresses the enemy elements that are the target of the attack and therefore any EADs that are accompanying them. Second, the flashes from the munitions provide the air crews with a visual reference of the location of the targets.

5-168. SEAD targets should be fired during egress in the same fashion as the ingress targets. Any targets discovered during ingress should be included in the egress program. The egress SEAD should be fired on-call if the attack aircraft can communicate with the FSO. If all communications with the helicopters is lost during the deep attack, then the egress SEAD should be fired on a planned time schedule. This allows the aircraft to know when it is safe to proceed down their egress route without being hit by SEAD fires.

CONSIDERATIONS

5-169. The battalion S3 and FDO work closely with the appropriate FSE, maneuver S3, and higher FA HQ to maintain current mission data. They review SEAD EFATs (and EFSTs) to ensure firing units will be in position, on time, with the necessary ammunition, able to fire the missions. They review the relative priorities, potential mission conflicts, and enemy threats to better anticipate how alternative or backup plans must be executed. The S3 verifies who has triggering responsibility, who has what authority to change mission factors, and who he or the firing unit must contact if problems develop. He ensures the battalion FDO and firing units (primary and backup) are properly briefed in all aspects of the SEAD mission.

5-170. Firing positions must not interfere with established air corridors or restricted operating zones (ROZs). ROZs are areas where aviation unit C2 aircraft operate (frequently over friendly terrain). S3s should query FSEs or force FA HQ early to identify air corridors, ROZs, and ACAs.

5-171. The primary and backup triggers for each SEAD EFAT should be evaluated during rehearsals. Timing is frequently important in SEAD fires to prevent fratricide of friendly air and obscuration of the main target. Aircraft may arrive early or late, targeting information may not develop, or the FA firing unit may be unavailable, delayed, or involved in another mission. The S3 must be able to quickly decide whether or not to fire or abort the mission. Since aborting a FA SEAD mission can have serious impact on the air mission, wargaming analysis and prior coordination are critical to understanding the commander's guidances and priorities that should guide the S3's decision. The FA battalion commander may retain abort decision-making authority on critical SEAD EFATs.

5-172. Aerial observer procedures should be reviewed in case immediate fires are requested. Requirements for fixed-wing observers will be different than for helicopter-based observers. Individual requests by flight leaders (pilots) for SEAD support are treated as targets of opportunity. These targets can be added to the current SEAD plan and fired during egress or during a re-attack of the target. The S3 and FDO must anticipate these missions, considering time, ammunition, firing units, and potential target types, and develop tentative fire orders for the more likely scenarios.

5-173. The S3 or FDO may have to recommend or make rapid adjustment to the SEAD fire plan to adjust for changing circumstances. When adjusting fire plans and servicing of immediate SEAD fire requests the S3 and FDO must carefully review the potential impact on other fires. Successful execution of adjustments depends on a complete understanding of the commander's intent, priorities, and the concept of operations, and a thorough review of branches and sequels during planning will facilitate these adjustments during execution, and accurate situational awareness (operational and CSS).

5-174. Smoke may be used to obscure enemy air defenses or to signal the lifting or shifting of fires to allow aircraft to attack. The S3 should ensure the use of smoke is well coordinated.

5-175. The S2 works closely with targeting officers in the FSEs and with S2s in maneuver, aviation, or higher FA HQ to ensure the battalion has the most current targeting information. If the battalion performs SEAD targeting, the S2 must submit requests for SEAD related intelligence and targeting information as early as possible. Direct coordination with aviation, air force, and MI elements may be necessary to get accurate information in a timely manner. The battalion S2 or targeting officer in a FA battalion may briefly move to the FSE responsible for planning SEAD support to an operation.

5-176. SEAD targets include C2, ADA weapons, and radars. Often, one C2 facility or radar will service several EAD weapons and are thus key targets. Because of the ranges involved in supporting deep operations, target locations must be as accurate as possible. During coordination of SEAD targeting, FA battalion S2s and S3s should discuss target location accuracy with FSEs when they identify potential problems.

5-177. The sources for development of SEAD targets in the close battle area are primarily visual observation by ground and air observers, electronic and imagery assets, or templating techniques. SEAD targets supporting deep air operations are provided primarily by Air Force tactical air reconnaissance flight reports, other aircraft reports, or satellite imagery available through corps and echelons above corps intelligence coordinators, all of which may require more coordination and/or special communications or automation arrangements.

5-178. The S6, working with the S3, reviews SEAD EFATs for unique communications and automation requirements. Due to the varied C2 arrangements, participants, and distances involved unusual communications arrangements may be necessary. Retrans or relay of voice and digital traffic may be necessary. Additional communications equipment may be warranted. Quickfire channels may be used. The battalion S6 may need to work directly with a ground or aviation force FSE to ensure communications arrangements are adequate. Alternate (backup) communications plans should be developed.

SECTION V – METEOROLOGY

5-179. Met data are one of the prerequisites for accurate predicted fire. With today's emphasis on first round fire for effect and trends toward longer distances, accurate met corrections for artillery fires are crucial to:
- Conserve ammunition.
- Decrease time in adjustment.
- Obtain a greater surprise effect.
- Reduce the potential for fratricide.

5-180. FA met involves the determination of current atmospheric conditions. Atmospheric conditions along the trajectory of a projectile or rocket directly affect its accuracy and may cause the projectile or rocket to miss the desired point of impact. A 5 to 10 percent effect on the firing tables is possible even with stable atmospheric conditions. For example, tests in Southwest Asia have shown that firing artillery at maximum ranges in extreme heat and low air density resulted in met corrections up to 4,700 meters.

5-181. While most FA battalions are primarily receivers and users of met information, FA battalions in separate maneuver brigades have an organic met section, and thus a responsibility for management of met operations. This includes preparation of the met plan as a part of the FASP/FSP (An example of a met tab is in Appendix A). During contingency or stability and support operations, any FA battalion could potentially have a met section attached. Detailed information on FA met is in FM 6-15, while use of met in gunnery solutions is covered in FM 6-40.

JOINT/COMBINED MET CONSIDERATIONS

5-182. During joint and combined operations, an FA battalion may need to rely on non-US Army met support. The following information will assist the FA battalion in understanding met availability in joint and/or combined operations. Requests for met support from joint or combined met elements should be coordinated well in advance. In coordinating this support the S3 should request assistance from corps or division met personnel to ensure that the data can be received in a useable format, that it will be conducted within the appropriate area, and that it will be provided on the needed schedule.

Joint Operations Met

5-183. The US Air Force (USAF) has numerous fixed and deployable weather teams deployed throughout the world capable of performing upper air soundings. The information they gather cannot be used for ballistic solutions to the gunnery problem. The FA battalion S3 should understand that the presence of a USAF met team does not provide a ballistic met capability.

5-184. The US Navy has mobile environmental teams capable of sounding he atmosphere and producing ballistic data. The message produced is in STANAG format. These teams are deployed on a mission basis. They typically support their own units, but also support joint operations and could be requested to support US Army artillery operations.

Combined Operations Met

5-185. The US and several of its allies have agreed on standard met message formats that allow the exchange of atmospheric data among member countries with the assurance that the same atmospheric standards were used. Combined force artillery commanders and S3s may be able to assist the FA battalion with met issues.

BASIC MET GUIDANCE

5-186. The basic decisions concerning met data involve the following:
- Verifying that the met message is free of major errors.
- Determining which met message to use when multiple messages are available.
- Determining how long the met message can be used before the data may no longer be valid.

5-187. Guidance is normally provided by TSOP or in the force FA HQ met tab of the FASP in the division or corps FSP. However, at times the FA Bn FDO, or the battery/platoon FDOs may need to make the key decisions concerning met usage. The general order of preference for determining which met data should be used is as follows:
- Current met message from a station within 20 km of the firing point.
- Current met message from the nearest station more than 20 km from the firing point.
- Met messages more than two hours old but from a station within 20 km of the firing points. A 4-hour old met message may be used except when day/night transitions or frontal passages are occurring.

MET MESSAGE VALIDITY CONSIDERATIONS

5-188. The validity of a met message decreases with time, distance, and weather. The accuracy of a met message decreases as the distance from the met sounding site increases. Local topography has a pronounced effect on the distance that met data can be reasonably extended. In mountainous terrain, or near large bodies of water, distinct variations in atmospheric conditions occur over short distances. Met messages for artillery are considered valid 10 to 20 km from the balloon release point depending on the nature of the terrain.

5-189. The passage of time decreases the accuracy of a met message because of the changing nature of weather. There are no specific rules for determining the usable time, since that determination will depend on the characteristics of the atmosphere, periods of transition, met section movement, personnel, supplies and equipment, and the altitude. Generally, the more the weather changes, the less valid the met becomes.

REGISTRATION

5-190. If the current applied met appears invalid and a valid met is not available the S3 and FDO should consider conducting a registration or using residual data from an adjust fire mission until a valid met is available.

Chapter 6

Movement and Positioning Considerations

The movement and positioning of FA battalions on today's fluid, crowded battlefield is a complicated process involving terrain management, selection of positions, movement planning and control, and the coordination of survey support for firing and TA operations. Clearance, coordination, and synchronization are operative terms that are critical to the successful conduct of FA movement and positioning. FA units are competing for battle space with all other elements, and the increased use of dispersed, scoot-and-shoot tactics by newer FA weapon systems creates a significant challenge for the FA battalion commander. This chapter provides the FA commander and staff with information to aid in planning the displacement and movement of the FA battalion. It has five major sections: Section I addresses terrain management, Section II focuses on positioning, Section III covers movement, Section IV discusses survey, and Section V provides a brief overview on deployment.

SECTION I – TERRAIN MANAGEMENT

6-01. Terrain management is primarily the responsibility of the unit that controls the ground in a particular area or sector. This is usually an Army maneuver unit, however, especially during stability operations and support operations, the controlling agency could be a host nation government or military force, or a UN-affiliated military force or civilian relief organization.

6-02. FA battalions are integrally involved in the terrain management process as the positions and routes that the FA requires to accomplish its mission must be carefully planned and coordinated with all the units who control or use the required terrain. Terrain management involves the planning and coordination of positions and movements for units and individual elements or teams that are part of, or in support of, a FA battalion. Terrain management coordination is primarily the responsibility of the S3, however the, S2, S4, S6, and, where applicable, FSOs all play a role in the planning and coordination of positions and movements. Because a maneuver unit usually controls the required terrain, FSEs play a critical role in terrain management for all FA assets that must operate within a particular maneuver unit's zone.

6-03. The S2 provides valuable advice on the terrain, road and weather conditions, security and threat considerations (military and civilian), obstacles, and any intelligence information related to positioning and movement. The S2 also frequently assists the S3 with coordination of MP support for moves, for reconnaissance of routes or PAs, and for acquiring maps or photographs of areas.

6-04. The FSEs with the maneuver units are responsible for assisting the maneuver S3 and the FA S3s in the coordination of positions and routes for FA units. The FSO is in the best position to monitor the current locations of all friendly units while simultaneously understanding FA requirements. Frequently, the brigade FSO will be working on behalf of and in conjunction with the FSCOORD/DS FA battalion commander. In addition to coordinating terrain management issues for supporting DS and R FA battalions, the brigade FSO may be involved in coordinating with division or corps FSEs or FA HQs for battle space for division and corps GS units operating within or moving through the brigade zone.

6-05. Corps and divisional GS/GSR units frequently coordinate terrain management through DIVARTY or Corps Arty. Occasionally, the higher level coordination will consist of general area coordination. The FA battalion will then conduct direct coordination with the lowest level maneuver unit to obtain the specific locations or routes needed for the battalion. Usually the brigade FSE is the best element with which to coordinate.

POSITION COORDINATION

6-06. Terrain management for a FA battalion involves the selection and coordination of numerous types of positions. The type of FA unit or element and the type of position required will have various implications for terrain management for PAs. (A PA is a general planning area within which a unit or element will position and operate, based on METT-TC and the actual terrain within the area. The boundaries of a PA describe the area within which a commander can select an appropriate position or positions. The size of a PA is dependent on METT-TC, especially the mission, type of unit and weapon system, echelon, and tactics. A battalion PA may contain smaller PAs for the HQ, trains, and subordinate units. A unit may designate separate smaller PAs for planning primary, supplementary, and alternate positions, or a single larger PA that allows for the siting of more than one of these position types within the limits of the PA.) While CP positions, hide locations, or assembly areas usually may be placed near other friendly units, weapon firing areas or radar operating positions should generally not be positioned close to other elements (e.g., BSAs, CPs, critical logistics or communications sites, populated areas) without appropriate consideration for the risks. As much as possible, S3s and FSEs should coordinate the use of PAs large enough to allow some flexibility in the final placement of the unit or element. Designation of too small an area may not provide enough terrain for the unit to properly site or camouflage all of its elements. Platoon or battery firing areas must be large enough to allow proper dispersion, and in the case of MLRS or Paladin, to allow for the selection of multiple firing points within the area.

6-07. Some weapon systems have special considerations. As an example, the danger area around an MLRS launcher, due to blast and flying debris during a launch, is 300m to the front and 400m to the rear of the launcher. FSOs must ensure that all unit commanders understand the risks and stay clear of

FA weapon systems. FA battery and platoon commanders must also understand terrain management priorities and allocations to avoid endangering or disrupting friendly units. The maneuver commander may designate specific sections of terrain as "No-Go" areas for FA weapon firing positions. This may be used more frequently for MLRS due to the larger firing signature and danger area.

6-08. When CP or trains positions must be placed near other similar elements (such as the BSA), consideration should be given to consolidating elements or, as a minimum, consolidating defensive plans. Both vehicular and electronic traffic should be considered in the planning and coordination of positions.

6-09. Terrain management is a three-dimensional process as firing locations must be coordinated with air corridors and other three-dimensional control measures. FSEs play a key role during planning by obtaining as much information as possible as early as possible from Army aviation and Air Force elements. Current and future operations must be considered as certain control measures, such as air corridors, may not go into effect until later in an operation.

6-10. FA battalion S3s should try to identify their PA requirements as early as possible so that FSEs can work with the maneuver units to prioritize and allocate battlespace early in the planning sequence. Alternate and supplementary position requirements must be considered and continuous coordination and communication is necessary. Alternate and supplementary positions are especially vulnerable to occupation by other Army units or even displaced civilians.

6-11. Frequently, coordination may also be required with local civilian governments. This coordination may be accomplished by the maneuver S3 as part of overall terrain coordination for the combined arms force, or the responsibility may fall to the FA battalion after general position requests have been approved by the maneuver S3.

MOVEMENT COORDINATION

6-12. FA battalions may move individually or as part of a larger force such as a maneuver brigade or a FA brigade. The movements may consist of administrative or tactical road marches, combined arms team movements or combat formations, or the short tactical displacement of elements.

6-13. Terrain management issues concerning FA movements include more that just ensuring that FA movements are synchronized with the battle plan. Since many Army units compete for limited routes, FA movements must be coordinated and synchronized as part of the overall force movement plan. Frequently a FA battalion will require several routes for movement of all battalion elements. Often, the time allocated for a FA unit to transit a given route or routes will determine the type of movement technique used, the speed traveled, and the number of rest stops. Careful coordination with the maneuver unit responsible for the routes is necessary to ensure that FA units are adequately prioritized and included in overall movement plans. Positions for assembly areas or rest/refuel stops may be necessary.

6-14. When the FA battalion moves as part of a larger force, the FA S3 must understand all larger unit TSOP issues, control measures, movement techniques, and the expected reactions to ground or air attack. In a combined arms force move, elements of the FA battalion may need to be dispersed throughout the larger force to allow adequate artillery support.

6-15. As with PAs, close coordination between FA battalion S3s and FSEs is critical to terrain management for moves. Conflicts that arise may be forwarded through maneuver channels as well as FA channels. FSEs usually try to monitor other unit movements to ensure they do not interfere with the FA movement plan. The FA battalion S4 is also in a good position to learn about the movement of other CSS elements and should pass on information to the S3 as appropriate.

SECTION II – POSITIONING

6-16. A FA battalion requires a wide variety of position locations in the accomplishment of its mission. The methods and techniques of organizing and positioning the elements of a FA battalion are usually situationally dependent. However, several standard positioning principles must be considered. Reconnaissance is also very important to the positioning and movement of the FA battalion. This section addresses position selection considerations, types of positions, and reconnaissance.

POSITION AREA SELECTION CONSIDERATIONS

6-17. Several factors influence the S3's decision on where and how to organize and position the firing batteries, trains and CPs. The specific details of many of these factors will be identified during MDMP and IPB development. Some of the factors the FA staff should consider in PA selection are:
- Mission.
- The tactical situation.
- Force mix and weapon capabilities and limitations (to include attached/R/GSR FA).
- Logistical considerations.
- Impact of ammunition constraints (types, quantities, achievable ranges).
- Survivability.
- Future operations.
- The zone of the supported unit.
- Communications.
- Enemy capabilities.
- Weather and terrain.

6-18. Firing units should be positioned laterally and in depth. This increases their survivability and their flexibility in responding to calls for fire across the zone of action of the supported unit. The S3 must also consider minimum and maximum range implications (weapons and ammunition) and requirements to mass fires. In static or offensive operations, where the FLOT is moving forward, the S3 generally wants to position firing elements so the majority of the range fan (such as 2/3's) is forward of the FLOT or forward edge of the battle area (FEBA). In retrogrades, or other operations where the FLOT is moving or may move rearward, the S3 may position firing units further behind the FLOT or FEBA. In all cases, the mission, METT-TC, and location of critical targets will be the primary considerations for positioning firing elements.

TYPES OF POSITION AREAS

6-19. The following list describes the types of positions that may be used by a FA battalion. CP locations are discussed in more detail in Chapter 2. CSS positions are discussed in Chapter 7. Positioning considerations for radar are covered in Chapter 5. Radio retrans sites are discussed in Chapter 3. Battery level positions are discussed in detail in FM 6-50, FM 6-60, and FM 6-70.

- Hide/firing positions/areas for cannon, rocket, and missile systems.
- Battery/platoon, battery operations center (BOC)/POC locations.
- CP locations: main CP, ALOC, BSOC, JTOC.
- Logistics locations: UMCP, refuel/rearm points, ammunition points.
- Assembly areas.
- Radar section or met section positions.
- Radio retrans sites.
- Primary, alternate, supplementary positions.
  - A **primary position** is one from which a unit will accomplish its assigned tactical mission.
  - An **alternate position** is one to which a unit moves if the primary position becomes untenable or unsuitable for accomplishing the mission. The alternate position must allow the unit to perform the same mission assigned to it in the primary position.
  - A **supplementary position** is one to which a unit moves to perform a specific mission. As an example, a firing battery may be instructed to use a supplementary position to fire a SCATMINE or smoke mission.
- Current and planned/successive positions.

6-20. Locations such as CPs and logistics positions may be established separately or may be located with each other, with other FA elements, or with non-FA elements. For example, a DS FA battalion CP may be co-located with the supported maneuver brigade CP; or the battalion trains may be co-located with the brigade trains. A DS and R FA battalion may consolidate UMCPs.

ASSEMBLY AREAS

6-21. A FA battalion may occupy an assembly area as an individual entity or as part of a larger force. DS and R units may occasionally occupy an assembly area as part of a combined arms force. GS and GSR units may be part of a FA brigade assembly area. There are two basic methods for organizing assembly areas:

- As a single assembly area divided into sub-sections.
- As separate, dispersed assembly areas for sub-elements or groups of sub-elements.

6-22. These methods are discussed below. While these paragraphs address combined arms assembly areas, the two techniques can also be used for establishing FA only assembly areas. GS and GSR FA battalions may sometimes occupy FA brigade assembly areas established on similar techniques. Additional information on maneuver brigade assembly areas can be found in FM 71-3, *The Armored and Mechanized Infantry Brigade*.

A Sectioned Assembly Area

6-23. In this method the force (in this case a maneuver brigade) divides the assembly area into subordinate areas of responsibility, with subordinate battalions around the perimeter. C2, CS, and CSS units and elements are located in the middle. This technique provides excellent perimeter defense. In a combined arms assembly area, the FA battalion may disperse its batteries within the center based on the situation. This can allow 360-degree FS, with each battery oriented on a maneuver battalion (see Figure 6-1).

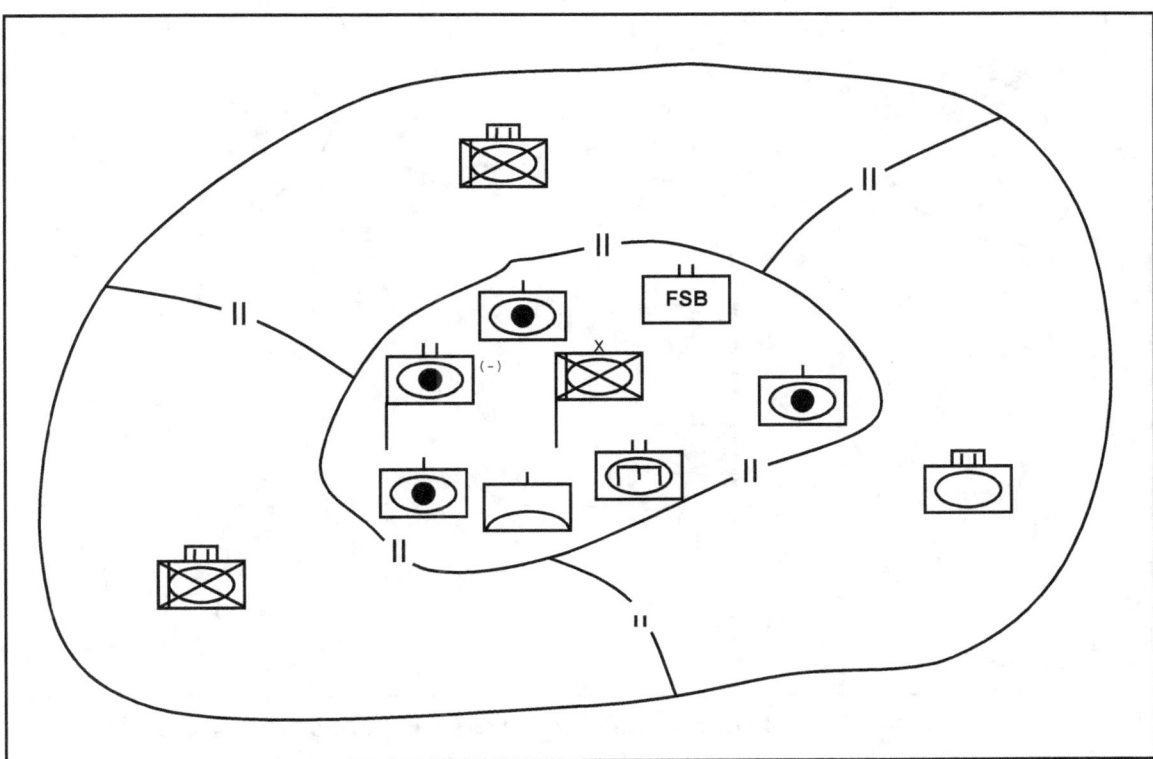

Figure 6-1. Example of a FA Battalion in a Sectioned Assembly Area

6-24. Depending on the size of the assembly area, minimum range limitations may require the battalion to rely on support from other FA battalions for close in fires. High angle fires may be required more frequently. Logistics operations, especially transfer of ammunition, are facilitated as all the FA units are within the same location.

6-25. As part of a FA brigade, a FA battalion may be assigned its own sector within the brigade assembly area, with the FA brigade HQ in the center section. As an individual unit, the battalion would assign sectors to each firing battery and place its C2 and CSS elements in the middle. In battalions with a consolidated CSS structure, ammunition and fuel may be dispersed to a larger degree, which may include placing them in firing battery sectors. This would facilitate CSS responsiveness and improve survivability.

Dispersed Assembly Areas

6-26. A brigade may assign separate assembly areas to subordinate elements (see Figure 6-2). In this method, subordinate elements provide their own 360-degree security. Areas between subunits would be secured through visual and electronic surveillance or patrols. Brigade C2 and the bulk of the CSS elements would occupy positions central to the outlying subordinate element areas.

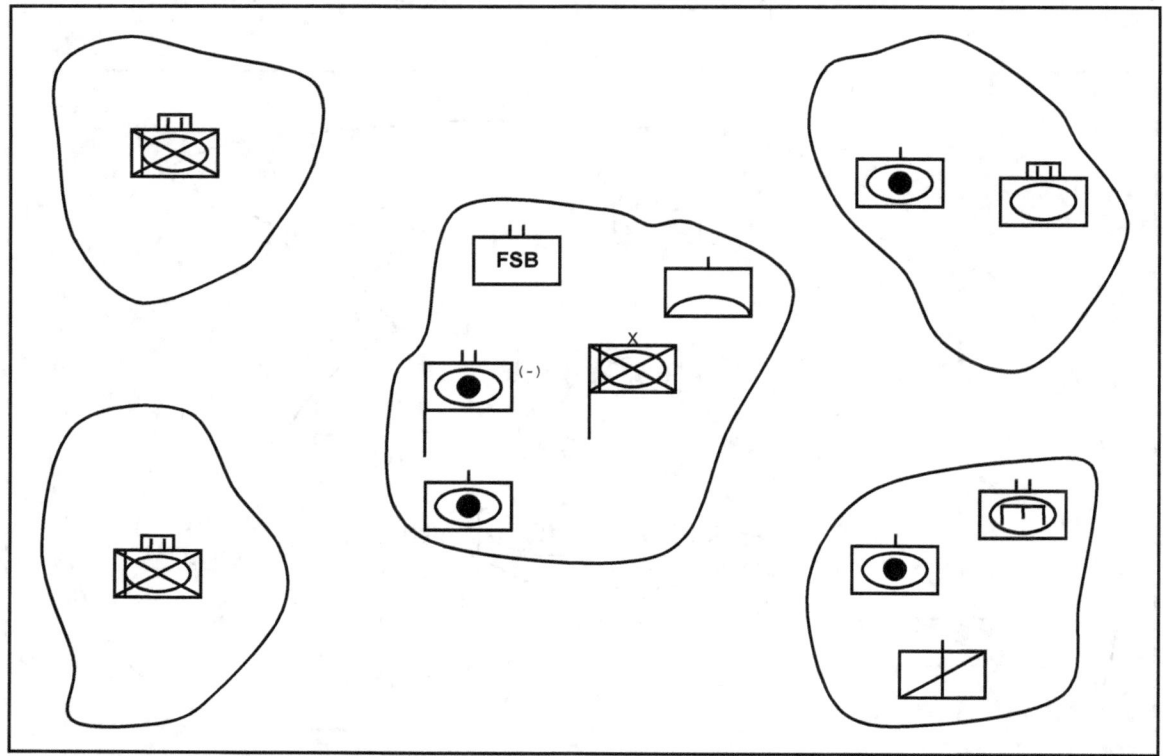

Figure 6-2. Example of a FA Battalion in Dispersed Assembly Areas

6-27. In a combined arms assembly area group, a FA battalion may disperse all of its firing batteries among the outer positions. The bulk of the battalion C2 and CSS would be located in the central position. This method increases overall survivability from air attack and provides better mutual support. However logistics is more complicated as CSS elements would have to traverse the unsecured ground between locations. Also, the firing batteries are more exposed to ground attacks on the maneuver battalion positions.

6-28. Another option is to locate the entire battalion within the central assembly area. This improves C2 and logistics but increases vulnerability to air or ground attack on the central position. It is also more difficult for the battalion to provide close in fires to the central location in case of attack and for the batteries to provide mutually supporting fires to each other.

6-29. A variation of both techniques can be used whereby the bulk of the battalion C2 and CSS is placed in the center and one or two firing batteries are dispersed to subunit assembly areas farthest from the expected enemy locations. At least one firing battery is positioned in the center location.

6-30. In a FA brigade situation, the FA battalion most likely would have it's own assembly area as part of the FA brigade assembly area group.

OCCUPATION OF BUILT-UP AREAS

6-31. When a FA battalion has the option of positioning within or outside of a built-up area, the S3 should consider the following advantages and disadvantages in making his decision.

ADVANTAGES

6-32. The enemy's TA capabilities are significantly degraded because of the effects of terrain masking on observation. The inherent heat and noise signatures of the cities distort sound ranging and IR detection systems. The inherent FM emissions make radio direction finding (RDF) difficult. Conventional photographic reconnaissance is more difficult because there is a greater demand on image interpretation with the clutter of an urban landscape. It is easier to hide in an environment where the unit equipment is less out of place than in a rural and more natural environment.

DISADVANTAGES

6-33. Some of the disadvantages of occupying built-up areas include:
- Urban areas are often on likely avenues of approach. To enhance survivability, FA normally avoids positioning along likely enemy avenues of approach. In urban combat, this may often not be possible because every road or alley is a possible avenue of approach. A battalion should use available obstacles, such as overturned vehicles and demolished structures, to delay an enemy force. The S3 must coordinate all obstacles with the supported maneuver force.
- Any unit deployed in urban terrain is vulnerable to human intelligence (HUMINT) and sabotage activities, especially by civilians and special forces.
- Survey is more difficult. Reduced line-of-sight and magnetic interference (metallic and power line interference) can interfere with conventional survey. Line-of-sight problems can interfere with laying in howitzers. Firing elements may use hasty survey technique more often. See FM 6-50 for hasty survey techniques.
- Communications with higher and supported units by FM radio is significantly degraded because of line-of-sight problems. Careful siting of antennas and retrans stations may be required to overcome the problem. Units may rely more on wire usage.
- FA firing units may find themselves surrounded by enemy forces as the result of the nonlinear nature of urban combat. The firing unit must be prepared to defend itself against enemy assault while performing its primary role of delivering FS. Depending on availability, a maneuver squad or platoon not committed elsewhere may be required to provide local security for a firing unit. However, it is likely that an FA battery must be prepared to prevent a breach in the line by defending its own position against enemy ground assault. This means that firing batteries must be trained and equipped to build barricades, prepare demolitions, lay minefields, and prepare Claymores and booby traps.
- Positioning FA units near urban structures may create site-to-crest problems. The height of some of the buildings along the gun-target line

directly in front of the battery position may have to be reduced to avoid the use of high-angle fires. Engineer support should be sought to ensure rubble doesn't hinder friendly movement. The S3 should ensure firing elements report site-to-crest problems so that he can anticipate the impacts and plan appropriate adjustments to fires. If several weapons are masked, the S3 may need to plan on increased volleys from available shooters and/or increased support from other FA assets.

- Lay and occupation times increase as a result of movement, construction, spade emplacement, and reduced line-of-sight. Units may need multiple aiming circles to lay a firing element. Also, the use of other lay techniques, such as referring between pieces, will be difficult because howitzers may not be able to see each other. Newer weapon systems with internal positioning systems are not as affected by this.
- Displacement may be difficult because of the rubbling effect and the width of roads in the urban area. In addition to site-to-crest problems, individual sections may have difficulty traversing and elevating weapons because of interference of buildings.

RECONNAISSANCE

6-34. Units conduct reconnaissance to identify the best battalion and firing unit positions, march routes, start and release points (SPs/RPs), CPs, OPs, and communications sites. This includes a thorough analysis of the terrain. Reconnaissance helps the unit move from one location to another as quickly and in as organized a manner as possible. At times, the reconnaissance effort may be part of a larger reconnaissance effort and will need to be coordinated.

PLANNING AND COORDINATION

6-35. Based on the tactical situation and METT-TC, the commander and the S3 will determine if reconnaissance is possible and if so, the type of reconnaissance and composition of the party. Normally, the S3, S6, and battery commanders, when available, form the reconnaissance party. In some cases, the S2 may go with the reconnaissance party to plan for radar positions, OPs, and all-around security. Composition of the reconnaissance party is generally prescribed in unit TSOPs. During the reconnaissance, the party makes decisions regarding:

- Ability to accomplish the mission.
- All PAs, communications sites, and observation posts.
- All-around security.
- Routes of march (primary and alternates) and rest/refuel sites.
- Survey requirements.
- Position entrances and exits.
- Concealment/defilade.
- Trafficability.
- SPs and RPs.
- Use of route markers or traffic control points.
- Order of march/ displacement.
- Enemy and friendly situations.

- Bridge capacity.
- Time of movement/travel times.

6-36. Concurrently, the staff (primarily the S3) coordinates with the maneuver HQ, normally through the brigade or regimental FSO, to:
- Verify the battalion can support the mission from its planned positions.
- Resolve any conflicts in positioning or movement between the FA battalion and the maneuver elements.
- Ensure all elements know the current and planned PAs.

6-37. Determine how specific maneuver operations, such as the obstacle and deception plans, affect the reconnaissance, its intended routes, and the subsequent tactical movement of the unit.

RECONNAISSANCE TECHNIQUES

6-38. The battalion commander and staff can use one or a combination of the three reconnaissance methods - map, ground, and air. The best reconnaissance is a combination of all three. Normally only a map reconnaissance is possible, frequently followed by a ground reconnaissance.

Map Reconnaissance

6-39. Any reconnaissance begins with a map reconnaissance, especially when time is short or when the enemy occupies the projected position. A map reconnaissance can identify potentially unsuitable routes, ambush sites, natural obstacles, and chokepoints. Some things to consider include:
- Actual terrain conditions cannot be determined.
- Roads, towns, and terrain features may have changed.
- Other units may be in the position.
- Military load classifications of bridges aren't listed on maps. Bridges must be physically inspected. The engineers may have a classification listing available; however, ensure it is not outdated.
- Enemy forces may be in the area.

Ground Reconnaissance

6-40. This is the best method of reconnaissance and is used whenever possible. Security may be an issue as most reconnaissance parties are small. When the ground threat is high, reconnaissance parties also must take actions to prevent fratricide with friendly elements in or near the area to be reconnoitered. Ground reconnaissance is the most time consuming technique.

Air Reconnaissance

6-41. Use air reconnaissance to support map and ground reconnaissance whenever possible, especially when time is short, air assets are available, and air superiority exists in the area to be reconnoitered. Considerations include:
- The physical condition of the ground is difficult to determine.
- The route to be used cannot be adequately reconnoitered.
- Key staff elements cannot accompany the commander.
- The reconnaissance could give away future plans and intentions.

FM 3-09.21 (FM 6-20-1)

SECTION III – MOVEMENT

6-42. This section addresses movement techniques and considerations common to most battalions. It also provides information on planning and controlling movement. Additional information can be found in FM 6-50, FM 6-60, and FM 6-70.

MOVEMENT TECHNIQUES

6-43. FA battalions may conduct several types of movement, individually or as part of a larger movement by a combined arms force or a FA brigade. DS and R FA battalions may participate in approach marches and combat formations, which are primarily maneuver or combined arms moves.
- Administrative movement.
- Tactical road march (close, open, infiltration and combined arms).
- Airborne or airmobile movement.
- Combined arms movements.
  - Approach march.
  - Combat formations.
- Tactical displacements.

ADMINISTRATIVE MOVEMENT

6-44. Units conduct administrative movement when contact with the enemy (ground or air) is unlikely. Movement emphasizes efficient use of organic and supporting transportation assets. The S4 plans administrative movements.

TACTICAL ROAD MARCH TECHNIQUES

6-45. The tactical road march is a unit move in a combat-ready posture normally conducted in the combat zone. Enemy contact is possible during the march or soon after arrival at the unit's destination. Units frequently move by tactical road marches to assembly areas to prepare for combat operations. Three techniques can be used during tactical road marches:
- Close column.
- Open column.
- Infiltration.

Close Column

6-46. In a close column, vehicles are spaced about 20 to 25 meters apart during daylight (maximum 50 meters). At night, vehicles are spaced so that each driver can see the two lights in the blackout marker of the vehicle ahead. Close column is normally used for marches under blackout driving conditions, in restricted terrain, when maximum C2 is required, or when necessary to quickly clear a bridge, intersection, or key route for other traffic. It is also useful during periods of limited visibility, or when moving through built-up or congested areas.

6-47. The advantages of the close column march technique include:
- Simplicity of command and control.

- Maximizes the traffic capacity of a route.
- Reduces march column length.
- Concentrates defensive firepower.

6-48. Disadvantages of the close column march technique include:
- Provides little dispersion.
- Increases vulnerability to enemy observation. Strength and nature of the column is more apparent to enemy observers.
- Increases vulnerability to attack, especially air attack.
- Increases risk of accidents, especially during night, periods of limited visibility or poor weather/road conditions, and during long moves.
- Reduces convoy speed and increases driver fatigue.

Open Column

6-49. In an open column, the commander increases the distance between vehicles to provide greater dispersion. The distance between vehicles varies from 50 to 100 meters, and may be greater if required. The open column technique is normally used during daylight and when traversing icy, slick, or steep roads where the accident risk is high. Units may also use it at night with infrared light, blackout lights, or passive night-vision equipment. This is the most common movement technique because it offers the most security while still providing the commander with a reasonable degree of control.

6-50. The advantages of the open column march technique include:
- Speed (the fastest march technique).
- Increases dispersion decreases vulnerability to effective enemy observation and attack, especially air attack.
- Lessens chance of an entire march column being ambushed.
- Eases passing of individual vehicles encountered during the move.
- Improves vision on dusty roads and reduces risk of accidents.

6-51. The disadvantages of the open column march technique include:
- Increases column length, requiring more road space, and increases passing times. This can complicate movement planning.
- Decreases C2 as communication within the column is more difficult.
- Decreases the ability of the column to quickly mass defensive fires against an ambush.
- Increases risk of column breakup if a vehicle breaks down or loses contact with the vehicle to its front.
- Increases risk of other traffic becoming interspersed in the column.

Infiltration

6-52. During a move by infiltration, vehicles are dispatched individually, in small groups, or at irregular intervals at a rate that keeps the traffic density down and prevents undue massing of vehicles. Infiltration is suited for tactical road marches when there is enough time and road space and when the commander desires the maximum security, dispersion, and deception.

FM 3-09.21 (FM 6-20-1)

6-53. The advantages of the infiltration march technique include:
- Provides least vulnerability to hostile observation.
- Provides passive defense against air and artillery attack.
- Deceives the enemy as to the size of the unit.
- Ideal for covert operations.

6-54. The disadvantages of the infiltration march technique include:
- Requires more time to complete a move.
- Is the most difficult to command and control.
- Smaller elements are more vulnerable to enemy ground attack.
- Individual vehicles or smaller groups may get lost.
- Complicates and protracts recovery of disabled vehicles.
- Unit integrity is not restored until the last vehicles closes. This can complicate the onward forward movement or deployment of the unit.

Combined Arms Road Marches

6-55. When the FA battalion moves as part of a combined arms force the battalion may move as a single serial within the overall force (see Figure 6-3). The position of the FA serial within the combined arms march is determined by the situation. The battalion may also move dispersed by battery within the movement. This technique may allow the battalion to place one battery more forward in the march column and to better disperse FA assets to provide mutual support, to support the force, and to increase survivability. When moving as part of the larger force, the FA battalion will need to coordinate reconnaissance and quartering party activities with the maneuver force.

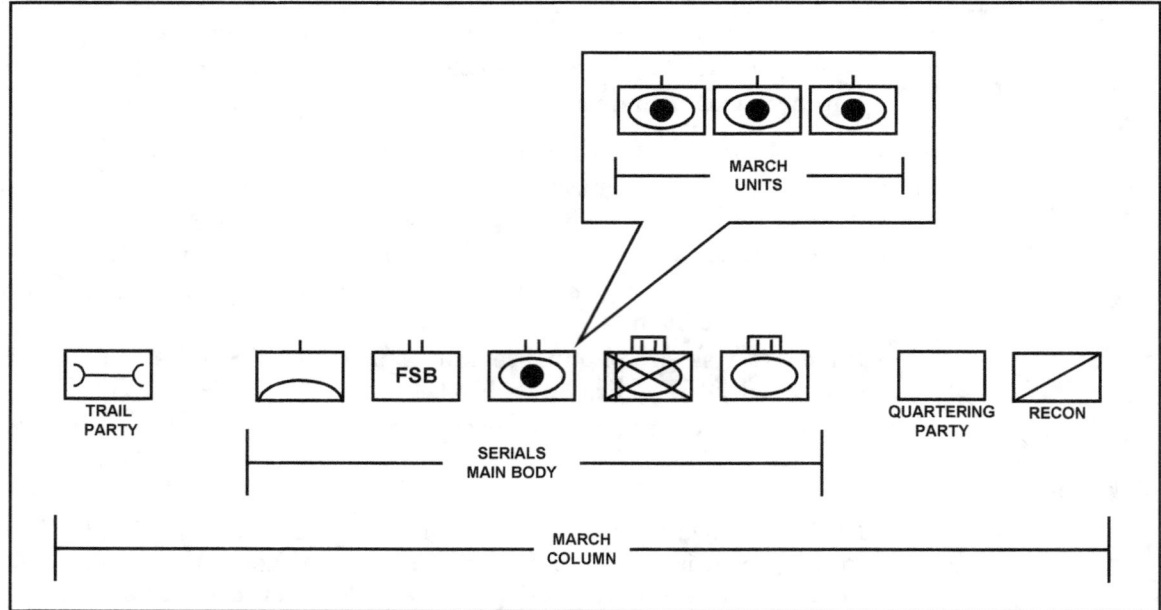

Figure 6-3. Example of a FA Battalion in a Combined Arms Tactical Road March

AIRBORNE/AIRMOBILE MOVEMENT

6-56. FA towed cannon battalions may be moved/inserted by way of airborne or airmobile operations. Airborne movements are usually conducted as part of a combined arms force operation. Airmobile moves are also frequently conducted as part of a combined force operation but may also be an FA only move. FA only airmobile operations may be used when ground movement isn't possible due to impassable terrain or enemy forces, to conduct an artillery raid, or to quickly shift firepower or reinforce an operation.

6-57. As air transportation assets are limited, airborne and airmobile movement frequently involves only the critical elements of the battalion, possibly only one or two firing batteries and a HQ/CSS slice. The remainder of the battalion may follow later. Reconnaissance is frequently difficult, and is an OPSEC issue as it can give away locations and plans. Additional information on airborne and airmobile operations is in Chapter 8.

COMBINED ARMS MOVEMENTS

6-58. FA battalions, especially DS battalions, may occasionally make their movement as part of a maneuver ground operation. Two types of combined arms ground movements are the approach march and combat formations.

Approach March

6-59. An approach march is a tactical movement that emphasizes speed over tactical deployment (see Figure 6-4). It is used when the enemy's location is known, which allows the force to move with greater speed and less physical security or dispersion. The approach march terminates in a march objective, such as an attack position, assembly area, or assault position, or can be used to transition to an attack.

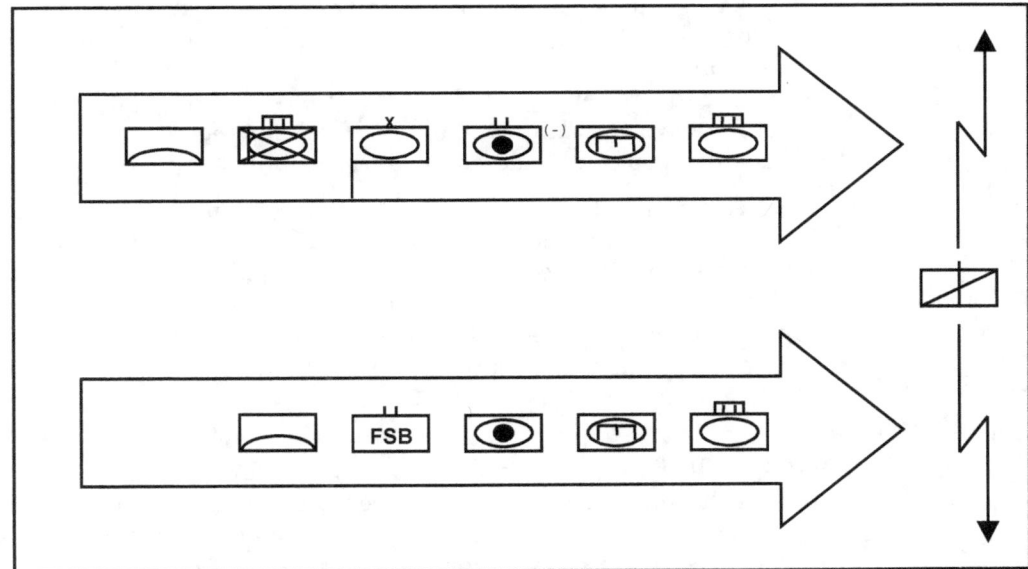

Figure 6-4. Example of a FA Battalion in a Combined Arms Approach March

6-60. There are several key differences between an approach march and a tactical road march. An approach march employs a larger security force. Units conducting an approach march are task organized before the march begins to allow them to transition to the mission without making major adjustments in the organization. Units conducting an approach march establish appropriate intervals between vehicles and normally do not employ a close column. In addition, more routes are used during an approach march.

6-61. As the approach march nears areas of likely enemy contact, the maneuver commander divides his main force into smaller, less vulnerable columns that move on multiple routes or cross-country while continuing to employ security elements.

6-62. A FA battalion that is part of an approach march will normally disperse among march columns based on how it expects to deploy during or at the end of the march. The ability to provide fires for the force is also a major consideration. If cross-country movement is expected, vehicles with limited mobility may need to travel in whichever column will use the more trafficable routes. These elements would link back up with their units as FA positions stabilize and better routes become available.

6-63. As the approach march disperses into smaller columns, security becomes an issue for FA units. At some point firing batteries and CPs may need to separate from the march column to establish firing capability to support the force. RPs should be used to identify where and when FA units are no longer part of the approach march. Generally, at least one battery will need to be in position at whatever point the maneuver commander desires support for the screening force in anticipation of enemy contact.

6-64. The requirement to provide fires may occur earlier than anticipated, before FA units have departed the march column to assume firing positions. The FA battalion should have a plan (battle drill) for this situation and should include this in the rehearsal plan. The plan may consist of one firing battery and the battalion jump TOC pulling out of the march column and assuming operations with further actions determined based on how the situation develops. The availability of reinforcing FA or fires from force FA units must also be considered during an approach march.

6-65. A DS FA battalion may also have to plan and coordinate march locations for a reinforcing battalion, and radars,. The later may be required in screening/security forces forward or to the flanks. Several EFSTs and EFATs will probably be planned in support of the approach march and many will involve linkages between COLTs/Strikers (or other security force elements) and the firing elements that will provide the fires.

Combat Formations

6-66. A FA battalion, especially one with a DS or R mission, may move as part of the supported maneuver force's combat formation. Combat formations are used for movement when the unit anticipates combat. Maneuver brigades use six basic combat formations:
- Column.
- Line.

- Echelon.
- Box.
- Wedge.
- Vee.

6-67. These formations and the guidelines for their use are described in more detail in FM 7-30, *The Infantry Brigade,* and FM 71-3. A diagram of a FA battalion moving in an infantry brigade echelon formation (Figure 6-5) is provided as an example of a combat formation.

6-68. The deployment of FA elements within a combat formation will be dependent on the situation and the maneuver commander's concept for fires. As with the approach march, the timing and execution of FA elements departing the formation to assume firing positions is a critical activity that requires detailed planning and rehearsal.

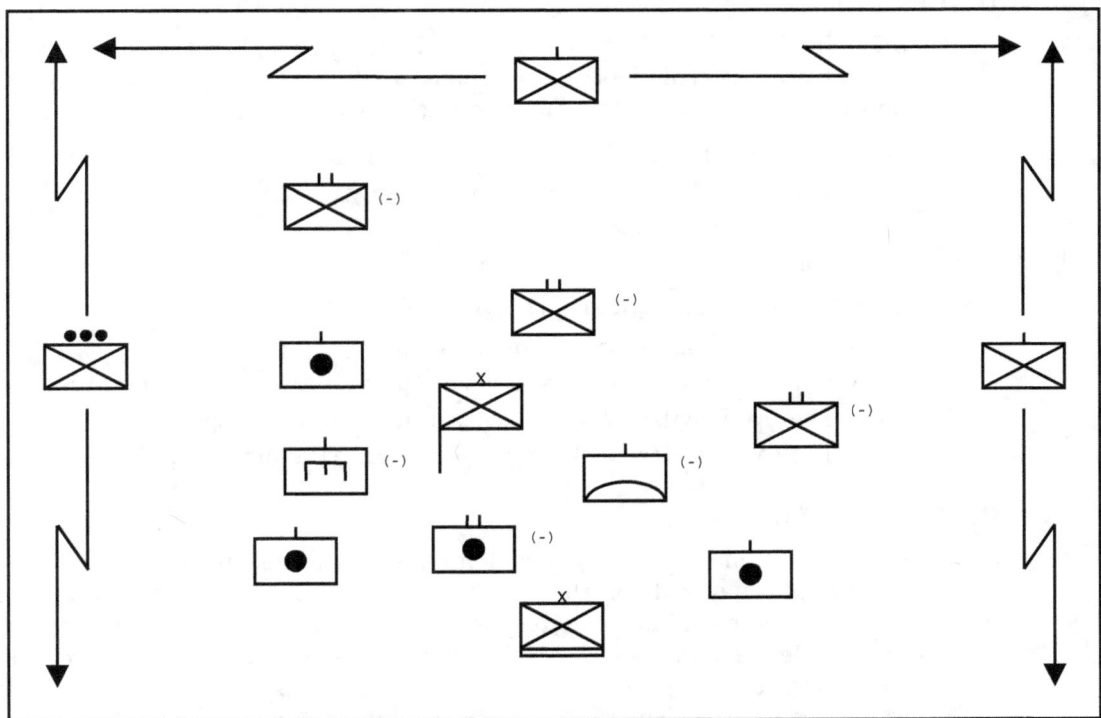

Figure 6-5. Example Combat Formation (Brigade in Echelon Formation)

MOVEMENT CONSIDERATIONS

6-69. Consideration for planning movements include:
- Current mission and future operations.
- Tactical situation (to include other movements).
- Communications (to include automation).
- Force mix and weapon capabilities.
- Survivability/security/threat.
- Time/distance.

- Routes.
  - Road/route capacities and conditions.
  - Bridge capacities.
  - Critical points, intersections/forks, and checkpoints.
  - Location of friendly/enemy/natural obstacles.
- Weather and terrain.

DISPLACEMENT TECHNIQUES

6-70. Whereas *movement* primarily concerns the method of transportation and the actual travel techniques used, *displacement* addresses the broader organization and sequencing of a unit move. The battalion can displace by unit, echelon, battery or element (that is, by platoon, section or vehicle).

DISPLACEMENT BY UNIT

6-71. In a displacement by unit, the battalion displaces with all elements moving at once. This method is best used when the battalion is supporting a unit not in contact or when augmenting fires are available.

6-72. The advantages of this method are as follows:
- This type of displacement is most easily controlled.
- It is the fastest method.
- Long moves are made more easily.

6-73. The disadvantages of this method are as follows:
- The battalion presents a big target.
- While moving, the battalion is not providing any immediate FS.
- The traffic will further congest already crowded roads.
- The commander has little flexibility once the movement has started.

DISPLACEMENT BY ECHELON

6-74. In displacement by echelon, the battalion usually moves in 2-3 groupings organized for the situation rather than by specific unit. As an example, the battalion may displace one or two firing batteries, a portion of the C2 element and some service elements in one echelon. The rest of the battalion stays in position to support the ongoing operation until the first echelon is in place. The remainder of the battalion moves as a second echelon.

6-75. The advantages of this method are as follows:
- The maneuver operation receives continued FA FS.
- The mutual support unit control of the remaining elements is simpler.
- Command and control are facilitated.
- The size of moving convoys is smaller than in a displacement by unit.

6-76. The disadvantages of this method are as follows:
- Each of the moving elements is relatively large.
- Support to the operation is degraded by as much as two-thirds, depending on the technique used.
- The commander's flexibility is limited.

DISPLACEMENT BY BATTERY

6-77. In a displacement by battery, each battery of the battalion moves only after the preceding battery has completed its move and is in place. The CP and trains move by a separate schedule. This method is used primarily to support a unit in contact.

6-78. The advantages of this method are as follows:
- Support to the maneuver operation is continuous.
- By use of the mutual support unit, C2 of fires are continuous.
- Command and control of the movement are centralized.

6-79. The disadvantages of this method are as follows:
- FA support to the operation is degraded by one-third throughout the movement of the battalion.
- The movement is slow.
- The movement of individual units presents a significant target.
- The commander's flexibility is not maximized.

DISPLACEMENT BY ELEMENT

6-80. In a displacement by element, the battalion displaces by individual elements as recommended by the battery commanders. Their recommendations are based on knowledge of the level of training of the battery.

6-81. The advantages of this method are as follows:
- Flexibility of the commander is increased.
- Maximum continued support to the maneuver operation is ensured.
- The signature of the moving unit is very small.
- The higher the level of training of the unit, the more effective this technique becomes.
- Command and control of the movement are decentralized. The C2 elements are released to concentrate on the conduct of the battle.
- Flexibility in selection of movement routes is unlimited.

6-82. The disadvantages of this method are as follows:
- Considerable time is required to complete the move.
- Control by the mutual support unit is not facilitated.
- Command and control problems are increased.
- The smaller elements are more at risk to ambush and attack by enemy elements or sympathizers.
- Information flow must be rapid and accurate.

MOVEMENT CONTROL MEASURES

6-83. Units use graphic and procedural control measures to control movement and positioning of forces. Common graphic control measures include objectives, phase lines, checkpoints, and boundaries. Procedural controls, such as periodic reports by subordinates, also assist with controlling movement. All subordinates should report crossing or occupation of key

FM 3-09.21 (FM 6-20-1)

graphic control measures and checkpoints, initiation of movement, and closure at designations. Units should immediately report problems that impact the movement plan. TSOPs will provide much movement guidance with movement plans addressing changes or additions as necessary. Refer to FM 101-5-1 for additional information on maneuver control measures.

START POINT

6-84. Each movement has an easily recognized SP. It should be far enough from assembly areas that units are organized and moving at the detailed rate by the time it is reached. Each unit should have a separate route to the SP. Each unit is responsible for reconnoitering its route to the SP and determining times of arrival and clearance of the SP. If the unit is displacing as part of a larger unit, the SP is also the point at which control of movement is normally assumed by the larger unit.

RELEASE POINT

6-85. The RP gives the march column a common point for reverting to own or parent unit control. It should be on the route and recognizable on both the ground and the map. It is important that units disperse quickly from the RP. Again, separate routes should be used from the RP to the new PA for each unit as much as possible.

CRITICAL POINTS

6-86. Critical points are points used for reference in giving instructions, places where interference with movement may occur, or places where timing may be critical. Movement should generally continue uninterrupted through these critical points unless one is designated as a planned stop (possibly to refuel, rearm, rest, or allow passing of a higher priority unit). Critical points may include key intersections or points along the route where direction of movement changes. Guides or signs may have to be used.

CHECKPOINTS

6-87. Checkpoints are features identifiable on the ground and on the map. They are used in reporting progress along the route. Checkpoints may be used as target reference points when planning defensive fires for the convoy.

RALLY POINTS

6-88. Normally a rally point is a geographical feature identifiable on the ground and on a map. It is used as a point of assembly and recovery from dispersion due to enemy attack. Some designated rally point(s) should be located near or on the alternate route to the new position.

RESTRICTIONS

6-89. These are points along the route, such as bridges or intersections, where movement may be limited or obstructed for specified periods of time. The planner must consider these restrictions and try to organize the move so minimal interference occurs at these points.

COMMUNICATIONS

6-90. Because OPSEC considerations may restrict use of radios during tactical movement, communications frequently relies heavily on personal contact, visual signals, code words, and signs, markers, or control measures. Use of radios may be restricted to emergencies. Progress at checkpoints may be reported by personnel manning the checkpoint, through use of a wire or digital communications network. TSOPs and rehearsals are especially important to the execution of tactical road marches during radio silence.

TRAFFIC CONTROL

6-91. Traffic control is the responsibility of the controlling HQ. The MPs are usually employed at critical points along the route to give directions and minimize delays. Road guides, posted by the quartering party, can help the MPs control traffic and resolve conflicts.

ROUTE MARKING

6-92. Route marking aids in movement control. The advance party or a route marking detail should post signs, and/or personnel at those critical points where elements of the march might make a wrong turn. Details concerning traffic control and route markings are in FM 55-30, *Army Motor Transport Units and Operations,* and FM 19-25, *Military Police Traffic Operations.*

SPEED CONTROL

6-93. It is critical that the head of the column not exceed the authorized speed of the slowest vehicle in the column in order to reduce column whipping. All personnel involved must maintain the correct interval, both between vehicles and between march units.

PREDETERMINED SIGNALS

6-94. Use established signals (in TSOP) to aid in convoy control (e.g., colored flags in daylight, and flashlights at night). See FM 21-60, *Visual Signals.*

HALTS

6-95. Halts may be made for rest, personal comfort, messing, refueling, maintenance, checking of equipment, allowing other traffic to pass, and for getting back on schedule. The time and length of halts are detailed in the movement order or in unit TSOPs. Activities performed during halts should be planned and conducted as drills and may be outlined in TSOPs or battle books. As much as possible, all halts should be planned based on time, distance, and speed estimates in order to determine where all halts may occur, whether potential locations are appropriate, and if special arraignments or changes to the movement plan are necessary. The are generally two types of halts

- A **short halt** is usually taken for 15 minutes after the first hour and for 10 minutes every two hours thereafter. All march elements should stop at the same time. The availability of sites, rather than time, may determine when short halts actually occur. For tactical road marches of 3 hours or less, the commander may elect not to use short halts.

- A **long halt** is a stop for an extended period, generally 30-60 minutes or more. Additional time must be added to the total travel time for a long halt. Locations for long halts generally require more extensive planning as security, dispersion, camouflage, and other requirements are more complicated. Also, long halts often include activities such as refueling, maintenance, section drills or training, team briefings, or other actions.

6-96. Dispersion and camouflage during halts are critical to survival. Wooded areas, built-up areas, and terrain features should be used as much as possible to conceal the column during halts. When possible, vehicles should disperse along opposite sides of the road to prevent a straight-line target for attack by enemy air. Columns generally should not stop near crossroads, railroads, and other easily identifiable reference points.

MOVEMENT PLANNING

6-97. Movement planning is part of the MDMP process. Movement times, sequences, and techniques should be evaluated, wargamed, and rehearsed as necessary to ensure that movement plans will support the operation. Much of the direction for movement should be addressed in unit TSOPs and battle books. METT-TC and situation specific factors will determine much of the movement plan. Movement planning consists of three major steps:
- Determine requirements for the moves.
- Analyze movement considerations, capabilities, and techniques.
- Establish movement priorities and control measures.

6-98. METT-TC usually dictates requirements for moves. During an operation, movements usually consist of short, tactical displacements or marches. However, when the battle tempo dramatically fluctuates, or when a FA battalion changes mission, longer moves are often required.

6-99. A FA battalion may plan and conduct its moves as part of a larger force. The following techniques, considerations, and control measures will assist the FA battalion in the planning and conduct of battalion level unit movement. FM 55-30 and the following references also contain useful information.
- By rail – FM 55-15, *Transportation Reference Data*.
- By air – FM 55-9, *Unit Air Movement Planning*, and FM 90-4, *Air Assault Operations*.
- By water – FM 55-15.

6-100. For movement as part of a combined force involving other nations or for movement conducted in allied nations, planners should also review.
- STANAG 2041 and QSTAG 520, *Operation Orders, Tables and Graphs for Road Movement* (see FM 55-30 for applicable details).
- STANAG 2154 and QSTAG 539, *Regulations for Military Motor Vehicle Movement by Road*.

PLANNING FACTORS

Distance

6-101. Distance factors include the following:
- **Vehicle distance** is the distance between two consecutive vehicles.
- **Column gap** is the space between two march elements. It is calculated in length or time units, measured from the rear of one element to the front of the next.
- **Traffic density** is the average number of vehicles in one mile or kilometer of road. It is expressed in as vehicles per mile or kilometer.
- Column/serial/march unit length is the length, including gaps, of the various march elements from front to rear.

Rate (Speed)

6-102. Speed factors are as follows:
- **Speed** is the actual rate of a vehicle at a specific moment. It is expressed in miles or kilometers per hour.
- **Pace** is the speed of a column set by the head vehicle to maintain the average speed prescribed in the movement order.
- **Rate of march** (ROM) is the average distance traveled in a period of time. It includes short halts.

Time

6-103. Time factors include the following:
- **Start time** is the time that the lead vehicle crosses the SP.
- **Arrival time** is defined as the time the lead arrives at a certain point.
- **Clearance time** is when the last vehicle passes a certain point.
- **Completion time** occurs when the last vehicle passes the RP.
- An **extra time allowance** (EXTAL) of 1 minute per 25 vehicles is normally allotted over and above the calculated pass time. If there are fewer than 25 vehicles in total, EXTAL is not added. If there are over 600 vehicles, 2 minutes per 25 vehicles is allotted.
- **Pass time** (PST) is the actual time between the lead vehicle of a column, serial, or march column passes a given point and when the last vehicle passes the same point.
- **Time distance** (TDIS) is the time needed to move a certain distance at a given rate of march.
- **Road clearance time** (RCT) is the total time a column needs clear a section of road. (RCT = TDIS + PST).
- A **time gap** is the time aspect of the column gap.

PLANNING FORMULAS

6-104. As the composition of each march column is different, the movement planner must determine time distance, pass time, arrival time, and completion time. The basic factors used in movement planning are distance, rate of march (speed), time, number of vehicles, and vehicle density.

Generally, the distance and number of vehicles is a given number, and the movement planner is primarily concerned with estimating total time required for the overall unit move, the total time for the road march portion of the move, and the rate of march and vehicle density.

6-105. When a FA battalion moves as part of a larger force, the S3 may be given the start and RPs, the anticipated rate of march, directions for open or closed column march, and guidance for short or long halts. He must then estimate his total march time – the time between when the first vehicle crosses the SP and when the last vehicle crosses the RP. Or the battalion may be given the start and RPs and a time allocation (normally designated by start time and RP clearance time). In this case the S3 must compute requirements for rates of march, vehicle density, column gaps, and halts. Since the battalion may move may be dispersed among several march columns, moving along multiple routes, the S3 and the battery commanders must work together to make the calculations.

6-106. Total movement time consists of three major segments:
- Assembly time is the time between when first elements depart their current positions and the start time (when the lead vehicle crosses SP).
- Total march time is the time between when the head vehicle of the march column crosses the SP and when the last vehicle crosses the RP.
- Occupation time is the time from when the last vehicle crosses RP and the time when all elements from the column have completed arrival in their new positions.
- Closure time may also be calculated to account for the recovery of vehicles that may drop out of the march column and cause the separation of the trail party from the main body of the march column. Closure time may be estimated as a specific hour or as a period of time after the RP clearance time. (i.e., Closure time is expected at 1700 hours or 3 hours after the last vehicle in the column crosses the RP.)

6-107. Estimate assembly time using the distance each unit must travel from current positions to the SP and the organization time each unit needs to get all vehicles in the proper order. TSOPs, movement rehearsals, and experience are critical to keeping assembly time to a minimum.

6-108. Total march time (TMT) is the sum of march TDIS plus PST plus long halts. These times are computed as follows (veh = vehicles, mph = miles per hour, kph = kilometers per hour):

$$\text{TMT (hours)} = \text{TDIS (hours)} + \frac{\text{PST (minutes)}}{60} + \text{Long Halts (hours)}$$

$$\text{TDIS (hours)} = \frac{\text{Distance (miles or km)}}{\text{ROM (mph or kph)}}$$

$$\text{PST (minutes)} = \frac{\text{Number of veh} \times 60}{\text{Density} \times \text{speed}} + \frac{\text{Number of veh}}{25} + \text{Time Gaps (in minutes)}$$

6-109. Occupation time is estimated based on the distance the elements must travel from the RP and the positions they must occupy. It is the period between the official end of the road march (when the last vehicle crosses the RP) and the time the last element has occupied its position. When possible, occupation time can be reduced by placing the elements with the most distant positions in the front of the column.

6-110. A battalion hasn't completed its move and fully closed on its new position until all elements have arrived. During longer moves or adverse conditions, recovery operations may extend final closure several hours beyond the march column's completion time. The trail party will try to recover all vehicles quickly enough to maintain contact with the main body of the march column, however, this may not be possible. Generally the trail party will try to consolidate all recovery teams that fall behind, traveling at the speed of the slowest vehicle. The trail party may compete with other units for routes and travel times. It may be incorporated into other unit march columns or may not be able to use the route until it become clear. Closure time is only significant if the battalion anticipates extensive recovery operations where the bulk of the battalion's recovery assets and a sizable maintenance effort cause the trail party to become separated from the march column.

6-111. The RP is normally the terminal point of a road march. Arrival time is computed by adding TDIS and long halts to the start time. If the unit passes the SP at 1000 and its TDIS was 6 hours and there was one long halt of 1-hour duration, the planner adds these and derives an arrival time of 1700. Completion time is calculated by adding PST to arrival time, or by adding TDIS, PST, and halts to the SP time.

DISSEMINATION OF MOVEMENT PLAN

6-112. Units disseminate a movement plan through the use of a **movement order**, which is a type of OPORD. The order covers the friendly and enemy situations, destination, routes, rate of march, maximum speed, details of air and ground alert guard, halts, vehicle distance, time gap, SP, RP, critical point, service support, and command and control. Other data such as route markers may be included as necessary.

6-113. A **strip map** or sketch of the route is usually included as an annex to the movement order. All key personnel, to include each driver, should receive a strip map. It should show the start and RPs, restrictions, and critical points with the distance shown between each.

6-114. A **road movement table** is an annex to the movement order. It consists of two parts. One part, the data paragraphs, shows information pertaining to two or more march elements, a list of march units, and all other information arranged in tabular form. The other part breaks information into specific march units and could include number of vehicles, load class of the heaviest vehicle, points of departure and destination, route, route to SP, critical points, route to the destination from the RP, and a remarks section.

SECTION IV – SURVEY

6-115. Survey is used to establish accurate locations and directional control for weapons and TA assets. It establishes a common grid that permits the massing of fires, the delivery of surprise observed fires, the delivery of effective unobserved fires, and the transfer of target data from one unit to another. With the increased availability of GPS devices in vehicles and weapon systems, requirements for survey support are decreasing. However, understanding of standard survey principles is critical for successful operations during degraded operations. See FM 6-2, *Tactics, Techniques, And Procedures for Field Artillery Survey* for additional information.

6-116. Survey control is a command responsibility. Each force FA HQ is responsible for establishing a common grid throughout its area of operations. During MDMP development, the supported maneuver commander, S3, and FSCOORD identify key survey issues. In advising the maneuver commander, the FSCOORD analyzes the commander's guidance, the scheme of maneuver, rate of movement, effects desired on HPTs, and accuracy requirements for weapons and TA sensors. The FSCOORD ensures that the FSP and FASP provide the necessary survey guidance and tasks. Details for survey support to mortars and non-FA TA assets may need to be addressed in both the FSP and FASP as the non-FA units may not receive the FASP.

6-117. A FA battalion may receive survey instructions and guidance directly from the FSCOORD/FSE/FA commander during direct involvement in the combined arms force MDMP or through their higher FA HQ in a FASP. The FA battalion commander, S3, and survey section chief are the key individuals involved in reviewing the instructions and guidance, identifying the battalion's total survey requirements, and developing battalion survey plans.

6-118. The FA battalion commander's guidance must provide the following:
- Priorities for survey to include survey methods.
- Accuracies required if other than TSOP. Modified survey techniques may be needed as the result of METT-TC.
- Times that critical tasks in the survey plan must be completed.
- Position requirements (primary, alternate and supplementary).
- Future plans.

6-119. The FA battalion S3 must coordinate continuously with higher-echelon staff and commanders and advise the battalion commander on any deviation from previous guidance. If the tactical situation or the absence of accessible survey control points (SCPs) requires use of hasty survey or field-expedient methods of establishing SCPs (position and azimuth system [PADS] in conjunction with the GPS), the force FA commander must be informed.

6-120. The S3, advised by the survey section chief, develops the survey plan using all available assets and techniques to best meet the guidance given by the commander. The S3s of both reinforced and reinforcing battalions must coordinate their efforts and plans. Survey assets may have to be pooled on occasion without regard to unit identity to achieve the mission. GS/GSR units will closely coordinate their survey requirements with DS units when operating in a DS unit's AO, especially during offensive operations. During defensive operations involving rearward movement, DS/R units may rely heavily on force FA and GS/GSR unit survey information to facilitate survey operations. The battalion survey plan must be coordinated with force FA HQ to ensure use of consolidated SCP data and to eliminate duplication of effort.

FA BN SURVEY SECTION

6-121. The survey section is responsible for providing survey control to all organic, assigned, and attached firing elements, TA assets, observers, or other elements (e.g., OH-58Ds, EW and intelligence units, and mortars). The section operates under the control of the operations section.

6-122. A battalion survey section usually consists of a section chief, an assistant and two surveyors, and the following equipment: a HMMWV, secure FM radio, HTU, a PADS, and a survey set.

6-123. The survey section chief is the primary advisor for survey operations within the battalion. He assists the S3 with survey planning and directs and supervises survey activities. Specific duties include:
- Coordinate and supervise battalion survey operations.
- Develop the survey plan with guidance from the S3.
- Coordinate directly with BCs concerning survey requirements.
- Perform general reconnaissance and observation as required by the S3.

6-124. (**NOTE:** The survey PADS team must also assist the S3 and S2 in acquiring combat information as they perform their normal mission. They are particularly useful in gathering information about the terrain.)

SURVEY PLANNING FACTORS

6-125. The FA commander and S3 must be aware of the basic capabilities and limitations of survey before they can issue effective guidance and/or orders to the survey section. They must be aware of the factors discussed below.
- Available survey assets and equipment.
- Total survey requirements.
    - Weapon locations – FA cannon/rocket/missile systems, and mortars.
    - TA locations – FA and non-FA radars, observers (FOs, COLTs/Strikers), MI equipment.
    - SCPs.
    - Force FA requirements.
    - Target area survey.
- Time and distance factors.
- Operational status of other positioning systems – those in weapon or TA systems and other vehicular and handheld systems.
- Weather and terrain.
- Availability and accuracy of existing SCPs.

SURVEY PLANNING TIMES

6-126. The following times are used in planning survey:

- PADS survey team:
  - Cross-country: 10 kph.
  - Unimproved road: 25 kph.
  - Improved road: 50 kph.
  - Maximum mission time: 7 hours (system shutdown and reinitialization require about 40 minutes). The system must be updated on an SCP after seven hours. This update takes approximately five minutes.
  - Maximum mission radial distance: 55 km (system will require update data).

PLANNING GUIDE

6-127. The battalion commander and S3 can use the following guide to ensure that most of the issues relating to survey planning are covered. It is not exhaustive and may have to be modified to meet a particular situation.

- Select primary, alternate and supplementary PAs for all assets requiring survey.
- Set time requirements associated with providing survey (planning, reconnaissance, fieldwork, and completion).
- Determine accuracy requirements for weapons and TA systems (third, fourth, or fifth order survey). Standard requirements should be reduced only if time is a critical factor. An example might be providing only direction to FA units and requiring other units to establish their own locations by use of hasty techniques.
- Set a survey priority for each asset requiring survey. This may mean that survey will be controlled at the highest feasible level and not be done independently by individual battalions and units.
- Determine the availability of starting SCPs, PADS update points and closing points and the accuracy of each point. If they are not readily available, include the requirement to emplace them in survey priorities.
- Consider performing survey updates at SCPs during rearm, refuel, and resupply (R3P) operations (sometimes referred to as R3SP operations).
- Coordinate at all levels. The requirements from higher HQ must be determined so that they can be included in the planning process.

DEGRADED SURVEY OPERATIONS

6-128. Degraded conditions for survey operations may occur due to unavailability of satellite systems or inoperable automated position/direction systems. During these times the FA battalion will rely more heavily on the use of PADS and on hasty survey techniques. During offensive operations, DS, R, and other forward FA battalions may require survey assistance from force FA HQ survey assets. During defensive operations, force FA survey teams can more easily assist DS and R units as they move rearward, however, this requires early identification and coordination of requirements.

6-129. Hasty survey techniques may be used during degraded operations or when adequate survey control is not available. See FM 6-2 for additional information on degraded and hasty survey techniques.

SECTION V – DEPLOYMENT

DEPLOYMENT READINESS

6-130. FA battalions must be capable of deploying anywhere in the world with little or no notice to provide fires for contingency forces. The following discussion is not intended to be all-inclusive but rather to highlight deployment planning considerations. Additional information can be found in:

- FM 25-5, *Training for Mobilization and War.*
- FM 55-9, *Unit Air Movement Planning.*
- FM 100-17, *Mobilization, Deployment, Redeployment, Demobilization.*
- FM 100-17-1, *Army Pre-Positioned Afloat Operations.*
- FM 100-17-2, *Army Pre-Positioned Land.*
- FM 100-17-3, *Reception, Staging, Onward Movement, and Integration.*
- TB 55-46-1, *Standard Characteristics (Dimensions, Weight, and Cube) for Transportability of Military Vehicles and Other Outsize/Overweight Equipment.*

FM 100-17-1 and FM 100-17-2 have "Commander's Guides" as appendices.

6-131. The key to proper deployment readiness is development of a detailed deployment TSOP and necessary deployment plans. Unit leaders should thoroughly analyze their potential deployment missions, evaluate various scenarios and options, and identify Army, post, and supported unit requirements. Plans and TSOPs should address all aspects of deployment, from training and preparation, to alert, recall, predeployment, deployment, and in-theater embarkation activities, and rear detachment requirements.

TRAINING

6-132. The battalion training plan should address training on all aspects of deployment. This includes everything from background briefings on the regional characteristics (weather, terrain, political/military, customs/laws, etc) and full, certification-type deployment exercises. Combined arms training strategies and mission training plans provide detailed training guidance.

ADMINISTRATIVE AND LOGISTICAL READINESS

6-133. The unit should establish and update unit movement plans, rear detachment plans, recall plans, and alert rosters. Recall plans should be practiced often and revised as necessary.

INTELLIGENCE/INFORMATION OPERATIONS

6-134. Early deploying units usually face a maze of complex information requirements--some relating to the enemy, others to local laws, availability of facilities, and similar considerations. Commanders and staff officers should quickly identify all sources of information and establish connectivity with appropriate agencies. Regional, deployment/staging, and CSS information should be obtained and incorporated into planning and training as early as possible, preferably during peacetime. This is critical in preventing information overload from interfering with core tactical mission planning.

FORCE TAILORING

6-135. A deploying FA battalion may be task organized as a composite battalion, with both cannon and MLRS batteries. Commanders must identify this potential during deployment planning and training. Leaders should give special attention to logistical and ammunition requirements.

LOGISTICS

6-136. Successful force projection requires flexible logistics and support systems. New supply channels will generally be established, and critical items, such as automated C2 parts and systems, may be in short supply initially. FA battalions should consider all classes of supply and logistical support when preparing to deploy as part of a force projection package.

JOINT OPERATIONS

6-137. FA units may support any of a number of components during joint operations. The most likely situations include support of a MAGTF, SEAD support for fixed/rotary wing aviation operations, and force protection fires. Unit leaders should review joint terminology and all applicable references identify C2 requirements (communications and automation). The S3 should carefully research requirements for control measures and clearance of fires procedures as unusual situations often require unusual FS arrangements.

COMBINED OPERATIONS

6-138. Contingency operations frequently involve operations with other nations. Commanders should ensure that all soldiers are aware of and sensitive to cultural differences that may impact their operations. Units should identify requirements for interpreters, digital C2, and liaison.

HOST NATION SUPPORT

6-139. The FA battalion must quickly determine the amount of host nation support it can expect and the conditions under which the staff will be interoperating with local government, municipal, or business leaders.

DEPLOYMENT

6-140. Usually, higher HQ develop deployment timeline based on METT-TC and reverse planning. These factors include but are not limited to: aircraft availability; type, size, and amount of equipment, and personnel and equipment attached. Movement officers must understand all aspects of deployment, and meticulously track automated unit equipment lists.

DEPLOYMENT PACKAGES

6-141. Since contingency forces are tailored to meet the specific mission requirements it is possible that only parts of a FA battalion will deploy as part of a force projection package. These packages assume that a battalion C2 slice will accompany each package. This facilitates support and rapid integration of the battalion's follow-on elements. Deployment packages will vary widely depending on the situation and the type of FA unit involved.

Chapter 7

Combat Service Support

The term "combat service support" describes the full range of personnel services and health services functions as well as the traditional logistical support of supply, maintenance, field services, and transportation. It includes all the requirements related to manning, arming, fueling, fixing, moving, and sustaining the force during military operations. The basic mission of CSS is to sustain the force. CSS planning must focus on maintaining and supporting the battalion's soldiers and weapon systems as it executes the commander's intent while conducting operations. This chapter has five sections. Section I addresses CSS organizations and functions in general. Section II covers CSS planning. Section III provides information on logistical support. Section IV focuses on personnel and health services support. And Section V provides an overview on reconstitution.

SECTION I – ORGANIZATION AND FUNCTIONS

7-01. This section outlines the CSS organizations within the FA battalion and the external support elements with which a FA battalion interfaces. TOE structure differences impact CSS. Some FA battalions have a HHSB while other battalions may have a HHB and a SB. FA battalions may also have a centralized CSS structure that places much of the CSS at battalion, or a decentralized structure with self-sustaining firing batteries that are assigned most of their own CSS.

7-02. Regardless, of the TOE/MTOE structure, the FA battalion commander can task organize the CSS assets for centralized or decentralized C2. Centralized CSS lightens the CSS burden on the firing batteries and can increase mobility. Decentralized CSS gives the firing batteries more control over their CSS, facilitates attachment of a battery to another FA unit or to a maneuver unit, and allows independent operations. In determining how much centralization will be required, the battalion commander considers:

- METT-TC.
- Personnel status (strength and experience) of these sections.
- Availability of equipment.
- Availability of external support.
- Capability of the battalion staff to supervise additional sections.

7-03. This chapter contains frequent references to the various classes of supply. Table 7-1 provides a brief description of each of the classes. FM 100-10, *Combat Service Support,* contains additional, detailed information on supply classes.

Table 7-1. Classes of Supply

CLASS	COMPOSITION
CLASS I	Subsistence, gratuitous health, and comfort Items (e.g., beef, sundry packs, vegetables, bread)
CLASS II	Individual clothing and equipment and general supplies (e.g., jackets, boots, tools)
CLASS III	Petroleum, oils, and lubricants (POL) (e.g., gasoline, oil, grease)
CLASS IV	Construction materials (e.g., wire, lumber, cement)
CLASS V	Ammunition (e.g., grenades, 7.62mm, mines, explosives)
CLASS VI	Personal demand items (e.g., candy, soap, cameras, cigarettes)
CLASS VII	Major end items (e.g., trucks, rifles)
CLASS VIII	Medical supplies (e.g., bandages, drugs, syringes, stretchers)
CLASS IX	Repair parts and components (e.g., batteries, spark plugs, axles, cotter pins)
CLASS X	Material to support nonmilitary programs (e.g., tools)

SECTION RESPONSIBILITIES

S1 SECTION

7-04. The S1 section is responsible for personnel services and the general administration of the battalion, to include support to the batteries. The S1 section manages strength accountability, casualty reporting, replacement operations, administrative services, personnel actions, legal services, finance services, and CP functions. The S1 section directly provides many of the services, while others, like legal and financial support often involve coordinating external support.

7-05. The S1 section also has primary staff responsibility for EPW operations and medical planning. It coordinates with the S2 for interrogation of prisoners and with the S4 for processing captured equipment and satisfying transportation requirements. The S1 coordinates with the medical section leader to ensure that patient treatment and evacuation are planned and coordinated throughout the battalion area.

MEDICAL SECTION

7-06. The battalion aid station (BAS) sorts, treats, and evacuates casualties or returns them to duty. It stocks medical supplies for the battalion and manages all Class VIII support. The BAS is also responsible for maintaining and evacuating the battalion's damaged medical equipment for repair.

7-07. The medical section (treatment team) officer, a field surgeon, or a physician's assistant, manages the BAS. He coordinates the operation, administration, and logistics of the medical section and combat health service support for the battalion. This includes coordinating patient evacuation to the supporting medical company and providing support to batteries.

S4 SECTION

7-08. The S4 section is responsible for supply, transportation, and field service functions. It coordinates requisition of supplies and their distribution to battery supply sections and turns in captured supplies and equipment. In combat, the S4 concentrates on nine classes of supply: Classes I, II, III, IV, V, VI, VII, IX and X.

7-09. The S4 section is responsible for obtaining water. The S4 uses organic transportation to transport water from the designated water supply point in or near the supporting CSS support area or from forward sources that are tested and approved by the medical section.

MAINTENANCE SECTION

7-10. The battalion maintenance section is responsible for unit maintenance on all battalion equipment except COMSEC and medical equipment. The section maintains Class IX (repair parts), The Army Maintenance Management System (TAMMS) records, and the prescribed load list (PLL) stocks. It also provides recovery and towing operations. In battalions with distributed CSS (firing battery maintenance sections), the battalion maintenance section supports the firing battery maintenance with higher level maintenance, major repairs, and contact teams.

7-11. Some battalions have consolidated maintenance activities; however, the responsibility for operator and crew maintenance remains with battery commanders. During maintenance operations, maintenance elements of the battalion are task-organized to maximize forward support to the batteries.

AMMUNITION SECTION

7-12. Some battalions have only a three-person ammunition management section (or support platoon HQ in light cannon units), and no battalion level ammunition sections. Other battalions have an ammunition platoon with a platoon HQs and three ammunition sections.

7-13. The ammunition management section (or platoon HQs) performs battalion level management of all ammunition requirements. It coordinates both external and internal resupply efforts. The BAO, working with the S3 and S4, coordinates the requisition, receipt, preparation, and delivery of Class V. The ammunition sections, where applicable, pick up and deliver ammunition, establish temporary ammunition points, and assist with residue removal when necessary. At times, battalion ammunition sections may be placed under battery control, or battery ammunition sections may be consolidated under battalion control.

BATTERIES

7-14. Battery CSS capability varies with the type of FA unit, and the TOE structure of the battalion. Normally, all batteries have their own supply sections. The battalion medical element provides a combat medic, who usually accompanies the battery, the S6 provides communications maintenance contact teams (on an as-needed basis), and the battalion S1 section provides personnel and administrative support on a GS basis.

7-15. In light (105mm) battalions, the firing batteries generally have their own ammunition sections, but receive maintenance, POL, and food service support from battalion. In 155mm battalions, each battery may have its own maintenance, food service, and POL sections, and firing batteries may additionally have their own ammunition sections. On some TOEs, battery maintenance sections may be on the service battery TOE. Some firing batteries also have a support platoon HQ that supervises battery CSS assets. In MLRS battalions, MLRS batteries usually have their own organic maintenance sections.

7-16. Firing battery and platoon leadership teams carefully monitor their unit's CSS status, plans, and requirements. When CSS assets are directly under their control (organic or attached), they proactively manage and direct this CSS as necessary. When most or all CSS assets are consolidated under battalion control, battery or platoon level CSS management consists primarily of reporting requirements, requesting support, ensuring that CSS is properly executed in the unit area, and on identifying potential CSS problems that may adversely impact mission accomplishment.

7-17. Because battery CSS capability varies by unit type and TOE/MTOE structure (which change), FA battalions working with other FA units should verify CSS organization.

FA BATTALION CSS

7-18. FA battalions receive CSS from various division and corps CSS elements, generally located in brigade, division, or corps CSS locations. To facilitate CSS operations, the force FA HQ, the division support command (DISCOM) or corps support command (COSCOM), and the division or corps G4s, frequently coordinate for the support to come from the closest CSS facility, such as a BSA, division support area (DSA), or a corps support group (CSG). When an FA battalion draws its CSS from the BSA or DSA, its may draw the support from either division or corps CSS elements located with those areas (dependent on command relationships and CSS arrangements).

DIVISIONAL FA UNITS

7-19. A FA battalion DS to a maneuver brigade usually receives its CSS from the BSA located in the brigade rear area, about 20-25 km behind the FLOT. The BSA will include the brigade rear CP, brigade and task force CSS assets, and division and corps CSS assets that support the brigade, division, and corps units operating in or near the brigade AO. The division, specifically the DISCOM, normally positions a forward support battalion (FSB) in the BSA to support the brigade, its supporting FA battalion, and other assets as directed.

7-20. The DS cannon battalion XO and S4 work closely with the maneuver brigade S4 and the FSB support operations officer to coordinate CSS and develop a logistics plan. The FA battalion commander and the brigade FSO assist the XO and S4 in communicating FA requirements to the brigade commander to ensure that FA requirements are adequately prioritized. If the DS battalion is supported by a R FA unit, the commander, XO, and S4 of the reinforcing unit will also participate in this CSS process, usually working through the DS battalion. The DIVARTY S4 assists the battalion in coordination with DISCOM elements.

7-21. Divisional GS FA units may receive some or all of their CSS from out of a BSA or the DSA, depending on distances and the arrangements coordinated by the FA battalion's S4. Divisional GS FA units may locate their trains locations in or near a BSA or DSA as appropriate. The DSA is normally between the BSAs and the division rear, and next to air-landing facilities and the MSR. The main support battalion (MSB) (or division support battalion [DSB] in newer CSS structures), operating from the DSA, normally provides much of the CSS support for the divisional GS FA battalion.

7-22. All FA units operating in the division rear, drawing support from the DSA, or desiring space in the DSA should coordinate with the DISCOM S2/S3 support operations branch, the division rear FSE, and/or the DIVARTY S4 as appropriate. More detailed information on DISCOMs can be found in FM 63-2, *Division Support Command, Armored, Infantry, and Mechanized Infantry Division*, FM 63-2-1, *Division Support Command, Light Infantry, Airborne, and Air Assault Division*, and FM 63-2-2, *Tactics, Techniques, and Procedures for the Division Support Command (Digitized)*.

NONDIVISIONAL/CORPS FA UNITS

7-23. The challenge for nondivisional/corps FA units is in maintaining consistent, timely CSS during movement between different division and brigade zones. FA battalions, or their FA brigades, may need to leave a small CSS element at a previous support area to close out any critical CSS issues that cannot be transferred to or assumed by supporting CSS elements in the new location. To overcome this problem, one technique used in at least one corps is the creation of corps forward logistical elements (FLEs) specifically designed to support a corps FA brigade. The FLE moves with the FA brigade in order to maintain better continuity of CSS support. The FLE will normally operate from within the nearest brigade, division, or corps support area. In corps that do not use the FLE concept, the FA battalion's CSS may come from the nearest support area.

7-24. Nondivisional FA units operating in the forward part of a division area may receive CSS from out of the BSA or the DSA. This support may come from either divisional or corps CSS elements operating within the BSA or DSA, depending on battalion's tactical mission, command relationships, the type and extent of the support and the arrangements coordinated by the HQs involved. The COSCOM determines the type and amount of corps level CSS needed in the BSAs and DSAs based on the amount of support the division needs and the number of corps units operating in the division zone. COSCOM CSS elements operating from a BSA or DSA may consist of a corps support battalion (CSB), elements from a CSG, or a smaller support element formed to provide forward support. The corps artillery G4 or FA brigade S4 will normally assist the nondivisional FA battalion in arranging CSS from a nearby BSA or DSA when necessary. The key distinction for a nondivisional FA unit receiving the CSS support is to determine whether the support is coming from divisional or from corps CSS elements, and to clearly identify the channels for submitting CSS requests.

7-25. Nondivisional FA units operating in the division or corps rear areas may receive their support through the nearest DSA, CSG, CSB, or other corps CSS element. Distance, operational requirements, and the CSS capabilities within each of the logistical support areas will be key factors in determining where the FA unit can be best supported. A nondivisional FA unit receiving support from within the DSA may receive that support from either division or corps CSS elements within the DSA. The FA battalion's higher FA HQs (FA brigade or corps artillery) will assist the battalion in coordinating the support with the DISCOM or COSCOM, as appropriate. The battalion will then primarily communicate directly with the appropriate CSS element and possibly the division or corps rear FSE. In some cases, a nondivisional FA battalion may receive CSS from both a DSA and from a CSG or CSB.

7-26. A major consideration for nondivisional FA battalions supporting light divisions is the spartan nature of the division's logistical support structure. Light divisions rely heavily on corps CSS packages, so the addition of nondivisional FA units usually requires well thought out CSS augmentation.

FA BATTALION TRAINS

7-27. The FA battalion trains is a grouping of equipment and vehicles to provide CSS support to the batteries. The organization of the FA battalion trains varies with METT-TC and available space. The battalion trains is normally made up of battalion CSS assets and may include elements of the FSB. Generally, trains can be organized for combat in a:
- Single location - All support operating under direct control of the unit is termed "unit trains."
- Dual locations – "combat" and "field" trains locations.
  - The combat trains contains those elements providing critical battlefield support forward with the batteries.
  - The field trains contains elements operating farther back with or near support units of the next higher HQ.

7-28. In either the single or dual location trains concept, C2 of CSS assets is primarily an S4 and S1 function, especially in HHSB based battalions. However, the HHSB leadership team, or where applicable the HHB and SB leadership teams, assist the S1 and S4 with management, movement, and security for the trains location(s).

UNIT TRAINS

7-29. When CSS resources are centralized in one location, they are called unit trains. This option provides:
- Centralized coordination and control of logistical personnel and equipment.
- Enhanced security and capability for ground defense.
- A single base for CSS activities.

7-30. Unit trains may be appropriate in slow-moving or static situations, when firing batteries have organic or attached support, when the tactical situation forces the trains to be a self-contained operation, when the battalion is in an assembly area or during an extended tactical march. Unit trains will normally consist of most of the battalion level CSS assets, except for those positioned with the battalion main CP, those detailed out to the firing batteries, and possibly a UMCP. The UMCP may be established closer to the firing batteries, possibly positioned near the main CP, in order to facilitate rapid repair and evacuation of equipment. The HHSB (or SB) commander commands the unit trains.

7-31. Towed FA units normally lack sufficient resources to effectively use the dual trains concept, and thus usually operate under a unit trains organization. The unit trains is normally in or near the BSA or closet support area. The operations center for the unit trains is the ALOC. The planning considerations for trains, logistics packages (LOGPACs), and other CSS operations for SP units are generally relevant to towed units as well.

DUAL (COMBAT AND FIELD) TRAINS

7-32. The preferred method of supporting a SP battalion is through dual trains. The use of the dual trains technique provides (Figure 7-1):

- Immediately responsive forward support tailored to the tactical situation.
- Flexible resource usage.
- Increased resource survivability.
- Enhanced responsiveness when the tactical situation is very fluid or when the supported unit is operating over extended distances.

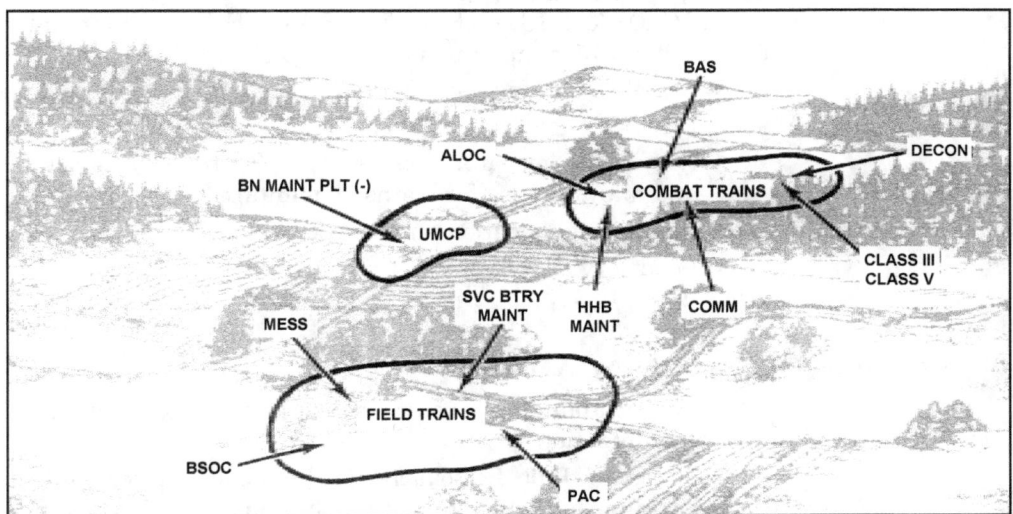

Figure 7-1. Dual (Combat and Field) Trains

Combat Trains

7-33. The battalion combat trains is organized to provide immediate critical CSS. It is the hub of CSS operations for the battalion. The HHSB (or HHB) commander usually commands the combat trains, which may include:

- The ALOC (which also serves as the CP for the combat trains).
- POL (awaiting distribution to the batteries).

- Ammunition (awaiting distribution).
- Maintenance contact teams with a recovery capability.
- Battalion aid station.
- Decontamination assets.
- Elements of the communications platoon.
- UMCP.
- Supporting elements from the FSB, MSB/DSB, or CSB.

7-34. The combat trains is located close enough to the FLOT to be responsive to the forward units; but, if possible, it should not be within range of enemy indirect fire. It generally occupies an area between the field trains and about 5 to 8 km behind the forward battery or platoon PAs. Combat trains must move often to stay in supporting distance of the firing units.

7-35. A FA battalion often establishes a UMCP to provide forward maintenance support to the battalion. The battalion maintenance technician supervises the UMCP. Under the dual trains concept, the UMCP may locate within the combat trains, especially when increased security is required. However, the unit may also establish the UMCP outside of but near the combat trains if necessary to better accomplish the mission.

Field Trains

7-36. The field trains includes those elements not in the combat trains and not required for immediate support of the batteries. It is usually in or near the BSA, DSA, CSG, or FLE. The SB (or HHSB) commander commands the field trains, which may include:
- The BSOC (which also serves as the CP for the field trains).
- PAC.
- Remaining maintenance sections (to perform scheduled maintenance and maintenance for trains elements).
- Remaining battalion ammunition trains.
- Food service sections
- Supply sections.

DETERMINING TRAINS ORGANIZATION

7-37. The commander must consider several factors when determining the trains organization.
- **Status of Unit Personnel and Equipment.** Shortages may hinder the battalion's ability to establish dual trains. This factor alone could dictate unit trains.
- **Phase of Combat.** During phases when fronts are relatively static or the battle area is condensed, unit trains may be preferable. During fast-paced offensive or defensive maneuvers, or operations over extended distances, dual trains may be advisable.

- **Survivability.** If a significant ground threat exists, the battalion should consider using unit trains, or combining the combat trains and the battalion CP to improve survivability. If air attack or indirect fire is the primary threat, dual locations increase dispersion and afford smaller targets. On a non-linear battlefield, with dispersed firing batteries, decentralization of CSS may reduce the trains to a relatively small element requiring the unit trains technique for security.

- **Location of the Support Area.** The battalion commander must consider the distance from the BSA, DSA, CSG, or FLE to the firing batteries and trains. Over short distances, the battalion can often provide responsive support from a single location. As the distance increases, responsiveness from a single location decreases. Although the use of dual trains does not decrease that distance, it decreases the turnaround time between battery and combat train locations.

- **Terrain.** Areas with paved, well-marked supply routes facilitate use of unit trains. Battalions should consider using dual trains when restrictive (e.g., mountainous or swampy) terrain slows CSS and hinders positioning or dispersal of unit trains and in desert areas where lack of natural camouflage increases vulnerability to air attack.

- **Amount of Centralization.** Decentralization of CSS to the batteries can facilitate use of unit trains if the distances are not too great. Because decentralization decreases the size of the battalion trains, dual trains may become difficult to operate and secure. Centralized CSS facilitates the use of dual trains, but can sometimes be less responsive if CSS management and coordination is not properly executed.

- **Responsiveness Versus Risk.** During wargaming and COA analysis the FA battalion commander and staff must evaluate the risk and responsiveness tradeoffs associated with dual and unit trains. If acceptable risk (within the maneuver/higher FA commander's guidance) is not achievable, the battalion commander should inform the appropriate HQs and coordinate the most effective solution possible.

TRAINS SECURITY

7-38. The HHSB (or HHB/SB) commander is responsible for trains security. When dual trains are used in units with a SB, the HHB commander is usually responsible for the combat trains and the SB commander is responsible for securing the field trains. When the battalion collocates the field trains with the BSA, DSA, CSG, or FLE, the HHSB (or SB) commander coordinates with the commander of the support area (and/or battalion) and the appropriate rear CP to integrate the battalion field trains into the overall defensive plan. In all trains areas, a perimeter defense is planned. Elements in the trains are assigned a specific sector to defend. Mutually supporting positions that dominate likely avenues of approach are selected for vehicles armed with heavy machine guns. Reaction forces and OPs are established. These are based on the unit TSOP. To enhance security, an alarm or warning system is arranged. Sector sketches, fire plans, and obstacle plans should be prepared. The HHSB commander directs rehearsals to ensure that all personnel know the parts they play in the defensive scheme.

COMMAND AND CONTROL OF TRAINS

7-39. C2 of CSS is the overall responsibility of the battalion XO. The S4 routinely coordinates all logistic operations while the S1 coordinates all personnel, administrative, and health services operations. Both follow the XO's guidance, and closely coordinate with each other. The battalion uses the ALOC, and sometimes the BSOC, as CSS C2 organizations.

7-40. When the battalion uses unit trains, it may establish only the ALOC, which will manage all CSS actions, especially if the unit trains are positioned in or near the BSA, DSA, CSG, or FLE. If the unit trains are away from the support area, the FA battalion may place a small CSS liaison element in the support area to facilitate coordination. When the battalion uses dual trains, it may establish both the ALOC and the BSOC. The BSOC, with the field trains, normally operates from in or near the BSA, DSA, CSG, or FLE.

7-41. The ALOC is the focal point of battalion CSS operations and the combat trains operations center. It should have the capability to serve as an alternate battalion TOC (less tactical FD capability). The ALOC concentrates on ammunition and POL resupply, priority equipment repair and salvage, and emergency medical care. The ALOC must:
- Stay abreast of the tactical situation (battle tracking).
- Monitor the battalion command net to identify CSS requirements.
- Receive requests, reports and requirements from subordinate elements.

7-42. ALOC personnel analyze, consolidate, and forward battalion requirements to the BSOC or to the appropriate supporting agency. The BSOC coordinates and directs elements in the field trains to take actions to meet the requirements of the forward units.

7-43. The BSOC serves as the operations center for the field trains and the key interface with supporting CSS elements in the BSA, DSA, CSG, or FLE. The BSOC coordinates all CSS actions that occur outside of the battalion. The BSOC may perform the following actions:
- Receipt/distribution of Class V from the supporting ATP.
- Receipt/distribution of mail and official documents.
- Receipt/preparation/distribution of Class I items (e.g., water, ice).
- Receipt/distribution of Class II, III, IV, VII, VIII, and IX from supporting CSS companies.
- Monitor repair operations performed by the supporting maintenance company.
- In-process new personnel.
- Process awards, personal and finance transactions, and legal actions.
- Provide FS planning for the rear area/CSS operations.

7-44. Both the ALOC and BSOC include S1 and S4 personnel cross-trained to ensure continuous operations. The S4, assisted by the personnel staff NCO (PSNCO), supervises ALOC operations. The S1, assisted by the S4 NCO in charge (NCOIC), usually supervises the BSOC. S6 section personnel may augment both operating centers to provide communications and automation support. Table 7-2 outlines one possible ALOC/BSOC organization.

Table 7-2. CSS Operation Center Manning

ALOC (Combat Trains)	BSOC (Field Trains)
S4 (ALOC OIC)	S1 (BSOC OIC)
PSNCO (ALOC NCOIC)	S4 NCOIC (BSOC NCOIC)
Battalion maintenance technician	Battalion maintenance officer
Ammunition officer	Ammunition NCO
Field surgeon or physician's assistant	

7-45. The ALOC and BSOC maintain control of vehicles moving forward to the logistic release points (LRPs) (Figure 7-2). The battalion TSOP establishes procedures for resupply without request in case of communications failure.

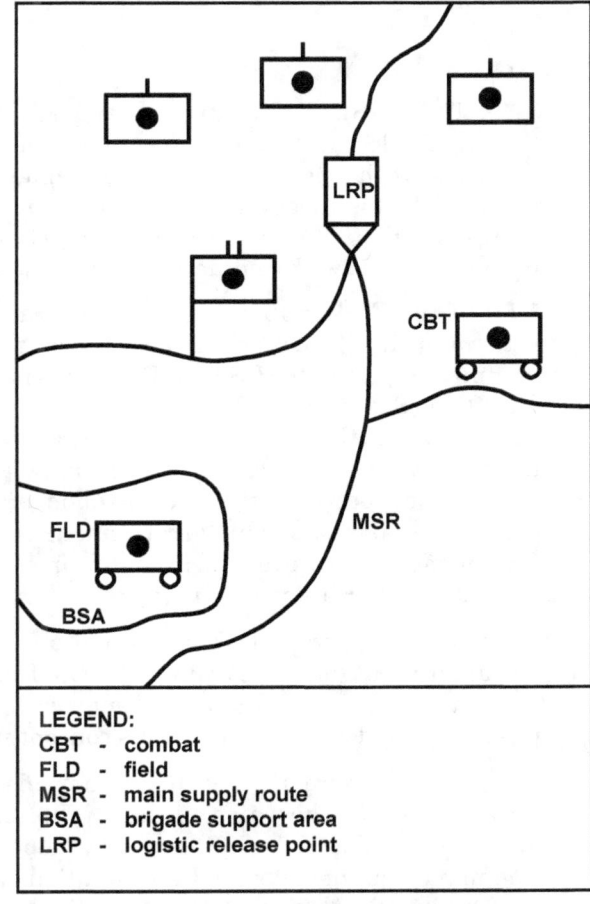

Figure 7-2. Logistic Release Point

TRAINS COMMUNICATIONS

7-46. Trains use a combination of FM radio, MSE, messenger, and wire for communications. The primary means for passing CSS traffic is the admin/log radio net, with the ALOC functioning as the NCS. The ALOC also relies heavily on the MSE/facsimile network.

7-47. The primary subscribers on the admin/log net are the S4, S1, HHSB (HHB/SB) commander, BMO, BAO, medical section, and others (as required). See Chapter 3 for an example admin/log net. The ALOC also monitors the FA battalion command net and supported FA/maneuver and higher HQS admin/log nets as appropriate.

7-48. Procedures for submitting routine reports (such as the personnel daily summary and the DA Form 2406 [Materiel Condition Status Report]) are established by TSOP. CSS reporting may be accomplished by any of the various C2 methods (voice/FAX/data), or in hard copy included as a part of LOGPAC operations. These reports are consolidated by the ALOC and disseminated as necessary. When messenger communications are necessary or used for hard copy backup, the battalion can prevent excessive travel by combining document and parcel delivery with CSS traffic as much as possible.

TRAINS POSITIONING

7-49. The HHSB (HHB/SB) commander coordinates with the XO, S3, S1, and S4 when selecting a trains location. The battalion must coordinate trains positions with the maneuver commander who owns the ground. It can accomplish this through a FSE at a main or rear CP, the force FA HQ, or a DISCOM/COSCOM support battalion. The basic options are: positioning the battalion trains with another element or separately.

7-50. If the FA battalion collocates its trains with another unit, it may have little input in the location. For example, if a FA battalion establishes its field or unit trains in the BSA or DSA, the brigade S4, or the division G4 and DISCOM S3, selects the location. Early planning and coordination are necessary for the FA battalion to provide input on selection of combined trains locations. Collocating the trains with the maneuver trains facilitates coordination between the FA battalion and the supporting division and/or corps CSS elements. This arrangement also enhances security for battalion CSS elements. However, turnaround time, communications, or other mission-related considerations may require location of the trains elsewhere.

7-51. In a low ground threat situation, an alternative is to position the battalion's unit (or field) trains separate from the BSA, DSA, CSG, or FLE, in a location more conducive to supporting the FA battalion. The actual locations will depend on the trains concept used and the distances involved.

7-52. Two or more FA battalions may also collocate trains elements when they operate in the same vicinity. This enhances security and potentially allows some mutual CSS support, depending on weapon system types, command relationships, and coordination. This technique is especially useful for DS/R battalions, and for nondivisional battalions operating near each other, or near a divisional FA unit.

7-53. A good trains location will have the following:
- Defensible terrain - allows selective use of limited personnel assets and avoids obstacles to CSS operations.
- Sufficient space - permits the dispersion of both vehicles and activities.
- Firm ground - supports heavy ammunition and POL vehicles.

- Landing pad - facilitates aerial resupply and medical evacuation.
- Road network - leads to the batteries and higher-level CSS elements; also, a suitable network within the position.
- Communications - extends both forward to the batteries and to rear CSS elements.
- Water source, if possible.

7-54. Built-up areas provide excellent locations for trains because they provide cover and concealment for vehicles and sheltered areas for maintenance operations at night. When built-up areas are used, trains elements should occupy buildings near the edge of the area to reduce the chance of being trapped. Seldom will a site be found that has all of the desirable traits. Priority is given to those considerations that are critical to mission accomplishment.

TRAINS OPERATIONS

7-55. The S4 is responsible for selecting battalion supply routes for resupply, evacuation, and maintenance support. Proposed routes should extend forward from the support elements/areas to the batteries. The S4, with the S3, identifies primary and alternate routes, and coordinates all routes with the maneuver unit responsible for the terrain (and for approving the routes). The S4 should also coordinate routes with adjacent combat, CS, and CSS units to avoid conflicts.

7-56. The S4, in coordination with the commander and S3, establishes CSS priorities that guide subordinate CSS leaders in executing their responsibilities. These guidelines address which supplies, resources, and units have priority, convoy size and security, supply routes used, trains mobility (uploaded ready for hasty moves, or downloaded/stockpiled), day/night movement restrictions, perimeter security, and other instructions necessary for efficient and effective trains operations.

TRAINS DISPLACEMENT

7-57. Proper positioning of trains minimizes displacements and increases the quantity and quality of support. In repositioning, the technique used to displace the trains may be the same as that used by the rest of the battalion, or may differ based on METT-TC. The trains may displace as one entity (independent of or as part of the rest of the battalion), by echelon, by section, or by infiltration.

SECTION II – PLANNING

7-58. CSS planning must address CSS support during all phases of an operation. The battalion staff develops the CSS plan concurrently with the tactical plan. Supporting CSS plans are as detailed as planning time permits. Use of TSOPs and contingency plans greatly help the CSS staff officers in the planning effort. The FASP addresses only the key what, where, when, why, and how CSS issues as well as deviations from the routine procedures established in the TSOP.

CSS PLANNING PROCESS

7-59. To develop and execute sound plans, CSS personnel must achieve and maintain a high degree of situational awareness and initiate actions well before the start of operations they are to support. Careful management of the information flow demands that information requirements be clearly identified early in the process, vigorously pursued, and shared with all involved.

LOGISTICS PREPARATION OF THE BATTLEFIELD

7-60. FA LPB is a conscious effort to identify and assess factors that facilitate, inhibit, or deny support to FA units at the tactical and sometimes operational levels. It involves a review of known EFATs for CSS tasks and the use of the S2's IPB products as an aid in analyzing the manning, arming, fueling, fixing, moving, and sustaining factors. The goal is to determine FA CSS requirements that will allow the development of a logistic estimate and feasible concept of support.

7-61. The process requires that the FA battalion commander, XO, and S3 understand data needed by CSS staff to plan and provide timely, effective support. It requires that the S1 and S4 understand the mission, the scheme of operations/fires, and battlefield time and space implications for support. The LPB is a coordinated effort which:
- Determines data requirements to support required actions.
- Identifies sources for pertinent data and collects raw or processed data.
- Analyzes collected data and develops it into decision information by assessing the impact on the mission and competing COAs.
- Integrates decision information into the MDMP by incorporating it into logistical estimates and FA plans and actions.

7-62. Sources that provide relevant logistical data include the following:
- Higher HQ briefings, plans and orders.
- FA commander's planning guidance and intent.
- Operations and intelligence briefings and overlays.
- Wargaming and rehearsals.
- MTOEs, subordinate status reports, and route reconnaissance overlays.
- Traffic circulation and highway regulation plans.

BATTALION LOGISTIC ESTIMATE

7-63. A logistic estimate, which includes LPB, is a continuous analysis of logistic factors affecting mission accomplishment. Emphasis is on how the status of CSS will impact on proposed COAs. Logistic planners use these estimates to recommend the best COA (that can be supported) and to develop plans to support the operations.

7-64. Logistic estimates at the battalion level are usually informal. As a minimum they are formulated in a briefing format that should address facts, assumptions, and conclusions in each of the following areas:
- Manning (e.g., quality of life, personnel and health service support).
- Arming (e.g., Class V status, restrictions, distribution system, RSR, CSR, and CCL).
- Fueling (e.g., Class III [bulk] status, distribution system, restrictions).
- Fixing (e.g., maintenance and Class IX status, repair times, and evacuation policy).
- Moving (e.g., status of transportation assets, critical LOC, and MSR status).
- Sustaining the soldiers and their systems (e.g., Class I, II, III [Package], IV, VI, VII, X, water, and field services status).
- COA(s) that can be supported.

7-65. Consumption factors and transportation requirements are fundamental parts of the CSS analysis. Guidance for computing these requirements can be found in:
- FM 55-15, *Transportation Reference Data*.
- FM 55-30, *Army Motor Transport Units and Operations*.
- FM 100-10, *Combat Service Support*.
- Operations Logistics Planner (distributed on two diskettes).
- TB 44-46-1, *Standard Characteristics for Transportation of Military Vehicles and Other Oversize/Overweight Equipment*.

7-66. To ensure effective support, CSS operators and planners must understand the commander's tactical plans and intent and develop plans that effectively and efficiently apply resources against requirements. General considerations include:
- Missions and tasks for each of the supported elements.
- When and how they will conduct operations.
- Current and proposed locations of the supported units, by timeline.
- The types and quantities of support required.
- The priority of support by time, type, and unit.
- The overall tactical situation and general unit status.

7-67. Support capabilities are assessed as follows:
- What CSS resources are available (organic, lateral, and higher HQ).
- Where the CSS resources are and when they will be available.
- Whether they will be delivered or must be picked up.
- Packaging, material-handling, loading, or transloading considerations.

7-68. On the basis of mission analysis, resources are compared with requirements. Shortfalls are evaluated in close coordination with operations planners to determine their effect on selected COAs.

7-69. The CSS staff must complete the CSS estimates in time for commanders to confirm the feasibility of the plan, modify plans and priorities as necessary, and calculate risks. Timely completion also facilitates the generation and coordination of supply and support requests.

PLANNING FOR CHANGING MISSIONS

7-70. Flexibility and innovation must characterize CSS planning and execution, as FA units often change missions, areas of operations, and command and support relationship during an operation. Transition from one area of operation to another normally results in a change in support areas and support elements. Therefore, units must forecast future needs with the gaining division or corps support element. Of particular interest are the planning requirements for classes V and IX and maintenance support.

- The FA battalion S4 must verify that the ATPs in its new area of operation will be able to support its requirements.
- The DISCOM/COSCOM may augment the gaining support element with authorized stockage list (ASL) push packages and maintenance support teams from the losing support element or other CSS assets.
- The battalion XO and CSS staff must ensure that adequate support is in the new location on time, without being removed from the old location too early.

SPECIAL CSS PLANNING CONSIDERATIONS

HEAVY-LIGHT FORCES MIX

7-71. Heavy-light or light-heavy force mixes make CSS arrangements especially challenging. When a FA brigade, with medium weapon systems, supports an infantry division, planners must consider that infantry division DISCOMs have little, if any, ability to provide the necessary support for the medium FA battalions. Even with COSCOM augmentation, infantry divisions have insufficient means to maintain and sustain a reinforcing SP FA battalion. In such situations, mission and/or unit specific CSS augmentation packages must accompany heavy forces' FA units. This includes POL, ammunition, and maintenance support with necessary repair parts, recovery and lift capabilities.

7-72. Class IX supplies and maintenance can also present unique CSS planning requirements. For example, a heavy division DISCOM does not have the ASL or maintenance personnel to support 105mm FA howitzer units. As FA battalions move from one brigade or division sector to another, gaining support battalions may require augmentation from losing support battalions, to include ASL push packages and additional maintenance support teams. Habitually associated maintenance support teams (MSTs) can facilitate this process. Also, COSCOM transportation assistance may be required to move ASLs from losing to gaining support units.

ARMY XXI/DIGITIZED FORCE CSS

7-73. CSS concepts and organizational structures are changing to reflect a paradigm shift from a supply-based CSS system in the past to an advanced distribution-based CSS system for Army XXI. These changes are leveraging advancements in technology and information operations.

7-74. The distribution-based CSS system combines situational awareness capabilities with efficient delivery systems to form a seamless distribution pipeline. This pipeline represents "inventory in motion" and the CSS imperative of increased velocity. In contrast, static inventories comprise a supply-based system. Storing this static inventory in large stockpiles at each echelon does not provide the mobility or flexibility required by the Force XXI maneuver commander. The Force XXI distribution-based system eliminates most stockpiles; substituting speed for mass. Logisticians control the destination, speed, and volume of the distribution system. With intransit visibility (ITV), total asset visibility (TAV), advanced materiel management, and advanced decision support system technology, Force XXI logisticians will have access and visibility over all of the items within the distribution pipeline. This visibility allows logisticians to redirect, cross-level, and mass CSS assets more effectively in support of the maneuver commander's intent. The distribution-based system gains speed through greater efficiency. Direct throughput from theater and corps to the brigade battlespace is the rule rather than the exception with distribution-based CSS. Throughput distribution bypasses one or more echelons in the supply system to minimize handling and to speed delivery to forward units. Supplies are tailored and packaged for specific supported units based on a specific time and location point of need, synchronized through support operation channels based on the combat commander's OPTEMPO. Advanced delivery platforms such as the palletized load system (PLS) and the container roll in/roll out platform (CROP), will use ITV/TAV to deliver directly from echelons above division to points as far forward as possible. Extensive use of "hub and spoke" transfer nodes will reduce transportation and material handling requirements.

7-75. Multi-functional, modular units in direct support of the combat, combat support, and combat service support units form the cornerstone of this concept and represent the CSS imperative of an agile CSS force structure. Force XXI battlefield CSS operations will provide support as close to the point of need as possible. A common operational picture coupled with information from the GCSS-A will allow the Force XXI CSS commander to anticipate requirements and project support further forward than ever before. CSS organizations will become modular, mobile, and multi-functional. They will be adaptable to support force projection and velocity of combat operations in both linear and non-linear environments.

7-76. These changes will impact FA CSS operations. FM 63-2-2, contains additional information on digitized division CSS operations.

SECTION III – LOGISTICAL SUPPORT

7-77. The four functional areas that are of primary interest for battalion logisticians are supply, maintenance, field services, and transportation.

SUPPLY

METHODS OF SUPPLY

7-78. The battalion always maintains combat-essential supplies and repair parts (basic loads and PLLs). The minimum stockage level is normally directed by division or higher. These supplies allow a unit to sustain itself in combat for a limited period without resupply.

7-79. The battalion has three methods by which to replenish its stocks:
- Supply point distribution.
- Unit distribution.
- R3P distribution.

Supply Point Distribution

7-80. In supply point distribution, unit representatives, using organic transportation, go to a supply point to pick up supplies. This is the normal method used by the battalion supply section to obtain supplies.

Unit Distribution

7-81. In unit distribution, non-organic transportation delivers supplies to a unit. The battalion often uses this method to resupply subordinate elements. When feasible, supplies are shipped directly from the issuing unit as far forward as possible. This means some supplies are issued directly to the battalion from COSCOM or theater Army level, especially classes III and VII. This issue usually occurs no farther forward than a BSA. CSS planners must consider material handling equipment (MHE) requirements for supply transfers.

7-82. The most efficient resupply of forward units is done by use of LOGPACs. LOGPACs are organized for each battery and element; usually in the unit or field trains under the supervision of the battalion S4 NCOIC (or the SB commander). They are moved forward to the LRPs daily for routine resupply. When possible, all LOGPACs are moved forward in a march unit under the control of an OIC or NCOIC. Special LOGPACs are organized and dispatched as required by the tactical situation and logistical demands. The S4 must plan and coordinate LOGPAC operations to ensure that they fully support the commander's tactical plans.

7-83. Battalion TSOPs establish the standard LOGPAC. Normally, a battery LOGPAC includes:
- POL trucks carrying bulk fuel and packaged POL products.
- Vehicles carrying additional supplies join the LOGPAC as coordinated by the S4 NCOIC and supply sergeant.

- Cargo trucks carrying Class I requirements based on the ration cycle. These may tow water trailers and carry full water cans for direct exchange. The trucks also carry supplies requested by the unit, incoming mail, replacement personnel, and other items required by the unit.

7-84. The battery LOGPAC moves forward under the control of an S4 representative. The convoy normally contains additional vehicles, such as maintenance vehicles with Class IX supplies to move to the UMCP or additional ammunition or fuel vehicles for the combat trains. The LOGPACs follow the MSR to an LRP, where the battery supply sergeant or a guide takes control of the battery LOGPAC.

7-85. The battery representative directs the LOGPAC to the locations where battery or platoon resupply occurs. The supply sergeant informs the S4 representative of requirements for the next LOGPAC. The LOGPAC returns to the LRP with outgoing mail, personnel, and identified equipment.

7-86. The S4, in coordination with the S3, determines LRP locations. Locations are based on the tactical situation and should be well forward and easily located. Normally, two to four LRPs are planned and are included on the operation overlay along with the MSR, combat trains, and field trains. The ALOC notifies subordinates and the BSOC well in advance, which LRP will be used. The battalion may establish TSOP standards for LOGPAC delivery (arrival time at the LRP) and the length of time it will remain in the battery or platoon area. If the tactical situation dictates changes, or if a LOGPAC is delayed, the S4 must notify units, the ALOC/BSOC, and the TOC.

7-87. A senior representative from the trains (S4, HHSB (HHB/SB) commander, or senior NCO) should be present at the LRP while the LOGPAC is in effect. The purpose is to meet with the supply sergeants for coordination of logistical requirements and to ensure that the LOGPAC is released and returned efficiently. A coordination meeting is normally held immediately before the supply sergeant picks up his LOGPAC. Coordination may include the following:
- Changes in logistical requirements, plans, or TSOPs.
- Battery reports on personnel, logistics, and maintenance.
- Updates on the tactical situation and logistical status.
- Delivery, receipt, and distribution of unit mail.

7-88. The S4 representative moves the LOGPAC convoy from the LRP to the unit or field trains. The battalion S4 NCOIC then begins organizing the next LOGPAC.

7-89. The HHSB (or HHB) first sergeant, normally operating from the combat trains, plans and coordinates resupply of the CP, combat trains, and attached elements. The platoon sergeant or the senior NCO at a facility must report his requirements to the HHSB (or HHB) first sergeant or to the ALOC. The methods of resupply are the following:
- Form small LOGPACs (the most desirable method). The platoon sergeant picks up LOGPACs at the LRP, as would a battery supply sergeant.

- Deliver the LOGPAC directly to the CP, combat trains, and attached elements.
- Resupply attached elements from a nearby battery LOGPAC. The S4 coordinates this resupply before dispatching the LOGPACs.

7-90. While the LOGPAC is the preferred method of resupply, other methods of resupply are sometimes required. These methods include:
- Resupply from the combat trains (emergency resupply). The combat trains has a limited amount of Class III and V supplies for emergency resupply. The S4 coordinates emergency resupply from the combat trains and then refills or replaces the combat trains assets. The S3, on the basis of recommendations from the S4 and on battalion operational requirements, determines distribution priorities for critical items. Normal supply priority is Class III, Class V, and Class IX.
- Prestocking. This is the placing and concealing of supplies on the battlefield. It is normally done during defensive operations when supplies are placed in subsequent positions (for example, ammunition for immediate consumption).
- Mobile prepositioning. This is similar to prestocking except that supplies remain on trucks, often positioned forward on the battlefield.

Rearm, Refuel, Resupply Point Distribution

7-91. This technique combines features of both supply point and unit distribution. It emphasizes Class III, V, and IX resupply, typically along the route of an extended battalion road march. However, resupply of all classes will occur whenever possible. R3P operations may also include survey update operations (R3SP). Close coordination between the S3 and S4 is essential to ensure the proper selection of the location and timing of this supply action. The S4 is responsible for the preparation of the R3P site; and coordinates with the S3 to schedule the movement of units through this site. The HHSB/HHB or SB commander or a CSS staff officer may supervise R3P operations. The battalion XO monitors all R3P planning and operations, with special emphasis on the communication and coordination between staff elements and with the firing batteries, to ensure effective, efficient operations in concert with the commander's guidance. While R3P distribution is rapid and often convenient, it does require that the unit take itself out of action to accomplish the resupply function. However, since the unit will normally perform R3P distribution in conjunction with a scheduled move, the overall loss of support capability is minimal.

CLASSES OF SUPPLIES

7-92. Each class of supply requires unique considerations, during logistics planning and operations, which helps speed requisitioning and distribution procedures. Battalion commanders and their staffs need to be aware of supply accountability procedures as presented in AR 710-2.

7-93. The FA battalion usually coordinates directly with the appropriate supply activity of the supporting division or corps support element. However, the DIVARTY or FA brigade monitors items of command interest by means of

TSOP-directed CSS reports. The following paragraphs briefly describe each class of supplies as it impacts on the FA battalion.

Class I: Rations

7-94. A battalion automatically requests Class I on the basis of daily strength reports for its units. The ALOC forwards the strength report to the BSOC or directly to the food service section (under unit trains). The food service section gets subsistence from the supporting Class I point in the BSA, DSA, CSG, or FLE. The S4 or his designated representative, in conjunction with the battery commanders, develops a feeding plan with instructions concerning how and when to feed.

7-95. Flexibility in ration cycles and meal preparation methods is necessary to effectively support fluid FA operations. Often, meal preparation is centralized in the trains location, with the senior food service sergeant supervising preparation and coordinating delivery arrangements with the ALOC. A- or B-rations are prepared in the trains and delivered to the batteries and attached elements as part of the LOGPAC. T-rations are prepared in the trains and sent forward, or they are pushed forward to the batteries and then prepared (heated) on site. The MREs stored on combat vehicles are eaten only when daily Class I resupply cannot be accomplished. The battery 1SG must monitor MRE usage to ensure prompt resupply action. At other times, especially during dispersed or non-linear operations, Class I operations may need to be decentralized.

7-96. Water is not a Class I supply item, but it is normally delivered with Class I. The battalion S4 NCOIC coordinates with the FSB, MSB, CSG, or FLE to pick up water from the designated water supply point. Water is delivered to the units by use of water trailers or blivets. Also, forward water points are tested and approved by the battalion medical officer. Each vehicle should carry water cans to be refilled or exchanged during Class I resupply and LOGPAC operations.

Class II: Supplies and Equipment

7-97. This class applies to all supplies and equipment (except cryptographic) prescribed by TOEs, common table of allowances, and PLLs. Class II supplies include clothing; individual equipment; tentage; organizational tool sets, kits, and hand tools; administrative and housekeeping supplies, and equipment (including battle dress overgarment (BDO) and decontamination items). The S4 section coordinates for pickup of Class II items from the appropriate supply element in the BSA, DSA, or CSG before normal LOGPAC operations. Expendable items, such as soap, toilet tissue, insecticide, clothing and TA-50 items, are provided during LOGPAC operations.

Class III: Petroleum, Oils and Lubricants

7-98. The brigade S4's POL forecasts form the basis for division and corps stockage levels. The FA battalion S4 section normally obtains POL from a Class III supply point in the BSA, DSA, CSG, or FLE. Batteries are not required to submit formal requests for POL and packaged products resupply, unless the products are unique or quantities unusually high. When necessary, the batteries send their requests to the ALOC.

7-99. POL tankers move forward with each LOGPAC. Each tanker may also carry packaged POL products. Depending on the tactical situation, DISCOM or COSCOM fuel vehicles may deliver fuel to the combat trains area. Battery refueling operations may be carried out in one of three ways:
- Fuel trucks move to each section or vehicle position.
- Each section or vehicle moves to a centrally located refuel point.
- Vehicles refuel during movement from one position to another.

7-100. Combat refueling (the use of 5-gallon cans) is an alternative to the above methods. It is slower; however, it may be required in some circumstances when bulk refueling is not available or feasible. The battalion TSOPs should prescribes procedures for all types of refueling. These procedures should be practiced during field training.

Class IV: Construction and Barrier Materials

7-101. This class of supply includes consumable items such as construction and fortification material and the lightweight camouflage support system. Requisitions for regulated Class IV items (fortification and barrier material) are submitted through command channels. Non-regulated items (small quantities of nails and common electrical, plumbing and similar hardware items) are requested or obtained from the appropriate support activity, of the supporting division or corps support element.

Class V: Ammunition

7-102. Some common ammunition terms include the following:
- The unit basic load (UBL) is that quantity of ammunition authorized and required to be on hand in a unit to meet combat needs until resupply can be accomplished. The UBL cannot exceed the haul capacity of the unit's organic vehicles. If the UBL exceeds the unit's organic haul capability, the battalion should notify its higher FA HQ immediately for assistance in resolving the situation. The basic load, specified by the theater army for the FA, is expressed in rounds, units, or units of weight, as appropriate. UBL size and composition are based on mission, enemy, and type unit supported, and normally varies among FA units.
- The RSR is the amount of ammunition a commander estimates will be needed to sustain tactical operations, without ammunition expenditure restrictions, over a period of time. The RSR is expressed as rounds per weapon (on hand) per day, or as a bulk allotment per day or per mission.
- The CSR is the rate of consumption of ammunition that can be allocated, considering the supplies and facilities available, for a given period. It is also expressed in rounds per weapon per day. Each tactical commander announces a CSR to the next subordinate tactical commander. The CSRs may be published in the OPORD or as a FRAGO. They may be included in the FSP or the FASP. To exceed its CSR, the battalion must obtain permission from the next higher commander, except in an emergency.

- Ammunition for immediate consumption is ammunition drawn for a specific purpose, such as a preparation. This ammunition is drawn in addition to the CSR. It is drawn to be expended within the next 24 hours and is considered expended when issued. If circumstances preclude expenditure as planned, the battalion must report this ammunition as excess daily until it is expended or reallocated.
- Ammunition transfer points are temporary sites where Class V materiel is transferred from corps or division transportation to issuing unit vehicles. ATPs, run by division or corps support units, are usually found in or near BSA, DSAs, CSGs, or FLEs.
- An ammunition supply point is an area designated to receive, store, and issue Class V material. It is normally located at or near the DSA or CSG and is operated by a corps ammunition company.
- A CCL is a single or multi-type load of ammunition built to the anticipated or actual needs of a firing unit, thereby facilitating throughput to the lowest echelon. CCLs are often designed to fit standard transportation assets and for transportation as a single unit. FA ammunitions are packaged and delivered in completed rounds (e.g., fuzes, primers, propellants and projectiles) and rocket or missile pods. See Table 7-3 for FA examples of CCLs.

Table 7-3. FA Sample CCL Packages

EXAMPLE PACKAGE G				
#	DODIC	NOMENCLATURE	QUANTITY	PERCENT
1.	D544	M107/M795 HE	4 Pallets (32 Projectiles)	18
2.	D563	M483A1 DPICM	18 Pallets (144 Projectiles)	82
3.	D541	M4, WH Bag,	2 Pallets (168 Prop Chgs)	74
4.	D533	M119A2, RB	2 Pallets (60 Prop Chgs)	26
5.	N340	M739, Fuze, PD	1 Box (16 Fuzes)	9
6.	N463	M728, Fuze, VT	1 Box (16 Fuzes)	9
7.	N289	M762, Fuze, ET	9 Boxes (144 Fuzes)	82
8.	N523	M82, Primer	1 Box (500 Primers)	100+
TOTAL WEIGHT: 13 Short Tons				
EXAMPLE PACKAGE J, SMOKE				
#	DODIC	NOMENCLATURE	QUANTITY	PERCENT
1.	D528	M825 Smoke	20 Pallets (160 Projectiles)	100
2.	D541	M4, WH Bag	1 Pallet (84 Prop Chgs)	53
3.	D533	M119A2, RB	4 Pallets (120 Prop Chgs)	75
4.	N285	M577, Fuze, MT	10 Boxes (160 Fuzes)	100
5.	N523	M82, Primer	1 Box (500 Primers)	100+
TOTAL WEIGHT: 12 Short Tons				

RSR Calculation

7-103. The RSR is the battalion's estimate of the amount of ammunition it will require for an operation. Determining the RSR is the responsibility of the battalion S3 and can be accomplished in a number of ways. These include personal experience, historical data from similar battles, and use of automated planning factors on the Operations Logistics Planner's diskettes. RSR reporting requirements may verify with TSOP and the tactical situation. Generally, the RSR is submitted through the supported maneuver force or senior FA HQs, with information copies to appropriate HQs. All RSRs are consolidated and reviewed at higher HQ, and used in determining the CSR for each unit. The FA battalion will generally receive its CSR through the same channels that it reports its RSR.

7-104. The manual method discussed here provides a method in computing an RSR for artillery ammunition. To determine the RSR, use the following steps:

- Step 1 - Determine the level of the operation using Table 7-4.

Table 7-4. Levels of Operation

LEVELS OF OPERATION			
Level of Operation	Percent of Commitment		Commitment of Higher HQ Reserves
	Maneuver	Fire Support	
Heavy	60+	100	Probable
Moderate	30+	50+	Not Anticipated
Light	30-	50-	No

- Step 2 - From Table 7-5, select the type of weapon system for which the RSR is being calculated. Rounds are expressed in number of rounds per tube per day (rounds/tube/day).
- Step 3 - Select the type of operation and level of operation in Table 7-5. If the type of operation is not listed, use the conversion table listed in Table 7-6.
- Step 4 - Compute ammunition requirements for the operation by using Table 7-5:
  - Day 1: Number of rounds required for the first day extracted from the first day column in the table.
  - Day 2-4: Number of rounds from the succeeding days column multiplied by the number of days to be computed (see Note (1), Table 7-5).
  - Day 5: Average the number of rounds from the succeeding and protracted days for the weapon system (see Note (1), Table 7-5).
  - Day 6-15: Number of rounds from the protracted days column multiplied by the number of days (see Note (1), Table 7-5).

Table 7-5. Daily Ammunition Requirements-Rounds Per Weapon and STON (Example)

Type of Operation	Level of Operation	First Day		Succeeding Days (1)		Protracted Period (2)	
		Rounds	STON(3)	Rounds	STON	Rounds	STON
105mm Howitzer							
Covering Force	1-Heavy	491	16.8	511	17.5	198	6.8
	2-Moderate	319	10.9	332	11.4	129	4.4
	3-Light	172	5.9	179	6.1	69	2.4
Defense of Position	1-Heavy	423	14.5	467	16.0	222	7.6
	2-Moderate	275	9.4	304	10.4	144	4.9
	3-Light	148	5.1	163	5.6	78	2.7
Attack of Position	1-Heavy	376	12.9	381	13.0	210	7.2
	2-Moderate	244	8.4	248	8.5	137	4.7
	3-Light	132	4.5	133	4.6	74	2.5
155mm Howitzer (Divisional)							
Covering Force	1-Heavy	254	17.2	274	18.6	174	11.8
	2-Moderate	165	11.2	178	12.1	113	7.7
	3-Light	89	6.0	96	6.5	61	4.1
Defense of Position	1-Heavy	203	13.8	207	14.0	183	12.4
	2-Moderate	132	9.0	135	9.2	119	8.1
	3-Light	71	4.8	72	4.9	64	4.3
Attack of Position	1-Heavy	146	9.9	153	10.4	140	9.5
	2-Moderate	95	6.4	99	6.7	91	6.2
	3-Light	51	3.5	54	3.7	49	3.3
155mm Howitzer (Nondivisional)							
Covering Force	1-Heavy	309	21.0	333	22.6	212	14.4
	2-Moderate	201	13.6	216	14.7	138	9.4
	3-Light	108	7.3	117	7.9	74	5.0
Defense of Position	1-Heavy	227	15.4	235	15.9	199	13.5
	2-Moderate	148	10.0	153	10.4	129	8.8
	3-Light	79	5.3	82	5.6	70	4.7
Attack of Position	1-Heavy	176	11.9	183	12.4	170	11.5
	2-Moderate	114	7.7	119	8.1	111	7.5
	3-Light	62	4.2	64	4.3	60	4.1

NOTE: (1) Succeeding days are the second, third and fourth days of the battle. For the fifth day ammunition requirements, take the average of the succeeding days rate and the protracted rate.
(2) Protracted period refers to days 6 through 15. For estimating ammunition requirements for periods greater than 15 days, use rates provided in SB 38-26, as amended by DA message 262258Z Aug 76.
(3) Short tons (STONS) are computed based on total weight per complete round:
105mm - 68.5 lb/rd , 155mm - 135.7 lb/rd

Table 7-6. Conversion Factor Table

TYPE OF OPERATION	CONVERSION FACTOR
Attack of position	100% of attack of position (deliberately organized)
Covering Force	100% of defense of position
Inactive Situation	80% of protracted period
Meeting Engagement	200% of protracted period
Pursuit	40% of protracted period
Retrograde Operation	59% of defense of position (succeeding days)
Assault of Hostile Shore	100% of defense of position (succeeding days)

- Step 5 - Beyond day 15, use SB 38-26.
- Step 6 - Divide the total rounds by the number of days in the operation. This will give the number of rounds/tube/day.

EXAMPLE

Divisional 155mm battalion conducting a heavy level, attack of position for **10 days**.

Requirement: Compute the RSR.

Day 1:	146
Days 2-4:	459 (153 x 3)
Days 6-10:	700 (140 x 5)
Day 5:	146 ((153 + 140)/2)
	1451 Total Rounds

Answer = **145 Rounds/Tube/Day** for this operation.
1451/10 (Total rounds divided by the total days)

Ammunition Resupply

7-105. The FA ammunition system involves the supply and expenditure of all ammunition that FA battalions are equipped to fire. Small-arms ammunition constitutes an insignificant portion of FA battalion daily tonnage requirements. It can be handled routinely with normal ammunition resupply. Thus a FA battalion focuses on its artillery ammunition.

7-106. The FA battalion S4 plans for and supervises Class V operations and the BAO supervises resupply operations. The S3, S4, and BAO must continually coordinate and exchange information concerning ammunition. Each must know the RSR submitted to higher HQ, the CSR established by higher HQ, and the authorized basic load. This information is provided to the battalion and battery commanders so they can plan resupply operations and set priorities.

7-107. Most of the ammunition in a theater is distributed through the corps storage areas (CSAs), which serve as the focal points of the corps ammunition system. Each corps will usually establish a CSA in the corps rear area and one behind each committed division. Allocation depends upon METT-TC and the size of the corps' stockage objective. CSAs provide corps-wide ammunition support. They serve as the primary source of high-tonnage ammunition for the division. Based on divisional forecasted needs, CSA personnel configure CCLs and ship ammunition to ASPs and ATPs. CSAs also provide support to units operating in the rear of the corps rear area as well as support for reconstitution operations.

7-108. The corps also establishes up to three ASPs and an ATP (the division RATP in the DSA) in each division rear area to support combat units and division ATPs. On occasion, the COSCOM may establish ASPs farther forward in the division area, especially when supporting covering force operations. The division operates up to four ATPs (one for each maneuver brigade, and one for the aviation brigade). The ATPs usually receive the majority of their ammunition in CCLs delivered directly from the CSA, with the remainder coming from the ASP.

7-109. The CSAs receive ammunition from the port and TSA in both breakbulk and containerized shipments, and in various load configurations. In the CSA, corps ammunition units configure much of the ammunition into standard CCLs specifically designed to fit on available transportation assets, such as PLS flatracks, or into mission/unit specific CCLs, often for throughput delivery. A smaller amount of ammunition may remain in breakbulk, container, or single DODIC configuration. The ammunition is stored or sent forward to the ATP, or ASP, or delivered directly to the field trains of FA units (METT-TC dependent). CCLs may also be configured in an ASP or ATP. As much as possible, downloading and handling of ammunition is kept to a minimum. An overview of the Class V distribution system is at Figure 7-3.

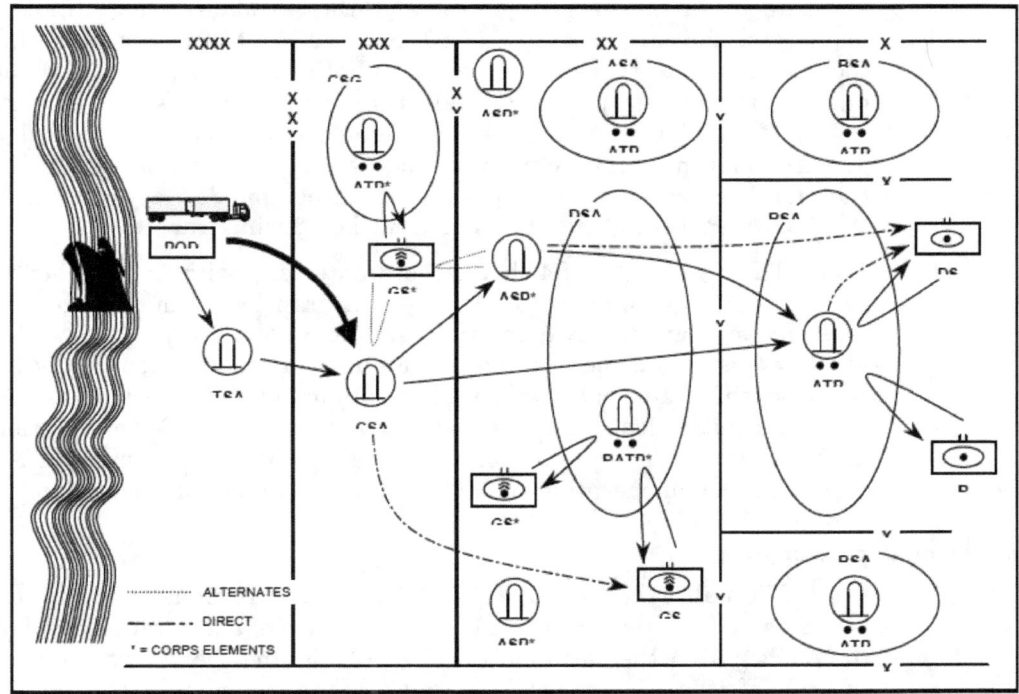

Figure 7-3. Class V Distribution

7-110. A FA battalion will submit its ammunition requests directly to the support operations officer of the supporting division or corps support battalion in the BSA, DSA, CSG, or FL, or to the supported maneuver S4 or senior FA HQs, depending on the situation and command/support relationships. Division and corps ammunition officers consolidate requests, verify CSRs can support the requests, and provide instructions on where and when the ammunition can be picked up or will be delivered.

7-111. A FA battalion will usually obtain Class V from an ATP operating in or near a BSA, DSA, CSG, or FLE. However, it may also obtain some or all of its ammunition from a corps ASP, or even directly from a CSA in some cases.

Also, with throughput distribution, corps and division assets may deliver ammunition directly to the battalion trains. This may be accomplished by vehicle, helicopter, or even parachute. Infrequently, the battalion may pick up ammunition directly from a seaport or airport.

7-112. At the designated ammunition site, FA battalion ammunition vehicles often have to go to only a single vehicle or trailer to get the items needed (because of CCLs). These are primarily transload operations using organic MHE. For FA cannon units this consists of pallets with complete rounds versus going to different trailers for each component, e.g., projectile, propellant, primers and fuzes. However, some ammunition may be picked up as individual items, or may require manual, forklift, or other handling procedures. For MLRS units ammunition transload involves launch pod containers.

7-113. Also, the ammunition vehicles used by the corps and division ordnance and transportation units may not match the battalion's ammunition vehicles one-for-one for cargo space. The S3, S4, and BAO must consider this when coordinating CCL requests. If overall quantity is important, CCLs should be built to maximize corps (or division) transportation assets and delivery to the ATPs. If rapid transloading or through-put delivery of a critical or low-density ammunition directly to an end-user is more important, the S4 must thoroughly coordinate the preparation, loading, and delivery of those CCLs at the ASP/ATP. They should be clearly marked during transit.

7-114. The FA battalion S4 should coordinate early with the support battalion or ammunition element to identify non-transload ammunition handling requirements and the availability of additional MHE support. The S4 should identify this before the battalion's ammunition sections depart the battalion trains so that additional personnel or equipment can be added as necessary and ammunition leaders briefed prior to departure for the ammunition point. This also gives the ammunition point leaders time to ensure that ATP/ASP organization and operations will meet the battalion requirements.

Battalion Ammunition Resupply

7-115. Normally, the BAO of each FA battalion is responsible for the resupply of the firing batteries. He must know all aspects of ammunition availability at the ATP or ASP, the battalion's RSR and CSR, and the locations (present and future) of the firing batteries and resupply points. He obtains this information from the OPORD (e.g., support annex, FASP) and close and frequent coordination with the battalion S4/ALOC and/or S3/operations section. The BAO can best perform coordination and management functions from the combat trains. The battalion XO or S4 NCOIC (or SB commander) must coordinate with the brigade S4, the DAO representative at the ATP, or the CSG representative at the ATP or ASP to ensure that correct locations, procedures, and handling requirements are identified and agreed upon.

7-116. The BAO plans how to most effectively use the batteries' ammunition hauling assets and how to use and control convoys for ammunition pickup and delivery. The load plans for each vehicle must allow for the delivery of CCLs and complete rounds and make maximum use of organic carrying capacity. In coordination with the S3 and S4, the BAO carefully plans for the delivery of the appropriate types and lots of ammunition to the right locations and the designated times. The capability of the battalion to mass fires must not be compromised by Class V incompatibility. Other aspects that must be considered include the following:

- The size of a convoy depends on the tactical situation and the level of training of ammunition personnel. If the unit is in heavy contact or the enemy has a good moving-target-acquisition capability, infiltration by groups of two or three vehicles may be best. Other situations (darkness, surge, or peak requirements) may dictate the use of larger convoys.
- Each convoy, regardless of size, must have one person in charge and a designated succession of control.
- Battery assets should be used and controlled consistent with the resupply option selected.
- Each firing battery reports the arrival of an ammunition convoy to the battalion operations section.
- Ammunition carrier loads must be configured to carry complete rounds of ammunition or proper launch pod loads.
- A series of standardized, preconfigured ammunition loads should be developed and the ammunition sections trained to use them. This allows flexibility and saves time when briefing crews and transloading.

7-117. On demand, ammunition is sent to a firing battery. There the XO, platoon leader, FDO, chief of firing battery, or platoon sergeant signs a hand-receipt for ammunition received. The battery is responsible for supervising and directing issue of ammunition to the firing sections. All ammunition supplied by an ammunition supply point will be signed for on a DA Form 581 (Request for Issue and Turn-in of Ammunition) or for training ammunition on DA Form 5515 (Training Ammunition Control Document).

7-118. Technological advancements in real-time forecasting of Class V sustainment requirements allow more effective ammunition planning. In addition, throughput distribution of Class V, packaged to weapon system requirements, reduces the need for high stockage of ammunition at ASP and the extent of ATP operations.

Class VI: Personal Demand Items

7-119. Class VI includes personal items sold through post exchanges (PXs). Requests for support are submitted by the S1 through administrative channels when PXs are not available. In some cases, ration supplementary sundry packs are issued along with normal ration distribution.

Class VII: Major End Items

7-120. The issuing of major end items (howitzers and ammunition carriers) is closely controlled through command channels. Issue priorities for the replacement of battle or other losses are based on item availability, unit mission, and the tactical situation. The DISCOM or COSCOM processes requests (usually in the form of battle loss reports) from requesting units. Class VII items may not be available in the early periods of a conflict because of limited pre-stocks and the lack of supply lines. These items may be delivered to the battalion, or the battalion may be required to pick up the items from a designated support unit. In some cases, weapon system replacement items (howitzers) may be provided to the battalion with crew, fuel, and ammunition, preferably during routine LOGPAC operations. Weapon system replacement operations (WSRO) are discussed in detail later in this chapter.

Class VIII: Medical Supplies

7-121. FA battalions obtain medical supplies through medical channels. A divisional battalion medical section gets supplies from the divisional clearing station in the BSA or DSA. A nondivisional battalion may obtain its supplies from a divisional clearing station or from corps medical assets in a BSA, DSA, or CSG. The battalion medical section provides organizational maintenance for medical items. Maintenance above this level is obtained by evacuating equipment through medical channels to the medical company in the BSA or to a comparable COSCOM element. For organizational maintenance, the medical section also stocks medical repair parts.

Class IX: Repair Parts

7-122. The FA battalion stocks repair parts based on a PLL. The battalion equipment maintenance clerk orders and stocks high-demand and combat-essential repair parts for vehicles, weapons (artillery and small arms), NBC equipment, and food service equipment. The battalion S6 section (or communications platoon) orders and stocks repair parts for C-E equipment.

7-123. Repair parts are issued in response to a specific request or by repairable (direct) exchange. The battalion gets repair parts from the Class IX supply point in the BSA, DSA, CSG, or FLE. Parts are moved forward during routine LOGPAC operations or as required to the UMCP. The maintenance section requests Class IX items (less repairable exchange) and major Class IX subassemblies, such as engines and transmissions. It submits requests to the supporting division or corps maintenance element of the appropriate support battalion (in the BSA, DSA, CSG, or FLE). Repairable exchange for selected items (including components and subassemblies) is handled as a simple exchange of the unserviceable item (with an attached request for issue or turn-in) for a serviceable item. In combat, exchange and cannibalization are the norm to obtain critical Class IX supplies.

Class X: Material to Support Non-military Programs

7-124. Material to support non-military programs, such as agriculture and economic development, is not included in Classes I through IX. Class X items are requested and obtained by the S4 on the basis of civil-military requirements. Specific instructions for request and issue of Class X supplies are provided by division or higher.

MAINTENANCE

7-125. Maintenance involves inspecting, testing, servicing, repairing, requisitioning, and recovering equipment. The FA battalion completes repair and recovery as far forward as possible, at the lowest capable echelon. When equipment cannot be repaired on site, it is moved only as far as necessary for repair. When all maintenance requirements of the battalion cannot be met, the XO determines maintenance support priorities for subordinate units. These priorities are based on operational requirements of the battalion and on recommendations of the S3, S4, and BMO.

7-126. Common maintenance terms include the following:
- A **MST** is a mobile team from the FSB, MSB, or CSG maintenance company organized and equipped to provide forward support.
- A **UMCP** is a facility established by the battalion maintenance section to collect equipment awaiting repair, evacuation, controlled exchange, or cannibalization. It is the first point to which battery maintenance teams recover equipment and at which some DS maintenance is performed. It is located next to the combat trains.
- **Controlled exchange** is the removal of serviceable parts, components, or assemblies from unserviceable, economically repairable equipment and their immediate reuse in restoring a like item to combat-operable or serviceable condition.
- **Cannibalization** is the authorized removal of parts or components from uneconomically non-repairable or disposable end items or assemblies and making them available for reuse.
- **Battlefield damage assessment and repair** (BDAR) is the act of inspecting battle damage to determine its extent, classifying the type of repairs required and determining the procedure best suited to make the equipment mission-capable. BDAR may involve the immediate repair of equipment by field-expedient methods; however, BDAR procedures shall be used only in combat, at the direction of the commander.
- In FA battalions with consolidated CSS, the **battery maintenance team** is a team from the maintenance platoon that is organized and equipped by MTOE to provide forward unit maintenance support. Normally, the team deploys a recovery vehicle and a maintenance truck forward with the battery, split between each platoon (when applicable). In battalions with a decentralized CSS structure the batteries have their own organic maintenance sections.

MAINTENANCE CONCEPTS

7-127. The following battlefield maintenance concepts illustrate how echelons overlap to provide continuous maintenance support to the batteries.

7-128. The BMO task-organizes the maintenance platoon according to his analysis of current and anticipated requirements. He is concerned with providing the appropriate support at battery, UMCP, CP, and trains locations.

7-129. Normally, (in centralized CSS battalions or during centralized CSS operations) the battalion provides each battery its habitually associated maintenance team. Usually, the battalion's recovery vehicles are positioned forward with each firing battery but remain under battalion control. This provides a quick-fix capability for those items that can be repaired in less than two hours and a recovery capability for those items requiring more extensive repairs.

7-130. The battalion normally establishes the UMCP next to the combat trains. It includes the maintenance platoon HQ (-), HHSB (or HHB) maintenance team and PLL, number 2 common tool kit and welding equipment and the DS MST (-). The BMO task organizes the UMCP according to the maintenance requirements and the tactical situation. The UMCP cannot become a collection point for non-operational vehicles to the extent that it cannot move with an hour's notice. Anything that cannot be repaired in the UMCP or that cannot be towed by UMCP assets is recovered to the field trains or sent directly to the FSB maintenance company in the BSA. The battalion maintenance technician (BMT) and the senior maintenance supervisor supervise the UMCP.

7-131. The rest of the maintenance platoon is in the field trains (or the unit trains) under the control of the BMO and the battalion motor sergeant. The battalion maintenance platoon organizes to support six elements - three firing batteries, the CP, the combat trains and the field trains (or unit trains) as follows:

- Each of the three firing battery maintenance trucks and PLL trailers provides tools and repair parts to support one battery. These vehicles also transport packaged POL to support repair operations. The HHSB maintenance truck carries tools and PLL to support the vehicles habitually located in the trains and at the CP. (In units with an HHB and SB, using dual trains, HHB maintenance supports the CP and combat trains while the SB maintenance truck with PLL items supports the vehicles and equipment located in the field trains.)
- The BMO sets direct support maintenance element priorities. Since the maintenance elements are equipped and trained to support the unit, task-organizing DS maintenance assets is not routine. The PLL parts, special tools, and test sets are not easily split.

NOTE: Direct support FA battalions organic to light divisions do not have the personnel or equipment assets to completely implement the procedures as described. However, the concept is valid for light units and must be adjusted on the basis of the unit's organic capabilities.

7-132. The battery maintenance vehicles are in the forward platoon locations. These vehicles carry the toolboxes, unit-level technical manuals, a limited number of special tools, and repair parts.

7-133. If a damaged vehicle cannot be repaired within two hours, it is recovered to the UMCP or the field/unit trains by the forward-positioned recovery vehicles. Recovery vehicles are directed by battalion maintenance to support recovery operations regardless of battery affiliation.

7-134. Maintenance elements from the FA battalion, FSB, MSB, or CSB repair damaged vehicles recovered to the UMCP. When not involved in on-site repairs, the battery maintenance teams may also repair vehicles in the UMCP. This is especially true of work requiring diagnostic test equipment that cannot be taken into the forward positions.

7-135. Vehicles that the unit can't repair within six hours, or if their repair would otherwise overload the capability of the UMCP, are recovered to the field/unit trains or taken directly to the FSB, MSB, CSB, or CSG collection point for repair. This recovery is done by the battery or battalion maintenance recovery vehicles, or with heavy equipment transporters (HETs). The use of HETs applies to FA units equipped with tracked vehicles. The BMT coordinates and directs the method to be used. The use of HETs is preferred; however, road conditions and availability restrict their use. HETs are requested through the FSB, MSB, CSB, or CSG. Some crew members go with the recovered vehicle to the rear to help mechanics repair the vehicle and return it to the unit when repaired. They also man operational weapon systems on the vehicle to provide additional security to rear areas. Installed C-E equipment remains in the vehicle when it is evacuated. Crewmen not going with the vehicle remove personal equipment and any special equipment before the vehicle leaves the area.

7-136. The UMCP usually displaces with the other elements of the combat/unit trains. During periods of frequent displacement, the BMT may direct that the UMCP displace by echelon. In this case, some personnel of the maintenance platoon, including the BMT, complete repair on vehicles at the old UMCP before displacing. Maintenance platoon assets not involved in repairs move with the rest of the combat trains and establish the forward UMCP. During rapid forward moves, such as exploitation, the UMCP conducts only essential repairs and simple recovery. Other disabled vehicles are taken to collection points on the MSR to be repaired or evacuated. Field trains and the maintenance elements of the FSB, MSB, CSB, and/or CSG displace forward to subsequent locations. The BMT coordinates the repair or evacuation with the battalion motor sergeant in the field trains.

7-137. In the field/unit trains, remaining elements of the battalion maintenance platoon perform other tracked and wheeled vehicle maintenance and class IX resupply. The battalion motor sergeant coordinates requirements with the S4 (and HHSB/SB commander) and with the maintenance element of the FSB, MSB, CSB, or CSG. He also coordinates maintenance requirements with the parent HQ of any attached or supporting elements working with the battalion.

FIELD SERVICES

MORTUARY AFFAIRS

7-138. Mortuary affairs services are provided by the MSB or CSG supply and service company. Mortuary affairs at battalion level consist of three functions: collection, identification, and evacuation. The soldier who has knowledge of the casualty should usually complete the appropriate forms. Subordinate elements send the forms to the field/unit trains with the returning LOGPAC. Unit personnel collect any military equipment and turn it over to the supply sergeant for forwarding during LOGPAC operations. Remains are placed in a human remains pouch, along with personal effects, and evacuated to the field trains. The battalion may establish a collection point, if necessary, at the combat/unit trains under the control of the S4. In any case, the unit should evacuate remains as quickly as possible to the collection point in the BSA, DSA, CSG, or FLE.

SHOWER, LAUNDRY, AND CLOTHING REPAIR

7-139. The MSB, CSB, CSG or FLE may provide shower, laundry, and clothing repair services. The FA battalion S4 requests clothing exchange (or gratuitous issue), laundry, and shower service through the brigade S4, FSB, MSB, CSB or CSG. The request must specify:

- The location of the unit making the request.
- The desired time for service.
- The range of clothing sizes for unit members.

7-140. The requesting unit must be prepared to furnish soldiers to help set up the shower, laundry, and clothing repair operation. Normally, there is one shower, laundry, and clothing repair service point per BSA, DSA, and CSG.

SALVAGE

7-141. The supporting CSS element will also provide salvage services. Salvage collection points are established in the BSA, DSA, CSG and FLE. They receive serviceable, unserviceable (repairable), discarded, abandoned, and captured supplies and equipment. The salvage point will not accept COMSEC or medical supplies, toxic agents, radioactive materials, contaminated equipment, aircraft, ammunition, and explosives.

LAUNDRY AND RENOVATION

7-142. COSCOM provides laundry and renovation services when the tactical situation permits. This service is coordinated through the brigade S4.

TRANSPORTATION

7-143. Should the FA battalion require transportation support beyond its organic capabilities, the S4 forwards a request to the maneuver brigade, or force FA HQ S4. They forward the request to the movement control officer (MCO) at the DISCOM or COSCOM. The MCO makes a determination based on requirements and existing priorities.

FM 3-09.21 (FM 6-20-1)

SECTION IV – PERSONNEL AND HEALTH SERVICES SUPPORT

7-144. Personnel and health services support functions sustain the morale and welfare of the soldier. At battalion level, these include personnel and administrative (P&A) services, legal services, finance services, postal services, chaplain activities, health services support, and EPW support.

PERSONNEL AND ADMINISTRATIVE SERVICES

S1 FUNCTIONS

7-145. P&A services are the responsibility of the battalion S1. The duties include the following:

Strength Accounting

7-146. Batteries and attached elements submit a personnel daily summary report to the S1 representative in the ALOC. The S1 forwards a battalion consolidated report to or through the maneuver brigade and/or force FA HQ S1. The S1 representative provides the TOC and PAC (in the field trains) with an information copy. These reports are the basis for individual replacements and Class I resupply. Accurate strength reports also give the commander and staff information to plan operations. Battalion TSOPs usually describe daily reporting requirements. Personnel strength reports should prominently note any critical skill shortages.

Casualty Reporting

7-147. The S1 ensures that both strength and casualty reporting are timely and accurate. Initial reports are usually verbal or plain text message. Written reporting occurs as soon as possible after the event. The section chief or any individual having knowledge of the incident initiates it. The DA Form 1156 is carried by all small-unit leaders and is used to report battle and nonbattle casualties. It provides initial information for notifying next of kin and for paying benefits. When a soldier is reported missing or missing in action or when the remains are not under US control, a DA Form 1155 goes with the DA Form 1156. The first sergeant collects the reports and forwards them to the ALOC. The S1 cross-checks the reports, requests any needed clarification, adjusts unit strength reports, and forwards the reports through the PAC to the maneuver brigade and/or force FA HQ S4 and informs the battalion TOC.

Replacement Operations

7-148. The PAC monitors replacement flow. The battalion S1 establishes a replacement receiving point (RRP) (usually in the field trains) and notifies the maneuver brigade and/or force FA HQ S1 of its location. All replacements or hospital returnees are brought to the RRP for initial processing. The division or corps adjutant general is normally responsible for delivering replacements to the RRP. Replacements are briefed on TSOPs and equipped with weapons and field gear before leaving the trains. They normally move forward to their unit with a LOGPAC.

Other Administrative Services

7-149. During lulls in the battle, the S1 and PAC complete all other P&A actions necessary. Special consideration is given to timely processing of awards and decorations.

LEGAL SERVICES

7-150. The S1 section coordinates legal services support for commanders, staffs, and soldiers. The division or corps staff judge advocate sections provide the actual support to the FA battalion on a GS basis. The support includes:

- Legal advice to commanders on all matters involving military law, domestic law, foreign law, international law, and administrative proceedings.
- Representation to soldiers accused and/or suspected in military justice matters and to personnel pending adverse military personnel action.
- Advice to soldiers on complaints, reports of survey, and the right to silence in administrative proceedings.
- Legal assistance to soldiers on personal civil legal matters.

FINANCE SERVICES

7-151. Mobile pay teams from the corps area finance support unit provide finance support to the FA battalion. During low-intensity operations, the mobile pay teams provide personal check cashing services and/or make combat payments to soldiers in amounts established by the theater army commander or in lesser amounts if the soldier so desires. The force FA commander may establish an amount less than the maximum for personnel assigned, depending on the tactical situation and the needs of the soldier. When and where the soldier is paid are determined by the commander and coordinated by the S1.

POSTAL SERVICES

7-152. A postal element, assigned by the corps DS postal company, receives and separates mail by battalion and then turns it over to the maneuver brigade or next higher FA HQ S1. The battalion mail clerk receives and sorts the mail by task organization. He distributes it to the unit supply sergeant (assistant mail clerk), who delivers it to the first sergeant or to the soldier himself (accountable mail) during LOGPAC resupply.

CHAPLAIN ACTIVITIES

7-153. The unit ministry team (UMT) (one chaplain and one chaplain's assistant) facilitates and coordinates religious support across the battalion AO. The UMT often operates out of the combat trains, however it positions itself based on its mission and METT-TC. The UMT may move forward with LOGPACs when visiting batteries or other battalion locations. This team is dedicated to serving the spiritual needs of soldiers. The UMT coordinates with all staff members, to include the S1, who receives messages and requests for religious support and ensures the necessary UMT information is published in paragraph 4 of the FASP. The UMT mission includes:

- Providing worship opportunities.

- Administering sacraments, rites, and ordinances.
- Providing pastoral care and counseling.
- Advising the commander and staff on matters of religion, morals, and morale.
- Ministering to casualties and those suffering battle fatigue.
- Providing spiritual fitness training to enhance soldier morale and unit cohesion.
- Routinely visiting unit soldiers in nearby hospitals.

HEALTH SERVICES SUPPORT

PLANNING

7-154. Battalion health services support is planned by the medical section OIC (battalion field surgeon or physicians assistant) and the S1. The battalion medical section provides the service. The FSB, MSB, CSB, or CSG medical company provides backup support. To support battalion operations, the field surgeon or physician's assistant and the supporting medical operations officer must understand the scheme of maneuver as well as the medical support plan.

ORGANIZATION

7-155. The FA battalion medical section is organized with a treatment team, an ambulance team, and a combat medic section. This organization allows quick evacuation of wounded soldiers for treatment by trained medical personnel within 30 minutes of the time they are wounded. The medical section in light units consists of the medical treatment team and a combat medic section. The medical treatment team establishes the battalion aid station, which operates from the combat trains. The ambulance team also operates from the BAS.

7-156. Combat medics habitually work with the same battery. It is often necessary to augment these medics with soldiers who have received intense medical training (combat lifesavers). The goal is to train one combat lifesaver per section throughout the battalion.

FUNCTIONS

7-157. The functions of the platoon medic are to:
- Provide emergency medical treatment and protection for the sick and wounded.
- Assist section crews in evacuating injured crewmen from their vehicles.
- Provide medical evacuation.
- Initiate field medical cards for the sick and wounded, and time permitting, complete cards for deceased personnel.
- Screen, evaluate, and treat patients suffering from minor illnesses and injuries; return to duty patients requiring no further attention; and notify the first sergeant of those requiring evacuation to the BAS.

- Inform the battery commander and the battalion surgeon of the status of patients seen and the overall status of health and welfare of the platoon.
- Train unit personnel self-aid and buddy aid.
- Provide trained combat lifesavers with medical supplies, as required.

7-158. The BAS has medically trained personnel to stabilize patients for further evacuation, to perform immediate lifesaving or limb-saving techniques, and to treat minor wounds or illnesses and return the patients to duty. Other functions of the BAS include the following:
- Receive and record patients.
- Notify the S1 of all patients processed and the disposition of casualties as directed by TSOP.
- Prepare field medical records and verify information on field medical cards.
- Request and monitor aeromedical evacuation.
- Monitor personnel, when necessary, for radiological contamination before medical treatment.
- Decontaminate and treat small numbers of chemical casualties.

CASUALTY REPORTING AND EVACUATION

7-159. Medical evacuations must be planned in detail. Too often, units rely unreasonably on aeromedical evacuation. If these limited assets are available, units must have standard procedures for their use. However, units must plan to care for and evacuate their soldiers by use of organic equipment.

Individual Casualties

7-160. Medics in forward platoon or battery locations treat casualties immediately after appropriate triage. Unit personnel prepare the appropriate documentation and notify the ALOC to prepare to receive casualties, to include preparation of litter teams. The unit transports the patients to the BAS in the combat trains or the nearest medical element/facility (forward aid station, main aid station or ambulance exchange point), depending on the arrangements coordinated by the medical section OIC or the S1.

Mass Casualties

7-161. Casualties in this category are beyond the capability of the unit to handle with organic assets. The affected unit notifies the TOC and the ALOC immediately, providing the general nature and extent of the casualties. The battalion XO normally coordinates and directs the battalion response. The battalion medical sections may require medical and transportation augmentation from other battalion elements in the trains, or from external sources. Following the medical treatment and evacuation, the battalion XO and unit leaders must direct reorganization and reconstitution operations as appropriate.

7-162. Mass casualty procedures must be clearly identified in unit SOPs and FASPs. During the MDMP, operational and risk assessments should identify the most likely times, places, and causes of mass casualties to allow planning of force protection and mass casualty measures. Internal mutual support plans are often addressed in SOPs, but arrangements for external mass casualty support are often based on the unique situation and available resources. The FASP should identify the internal and external mass casualty mutual support arrangements (not covered by SOP), available assets, triggers, C2 considerations, and timeline or phase considerations.

NBC-Contaminated Casualties

7-163. These casualties fall into two categories:
- Soldiers suffering the effects of an NBC attack.
- Soldiers, although fully protected in MOPP 4, suffering a conventional wound.

7-164. For both circumstances, the casualty must be decontaminated before he is entered into the unit's casualty evacuation system. The initial procedures include taking appropriate protective measures as well as notifying the TOC and the ALOC.

7-165. The battalion establishes a hasty decontamination site, organized under battalion control, and augmented by battery personnel as appropriate. The focus of this initial effort is on the decontamination of casualties. Decontamination of remaining unit personnel and equipment follows, when appropriate, after coordination by the battalion S3.

MEDICAL SUPPLY AND PROPERTY EXCHANGE

7-166. The medical section maintains a three-day stock of medical supplies. To prevent unnecessary depletion of blankets, litters, splints and the like, the receiving medical facility exchanges like property with the transferring agency. Medical property accompanying patients of allied nations is disposed of in accordance with STANAG 2128, Appendix C.

PREVENTIVE MEASURES

7-167. Experience in World War II, Korea, and Vietnam indicates that most hospital admissions were for disease and nonbattle injury. Commanders can reduce disease and non-battle injury by emphasizing preventive medicine, safety, and personal hygiene. See FM 21-10, *Field Hygiene and Sanitation*, and FM 21-10-1, *Unit Field Sanitation Team*.

PRISONERS OF WAR

7-168. The S1 plans and coordinates EPW operations, collection points, and evacuation procedures. Prisoners of war are evacuated from the battalion area as rapidly as possible. The capturing battery is responsible for:
- Guarding prisoners until relieved by proper authority.
- Recovering weapons and equipment.
- Removing documents with intelligence value.
- Reporting EPW events and status to the TOC and ALOC.

7-169. Prisoners are evacuated to the vicinity of the combat trains or UMCP for processing and initial interrogation. Crews of vehicles undergoing repair or unoccupied mechanics act as guards. Prisoners are then moved to the brigade EPW collection point on returning LOGPAC vehicles or by transportation coordinated through the S4. As necessary, the S2 reviews and reports any documents or information of immediate value. The S4 coordinates evacuation of enemy equipment. Wounded prisoners are treated through normal medical channels but are kept separated from US and allied patients. For additional information on treatment and handling of EPWs, see FM 19-40, *Enemy Prisoners of War, Civilian Internees, and Detained Persons*, and FM 27-10.

SECTION V – RECONSTITUTION

7-170. Planners must be prepared for mass casualties, mass destruction of equipment, and the destruction or loss of effectiveness of entire units. Battalion units that have been catastrophically depleted or rendered ineffective are returned to combat effectiveness through reconstitution.

7-171. Reconstitution consists of the actions to restore units to a desired level of combat effectiveness commensurate with mission requirements and availability of resources. Reconstitution differs from sustaining operations in that it is undertaken only when a unit is at an unacceptable level of combat readiness; sustainment operations are routine actions to maintain combat readiness. Commanders reconstitute by either reorganization or regeneration. See FM 100-9, *Reconstitution*.

REORGANIZATION

7-172. Reorganization is the action taken to shift resources within a degraded unit to increase its combat power. Measures taken include the following:
- Cross-leveling equipment and personnel.
- Matching operational weapon systems with crews.
- Forming composite units.

7-173. Immediate battlefield reorganization is the quick and often temporary restoration of units during an operation.

7-174. Deliberate reorganization is a permanent restructuring of the unit. It is the type of reorganization considered during reconstitution planning. Deliberate reorganization is supported with higher echelon resources (such as maintenance and transportation). Additional replacements and other resources are made available. The parent-unit commander, one echelon higher than the unit being reorganized, must approve a deliberate reorganization.

REGENERATION

7-175. Regeneration is not a battalion commander's prerogative. It consists of:
- Incremental or whole-unit rebuilding through large-scale replacement of personnel, equipment, and supplies.
- Reestablishing or replacing essential command, control, and communications.
- Conducting the necessary training for the rebuilt unit.

7-176. The intensive nature of regeneration requires that a unit be pulled out of combat for this purpose.

WEAPON SYSTEM REPLACEMENT OPERATIONS

7-177. WSRO is a method to supply the combat commander with fully operational replacement weapon systems. Three terms that are often used in describing WSRO are a ready-for-issue weapons system, a ready-to-fight weapon system, and linkup:

- A ready-for-issue weapon system is a weapon that is mechanically operable according to current standards and has all ancillary equipment (fire control, machine guns, radio mounts, and radios) installed. The vehicle has been fully fueled and basic issue items are on board in boxes. There is no ammunition on board and the gaining unit must provide the crew.
- A ready-to-fight weapon system is a crewed, ready-for-issue weapon with ammunition stored on board. For a cannon system, the weapon has been boresighted and boresight has been verified.
- Linkup is the process of joining a ready-for-issue weapon with a trained crew.

7-178. WSRO is simply a procedure for bringing a weapon system to a ready-to-fight condition and handing it off to the combat unit. It involves making a vehicle ready to issue and marrying it to a complete crew, who makes it ready to fight. WSRO is an intensively managed process for giving the commander usable weapon systems in the shortest possible time.

7-179. To manage weapon systems, a common weapon system manager (WSM) is required. A WSM is designated at each level of command. The mission of the WSM is to maximize the number of operational weapon systems in accordance with the commander's priorities. The WSMs at all levels are charged with quick-fix responsibility; they match serviceable vehicles and surviving crews.

7-180. Primary linkup points for weapon systems (weapon with crew) are in the DSA, CSG, or assembly areas for formations in reserve. The DISCOM, COSCOM, or support group commander organizes the linkup point and provides personnel to make the weapon system ready for issue. The crew, working with division or corps elements, readies the weapon system to fight.

7-181. Conditions permitting, some familiarization training may be provided to crews in the linkup area. Such training should include:
- Refresher gunnery.
- Tactical driving.
- Enemy and allied vehicle identification.
- Passive air defense procedures.
- Local TSOPs.
- Any other subjects appropriate to the operational area.

7-182. It is not intended that such wartime training should be elaborate or should substitute for crew qualification. The intent is to familiarize crews with conditions in the combat area and with any key model differences if the weapon is a newer or modified version than others in the unit.

7-183. Whenever possible, experienced soldiers should be mixed with replacement soldiers to form complete crews. New crewmen can join a partial weapon crew (those whose weapon has been destroyed or evacuated) at linkup points to form complete crews. There they pick up a replacement weapon, make it ready to fight and rejoin their unit.

Chapter 8

FA Operations

Chapters 1-7 described the basics of how a FA battalion is structured and how it shoots, moves, communicates, and sustains. This chapter discusses how a FA battalion applies those techniques and principals in the context of FA operations in a variety of operational situations. Section I discusses FA considerations common to all operations. Sections II and III cover FA operations in support of offensive and defensive operations, respectively. Section IV details FA support of other unique tactical operations, such as airborne operations. Section V addresses FA support of stability operations and support operations. And Section VI discusses climate and terrain considerations that impact on FA operations. Each section addresses tactics, techniques, procedures, and considerations in relation to the six tactical task areas discussed in Section I, Chapter 1. The focus of this chapter is on FA operations. Fire support tactics, techniques, and procedures are included in FMs 6-20, 6-20-10, 6-20-30, and 6-20-40.

SECTION I – COMMON FA CONSIDERATIONS

8-01. There are several FA considerations that may be applicable in all or most types of operations. Those are addressed in this section. Actions unique to a specific type of operation are addressed in the appropriate section.

DEPLOY/CONDUCT MANEUVER

- During wargaming and during the battle, anticipate when tactical movement vice tactical maneuvering of the battalion or batteries may be necessary.
- When speed is necessary, consider moving the battalion on multiple routes if possible.
- Thoroughly identify terrain management issues during planning, wargaming, and rehearsals. Conduct movement and positioning coordination early to reduce conflicts.
- Consider using the hours of darkness for movement and resupply.

DEVELOP INTELLIGENCE

- Develop information on both military and civilian threats.
- Identify and template all enemy FA assets that can affect combined arms operations and the FA battalion's operations.
- Develop and submit prioritized FA related intelligence and target acquisition requirements as early as possible.
- Request and collect intelligence information from maneuver units, MPs, nearby units, and host nation civil/military elements as necessary to protect FA battalion assets from ground attack.

EMPLOY FIRES

DETECT AND LOCATE TARGETS

- Identify all specified and implied targeting responsibilities.
- Develop targets and targeting information to support counterfire and SEAD operations.
- Identify which observers (primary and backup) will trigger FA events (e.g., fire missions, cueing).
- Coordinate the support of external FA and non-FA intelligence and TA assets to acquire targeting information and BDA.
- Plan and direct counterfire radar operations in coordination with force FA radar operations.

DELIVER FIRES

- Destroy, neutralize, and suppress enemy indirect fire systems with proactive and reactive counterfire.
- Provide close and deep fires to support maneuver operations and to destroy and disrupt enemy C2.
- Provide FA illumination to assist friendly force night operations, to mark locations or targets, to provide friendly direction orientation, or to degrade enemy night vision equipment.
- Mass fires to gain maximum efficiency and effectiveness.
- Interdict and disrupt enemy CSS efforts and troop movements.
- Continuously review and adjust primary and backup EFAT responsibilities. In DS battalions the S3 must also maintain close coordination with the brigade FSE to monitor changes in EFST and trigger responsibilities. When responsibilities change, the S3 must ensure the responsible unit quickly receives all frequencies, lasing codes, or quickfire/sensor-to-shooter linkage information. The BAO may need to deliver or redistribute ammunition, to include emergency CCLs.
- Provide fires in support of aviation operations (attack helicopters, air cavalry, air assault, CAS, and JAAT). Provide SEAD.
- Provide rapid, SCATMINE minefields to support maneuver operations.
- Provide smoke for obscuration, suppression, screening, and deception to support maneuver operations.
- Coordinate for meteorology and survey data.

PERFORM LOGISTICS AND CSS

- Stockpile ammunition to support major firing events (such as preparations or counterpreparations).
- Time key ammunition deliveries of low-density ammunition (such as illumination) and stockpiled ammunition (for fires such as preparations) to arrive soon before the time it is required.
- Use helicopter resupply for critical items, especially when supply lines become extended.

EXERCISE C2

COMMUNICATE

- Closely monitor distances during planning and execution to determine when digital and voice radio range limitations may become excessive.
- Employ alternate digital routing and voice capability to back up critical digital communications.
- Carefully position and move retrans teams to maintain communications in offensive and defensive situations.
- Use decentralized techniques such as direct routing and quickfire channels to provide immediately responsive sensor-to-shooter linkages for critical fires.

COORDINATE FIRE SUPPORT

- Make maximum use of available FSEs to gather friendly and enemy information and coordinate movement and positioning.
- Use liaison as much as possible to ensure effective coordination with other FA units and other military and civilian elements as necessary.
- Increase frequency of information/database updates during fast moving operations, and whenever danger close fires are planned or anticipated.

PROTECT THE FORCE

- Coordinate support from maneuver units, MPs, nearby units, and host nation civil/military elements to assist in defending FA battalion assets from ground attack and in repelling attacks.
- Consider using supplementary positions for lengthy, preplanned missions, especially when the counterfire threat is high.
- Make maximum use of mask to shield fires and communication from enemy acquisition.

SECTION II – FA SUPPORT OF OFFENSIVE OPERATIONS

8-02. This section describes FA tactics, techniques, procedures, and considerations for FA support of offensive operations. It addresses those principles that are generally common to all offensive operations, and discusses FA considerations unique to specific types of offensive actions.

BASIC FA TASKS IN THE OFFENSE

8-03. FA prepares the way for the maneuver force by suppressing, neutralizing, or destroying the enemy as well as obscuring his vision of friendly movement. FA fires are planned to soften enemy defenses before the attack. Short, violent preparations are planned and targeted against front-line defenses, OPs, C2, indirect fire weapons, and reserves.

DEPLOY/CONDUCT MANEUVER

8-04. Offensive operations frequently involve an ebb and flow of forward, rearward, and lateral movement. During periods of rapid advance, battle space may open up, and PAs may be relatively easier to find. When advances stall, or attacking forces are counterattacked, battle space may condense. Movement may become a series of shorter tactical maneuvers, occasionally involving increased lateral or even rearward movement.

- Plan to use more hasty occupations to support rapid movement.
- Plan to use increased map reconnaissance, since time available for ground reconnaissance will likely decrease, and the terrain will not be available while it is in the enemy's possession.
- Request photographic reconnaissance or copies of the products from other reconnaissance efforts.
- Consider air reconnaissance, if available.
- Consider locations that the enemy used for his FA units. It may be an indicator that the terrain is suitable. However they may contain hazards due to ICM duds or SCATMINE from friendly FA attacks.
- FA battalions supported by a single counterfire radar may have difficulty maintaining radar coverage during fast moving offensive operations. DIVARTY or Corps Arty assistance may be necessary.
- FA battalions may rely more heavily on the faster movement techniques, especially in the faster-paced offensive operations.
- Position firing units well forward to range beyond maneuver objectives. Identify requirements for extended range munitions.
- Plan alternate routes to bypass enemy obstacles. Request engineer mobility support.
- Consider repositioning light units by air.

DEVELOP INTELLIGENCE

- Identify and prioritize enemy indirect fire assets that can potentially impact friendly offensive operations. Develop and provide counterfire targets for preparations, counter-preparations, and other proactive and reactive counterfires.

- Find canalizing terrain or road networks in the vicinity of enemy FA that can be blocked or interdicted to prevent retreat of enemy artillery, to entrap enemy FA, or create TAIs and kill zones. Coordinate intelligence/TA coverage of the area. Consider attacking entrapped enemy FA by air or ground forces as an alternative to FA attack.

EMPLOY FIRES

Detect And Locate Targets

- Plan for frequent repositioning of TA assets based on FLOT movement.
- Use CFFZs to provide TA coverage on suspected enemy firing positions.
- Ensure radar is in position in time to support the assault on the objective and consolidation.

Deliver Fires

- Provide fires at the time and place required by the maneuver commander, to include suppressive fires on the objective.
- Isolate the objective with fires beyond and to the flanks.
- Provide fires to support breaching operations. Use ICM, HE, and smoke to suppress enemy forces overwatching obstacles. Use smoke to screen the breaching operation, and aggressive counterfire and CFZs to reduce the enemy indirect fire threat against the breeching force.
- Plan for increased use of hasty survey -- survey availability decreases in relation to the speed of the advance.
- Prepare to receive and execute hasty fire plans to support changes in objectives, to support in repelling enemy counterattacks, or to support developing penetrations and exploitations.
- Put survey with lead FA units. Regularly forward updated survey data to force FA HQ to facilitate emplacement of following FA assets.
- When the FA battalion supports lead elements, especially during penetrations and exploitations, it must increase coordination with its higher FA HQ to maintain effective meteorology support.
- Consider using Copperhead against counterattacking forces or against armored forces in strongpoints. Anticipate hasty planning procedures.
- Coordinate with division and corps TA assets to identify deep targets.
- Offensive operations may require increased DPICM and less SCATMINE. Anticipate changing ammunition requirements as the battle reaches a culminating point, and transitions to the defense.

PERFORM LOGISTICS AND CSS

- Coordinate stockpiling of ammunition for preparations.
- Plan for increasingly extended lines of resupply.
- Plan for more frequent moves of the combat trains.
- Synchronize resupply of ammunition and POL. Push well designed CCLs far enough forward to quickly link up with firing units.
- Consider aerial resupply using Army air, container delivery system (CDS) and/or mass supply (light forces).

EXERCISE C2

Communicate

- Plan retrans capability to cover extended lines of communication (LOC).
- Rely primarily on radio (voice/digital) communications, since establishing wire links becomes more difficult in mobile situations.

Coordinate Fire Support

- Plan fires to prevent reinforcement, disengagement, and resupply of the objective.
- Plan fires to protect units as they reorganize on the objective.

PROTECT THE FORCE

- Plan for unit defense in a 6,400-mil environment, since encountering bypassed enemy elements becomes more probable.
- Plan counter-counterpreparation fires. Include this requirement in ammunition requests and distribution plans. Ensure ammunition plans address movement and use of the ammunition if it isn't needed.
- Within the framework of the maneuver deception plan, consider deception techniques to confuse the enemy's intelligence assets.
- Consider using Firefinder CFZs for increased force protection.
- Prepare to provide continuous FS in an NBC environment. The threat of an enemy NBC attack may increase as his defeat becomes imminent.

FORMS OF MANEUVER

8-05. Maneuver units use five forms of maneuver in the offense:
- Envelopment.
- Turning movement.
- Penetration.
- Frontal attack.
- Infiltration.

8-06. FA battalion commanders and staffs must understand the differences in these forms of maneuver and the implications for supporting FA battalions.

ENVELOPMENT

8-07. Envelopments are usually fast-paced, fluid operations, requiring hasty planning techniques and increased reliance on battle drills and fire plans for branches or sequels. A DS or R FA battalion supporting a maneuver brigade envelopment will plan and provide fires for both the fixing force and the enveloping force. The depth of the envelopment will generally be relatively shallow. The following considerations apply:

- A primary consideration is how much FA (if any) to send with the enveloping force. Battlespace along the corridor used by the enveloping force will be tight and security tentative. Consider the depth of the envelopment, and branches and sequels. The battalion may be able to provide much of the needed support from close behind the fixing force.

- GS/GSR FA may be pushed well forward to support the enveloping force and to provide deep fires to prevent reinforcements, to disrupt C2 and support SEAD for supporting air assets.
- Consider using RFLs to control fires of converging forces. S3s should monitor the frequency of RFL and FLOT updates and request updates if he determines data may have become outdated. The unit may use quickfire voice channels to obtain the most current FLOT information.
- CSS support for FA in the corridor of advance may be difficult, as interdiction of LOCs may be likely.

8-08. In larger operations, DS/R FA battalions may support either the fixing force or the enveloping force. GS/GSR battalions may support either force or provide support to both operations. FA units should consider the following:
- Since the enveloping force is usually the main effort, the DS FA battalion supporting it may frequently receive reinforcement, while the DS battalion supporting the fixing force may not.
- DS/R FA battalions supporting enveloping forces may experience limited battlespace and tentative security in the corridor of advance. Shoot-and-scoot tactics may be difficult, especially if the advance slows or stalls. The FA unit should increase force protection measures due to the threat from bypassed and counterattacking forces.
- Some GS/GSR FA battalions may follow closely behind lead enveloping forces in order to support DS/R units and facilitate their movement; to facilitate attack of deep targets; and to take the bulk of the counterfire and SEAD responsibilities off the lead DS/R FA battalions.
- Many FA battalions may have o/o missions: DS battalions supporting lead forces may become GS if their unit relinquishes its lead role and goes into reserve. R FA battalions may support two or more DS FA units in succession as follow-and-assume forces take the lead role.
- Planning and rehearing require careful coordination, as R/GSR units may support multiple planning efforts. Battalions may need to create additional liaison teams out-of-hide to cover liaison responsibilities.

TURNING MOVEMENT

8-09. A turning movement is somewhat similar to envelopment. While a small fixing force keeps the enemy in his defensive positions, the main force passes around the enemy defenses and secures an objective deep in the enemy's rear area. Many of the considerations for an envelopment apply to a turning movement, with the following additions:
- The unit may use short-destruct SCATMINE, fired by FA supporting the fixing force, to keep the enemy in his positions or to channel the direction of his withdrawal.
- Depending on the size of the objective area(s), after the friendly force takes and secures the objective, DS/R FA battalions may have little secure battlespace over which to disperse. They may have difficulty supporting the friendly force from inside the newly established battle position. Support may be necessary from GS/GSR units within range or DS FA units on other objectives in the area. FA battalions may require maneuver support to secure adequate firing positions.

- The turning force may need defensive fires after it seizes its objective. This may include the use of EAs involving Copperhead, SEAD for air attacks, and hasty SCATMINE.
- CSS may be more difficult. Temporary interdiction of LOCs may occur as the force concentrates on consolidation and defense of the objective.

PENETRATION

8-10. In a penetration, the friendly force concentrates firepower and forces to rupture defenses along a narrow front to create an assailable flank and/or to gain access to the enemy's rear. Often one maneuver unit will achieve the initial penetration, and following units will widen or deepen the penetration or will conduct exploitation or pursuit operations as appropriate. A FA battalion supporting a penetration may support both of these forces (e.g., a DS battalion supporting a brigade level penetration or a GS FA unit supporting division or corps level penetrations). In division and corps penetrations, a DS FA unit may support the penetrating force or a following force. In large unit penetrations FA battalions will frequently have o/o missions.

8-11. FA units supporting a penetration should consider the following:
- FA battalions may participate in short, intense preparations, coordinated with air attacks, focused on the point of desired penetration. This will frequently include fires on second and third echelon defensive positions.
- The penetration unit will frequently be the main effort. DS FA units supporting this effort can expect one or more reinforcing units. FA units supporting follow-and-support and/or follow-and-assume forces may establish liaison with forward DS units to better coordinate survey, positioning, and fire coordination as following units assume the lead.
- Exchange of zones of fire responsibilities between FA units is a critical event when maneuver forces change roles and conduct passage of lines. Responsibility for EFATs may change from one FA unit to another when mission changes do not occur according to plan. Liaison and thorough evaluation of branch/sequel possibilities during the MDMP are essential to effective battle handoffs.
- The penetrating force will usually have priority of fires, and multiple FA battalions, in various roles, may work together as part of a consolidated counterfire plan directed from DIVARTY or Corps Arty. The higher FA HQ may use CSBs extensively to better assign counterfire radar responsibilities.
- GS FA units may support SEAD operations for attack helicopter and/or airforce attacks to destroy, suppress, or fix enemy reserve forces.
- Fire planning for branches and sequels must be thorough, with adjustments during the penetration to account for changing factors.
- FA battalions may participate in massed fires involving groups and series of targets designed to widen the penetration or destroy/suppress enemy units on the flanks of the penetration.

FRONTAL ATTACK

8-12. Units use the frontal attack to attack the enemy across a wide front, along the most direct approaches in an attempt to overwhelm and destroy a weakened enemy force or to fix an enemy and restrict his movement.

- Frontal attacks usually present the least force protection concerns for a FA unit unless they develop into exploitations or pursuits.
- A frontal attack frequently has a main attack and one or more supporting attacks. FA battalions DS to the main attack forces are more likely to receive a reinforcing unit. FA support to the main attack force, a follow-and-assume force, or the reserve force may evolve into support for a penetration, exploitation, or pursuit. Main force attacks may be deeper and thus LOCs more extended.
- The main effort, or the most successful friendly attacking force, will most likely draw the most fire and larger enemy counterattacking forces. Anticipate higher CSRs, greater attrition rates, and increased requirements for transportation and maintenance support.

INFILTRATION

8-13. Infiltration is the covert movement of all or part of the attacking force through enemy lines to an objective in the enemy's rear area. It is a form of maneuver normally used with and to support other forms of maneuver. Infantry, cavalry, and reconnaissance forces use this form of maneuver more frequently than do armored or mechanized forces.

- An infiltration generally presents FA units the highest force protection risk of the five forms of maneuver. In smaller operations, FA units may not move forward with infiltrating forces. However, FA units may need to use positions well forward to range objectives and deep targets. FA units may need intense counterfire programs to reduce the counterfire threat. If FA is infiltrated with maneuver forces the battalion may need maneuver forces for security. The S3 and S2 must make maximum use of all force protections measures during an infiltration.
- FA units may use FA raid tactics and airmobile movement of light FA.
- Judicious use of FSCMs, carefully planned clearance of fire procedures, and frequent force location updates are necessary as an infiltration has increased risk of fratricide due to intermingled friendly and enemy forces. Consider using hasty NFAs, or RFAs for forces that become cut off while infiltrating. The S3 and battalion FDO must ensure the TOC maintains accurate situational awareness (manual and digital), and quickly disseminates position updates.

MOVEMENT TO CONTACT/SEARCH AND ATTACK

8-14. A movement to contact operation develops a situation and establishes or regains contact. A movement to contact may involve the following actions:

- **Search and Attack.** A search and attack is a variant of the movement to contact. It is conducted by small, light maneuver units, air cavalry, or air assault forces over large areas. A search and attack shares many of the characteristics of an area security mission.

- **Meeting Engagement.** This is a combat action that occurs when a moving force, incompletely deployed for combat, collides with and engages an enemy at an unexpected time and place.
- **Approach March.** Units may use an approach march when the enemy's location is known, thus allowing the friendly force to move with greater speed and less physical security or dispersion than occurs with use of the traveling movement technique.

8-15. In supporting a movement to contact or a search and attack type operation, a FA battalion should consider some of the following actions:
- Provide immediate fires to leading elements/elements in contact.
- Use priority of fires and quickfire channels.
- Attack deep targets with massed fires to prevent enemy reinforcements.
- Since the enemy situation is usually vague, CFZs on lead elements may be more useful than CFFZs.
- Plan for hasty attack contingencies.
- Anticipate frequent moves and hip shoots.
- Keep ammunition uploaded.
- Numerous requests for immediate smoke may occur when contact is established. The S3 will need to carefully monitor expenditures. Smoke resupply may need to be put on the road as soon as the S3 confirms major contact has begun.
- Plan fires along the route and on the flanks to protect the force.
- S3s must watch for rapid changes in the situation, which can occur more easily in developing situations. Hasty FPFs or blocking fires can help lead elements to disengage or establish hasty defensive positions.
- Since the intelligence situation is often vague, it may be difficult to knock out enemy FA until it begins firing. Thus his initial counterfire capability may be strong. FA battalion S3s may need to plan/request additional counterfire support early to ensure the enemy does not gain an advantage in the early counterfire battle.
- Air reconnaissance (fixed or rotary-wing) may support the operation. The S2 should coordinate rapid communication of enemy FA locations to counterfire planners. The S3 and supported FSE may decide to develop some or all of these targets into an on-call counterfire program than firing them as they are acquired.
- Before the maneuver force has established contact, a good time to fire proactive counterfire targets is just prior to a friendly FA unit's next planned move. That way the firing unit doesn't give away a position location that may be needed to support forces making contact. The same applies to SEAD or other deep planned targets.
- Place coordinated fire lines (CFLs) well forward of friendly maneuver elements. Plan o/o CFLs on phase lines to facilitate rapid shifting as the force moves.

ATTACKS

8-16. The attack differs from a movement to contact in that information on enemy dispositions is more developed, which allows the maneuver commander to achieve greater synchronization. Attacks are characterized as hasty or deliberate. There is no clear distinction between a deliberate and hasty attack. They differ mainly in the level and detail known about the enemy. Also, deliberate attacks are characterized by a more extensive preparation period prior to execution.

HASTY ATTACK

8-17. The hasty attack is the most common type of attack. Hasty attacks normally result from a movement to contact, successful defense, or continuation of a previous attack.

8-18. FA considerations associated with a hasty attack include the following:

- There may not be time for an extensive counterfire program prior to the attack, or the servicing of many counterfire targets during a preparation (if one is conducted). There will also be less time to collect and develop intelligence on counterfire targets. This may result in more reactive counterfire missions and greater reliance on counterfire radars.
- The unit may not use a preparation due to limited planning time or the need to achieve surprise. Short, intense programs, series, or groups may be used to mass fires on critical areas or targets sets.
- Anticipate immediate suppression and quick smoke fire missions.
- Expect the rapid shift of massed fires to exploit identified enemy weak points.
- DS/R TOCs must work quickly with the brigade FSE to coordinate fires in support of multiple brigade/battalion hasty fire plans. GS/GSR battalions may participate in hasty fire plans for forward maneuver units, SEAD for air force or Army aviation operations, or deep attacks.
- Low-density ammunition types may be in short supply as a hasty attack often occurs as a branch or sequel to an earlier operation. The S3 may want to immediately request a certain number of CCLs be brought forward and prepositioned in pickup areas while actual ammunition requirements are being determined.
- Targeting officers in R units may temporarily move to assist the brigade FSE and maneuver S2 with targeting. This may allow the FSE to concentrate on FS coordination and facilitate getting targeting decisions made and passed to firing units in the short time available.
- Rehearsal time will be extremely limited. The S3 should use WARNOs to quickly disseminate EFATs. DS/R units may only have time for one consolidated rehearsal with the combined arms team. A digital rehearsal may not be advisable if there is a chance units can't purge rehearsal information and reconfigure automation systems with actual attack information in a timely manner.
- The staff must aggressively seek out the information needed to update and disseminate AFATDS guidances. FSEs and FSCOORDs are primarily responsible for developing and coordinating the necessary information, however FA battalion S3s must drive the process to receive the information as early as possible. Guidance on the use of SCATMINE, ICM, and smoke is especially critical.

DELIBERATE ATTACK

8-19. Deliberate attacks normally include high volumes of planned fires, major shaping operations, and the forward positioning of logistics. Deliberate attacks follow a distinct period of preparation used for extensive reconnaissance, detailed planning, task organization of forces, rehearsals, and plan refinement. FA battalion considerations include:

- Deliberate attacks may involve an extensive FA preparation, and/or counterfire and SEAD programs if enough ammunition is available. Stockpiled ammunition should not be brought forward and downloaded too early and should be well protected to prevent loss to sabotage or an enemy counterpreparation.
- Long preparations increase the unit's vulnerability to counterfire. A counterfire program shortly before the preparation or during its early phase may reduce the threat. The battalion should consider using supplementary firing positions for counterfire (or SEAD) programs and preparations. If time and resources permit, units should also harden firing positions used for long preparations.
- Plan to expend large amounts of smoke to screen friendly movements and obscure enemy observation.
- Expect an emphasis on thorough rehearsals. There may be time for several FA battalion level FA/FS only rehearsals before and/or after larger combined arms or force FA rehearsals.
- Prepare to support the deception plan before the main attack begins by massing fires and firing smoke on forward enemy units not in the area of the main attack.

EXPLOITATION

8-20. Exploitation results when a successful attack presents an opportunity for the friendly force to take significant advantage of a weakened, collapsed, or disorganized enemy force. Exploitations can have several objectives: secure deep objectives or destroy specific enemy forces or functions.

8-21. Units usually conduct an exploitation with two or more missioned maneuver forces. The primary force is the lead or direct pressure force, which must quickly destroy or bypass any enemy forces in route to the main objective. One or more forces follow the lead unit with the missions of follow-and-support and/or follow-and-assume. Depending on the situation and the plan, one of the forces may also be tasked to block and defeat a responding enemy reserve force.

8-22. A supporting FA battalion commander must understand the battalion's role. In larger exploitation operations (division and higher), the FA battalion may support a brigade-sized task force with one or more of the discussed missions. The battalion may need to follow the brigade at a distance that allows support, but without interfering with follow-on forces. If the advance stalls, battlefield space becomes limited, and hinders shoot-and-scoot tactics.

8-23. In brigade or smaller exploitations, the FA battalion supports battalion level forces advancing on a narrower corridor to less depth. It will be more difficult for all FA battalion elements to follow, and it may not be necessary for more than one or two firing batteries to move with forward elements, depending on the size of the corridor, the depth of the advance, and the availability of reinforcing fires from MLRS.

8-24. In exploitation and pursuit operations a DS cannon battalion may have one or more reinforcing FA units to facilitate the rapid movement, and to provide deep fires. However, due to limited battlespace, the reinforcing unit may be an attached MLRS battery, or a composite 155mm/MLRS battery. Exploitations often involve o/o missions, to shift reinforcing FA from the lead unit to the follow-and-assume unit.

- Place additional emphasis on 6,400-mil capability to support units in contact with enemy located out of zone. METT-TC will dictate how to achieve this (one or more platoons, a firing battery, etc).
- Plan for frequent moves to keep pace with the target array.
- Keep ammunition uploaded and provide for emergency resupply of POL and ammunition.
- Maintain perimeter security since bypassed enemy units will try to break out and return to their own lines.
- Target deep to sever escape routes or to prevent reinforcements.
- SCATMINE, crater producing munitions (HE/PD), and dud producing munitions (ICM), should be carefully controlled to ensure commander's guidances are followed. These munitions could delay the exploitation if not properly employed. They may primarily be used on the flanks, for deep fires, or on positions to be bypassed.
- In a rapidly advancing exploitation, a DS or R FA battalion may need two counterfire radars to ensure coverage as frequent moves may be required. If the advance is not too deep, a DIVARTY or Corps Arty controlled radar could support the initial phase and pass targets to a GS unit while the DS/R controlled radar moves to a forward position in cleared terrain.
- The S2 should closely monitor intelligence reports for information on enemy FA moving in to attack the exploitation.
- Aerial resupply can facilitate CSS efforts and assist in evacuation of wounded personnel. Regular medivac helicopters may be best for serious wounded personnel, and requirements for this support may increase during pursuit and exploitation operations.

PURSUIT

8-25. An attack or exploitation frequently evolves into a pursuit, when the enemy tries to withdraw to a more defensible location. The friendly force exerts unrelenting pressure to keep the enemy from reorganizing and preparing defenses. Usually, a direct pressure force applies aggressive attacks against the withdrawing enemy force to prevent unhindered withdrawal while another highly mobile friendly force encircles the enemy. The encircling force cuts off his retreat and, in coordination with the direct pressure force defeats the enemy.

- FA fires may attack targets in the enemy's rear to slow his withdrawal and to cut off avenues for retreat.

- Plan fires on enemy high-speed avenues of withdrawal.
- Use FA at canalizing points and hasty river crossings where the enemy cannot easily bypass destroyed vehicles. These may be TAIs or NAIs with targeted intelligence and TA assets and quickfire links to the FA battalion. FA may also provide SEAD at these locations while air assets attack.
- Destruction of enemy bridging equipment may destroy or degrade his ability to cross subsequent water hazards.
- The FA unit should carefully control SCATMINE, crater producing munitions (HE/PD), and dud producing munitions (ICM), to ensure commander's guidances are followed. These munitions could delay friendly pursuit if not properly employed.

- FA fires will support the encircling force. If the encircling force is large, (brigade or larger) the entire FA battalion may follow and support. For smaller operations, the FA battalion may need to provide support from locations behind the direct pressure force. If adequate security is provided, it may be possible for one firing battery to closely follow the encircling force.
  - Increased smoke and suppressive fires may be required by the encircling force to assist them in bypassing elements that cannot be quickly overwhelmed.
  - The encircling force's flanks and/or rear may be more vulnerable to attack that those of the direct pressure force.
- Massed FA fires assist in maintaining pressure on the enemy, demoralizing him, and destroying his will to fight.
- Plan to move as an integrated element of the maneuver force.
- Establish FSCMs along the axis of advance to avoid possible fratricide.
- The pressure from maneuver forces will force enemy FA to move frequently. Use CFFZs to quickly target and attack enemy FA when it does stop to shoot. However, if the FA with the main force is significantly damaged, disorganized, or kept on the move, the major threat may come from longer ranging enemy FA units to the enemy's rear or on the flanks.
- CFZs on the lead force may be more useful than CFFZs on suspected enemy firing locations. Because of the nature of an exploitation, enemy fires could come from many directions.
- Streamline firing units to displace as quickly as possible.
- Position well forward so the unit can promptly deliver effective fires.
- Prepare for increased reliance on radio retrans and/or relay, since communications capabilities decrease with distance.
- Have a contingency plan for linkup operations. Maneuver elements may be airlifted to deep objectives to cut off the enemy at choke points.

RESERVES

8-26. Reserve operations frequently involve fast moving attacks into developing situations, often to support a branch, sequel, or unanticipated event. FA battalions supporting reserve force operations should consider:

- Increased involvement in coordinating and supporting hasty fire plans and making last minute changes to existing plans just prior to kick-off.
- One or more o/o missions as the FA unit may be used in a GS or GSR role prior to executing a DS or R in support of the reserve force.
- Clearance of fires challenges due to intermingled forces, fluid FLOT changes, RFLs/NFAs/RFAs, and unusual maneuver force boundaries.
- Deception fires may be used to mislead the enemy as to the timing and location of a counterattack.
- Fast tactical march may be necessary to position the FA battalion.
- Forward passage of lines operations as the reserve moves through forward forces.

SECTION III – FA SUPPORT OF DEFENSIVE OPERATIONS

8-27. FA allows the defending maneuver commander to attack the enemy before he moves within range of direct fire weapons, to maximize the effectiveness of combined arms kill zones and engagement areas, to economize maneuver forces for a planned counterattack and to swiftly shift firepower to critical points on the battlefield. FA can attack enemy follow-on echelons before they close with his maneuver units, thereby preventing the enemy from massing overwhelming firepower and allowing the supported maneuver force to defeat the enemy in detail.

ORGANIZATION OF THE DEFENSIVE BATTLEFIELD

8-28. Brigade, division, and corps defensive battlefields are often organized along three major functional areas – a security area, a main battle area (MBA), and a sustainment area. FA battalions operate in and provide support to forces throughout all three areas.

SECURITY AREA

8-29. Maneuver operations in the security area provide early warning and reaction time, deny the enemy reconnaissance, and protect the MBA. Operations in the security area are very fluid and fast moving. They often involve covering force operations, screens, guards, counter reconnaissance, delays, and passage of lines. FA battalions supporting brigade, division, or corps controlled security area operations, should consider the following:

- Maintain superior situational awareness to prevent being overrun or suffering significant damage from enemy advance elements that may infiltrate through dispersed security area forces.
- Minimize the supplies and equipment taken forward. Consider positioning most of the battalion trains farther than normal to the rear.
- FS coordination may require more attention to detail, as security operations frequently bring together units that may not regularly operate together. Requirements for liaison may increase.
- Increased smoke and SCATMINE may be required to slow the enemy, create kill zones, and allow security forces to disengage and move to successive defensive positions.
- Consider augmenting security area elements with additional observers and COLT/Striker teams.
- Plan counter preparation fires. Anticipate high reactive counterfire requirements immediately before and after initial enemy contact.
- Since many attacks begin during darkness, security operations may require significant coordinated illumination missions.
- Consider the effects of night attack, and enemy use of smoke on Copperhead EFATs.
- Distribution and expenditure of low-density, improved munitions must be carefully managed as batteries may be more dispersed. This limits the ability of batteries to backup each other's EFATs.
- Security area operations often culminate in a rearward passage of lines.

MAIN BATTLE AREA

8-30. The battle normally matures in the MBA, which contains the bulk of the maneuver force's combat power. Boundaries usually delineate major unit areas or sectors of responsibilities within the MBA. Forces may be arrayed in linear or non-linear (area) defensive posture. Units may use task force or brigade size BPs or strongpoints. Considerations for FA battalions supporting MBA operations include:

- Thoroughly plan to accept battle handoff from withdrawing security force FA and support their passage of lines. Units may use SCATMINE to close lanes behind withdrawing forces.
- Thoroughly understand the MBA obstacle plan, which may be extensive, and monitor battle progress to better anticipate unplanned requirements for FA fires supporting obstacles.
- Anticipate frequent planned and unplanned massed fire missions early, especially in EAs, as the force attempts to quickly disrupt, delay, and defeat the attacker with fires.
- GS/GSR MLRS units may occupy positions well forward in the MBA, or just beyond it to allow early, intensive counterfires and attrition of enemy FA.
- FA battalion S3s should closely monitor the battle for signs indicating transitions to branches and sequels – counterattacks, retrogrades, withdrawals. Review positioning and ammunition considerations.

SUSTAINMENT AREA

8-31. The sustainment (rear) area normally contains the bulk of the CSS capability of the force and may include artillery units, uncommitted combat forces, CS elements, and C2 facilities. FA units may occasionally maneuver and fire from within sustainment areas, especially in blunting penetrations in the MBA, in providing security to forces in the sustainment area, or when firing missiles against deep targets. See the section on rear area operations for additional information on FA fires in the sustainment area.

BASIC FA TASKS IN THE DEFENSE

8-32. Several tactical techniques and considerations are common to FA support of all types of defensive operations. These are discussed below.

DEPLOY/CONDUCT MANEUVER

8-33. Movement during early stages of the defense may often be reactive. The battalion may experience increased lateral and rearward movement, frequently unplanned, until the friendly maneuver force can regain the initiative, slow the advance and/or better anticipate enemy actions. The faster the defense is pushed back, the more congested the battlefield becomes as friendly units fall back onto one another. All personnel involved in movement planning must understand the impacts of battle tempo on movement.

- FA units supporting brigade and division size counterattacking forces may need to make a tactical move as part of the brigade or division movement into attack position. Integrate FA movement so that the FA units are in their firing positions in time to support the attack.

- Identify potential rearward and lateral chokepoints that may best be circumvented by early tactical movement.
- FA units should consider the possibility that civilian exodus/evacuation during defensive operations may interfere with tactical movement. Request MP support when necessary.
- Coordinate movement plans with the maneuver HQ. Consider the obstacle plan in planning movements.
- Conduct aggressive ground reconnaissance, selection, and occupation of position (RSOP) whenever the defense is forced into unexpected lateral or rearward moves. Other units may be slow to react, which can cause congested battle space. FA units may use alternate locations more frequently in the defense.
- Use lateral maneuver to methodically move some FA units away from enemy penetrations. This facilitates dispersal of FA units while allowing both continued support to forward defenses and massing of fires onto penetrating forces. However, logistic support may be complicated if the penetration becomes large enough that batteries are widely separated, especially if FA trains are forced to move rearward.
- Controlled sequencing of FA unit tactical maneuvering can facilitate positioning of FA units for follow-on missions (such as support of counterattacks). This can reduce the need for longer, tactical moves.
- Request advance preparation of all possible PAs that the battalion anticipates falling back into.

DEVELOP INTELLIGENCE

- Monitor threat posed by enemy reconnaissance and special purpose troops infiltrating into friendly territory in advance of main force.
- Determine potential enemy offensive use of NBC capabilities.
- Identify indicators of enemy massing of FA.

EMPLOY FIRES

Detect and Locate Targets

- Reliance on external TA assets to identify deep targets may increase.
- Anticipate movement of CFFZs based on S2s SITEMP and expected rate of enemy advance.
- Higher FA HQ/TA units can assist front line TA assets in identifying and reconnoitering TA positions toward the rear.

Deliver Fires

- The FA battalion may participate in targeting and scheduling for larger counterpreparations. The S3 must anticipate how these fires could impact other battalion missions.
- Provide target area survey to ensure accurate placement of FPFs, smoke screens, SCATMINE minefields, and fires supporting obstacles.

- Identify survey requirements early and request force FA assistance with survey points to the rear. Make maximum use of digital equipment to obtain and disseminate all known survey points.
- Deliver massed fires to support – planned kill zones, blunting enemy penetrations, counterfire/counterpreparation programs.
- Support rear operations against smaller infiltration forces or larger penetrating forces.

PERFORM LOGISTICS AND CSS

8-34. In the defense, supply lines are frequently shorter. During rearward movement, the battalion has the advantage of falling back into friendly territory. This allows advance preparation of many PAs and the battalion can fall back onto personnel, supplies and equipment. However, civilian evacuations and enemy fires can interfere with LOCs.
- Preposition ammunition for immediate consumption.
- Plan for surge use of CSS. Maximize benefits of shortened supply lines.
- If the batteries of a battalion become widely dispersed around the flanks of a penetration, the battalion may need to run a modified dual trains operation or coordinate support through other FA units until normal resupply lines are restored.
- Coordinate for forward triage of wounded personnel and forward repair of damaged equipment to return both to combat effectiveness rapidly.
- Consider means for channeling EPWs and refugees to the rear area.

EXERCISE C2

Communicate

- Use internal wire communications when possible.
- Plan redundant communications means.

Coordinate Fire Support

- Coordinate additional FA fires when survival or unplanned tactical moves temporarily hinder battalion or battery mission support.
- Identify FS requirements for stay-behind forces.
- Ensure commander's guidances address control of SCATMINE and dud/crater producing munitions, especially when general or focused friendly counterattacks are expected.

PROTECT THE FORCE

- Harden positions whenever possible.
- Coordinate for engineer support and Class IV materials.
- Plan for use of direct fire in support of battery defenses.
- Use CFZs to increase protection of key friendly units.
- Pay increased attention to OPSEC considerations concerning trash and abandoned equipment. Review emergency destruction procedures.
- Anticipate the need for survivability moves after the battalion has provided extended and/or intense massed fires (planned or unplanned).

MOBILE DEFENSE

8-35. The mobile defense actively orients on the destruction of the enemy force versus the retention of terrain. It employs a combination of fire and maneuver, offense, defense, and delay to defeat the enemy attack and destroy the enemy force.

8-36. The main effort and key to the mobile defense is usually a striking force (which is not a reserve force). Strike force operations may involve ground, airborne, air assault, amphibious, attack helicopter, and CAS operations, to include airmobile FA raids.

8-37. FA battalions play a key role in supporting mobile defense operations. DS/R FA battalions will participate in planning for all phases of the mobile defense. In division or larger operations, DS/R FA battalions may support one of the main defensive units or the strike force unit. In both small and large mobile defenses, GSR and GS units may have a wide range of support requirements, but often are involved in deep targeting and counterfire. Other considerations for FA battalions supporting a mobile defense include:

- Position batteries in depth for continuous support as batteries displace.
- Move batteries that will support the striking force into forward positions immediately prior to the attack. Anticipate passage of lines.
- Use positioning methods that maximize force protection in non-linear environments (larger groups, positioning with or near other elements, off high-speed approaches).
- Anticipate long range fires to support the striking force. Plan extended range ammunition or reinforcing (155mm/MLRS) fires accordingly.
- Anticipate participation in mass fire missions to support the striking force attack.
- Consider requesting infantry or MP support for increased force protection where non-linear conditions exist.
- Place increased emphasis on mutual support by fire between firing elements.
- Plan for increased use of hasty fire planning techniques, immediate smoke, suppressive fires, and target of opportunity minefields.
- Plan for fast-paced mobile warfare, operating frequently on the move or from vehicular CPs rather than dismounted shelters or tents.
- Place increased emphasis on monitoring security of LOCs. Reroute CSS and use air resupply as more frequently.
- Plan for increased use of RFLs, RFAs, and NFAs, especially during strike force operations.

AREA DEFENSE

8-38. Area defense focuses on denying the enemy access to designated terrain or facilities for a specific time, rather than outright destruction of the enemy. The area defense is normally organized around static defensive positions in depth, seeking to destroy the enemy forces with interlocking fires. There are two general forms of maneuver for an area defense – forward or in depth.

8-39. **Forward defense** emphasizes maintaining forward positions. FA considerations for a forward defense include:
- Hasty fire plans for frequent counter attacks forward of the FEBA.
- Increased reliance on massed fire missions to prevent penetrations.
- Longer, more lethal FPFs and anti-breaching fires to support more static defenses (increased HE/ICM/SCATMINE, decreased smoke).
- Increased need to harden and camouflage positions due to decreased movement options. Greater reliance on counterfire for force protection.
- Use lateral movement and infantry or MP support in response to enemy penetrations as terrain may not allow rearward displacement.
- Increased potential for direct fires, anti-armor teams, and other self-defense measures.
- Clearly stated guidelines regarding conditions and approving authority for FA survival moves.
- Increased use of wire and communications techniques to reduce electronic signatures.

8-40. **Defense in depth** makes maximum use of the depth of the AO to prevent enemy penetrations. FA considerations for a forward defense include:
- Increased use of smoke and SCATMINE to assist disengagements.
- Rearward and lateral displacements to support kill zone operations, followed by forward movement to support counterattacks.
- Increased use of vehicular TOC operations, and uploaded, on time delivery of ammunition.
- Increased reliance on established triggers for planned FA movements.
- Maximized prior development of successive, rearward positions.
- Maximum use of terrain for alternate and supplementary positions, and of relatively small movements in the FLOT for FA moves.
- CSS positioning and movement plans that consider FLOT movements.

RETROGRADE OPERATIONS

8-41. Considerations for retrograde operations include:
- Develop fires for delay plans early.
- Arrange a withdrawal schedule for the FA with supported units.
- Fire long-range fires from initial positions.
- Ensure continuous, responsive FA support is available for all sectors.
- Reconnoiter routes and positions to the rear, primary and alternates.
- Maintain high mobility throughout the delay.
- Monitor the delaying actions in adjacent sectors.
- Contribute to the obstacle and deception plans with FA fires.
- Consider use of CFZs on critical points or withdrawal routes; for example, river-crossing points and bridges.

ADDITIONAL FA CONSIDERATIONS FOR DEFENSIVE OPERATIONS

8-42. FA battalions may support the following defensive techniques, which may be conducted as part of larger defensive operations.

DEFEND IN SECTOR

8-43. This mission is characterized by an extremely fluid tactical situation in which friendly and enemy units may often be intermixed. To support the sector defense, the FA battalion must:
- Position batteries in depth for continuous support as units displace.
- Position batteries off high-speed avenues of approach.
- Track the battle continuously and keep batteries informed as enemy forces approach.
- Plan for rearward displacement. Coordinate routes and recognition signals with the supported maneuver unit.
- Ascertain and disseminate locations of existing and planned obstacles.
- Preposition ammunition for counterpreparations and immediate consumption. Keep all other ammunition uploaded for rapid movement.
- Conduct communications reconnaissance for fallback positions and preposition retrans capability if necessary.

DEFEND A BATTLE POSITION

8-44. BPs are used to focus and control a maneuver unit's fires, maneuver, and positioning. BPs prescribe a primary direction of maneuver fire by orientation of position. They are often placed on well-defined, enemy brigade or larger avenues of approach. The commander designates the conditions under which the force can abandon the BP. Frequently, the maneuver forces CS and CSS elements may operate outside of the BP.

8-45. A battle position defense is generally less fluid than the sector defense. When supporting a defense of a battle position, consider the following:
- Position units/batteries to ensure FS is available to security forces.
- Harden unit/battery positions to the maximum extent possible. Request engineer support when it is available.
- Ensure the locations of all friendly obstacles and engagement areas are known and plotted in battalion and battery CPs

DEFEND A STRONGPOINT

8-46. A strong point is a heavily fortified BP tied to a natural obstacle or restrictive terrain to create an anchor for the defense. It is designed to control key terrain and/or block, fix or canalize enemy forces. Strongpoints are prepared for all-around defense and rarely are used for armored or mechanized brigade or smaller forces. Strongpoints require extensive engineer support.

8-47. Defense of a strongpoint is seldom a stand-alone mission. Normally, the strongpoint is a part of a larger operation. The FA considerations for the strongpoint are in addition to those for the overall mission and may include:
- Position units/batteries so all or at least a substantial majority of available fires can be massed in support of the strongpoint.
- Consider use of a quickfire net for the unit manning the strongpoint.
- Position observers to overwatch the strongpoint and for controlling fires if communications are lost or the position is overrun.

SECTION IV – FA SUPPORT OF OTHER TACTICAL OPERATIONS

8-48. The operations discussed in this section occur often during combat. Some actions, such as passage of lines, crossing water obstacles, relief in place, and amphibious operations, are usually one phase of an operation. These operations are common to both the offense and the defense.

AMPHIBIOUS OPERATIONS

8-49. An amphibious operation is an attack launched from the sea by naval and landing forces embarked in ships or other watercraft for the purpose of landing on a hostile shore. A successful amphibious assault achieves surprise and concentrates an overwhelming force at a point of enemy weakness. The amphibious operation requires detailed planning, precise timing in coordinating CAS, NSFS, FA support, and effective command relationships. A naval officer is normally the commander of an amphibious task force (CATF). The landing force consists of both ground and air components. The CATF exercises the degree of authority over the entire force necessary to ensure success. The responsibility for conduct of operations ashore lies with the landing force commander (LFC). Planning and execution of the landing and assault are his concern. An amphibious operation is conducted in five phases: planning, embarkation, rehearsal, movement and assault.

8-50. The FA battalion is not simply a passenger on a ship-to-shore transport; it is an active component of the operation. Its active involvement before, during, and after the movement and assault is essential to the success of the landing force. When coastal topography permits, FA can be positioned on offshore islands to provide fires to support the assault element. As part of the landing party, DS artillery provides close support with direct and indirect fires to support the amphibious operation. For additional information refer to JP 3-02, *Joint Doctrine for Amphibious Operations*.

DEPLOY/CONDUCT MANEUVER

- Complete initial reconnaissance by map and air.
- Advance parties arrive with assault elements to prepare positions.
- Occupy firing positions quickly to support assault forces during the early stage of beachhead operations.
- Deploy recovery and/or engineer assets to facilitate FA occupation.
- Coordinate for PAs with the landing force commander.

DEVELOP INTELLIGENCE

- S2s should become familiar with Navy and USMC intelligence assets and information and determine channels for requesting intelligence and TA support during both pre-operation planning and execution.
- Anytime the FA battalion is operating in proximity of the ocean the S2 should maintain awareness of potential threats from enemy naval or marine forces.

EMPLOY FIRES

Detect And Locate Targets

- Coordinate with naval sources for initial targeting data.
- Aerial observers are used extensively during ship-to-shore movement.
- Plan TA handoff from the supporting arms coordination center (SACC) to the LFC.

Deliver Fires

- Obtain ballistic met support from Navy shipboard met stations.
- Coordinate with landing force HQ for available survey information.
- Use hasty survey techniques until survey assets are operational. Send survey ashore early to establish and extend a common grid.
- Decentralize tactical and technical FD to allow for flexibility until units are established ashore.
- Plan to process interservice calls for fire.
- Use engineers to stabilize gun positions, especially on sandy beaches.

EXERCISE C2

Communicate

- Establish radio as the primary means of communications during ship-to-shore movement.
- Plan communications to support aerial observers in ship-based aircraft.
- Exchange of interservice SOIs is imperative.

Coordinate Fire Support

- Provide movement plans for early landing and employment of FA units.
- Coordinate fires for the landing force with the SACC prior to landing. Once ashore, the LFC assumes responsibility for coordinating all fires.
- Plan SEAD in support of the landing.
- Ensure logistical support planning is an integral part of the FSP.

PERFORM LOGISTICS AND CSS

- Plan for high ammunition expenditure during the initial landing stages.
- Protect equipment and ammunition from salt water.
- Plan for resupply and evacuation by ship, plane or helicopter.
- Allocate vehicle recovery assets to help in resupply operations.
- Coordinate supply and/or logistic activities with naval logistic agencies.
- Cross-load to ensure availability of FA assets ashore.

PROTECT THE FORCE

- Disperse FA throughout the assault elements during movement ashore, however, unit integrity must be maintained.
- Equip personnel with life vests and other life support equipment.

AIR ASSAULT OPERATIONS

8-51. Division (or higher) HQ usually directs the formation of an air assault task force (AATF). The task force is designed for a specific mission and will be tailored for the specific mission. As an example, it may consist of an infantry battalion, an aviation company, and a FA battery. Overall command goes to the AATF commander. Air assault operations are used to seize deep objectives and to conduct penetration, covering force, or surveillance operations. They can operate in urban areas, jungles, and mountains and are used to reinforce threatened sectors.

8-52. FA participation in air assault operations is characterized by maximum decentralization of C2. Firing units move to quickly provide FA fires to attack deep targets, to bypass enemy concentrations or untrafficable terrain, and to facilitate future operations. FA units can expect to conduct SEAD, landing zone (LZ) preparations, and artillery raids. Artillery raids involve the rapid movement of artillery assets by air into position to attack a high-priority target. A FA raid normally requires operations across the FLOT, is short in duration, and does not involve sustained operations. Detailed planning, surprise, and speed of execution are key factors for success. FM 90-4 provides more information on air assault operations.

DEPLOY/CONDUCT MANEUVER

- Coordinate load plans to ensure critical elements are cross-loaded to prevent catastrophic loss in the event of downed aircraft.
- Conduct reconnaissance by map and air initially.
- Plan for air or ground displacement.

DEVELOP INTELLIGENCE

- Imagery can aid in identifying potential firing points, the general lay of the land, and major routes in the area.
- The supported maneuver unit S2 and force FA S2 can assist in templating FA and non-FA enemy forces in the air assault area and in identifying primary threats.

EMPLOY FIRES

Detect And Locate Targets

- Assign or attach FOs to accompany leading elements of the assault force to observe and adjust SEAD fires and execute the FSP.
- Coordinate with air reconnaissance and aerial scouts for target identification and attack.

Deliver Fires

- Execute fires to support the air movement plan under procedural or positive control (procedural control is the preferred method):
  - Initiate and terminate procedural-control of fires according to a strict time schedule.

- Positive-control of fires relies on phase lines, air control points and/or other control measures to initiate, shift, and terminate fires.
- Coordinate for met in the new PA.
- Utilize the NSG and PLGR, or use hasty survey techniques until PADS is brought forward.
- Plan SEAD fires to support reinforcement, resupply, and medivac for the FA battalion as necessary.
- Give priority to intelligence collection in air assault AO to ensure accurate location of EAD.
- Support overall SEAD efforts and ensure priorities for SEAD, relative to other fires, are well understood by the TOC and battery FDCs.
- Plan fires for false insertions in support of the deception plan.

EXERCISE C2

Communicate

- Use C2 aircraft and coordinate retrans as necessary during the movement to ensure continuous communication between the FSE controlling fires and the assets providing those fires.
- Plan and coordinate visual signals (flares and colored smoke).
- Coordinate SOIs between air assault forces and supporting forces.

Coordinate Fire Support

- Coordinate short and intense SEAD fires along the flight route(s) to aid aircraft flying past areas of known or suspected enemy positions.
- Consider all SEAD assets: EW, FA, CAS, and attack helicopters.
- Plan to lift and shift fires, ACAs (formal and informal), and other FSCMs as needed to coincide with arrival times of aircraft formations.
- Ensure use of FA or mortar smoke on or near LZs meets commander's guidances and does not interfere with air or ground operations.

PERFORM LOGISTICS AND CSS

- Ensure adequate ammunition is available for the assault force artillery.
- Plan, prioritize, and synchronize resupply of all CSS, primarily Class V.
- Evacuate casualties by air.

PROTECT THE FORCE

- Consider enemy air, ground, and artillery threats when planning moves because units are most vulnerable in pickup zones (PZs) and LZs.
- Consider the effects of munitions in the LZ or PZ (ICM – duds, HE/PD – cratering) that may make the area unusable.

AIRBORNE OPERATIONS

8-53. Airborne operations are joint operations conducted between the Army and Air Force. The Air Force provides airlift, CAS, and aerial resupply for airborne ground forces. Airborne units represent a contingency force that can be deployed worldwide on short notice.

8-54. FA units are normally attached to maneuver units for airborne operations (e.g., FA battery attached to a maneuver battalion). Parent FA units will assume control of subordinate units upon arrival in the airhead and will then establish standard command relationships. During brigade airborne operations, the FA battalion will provide an assault command post (ACP) to C2 batteries. FM 90-26, *Airborne Operations*, provides more information on airborne operations.

DEPLOY/CONDUCT MANEUVER

- Conduct initial reconnaissance by map or air.
- Plan displacement using air assets.
- Consider decentralized control for unit movement.

DEVELOP INTELLIGENCE

- Aerial photography can be extremely helpful in identifying potential firing points, better understanding the general lay of the land, and major routes in the area (from friendly and enemy perspectives).
- The supported maneuver unit S2 and force FA S2 may be able to assist in templating FA and non-FA enemy forces in the air assault area.

EMPLOY FIRES

Detect And Locate Targets

- Use aerial observers (Army aviation and Air Force AC-130).
- Deploy Firefinder radars as soon as practical after the initial assault.

Deliver Fires

- Plan noncratering munitions on airfields.
- Mass all available indirect fire systems, to include mortars.
- Ensure all units have a 6,400-mil capability.
- Prepare to use hasty survey techniques in the drop zone.
- Establish a common grid for FA and mortars as soon as possible.
- Coordinate met for the AO.

EXERCISE C2

Communicate

- Initially use primarily FM communications.
- Communicate by TACSAT, when available.
- Establish AM radio communications for use over long distances.
- Use visual signals and messengers for short-distance communications.

Coordinate Fire Support

- Rely on aerial photography when maps are not available.

- Ensure positive clearance of all fires (that is, silence is not consent), which is essential during initial stages of the operation.

PERFORM LOGISTICS AND CSS

- Resupply requires careful planning and coordination, especially Class V, as airborne units have limited CSS capability. Supplies are usually air-dropped or air-landed (containerized delivery or mass supply).
- Inspect weapons and equipment for damage after an airdrop.
- Conduct medical evacuation by air.

PROTECT THE FORCE

- Position units based on enemy ground, air, and artillery threats, as well as, the amount of space provided by the expanding airhead.
- Be prepared to provide 6,400-mil firing capability if necessary.
- Position units for mutual defense.
- Prepare unit defense taking maximum advantage of available intelligence and aerial photographs.

MILITARY OPERATIONS IN URBAN TERRAIN

8-55. Military operations in urban terrain (MOUT) are characterized by extreme limitations on freedom to maneuver. Both attacking and defending forces must use available cover and concealment offered by urban areas, but both are equally hampered by reduced visibility. While the defender normally has the advantage, operations are slow and deliberate and small-unit operations predominate. The defender enjoys superior protection as well as concealment and covered routes of movement. The attacker can isolate and bypass certain areas; but he is forced to fight into other, well-defended areas.

8-56. FA units can use positions in villages and small towns to great advantage. Barns and other large buildings offer complete concealment of weapons and equipment. Normally, decentralization is required. Detailed orders and TSOPs are necessary due to decreased communication ranges and extended frontages for firing units. FA techniques of assault fire and direct fire may be required more often on urban terrain than elsewhere. FM 90-10, *Military Operations on Urbanized Terrain (MOUT) (How to Fight)*, and FM 6-20-40 contain additional information on MOUT.

DEPLOY/CONDUCT MANEUVER

- Ensure PAs are identified that will support emplacement since there is a predominance of concrete surfaces in urban areas.
- Anticipate the possibility that street rubble may hamper movement.
- Anticipate increased movements to overcome obstruction/dead space.
- Ensure howitzer positions allow for high-angle firing.
- Position FA on the edge of the urban area, if possible.
- Provide multiple routes of escape from the position.
- Select howitzer positions that allow direct fire capability.

DEVELOP INTELLIGENCE

- Closely coordinate targeting efforts to ensure all protected areas and FSCMs are identified and posted to automated and manual systems.
- Determine the status and disposition (friendly, enemy, neutral) of the indigenous population and whether or not the enemy is using the urban population for cover.

EMPLOY FIRES

Detect And Locate Targets

- Identify size and location of dead space (where indirect fires cannot reach). Dead space is generally five times the height of buildings for low-angle fire and one-half the height of buildings for high-angle fire.
- Plan radar coverage to take advantage of the increase in high-angle fires. Radars lose effectiveness if positioned too close behind buildings.

Deliver Fires

- Careful use of VT is required to avoid premature detonation.
- Use caution in the adjustment of fires. Rounds can be lost behind building or other structures.
- The battalion may support more small-scale battles than normal. This involves frequent shifting of fires from one mission to the next. The battalion may need to shift ongoing missions between firing units if battle movements or adjustments move the fires into the dead space of the initial firing unit.
- More frequently, FDCs must account for bursting radius, delivery errors, and standard deviations. Reference cards, TSOPs, and rehearsals are critical in ensuring that clearance of fires doesn't become a slow, cumbersome process.
- Commanders may require close control of WP since it may create unwanted fires and smoke.
- Use fuze delay to penetrate fortifications and buildings.
- Plan for increased use of high-angle fires (cannon units).
- Consider an increase in ammunition expenditure, especially if other FS assets are not available.
- To provide maximum flexibility in MOUT's diverse situations, the reinforcing FA unit may be a composite heavy/light/MLRS force.
- Use precision-guided munitions to minimize rubbling.
- Consider the limitations of laser designators in urban terrain, such as:
  - The difficulty in maintaining a continuous laser track on moving targets because of structure interference.
  - Obstructions may limit the battalion's ability to mass fires.
  - The presence of highly reflective surfaces, such as windows that may refract laser energy and/or pose a hazard to friendly troops.
  - Presence of highly absorptive surfaces such as open windows or tunnels, which may degrade designator effectiveness.

- It may be hard to position designators to ensure Angle T does not exceed 800 mils.
- The need to plan for an increase in hasty survey since conventional survey is hampered by decreased line of sight.
- Determining accurate locations by map spot can be difficult.
- The need for multiple SCPs. Anticipate survey difficulties due to obstructions, rubbling, and electro-magnetic interference (e.g., metal, powerlines, transformers)

EXERCISE C2

Communicate

- Anticipate reduction of radio ranges due to line of sight problems.
- Increase use of wire, messenger and visual signals.
- Route wire through sewers and buildings for protection.
- Plan to remote antennas to upper floors to increase their range. Do not position antennas on rooftops since they will be vulnerable to fires and possibly give away unit locations.
- Locate generators near existing walls outside occupied buildings.
- Use existing civilian telephone systems for unsecured communications, when possible.

Coordinate Fire Support

- Avoid collateral damage to civilian populations, if possible.
- Well-defined priorities of fire are extremely important in MOUT.
- Consider use of aerial observers.
- Consider placing observers on overlooking terrain outside the city and using external routes for observer movement.
- FSCOORDs and FSOs will encounter more detailed rules of engagement and lists of protected or restricted sites and areas during MOUT. FSCM usage may increase.
- Identify potentially hazardous industrial sites that may require restrictive FSCMs.
- Consider underground dangers, gas, water, and power lines. A natural gas explosion or electrical fire in the vicinity of a protected structure, civilians, or friendly troops can become an ROE violation.
- Coordinate FA fires carefully due to the close proximity of friendly and enemy units (e.g., use of a numbering system for each building may aid in coordinating fires within close proximity of friendly troops.

PERFORM LOGISTICS AND CSS

- Anticipate an increased use of certain munitions (delay and concrete piercing fuzes, HE, or smoke).
- Use several smaller resupply convoys if movement is restricted.
- Anticipate difficulty moving large CSS vehicles inside firing positions.
- Use locally available power sources and supplies, when available.

- Plan for increased time for resupply actions.
- Consider use of prestocked supplies.

PROTECT THE FORCE

- Use existing structures as hardened positions. Ensure stability of building structure prior to occupation. Shock waves may cause weak walls and ceilings to collapse.
- Plan to increase OPs and listening posts (LPs), as terrain allows threat forces to infiltrate and get closer to artillery positions.
- Plan foot traffic routes to minimize exposure from observation and sniper fires from tall buildings.
- Consider using supplemental positions for battery defense.
- Avoid obvious positions if possible (e.g., parks and schoolyards).
- Establish guidance/drills for key situations (e.g., snipers and minefields).
- Consider unseen dangers (e.g., underground gas, water, or electrical lines).

ENCIRCLED FORCES

8-57. FA battalions may support the breakout of encircled forces as part of the encircled force, or from outside the encirclement. When the FA battalion is part of the encircled force it should:

- Quickly identify all FA/FS/TA assets within the encirclement and direct or participate in the reorganization. Ensure centralized control where possible and establish a force FA HQ if necessary.
- Complete 6,400-mil coverage.
- Retain the capability to mass fires where practical.
- Plan for aerial resupply of ammunition and critical items.
- Identify FA outside the encirclement that can range the FA battalion's zone of fire and coordinate support if possible.
- Reorganize FS communications to minimize overloading of these nets.
- Stress survival techniques.
- Identify appropriate FSCMs, such as a RFA or a RFL.
- Use CZs for Firefinder radars in both the encircled force and the main force areas to prevent fratricide.

8-58. The FA should be neither the first nor the last unit out of the perimeter during a breakout of an encirclement. If more than one firing element is within the perimeter, withdrawal should be phased to maximize the time FA fires are available. Consider external FA support if available. Maintain unit integrity at platoon or battery level if at all possible. The FA commander must keep in contact with both the lead element commander and the forces remaining in the perimeter. Moving units must anticipate hip shoots.

8-59. During linkup, the FA commander should:

- Integrate fires with the battle plans and establish FSCMs.
- Position weapons to support the relieving force.

- Plan for subsequent actions to include new missions for the FA.
- Establish and exchange sensor zones for Firefinder radars.

PASSAGE OF LINES

Forward Passage

8-60. During an offensive passage of lines, responsibility for FA fires passes from the stationary force to the passing force at the same time control is passed to the maneuver units. The stationary FA force may be attached to the passing FA force or it may be ordered to reinforce the passing FA force from its present positions, until the passing force has moved out of range.

8-61. During a forward passage, the FA commander should:
- Establish liaison and communications with the stationary FA HQ.
- Obtain and review the passage plans of the supported force.
- Determine security requirements.
- Obtain available target lists and fire plans from the stationary force.
- Plan and review PAs and routes.
- Review possible enemy observation capabilities in the area.
- Review FSCMs in effect and needed.
- Consider resupply operations for the future.
- Coordinate elements that are needed forward.
- Exchange survey data with the stationary force FA SPCE.
- Exchange Firefinder zone data, particularly CFFZs and ATIZs.

Rearward Passage

8-62. Withdrawal actions in the defense often involve a rearward passage of lines. This often occurs when a covering force withdraws behind the FEBA. FA units with each force exchange liaison and critical information as early as possible. They coordinate fire plans to synchronize and maximize their combined firepower. This includes the transfer of FA support responsibilities within the maneuver unit's sector. This transfer usually coincides with the passing of maneuver control. The withdrawing FA commander should:
- Exchange FA fire plans.
- Establish communications requirements.
- Coordinate clearance of PAs and routes, if needed.
- Coordinate resupply, if appropriate.
- Exchange survey data in the area with the passing FA SPCE.
- Establish and exchange recognition signals with the stationary force.

RELIEF IN PLACE

8-63. During a relief in place, the FA commander should:
- Establish liaison and communications between FA units.
- Provide existing fire plans to the incoming FA unit. Exchange LNOs.
- Establish procedures for the relief.

FM 3-09.21 (FM 6-20-1)

- Establish the contribution of the outgoing FA.

8-64. Normally, the FA units will not be relieved at the same time as the maneuver forces. The change of FA responsibilities is as agreed upon by the two FA commanders unless otherwise directed.

8-65. The outgoing force passes fire plans to the incoming force so those plans can be continued. Both FA commanders should:
- Exchange SOI Information.
- Prepare and disseminate fire plans to support the incoming force.
- Disseminate specific TSOP items of the incoming force.
- Disseminate the current target list to the incoming force.
- Plan fires to support or emplace a barrier or obstacle, as necessary.
- Plan smoke to screen friendly movements.
- Support the deception plan.

RIVER CROSSING OPERATIONS

8-66. During an offensive river crossing, FA units should consider:
- Aerial observers can provide surveillance beyond the river depending on availability and visibility. Smoke may limit ground observation.
- Consider using CFZs, with well thought out cueing techniques, on the river-crossing site, associated assembly areas, and air defenses.
- Fire series and groups to neutralize the bridgehead area and then to isolate it. Deep fires can also prevent or delay reinforcements.
- Positioning should facilitate rapid crossing.
- Ammunition expenditures, especially smoke and illuminating projectiles, will be high during a deliberate crossing. Consider aerial resupply initially to the far bank to offset congested crossing sites.
- Maintaining communications is critical when units are split on the two banks of the river crossing.
- DS FA units should displace to far bank positions as soon as the maneuver unit seizes first-phase objectives on the far bank and secure FA positions are available. Other FA units must cross the river before their supported maneuver units move out of range. FA crossings require well-planned integration into the overall combined arms movement plan.
- Survey assets should cross as soon as possible. When a survey team equipped with PADS crosses by river barge or boat, ensure plans allocate time for it to do a 10-minute zero-velocity update just before crossing. If the crossing will take longer than 10 minutes (total of loading, transport, and unloading times), then a conventional team must put in a starting control point on the far shore.

8-67. During a rearward river crossing, under pressure, consider:
- Anticipate fires to the flanks on enemy crossing sites and infiltrating forces involved in enemy flanking efforts.
- Consider using CFZs, with well thought out cueing techniques, on the river-crossing site, associated assembly areas, and air defenses.

- Use CFFZs and templating to locate enemy FA that attempts to interdict friendly routes of withdrawal, reinforcement, and resupply.
- Plan for increased close fires (FPFs, smoke, and SCATMINE) and massed fire missions to assist disengagement and withdrawal of the last maneuver elements across the river.
- Cross FA as soon as possible, while maintaining mission capability, to avoid entrapment and/or congestion.
- If the maneuver force plans to establish defensive positions on the far side, and stabilize the FLOT, consider engineer support to harden FA and FO/COLT/Striker positions on the far side.
- DS FA units may be able to move into hardened positions vacated by R/GSR/GS units. However, consider the risks that the previous fires may have compromised the positions.

SECURITY OPERATIONS

8-68. Units conduct security operations to provide early warning of enemy operations, to provide the force being protected with time and space within which to react, and to develop the situation for the protected force. The four forms of security operations are cover, guard, screen, and area security, which respectively contain increasing levels of combat power and security.

COVERING FORCE OPERATIONS

8-69. A covering force operation is usually a division or higher-level operation involving cavalry regiments and other forces specifically intended for these types of operations. The covering force is a tactically self-contained security force operating a considerable distance to the front or rear of a moving or stationary force. Offensive covering force operations emphasize reconnaissance along the main body's axis of advance and attempt to destroy the enemy's reconnaissance and security forces, determine enemy force dispositions, identify gaps or weaknesses that the main body can exploit, and to defeat and destroy forces as directed. Defensive covering operations focus on counter reconnaissance. They attempt to prevent the main body from being surprised, to defeat the enemy's reconnaissance and advance elements, determine the size and direction of the enemy's main attack, and delay and disorganize enemy forces in order to allow the main body more time to prepare its defense. Covering force operations are frequently fast-paced operations involving extended forces operating over long distances.

8-70. A FA battalion may be part of a larger covering force operation where a FA brigade, DIVARTY, or Corps Arty functions as the force FA HQ. The battalion may be DS to one of the maneuver forces or may be in a R, GSR, or GS role. Or the battalion may be DS to, and serve as force FA HQ of the covering force. In either case, the FA battalion may have one or more howitzer batteries from a cavalry regiment attached under battalion control. FA units involved in covering force operations should consider the following:
- Locate the enemy and provide immediately responsive fires to leading elements/elements in contact.
- Use priority of fires and quickfire channels.
- Attack deep targets with massed fires to prevent enemy reinforcements.

- Plan for hasty attack contingencies.
- Anticipate frequent moves and hip shoots.
- Keep ammunition uploaded.
- Plan for employment of hasty smoke and/or illumination, and increased suppressive fires.
- Plan to use SCATMINE to delay enemy formations and employ Copperhead for HPTs.
- Prepare for the use of permissive, o/o FSCMs and for rapidly moving FLOTs requiring frequent position updates.
- Plan for a passage of lines. Review passage of lines procedures.
- Position supporting FA forward. Consider future missions in selecting FA positions when the covering force operation nears completion.

SCREEN

8-71. Screen describes a force whose primary task is to observe, identify, and report information. A screen force fights only in self-protection. The screening force maintains surveillance, provides early warning to the main body, destroys enemy reconnaissance elements within its capability, and impedes and harasses the enemy. Indirect fires are a significant means of impeding and harassing the enemy. FA planning and execution in support of a screen mission is similar to that for a defend in sector mission.

GUARD

8-72. Guard describes a force whose primary task is to protect the main force by fighting to gain time, while also observing and reporting information, and to prevent enemy ground observation of and direct fire against the main body by reconnoitering, attacking, defending, and delaying. A guard force normally operates within the range of the main body's indirect fire weapons. The FA battalion supporting this operation, plans, prepares, and executes this mission as it would for a movement to contact or other offensive operations.

AREA SECURITY

8-73. Units conduct area security operations to protect friendly forces, installations, and actions in a specific area. Area security preserves the force commander's freedom to move his reserves, position FS assets, conduct C2 operations, and provide for sustainment operations. Area security actions, which may be offensive or defensive in nature, could include area reconnaissance; rear operations; and security of designated personnel, equipment, facilities, and critical points. Applications of area security missions are convoy and route security. FS considerations, for area security, are similar to those identified to support rear area operations.

REAR AREA OPERATIONS

8-74. Rear operations (sustainment area operations) are those activities from a maneuver unit's rear boundary forward to the rear boundaries of subordinates forces, which are conducted to ensure the unit's freedom of maneuver and continuity of operations, including continuity of sustainment and C2. The unit must synchronize the rear operations functions of terrain management, security, sustainment, and movement in consonance with the higher HQ commander's concept and intent.

8-75. A DS FA battalion must plan fires throughout the supported brigade's AO, to include defense for the BSA (e.g., base clusters). The S1, S4, or HHSB commander (or SB commander) will normally function as the FSO for the BSA. He is responsible for planning fires and forwarding them to the brigade FSE. As the rear area FSO, he should coordinate other FS assets through the brigade FSE as well. The battalion S3 should consider the following when developing plans to execute FA fires in support of a BSA: PA selection, nonstandard mission assignment, o/o mission of R FA.

8-76. While the division and corps rear FSEs are the primary planners and coordinators of division and corps rear area fires, R, GSR, and GS FA battalion may participate in the process. They may assist in coordinating fire plans with nearby CSS units or host nation military, paramilitary, or civil authorities. They may also provide call for fire training to key personnel, especially those responsible for base cluster defenses.

8-77. Three levels of response to rear area threats serve as guides for planning rear area operations. These levels focus on the nature of the friendly actions needed to defeat the threat.

- **Level I.** Smaller threats that the base or base cluster self-defense measures can defeat.
- **Level II.** Threats beyond the capability of the base or base cluster self-defenses but that relatively small response forces (e.g., MPs) can defeat.
- **Level III.** Threats that require commitment of a combined arms tactical combat force (TCF) to defeat them.

8-78. Commanders will generally reserve FA fires for Level III threats or in supporting a MP force engaging a Level II threat in an area where collateral damage is reduced. FA units should also consider the following factors.

DEPLOY/CONDUCT MOVEMENT

- Rear FSOs can assist FA battalions with terrain management issues.
- Level III threats may cause significant traffic as CSS units and civilians move away from the threat. FA battalions may need to request priority for movement and MP assistance (if available).

DEVELOP INTELLIGENCE

- The S2 should closely monitor developing situations in the rear to better anticipate potential battalion involvement and determine the nature and extent of enemy rear area threats.

EMPLOY FIRES

- Because FA units are not usually given rear area support as a primary mission, responding FA units must quickly review assigned EFATs and other tasks to determine the impact when given rear area missions. If backup plans are not adequate the unit should notify FSEs and force FA HQ so the EFATs can be reassigned or terminated.

- Ammunition restrictions on SCATMINE and dud producing munitions may limit FA to HE, except for major penetrations. Illumination may require high-angle fire to allow safe firing. Consider fire hazards.

EXERCISE C2

Communications

- Communication with the division or corps rear FSE may be difficult due to distances. A FA battalion may need to relay fire planning and/or fire coordination information through another FA battalion.
- Nonstandard communications arrangements may be necessary. CSS units may not have digital equipment that interfaces with FA systems. Host nation civil or paramilitary force may not have compatible radios.

Fire Support Coordination

- Commander's guidance, FSCMs, and ROE for FA fires in rear areas are generally restrictive in nature (RFAs, NFAs).
- Commanders may task FA battalion's in rear areas to provide FOs or FSOs to assist with rear area operations. Fire mission requests in rear areas may frequently involve untrained observers.
- A FA battalion may participate in development of a hasty fire plan with the FSO of a responding TCF, MPs, and other response forces. Consider using RFLs to control fires between converging friendly forces.

PROTECT THE FORCE

- FA units requiring force protection fires may request attack helicopters and slower fixed-wing CAS support when available.

LINKUP OPERATIONS

8-79. Linkup operations join two friendly forces. Both forces may be moving toward one another or one may be stationary. Often, a linkup operation requires a passage of lines. When the linkup is made, the linkup force may join the stationary force or it may pass through or around and continue the attack. The controlling HQ of both forces establishes the command relationship between the two forces and the responsibilities for each. It also establishes the control measures. FA considerations include:

- As the linkup nears completion, consider future operations in positioning of battalion elements.
- Plan for the increased use of o/o RFLs and CFLs.
- Place increased emphasis on maintaining updated position and FSCM locations in both automated and manual systems.
- Anticipate blocking fires to prevent trapped enemy forces from escaping the linking forces.
- Ensure clearance of fires procedures address all contingencies and FA forces. GS/GSR units may need to clear fires with both linking forces.
- Exchange targeting and communications information, triggers, quickfire channels, laser designation codes, and other essential items.

- Exchange recognition signals and disseminate to all personnel.
- FA units supporting linking forces should consider exchanging liaison. If the linkup involves a stationary and moving force, the moving force FA should provide liaison to the stationary force FA

BREACHING OPERATIONS

8-80. Breaching is a synchronized combined-arms operation under the control of a maneuver commander. Breaching operations begin when friendly forces employ suppressive fires and end when battle handover has occurred between a unit conducting the breaching operation and follow-on forces. FA considerations in supporting breaching operations include:

- Anticipate high volumes of suppressive (HE/VT, DPICM) and obscuration ammunitions. Develop CCLs to support breaching EFATs and schedule delivery to maximize ammunition resupply operations.
- Provide fires during all phases of the breaching – suppress, obscure, secure, reduce (SOSR). See FM 6-20-40 for more information on SOSR.
- Backup plans are especially critical to maintaining suppressive and obscuration fires while the breaching team is exposed.
- Unplanned breaching operations may require that the S3 quickly review ammunition status for impact on other EFATs.
- Position a FO or FIST member forward to coordinate fires for the breaching team. Plan for observers in depth.
- Primary and backup FA firing units must understand the primary and backup triggering plans to shift fires to the assault force.
- If Copperhead is used against armored vehicles protecting the obstacle site, it may be better executed early, as preparatory fires, to prevent interference to lasing from the obscuration fires.
- Anticipate SEAD fires if air assets participate in the operation.
- Consider using SCATMINE to prevent reinforcement or counterattack. Ensure it does not interfere with the breaching or the follow-on assault.

ARTILLERY RAID OPERATIONS

8-81. An artillery raid is a type of spoiling attack that uses FA as its primary attack mechanism. Raid missions support the higher HQ objectives by sending firing elements forward to engage enemy targets that are currently beyond the maximum range of available FA weapons. Raids may occur in conjunction with a large ground attack that seizes the terrain needed for the firing unit, with a small force that creates a relatively small moving pocket, or even without a significant ground force (if the threat is low). Light FA units may conduct airmobile FA raids. An artillery raid is frequently a platoon or battery size operation, but can involve an entire battalion.

PROCEDURES

Unit Selection

8-82. If higher HQ does not specify the firing element, the battalion S3 determines which unit/firing element will conduct the raid mission based on:

- Weapon system availability (desired effects on target).
- Ammunition availability (number and type of rounds).
- Location of firing element (proximity to firing points).
- Tactical situation.

Raid Briefing

8-83. For cross FLOT operations, the battalion HQ will conduct a raid briefing with the battery commander of the selected battery. If available, the commander of the maneuver security force should be present during the briefing in order to affect coordination. Due to time constraints or travel distance involved, a face-to-face meeting with the maneuver commander may not be feasible. For raids to be conducted behind the FLOT with minimal external assistance, raid missions may be passed via FM radio (voice or digital). At a minimum, the battalion commander or S3 will brief:

- **SITUATION.** Friendly, enemy, attachments, and detachments.
- **MISSION.** Who, what, when, where, and why to include the size of the element to conduct raid, method of control, and target/FP grids.
- **EXECUTION.**

    Behind the FLOT operation:
    - Route to operations area (OPAREA).
    - SP/CP/RP locations.
    - Firing point OPAREA.
    - Rally point after mission.
    - Target grids.
    - Firing window or TOT.
    - Number/Type rounds per target.
    - Number of howitzers/launchers authorized.
    - Call signs and frequencies.
    - FSCMs.
    - Abort authority and abort code word.
    - Emergency destruction (ED) criteria.
    - FS assets available.

    Cross FLOT operation. In addition to the elements involved in a behind the FLOT operation, the following must be considered:
    - Link up-point with maneuver element guides.
    - Force protection (ADA, EW, FS assets, escort).
    - Passage lane/passage point.
    - Procedures/Signals for passage of lines.
    - Maneuver call signs and frequencies.
    - Maneuver commander name and rank.

- **SERVICE SUPPORT.**
    - Maintenance support/contact team requirements.
    - Survey support available.
    - Reload requirements.

- Amount of ammunition to be brought forward.
- Refuel support.
- **COMMAND AND SIGNAL.**
  - Retrans location and frequency.
  - C2 (e.g., FDC vehicle, OE254).

Execution Of The Raid

8-84. The following procedures identify responsibilities and outline steps for the actual execution of the raid:
- Firing units will carry forward only the number of vehicles necessary to accomplish the mission as designated by battalion. (Depending on the importance of the target, one additional howitzer/launcher will be brought forward and laid on the target in case of technical/ mechanical difficulties). Weapons platforms with automated fire control systems will move forward with the mission in their system and a hardcopy of the mission in case manual fire mission processing is required.
- Firing unit(s) arrive at the link-up point.
- The OIC/NCOIC of the raid party will brief the maneuver unit commander or representative at link up point or via FM communications as directed.
- Once the brief is conducted, the leader of the raid unit or a maneuver escort will bring the firing elements to the link-up points.
- Security force will move forward and clear the route to the FP.
- If possible, report link-up, movement/checkpoints, and in position to BOC. If necessary, a vehicle will be brought forward with the raid element to act as a relay between the raid element and the controlling raid HQ if constant communications is required. If not, the communication will be maintained between the supported unit HQ, the battalion TOC, and the raid OIC. The raid OIC must be prepared to accept target updates prior to the designated time.
- Once the maneuver security force has cleared the route and OPAREA, the firing element will be called forward to the firing points.
- The mission(s) is (are) fired. Units will report shot on each target and rounds complete to the controlling HQ.
- Firing elements will then withdraw to a pre-designated rally point.
- If the firing unit was briefed that it was to perform a follow-on mission, the unit would proceed to the next location and fire the mission. MLRS launchers may need to reload between missions. Upon rounds complete, the firing element will withdraw to the rally point.
- Battalion will provide abort criteria.

CHECKLISTS

8-85. The use of checklists can assist raid planners. These can be developed as part of the unit TSOP or battle books. An example of a battalion level checklist for an artillery raid operation is provided in the following table.

Table 8-1. Artillery Raid Planning Checklist (Example)

\multicolumn{2}{c}{ARTILLERY RAID PLANNING CHECKLIST (BATTALION)}	
ITEM	ACTIVITY
1	Verify raid order contains all pertinent data.
2	If not specified by higher HQ, what size FA unit is necessary for successful mission?
3	Who is the raid force commander (maneuver? FA?).
4	What force protection will support the raid force?
	• Maneuver Force?
	• FS Plan?
	• Air Defense? (attack helicopter/CAS Spt)
	• Reconnaissance and Security?
	• Radar?
	• Observers?
5	What are the ABORT criteria?
6	What frequencies will be used to C2 the raid?
7	Any updates on enemy/friendly situation that impact on raid?
8	What is the route (does it require clearance by a maneuver commander)?
9	Passage of Lines.
	• Linkup Grid and Time?
	• Routes?
	• Maneuver Graphics?
	• Engineer Plan (mobility/countermobility)?
	• Air Defense Plan and Coverage?
	• FS and Observation Plan?
	• C2 (Raid Battle Handover Line)?
	• MEDEVAC Support?
	• Maintenance Support?
10	What survey support is optimal/adequate for raid force?
11	Is met available/valid?
12	Will ammunition need to be brought forward? How much?
13	What is the reload plan (approved location for reload operations)? Need to conduct reload to complete the mission?
14	Will the Firing Point require clearance by a maneuver force? Will this be in addition to the security force?
15	What is the link-up grid for coordinating with the raid force commander? When will link-up take place?
16	What is the name, frequency, and call sign of the raid force commander/security force?
17	Notify the raid BC of the raid mission and time/place of briefing.
18	Plot firing positions, passage lanes/points/ routes to OPAREA.
19	Determine/verify firing elements, # of howitzers/launchers and C2 structure.
20	Develop timetable (SP, TOT).
21	Brief the BC of the raid element battery.
22	Track planning and rehearsal schedule coordinated by battery.
23	Monitor & track progress of raid

SECTION V – FA SUPPORT OF STABILITY OPERATIONS AND SUPPORT OPERATIONS

8-86. The FA battalion may support a wide variety of stability operations and support operations that may or may not involve traditional combat. Because stability operations and support operations involve significant political considerations, and are often multinational, joint force operations, the FA battalion leadership should understand the nature of the joint, multinational, civil, and military relationships, and the cultures of our allies and the host nation. The FA battalion's success relies in large part on the legitimacy provided by international agreements, in the battalion's ability to abide by established agreements and ROE, and, often, in the unit's ability to remain neutral while executing assigned tasks.

8-87. Stability operations and support operations may encompass activities where FA organizations are employed in areas outside the US in support of operations in nontraditional, noncombatant roles without primary weapons. Disaster relief and humanitarian assistance and security are examples. The FA battalion's communications infrastructure, coordination skills, and inherent mobility can enhance and assist a command's overall coordination and liaison effort. Potential responsibilities include enhancing effective C2, convoy operations, local security operations, and liaison in support of civil-military affairs.

STABILITY OPERATIONS

8-88. Stability operations involve the application of military power to influence the political environment, facilitate diplomacy, and interrupt specified illegal activities. They include both developmental and coercive actions. Developmental actions enhance a government's willingness and ability to care for its people. Coercive actions apply carefully prescribed, limited force and the threat of force to achieve objectives. The types of stability operations that a FA battalion may participate in include, but are not limited to the following:

- Peace operations (peacekeeping, peace enforcement, peacemaking and peacebuilding).
- Foreign Internal Defense.
- Security assistance.
- Humanitarian and civil assistance.
- Support to insurgencies.
- Support to counterdrug operations.
- Combating terrorism (counterterrorism and antiterrorism).
- Noncombatant evacuation operations.
- Arms control.
- Show of force.

8-89. While each operation is unique, seven broad imperatives help forces develop concepts and schemes for executing stability operations:

- Stress force protection.

- Emphasize information operations.
- Maximize interagency, joint, and multinational cooperation.
- Apply force selectively and discriminately.
- Display the capability to apply force in a nonthreatening manner. Demonstrate strength without provoking a potential adversary to act.
- Understand the potential for disproportionate consequences of individual and small unit actions.
- Act decisively to prevent escalation.

FA SUPPORT OF STABILITY OPERATIONS

DEPLOY/CONDUCT MANEUVER

- Select hard surface roads whenever possible to minimize the risk of encountering mines and booby traps.
- Coordinate cleared and approved routes before departure.
- Maps may not be accurate. Aerial reconnaissance may facilitate movement planning.
- Helicopters can quickly emplace advance party teams.
- Closely monitor vehicle locations as they move throughout the AO. Ensure convoy leaders report departures, maintain communications during movements, and report arrival at the destinations.
- Keep vehicles on hard surfaced roads if stopped. Do not "herringbone" off the road unless a credible air or indirect fire threat exists.

DEVELOP INTELLIGENCE

- The S2 should obtain a clear understanding of the intelligence/TA assets available and the channels for requesting and reporting intelligence information.
- The S2 should receive a thorough intelligence briefing on the military, political, and social factors that may impact on the mission.
- Develop an intelligence collection plan that addresses both military and civilian elements.
- The S2/S3, in coordination with appropriate FSEs, should develop or obtain a list of protected/restricted areas that are or may be protected with FSCMs. This is necessary in targeting, and can identify potential "sanctuary" areas the enemy may try to exploit to his advantage.

EMPLOY FIRES

Detect And Locate Targets

- Integrate all information sources to identify potential targets.
- Coordinate TA assets to locate potential targets; potentially in a 6,400 mil capability.
- Develop an observation plan that includes priority intelligence requirements, addresses both military and civilian activity, is objective oriented, and focuses on monitoring critical areas.

Deliver Fires

- Ensure accurate target locations by using 1:25,000 or 1:12,500 scale maps for greater accuracy.
- Plan and execute fires within the confines of established ROE and commander's guidances. Plan to provide defensive fires to protect the force, and offensive fires as required by the nature of the operation.
- Plan to provide fires in a dispersed, non-linear environment, using battery or platoon size firebases.
- Plan to provide fires to support convoys as they move through the AO.
- Control the use of hasty survey techniques.
- When required, use precision munitions and centralized fire control procedures to minimize collateral damage.
- Plan and rehearse clearance of fire drills. Clearance of fires may include coordination with designated civilian agencies.
- Plan for 6,400-mil capability since a well-defined front line is unlikely.

PERFORM LOGISTICS AND CSS

- The S4 should identify all joint, multinational, and host nation sources of supply and any guidelines, especially to use of host nation resources.
- Plan for surge use of specific classes of CSS, increased consumption of Class I and VII, and increased use of Class IV barrier material.
- Ensure mine detectors are operational and soldiers trained in their use.
- Consider means for channeling refugees to collection points.

EXERCISE C2

Communicate

- The S6 should review anticipated tactical situations and EFATs for unique communication and automation requirements involving joint and multinational forces.
- The dispersed nature of the operations may necessitate additional retrans capability. Consider security for retrans teams.
- Plan to use unsecured communications with allied and NATO forces.
- Plan to use local telephone networks, if available.

Coordinate Fire Support

- Identify and develop/obtain a list of locations that have political, religious, or other significant considerations that must be accounted for during FS planning and development of commander's guidances.
- Identify ROE.
- Ensure targeting, clearance of fire procedures, and use of FSCMs minimize collateral damage and adhere to ROE.
- Identify unique liaison requirements with joint, multinational, and/or civilian agencies and units.

- Identify information operations requirements, assign tasks, and prepare plans as appropriate.
- Consider distribution of the FSP down to the lowest level possible – to include checkpoints, patrols, and logistics convoys.

PROTECT THE FORCE

- Position units to protect them from potential enemy indirect and direct harassing fires, and allow mutually supporting fires.
- Harden positions whenever possible.
- Consider using CFZs on key friendly forces to facilitate counterfire against attacking enemy indirect fire assets.
- Train all soldiers on booby trap and mine identification, likely locations, and marking procedures.
- Ensure an advanced party clears PAs of mines prior to the main body arriving. Initially clear lanes for critical vehicles to move into position (e.g., FDC, howitzers.). Clear noncritical areas as time permits.
- Use proper reporting procedures when mines are located. A good method is using the acronym HARMM:
  - **H**alt all movement.
  - **A**void disturbing the mine(s).
  - **R**eport the location of the mine(s).
  - **M**ark the location.
  - **M**ove out of the area.
- Develop and practice battle drills for responding to mounted and dismounted mine strikes.
- Establish a secure perimeter to guard against ground attacks, displaced civilians entering the perimeter, and thieves.
- Ensure vehicles never travel alone.

SUPPORT OPERATIONS

8-90. Support operations provide essential supplies and services to assist designated groups. They are conducted to help foreign and civil authorities respond to crises and include action to save or protect lives, reduce suffering, recover essential infrastructure, and improve quality of life. The types of support operations that a FA battalion may participate in include, but are not limited to the following:

- Humanitarian assistance in dealing with starvation, epidemics, and similar emergencies.
- Environmental assistance in responding to floods, earthquakes, and other natural or manmade disasters.

8-91. Although each support operation is unique, seven broad imperatives generally guide involvement:

- Secure the force, equipment, and supplies.
- Provide essential support to the largest number of people.
- Hand over assistance operations to civilian agencies as soon as feasible.
- Establish measures of success.

- Conduct robust information operations.
- Ensure operations conform to legal requirements.

FA SUPPORT OF SUPPORT OPERATIONS

8-92. If support operations involve the potential use of force or traditional combat, many or all of the considerations applicable to stability operations will also be appropriate to support operations. However, support operations usually involve reduced potential for use of significant force.

DEPLOY/CONDUCT MANEUVER

- Anticipate dispersed operations and small unit positions. Terrain management may involve both military and civilian agencies.
- Road conditions may be poor, especially on frequently used routes. Develop a prioritized list of engineer support requirements.
- Consider refugee and military/civilian emergency vehicle traffic.

DEVELOP INTELLIGENCE

- The FA battalion TOC can assist civil authorities with collection and dissemination of vital information, requirements, and status reports.
- Ensure the lack of a threat does not make unit soldiers complacent to OPSEC procedures. Adversarial intelligence collection activities may occur. Conduct a thorough OPSEC review to identify issues. Brief all soldiers on OPSEC precautions and reporting procedures.
- Establish close coordination with MPs, the Criminal Investigation Division, and other military and civil authorities to monitor threat levels and criminal activities that may impact battalion operations. These include theft of military supplies and equipment, black-market activities, racial/sexual/ethnic assaults, and similar issues.

PERFORM LOGISTICS AND CSS

- The battalion must plan, coordinate, and provide CSS on a dual support basis – direct mission-related CSS, and normal battalion-oriented CSS.
- Plan for dispersed maintenance and recovery operations.
- Identify available host nation and multinational support.
- Some relief convoy operations may involve both military and civilian agencies and vehicles. This requires careful coordination and security.

EXERCISE C2

- Unit communications equipment may be multi-tasked, assisting with support operations as well as in coordinating the battalion's operations.

PROTECT THE FORCE

- Conduct detailed, comprehensive risk analysis to identify all potential hazards and unique situations encountered in support operations.

- Disease and sanitary precautions may be higher force protection priorities than normal. Pre-deployment medical reviews should ensure all soldiers are inoculated and free of major health problems. In country, preventative measures include proper positioning of forces, good sanitary practices, and guidelines on interaction with the host nation populace and multinational force personnel.

SECTION VI – CLIMATE AND TERRAIN CONSIDERATIONS

8-93. Both climate and terrain can vary widely between different operational areas, and even within the same operational area. FA battalions frequently adjust their TTP to account for these differences. Some of the climate and terrain factors that FA battalions should consider are discussed in the following paragraphs.

NIGHT OPERATIONS

8-94. Effective operations during hours of darkness are essential in combat. The basic ingredient of successful offensive or defensive night operations is the confidence of the individual soldier in his ability and equipment in the night environment. This confidence stems from detailed planning and effective training. The adverse effects of darkness require a change in techniques and procedures. However, it is important to note that darkness imposes limitations equally on enemy forces.

8-95. The objectives of night operations are to:
- Achieve surprise and avoid losses that might be incurred in daylight over the same terrain.
- Compensate for advantages held by a numerically superior enemy who has air superiority.
- Retain the initiative by defeating enemy night operations.
- Exploit our technological advantage at night over a less sophisticated enemy.

8-96. Planning considerations for the basic FA tasks in support of night operations are discussed in the following paragraphs.

DEPLOY/CONDUCT MANEUVER
- Plan and rehearse RSOP procedures for night occupation.
- Plan for increased movement times at night.
- Plan for the increased use of traffic control points to ensure the correct direction of travel is maintained during movement.
- Guide every vehicle into position according to the track plan.
- Erect tentage before darkness and check for light leaks.
- Install generators and light sets before darkness.

DEVELOP INTELLIGENCE
- Scout high traffic routes during daytime to identify potential ambush sites and intersections or turns where vehicles and convoys may become misdirected or where large vehicles may have difficulty traversing.
- Identify locations of MP, maneuver, and other friendly force checkpoints and patrols. Also identify host nation checkpoints. Verify clearance procedures in place to ensure there are no misunderstandings in the dark.

EMPLOY FIRES

Detect And Locate Targets

- Limited sound flash observations by FOs, COLTs, and Strikers may be possible to supplement radar.
- Provide OPs with night vision devices.

Deliver Fires

- Adjust FPFs and danger close targets during daylight, if possible.
- Establish procedures for marking the end of the orienting line (EOL) and the orienting station (OS).
- During periods of relatively low activity and stable fronts consider firing from supplementary positions at night to reduce night survival moves of the entire battery.
- Review commander's guidances on use of illumination and smoke.
- Anticipate requests for illumination in the rear when enemy infiltration risk is moderate to high. Coordinate FSCMs and clearance of fire procedures. Obtain current friendly force locations.
- Plan for the increased time to perform hasty survey techniques.

PERFORM LOGISTICS AND CSS

- Plan resupply operations at night to decrease vulnerability.
- Ensure adequate amounts of illuminating and smoke projectiles are on hand and in the proper locations.
- Perform noisy operations while the unit is firing. Firing will mask the noise of heavy vehicular traffic and material handling equipment.

EXERCISE C2

Communicate

- Install and check communications equipment prior to darkness.
- Inspect operation of wire/LAN systems prior to darkness.

Coordinate Fire Support

- Determine the specific area in which the commander desires to use smoke to degrade enemy night vision capabilities. Ensure it does not degrade friendly night vision capabilities.
- Develop and distribute illumination and smoke plans early enough that the cannon units can deliver and prepare as much of the ammunition as possible during daylight hours.

PROTECT THE FORCE

- Plan and adjust on-call FPFs around unit positions prior to darkness.
- Establish direct fire sectors prior to darkness.
- Stress light and noise discipline.
- Include self-illumination in the unit defense plan.

COLD WEATHER OPERATIONS

8-97. Cold weather operations involve unique weather and climate considerations. Summer has long periods of daylight; while winter has long nights, deep snow, and extreme cold. Spring thaws turn low-lying areas into a morass of mud, which severely degrades surface mobility. Weather phenomena such as whiteouts and greyouts cause loss of depth perception, which increases the hazards of driving. Ice fogs often form over troop concentrations and disclose their location. In extreme cold, metal becomes brittle, hydraulic oil thickens and parts breakage rates increase. Rates of fire for indirect fire weapons decrease as a result of heavily clothed gun crews, cold weapons, and fogged lenses on fire control devices. The enemy force is equally affected by these extreme conditions of subzero weather and snow.

8-98. Winterization of equipment is critical for sustaining combat effectiveness. Indoctrination, training, and acclimatization of individual soldiers in northern region environments are essential first steps to overcoming these adversities. Thorough planning and preparation will help a FA unit fulfill its mission while facing the extremes of this environment. In winter, when daylight is shorter, maximize its availability for preparations, reconnaissance, rehearsals, and other key activities. Refer to FM 31-70, *Basic Cold Weather Manual*, and FM 31-71, *Northern Operations*, for more information on cold weather operations.

DEPLOY/CONDUCT MANEUVER

- Consider route reconnaissance by both ground and air.
- Determine ice thickness and load-bearing before crossing frozen lakes and rivers.
- Determine PAs prior to movement since frozen, snow-covered terrain may limit the number of available positions.
- Anticipate icy road conditions and blocked routes in mountain passes during cold weather. Conduct prior reconnaissance.
- Hot springs exist in some cold weather locations. They may freeze during extreme cold, but will weaken and thaw before other areas,.
- Plan for increased movement times due to local conditions.
- Use air assets to position artillery weapons, if available.
- Train soldiers to operate equipment on ice and snow.
- Enforce track plans in the PA.

DEVELOP INTELLIGENCE

- Increase air reconnaissance, especially when adverse road conditions.
- Photographic reconnaissance may provide valuable information on possible enemy FA locations, especially after fresh snow.

EMPLOY FIRES

Detect And Locate Targets

- Provide amber filters for binoculars and observation devices to help reduce the incidence of snow blindness.

Deliver Fires

- Anticipate degradation of radar operations due to extreme cold weather
- Update meteorology data when abrupt temperature changes occur.

- Plan for increased use of airburst munitions. HE-PD, HE-delay, ICM, and SCATMINE are ineffective in deep snow and frozen ground. Snow smothers at least 40 percent of the blast from these munitions.
- Use WP as marking rounds; however, phosphorus may burn undetected in the snow for extended periods and create a hazard to friendly troops.
- Plan to use VT fuzes for cold weather operations. However, snow and ice may cause premature detonation. Also, extreme cold causes an increase in the dud rate among VT fuzes. Use the new improved VT fuze (M732) to reduce this problem.
- Plan for decreased rates of fire as a result of heavily clothed gun crews, cold weapons and fogged lenses on fire control devices.
- Place additional emphasis on monitoring propellant temperatures.
- Plan on an increase in the use of high-burst or radar registrations and met plus velocity error (VE).

PERFORM LOGISTICS AND CSS

- Plan for decreased logistical resupply due to reduced mobility and difficulty in determining grid locations.
- Ensure supply convoys travel in close columns during whiteout conditions and prolonged darkness.
- Plan for an increase in parts breakage as metal becomes brittle in extremely cold temperatures.
- Plan maximum use of aerial resupply.
- Order larger quantities of POL due to an increased use of personnel heaters and vehicle warm-up operations.
- Check vehicle winterization often to ensure continued protection.
- Exercise weapon recoil systems often between fire missions.
- Adhere to preventive maintenance checks and services (PMCS) as prescribed for cold weather operations.

EXERCISE C2

Communicate

- Plan for decreased communications effectiveness.
- Replace batteries, both dry-cell and nickel-cadmium, more frequently since they become less effective with the decrease in temperature.
- Cover the mouthpieces of microphones to prevent frost from forming.
- Plan for difficulty in establishing a good electrical ground in permafrost and deep snow.
- Keep antennas free of snow and ice.
- Check TMs for radios and power sources for special precautions during operation in extremely cold climates.

- Ensure retrans teams are well supplied to endure longer periods without resupply during inclement weather. Monitor storms that could cause them to become snowed-in in high altitude or mountainous cold weather regions.

Coordinate Fire Support

- Plan for limited ground mobility of artillery weapons and ammunition supply vehicles and increased time preparing for operation.
- Frequently relieve observers in exposed, extremely cold static positions.
- Establish a marking system for friendly locations.

PROTECT THE FORCE

- Provide firing areas with firing platform stability.
- Avoid emplacement in avalanche-prone areas. The sound produced by firing can cause an avalanche.
- Maintain seasonal camouflage for use by units.
- Train soldiers on the prevention of cold weather injuries.
- Provide warming areas for soldier use.

DESERT OPERATIONS

8-99. Military operations in desert regions are characterized by rapid, highly mobile warfare conducted over great distances. These fast-moving battles, with long-range visibility, are more suited to mechanized rather than light forces. Deserts offer little life support. Extreme weather conditions in the desert make combat operations demanding on both equipment and personnel.

8-100. Active deception techniques play key roles in the concentration and dispersal of FA units and security takes on added importance. Long-range engagements are common due to terrain, weather, and fields of fire. However, heat waves, mirages, and sandstorms can hamper ground observation. Air observation is highly effective in this environment; however, the absence of prominent landmarks in some areas degrades this capability. Also the lack of trees and hills makes aircraft more vulnerable to enemy air defenses. FM 90-3, *Desert Operations*, provides more information on desert operations.

DEPLOY/CONDUCT MANEUVER

- Position radars to provide the maximum screening crest.
- Consider the effect of sand and dust on visibility and convoy speeds.
- Position howitzers in defilade.
- Avoid predictable FA positions.

DEVELOP INTELLIGENCE

- Friendly ground observation is enhanced but additional early warning is required due to rapid movement rates. Quickly disseminate notifications of enemy penetrations or infiltrations to affected FA units.

EMPLOY FIRES

Detect And Locate Targets

- Anticipate terrain association and navigation errors that increase target location errors.
- Use G/VLLDs to perform target area survey.
- Emplace and camouflage radars and equipment at night, if possible.
- Exploit situational cueing.
- Anticipate increased survivability moves.
- Use PADS to establish OP location and directional reference.

Deliver Fires

- Request met support for transitional periods because of abrupt weather changes (especially temperature) in the morning and evening.
- Consider range requirements for meteorology support.
- Plan to provide survey control over extended distances.
- Plan for increase in hasty survey. Consideration should include:
  - Graphic resection if maps are available and accurate.
  - Simultaneous observation.
  - P-2 reticle and Polaris-Kochab use.
  - Use of PADS to determine direction and GPS for location in establishing SCPs.
- Consider the location of SCPs and their affect on providing control.
- Stress uniform storage and frequent measuring of propellant temperature due to high surface temperature effect on propellants.

PERFORM LOGISTICS AND CSS

- Plan for extended supply lines.
- Plan for increased water consumption.
- Plan for increased vehicle overheating, electrical component breakdown, and faster tire wear-out.
- Stockpile filters, coolants, lubricants, cleaning materials, and tires.
- Train soldiers in the prevention of heat and cold weather injuries.
- Plan for night and/or aerial resupply. However, dust clouds from helicopters must not give away PAs.
- Check vehicles batteries often and maintain adequate supplies of distilled water. Electrolyte in wet-cell batteries evaporates quickly.
- Perform frequent PMCS on vehicles, equipment, and weapons.

EXERCISE C2

Communicate

- Consider increased ranges for radio communications.
- Plan for early emplacement of retrans assets.

- Protect radio equipment. Failure rates increase due to blowing sand and large temperature variances.

Coordinate Fire Support

- Anticipate rapid enemy movement.
- Provide SEAD fires in support of CAS and attack helicopters.
- Prepare to support forces dispersed over wide expanses of terrain.

PROTECT THE FORCE

- Anticipate more heat and burn cases and snake and insect bite victims.
- Use the terrain to provide depth and dispersion.
- Use wadis for concealment.
- Use desert camouflage nets.
- Request attachment of anti-tank teams if contact with enemy armor or mechanized forces is anticipated.
- Employ crew-served weapons to maximize effective ranges.

JUNGLE OPERATIONS

8-101. Jungle operations involve a greater, but not exclusive, reliance on air assets for mobility, observation, and resupply of engaged forces. Surface mobility (wheeled and tracked) is limited. Light forces are best suited for jungle operations. They can be inserted and extracted by helicopter. High temperatures and humidity take their toll on equipment and soldiers. Frequent jungle operations include ambushes, raids, and small unit patrols. They seek to attack and destroy enemy forces, their bases, and their supplies.

8-102. Close in fighting is common in jungle terrain. FS may be limited to high-angle indirect fires and CAS. If the friendly force has a substantial advantage in FS, the enemy will most likely try to establish and maintain extremely close contact. This limits the effectiveness of FA because of the fratricide danger. For the FA battalion commander, the challenges are varied and many. His greatest frustration may be in trying to mass the weapons of the battalion because frequently firing units are dispersed over large areas in order to support small-unit operations. FA considerations for operations in jungle environments are discussed in the following paragraphs. FM 90-5, *Jungle Operations*, provides more information on jungle operations

DEPLOY/CONDUCT MANEUVER

- Select positions accessible by roads, when available.
- Plan to reposition using air assets.
- Anticipate difficulty in mobility for wheeled and tracked vehicles.
- Anticipate weather conditions and its effects on mobility.
- Plan equipment loads to maximize available air assets.

DEVELOP INTELLIGENCE

- Consider increased ground reconnaissance in and around FA PAs and routes and security assistance from MP and maneuver units.

EMPLOY FIRES

Detect And Locate Targets

- Ensure safety considerations are stressed since map reading (self-location, target location and friendly unit location) is difficult.
- Plan for increase use of Firefinder radar for counterfire missions.
- Use ground surveillance radars and remote sensors, if available.

Deliver Fires

- Understand the following ammunition considerations:
  - HE-delay penetrates the treetops and splinters the trees, creating additional fragmentation.
  - Smoke has limited effectiveness in dense vegetation.
  - WP is effective as a marking round. Consider using an airburst WP round as the initial round in adjustment.
- Plan for a reduction in illumination effects because of vegetation.
- Anticipate increased hasty survey techniques as SCPs may be scarce and difficult to establish.
- Use creeping fires in heavy vegetation.

PERFORM LOGISTICS AND CSS

- Anticipate increased maintenance problems due to moisture and rust.
- Expect ammunition expenditure to be high and plan accordingly.
- Use air as the primary means of resupply, when possible.

EXERCISE C2

Communicate

- Plan for communication degradation in a triple-canopy jungle.
- Ensure antenna cables and connectors, as well as power and telephone cables, are off the ground. This minimizes the effects of moisture, fungus and insects.
- Elevate antennas above the jungle canopy when possible.
- Coordinate for aerial observers or airborne C2 platforms to act as relay stations, when possible.
- Use directional antennas to increase the range of FM communications.
- Plan the use of retrans assets.

Coordinate Fire Support

- Plan to fire high-angle missions.
- Plan for an increase in requests for SEAD.

PROTECT THE FORCE
- Position units for mutual defense, especially when thick vegetation increases vulnerability to ground attack.
- Plan and adjust for mutual support.
- Prepare to use anti-personnel mines (Claymores) and direct fire cannon munitions (105mm, Beehive) for immediate use while in position.
- Establish local all-around security.
- Select alternate and supplemental positions.
- Plan for increased health hazards, disease, and snake and insect bites.

MOUNTAIN OPERATIONS

8-103. Mountain operations include many of the same problems found in cold weather regions. Mountainous areas typically have rugged, compartmented terrain with steep slopes and treacherous mobility. Weather may span the entire spectrum from extreme cold with ice and snow in winter to extreme heat during the summer. In mountain operations, the advantages favor the defender, and the focal point is the battle to control the high ground. Infantry units are the most suitable force for this type of combat, particularly when properly supported. Also, the terrain promotes isolated battles that make C2 difficult. Small-unit commanders often operate semi-independently

DEPLOY/CONDUCT MANEUVER
- Position FA in defilade to increase their survivability. But beware of snow and rock slides in these positions.
- Give SP units priority in PA selection due to terrain limitations.
- Maximize helicopter airlift for movement, especially for elements such as retrans sites, observers, and PADs.
- Plan for air reconnaissance of routes and positions, when possible.
- On narrow mountain roads, turnaround locations for large vehicles and those pulling trailers may be scarce. Locate potential turnaround points during route reconnaissance.
- Plan for increased hasty survey. Place special emphasis on accurate altitude.

DEVELOP INTELLIGENCE
- Increase use of aerial reconnaissance and intelligence platforms and internal and external intelligence reports to compensate for reduced visibility and ground reconnaissance.
- Placed increased emphasis on terrain considerations (such as use of defilade) in templating enemy FA.
- Don't underestimate the enemy's ability to position mortars in difficult terrain. Range capabilities are more useful in templating.

EMPLOY FIRES

Detect And Locate Targets

- Place FOs on high ground to maximize visibility; however they may need to be staggered at different levels if low-level clouds are possible.
- Anticipate poor visibility due to clouds, fog, or snow blindness.
- Employ Firefinder radar to detect high-angle fires.
- Position Firefinder radar to maximize terrain masking.
- Plan for ground surveillance radars and remote sensors, if available.

Deliver Fires

- Choose shell/fuze combinations based on terrain, e.g., HE-PD, HE-delay and ICM are ineffective in snow; but are highly effective in rocky terrain. Also, consider slope or unevenness of the terrain and the adverse impact on both SCATMINE and ICM effectiveness:
  - RAAMS and ADAM must stabilize within 30 seconds of impact for the submunitions to arm.
  - Uneven terrain (plowed ground, jumbled rocks and so forth) may keep ADAM trip wires from deploying properly.
  - DPICM does not function if the angle of impact is greater than 60°.
- Anticipate difficulty in adjusting fires due to the mountainous terrain.
- Anticipate increased fire high-angle fires, and high-angle registration.
- Plan high-angle fires with airburst munitions on reverse slopes of hills and mountains.
- Use SCATMINE to restrict routes, especially at chokepoints.
- Anticipate difficulty in transfer of firing data due to the wide variance in altitude of firing units.
- Plan frequent met updates due to rapidly changing weather conditions.

EXERCISE C2

Communicate

- Consider the masking effects of mountains or hills on communications.
- Use directional antennas to increase range.
- Maximize line-of-sight radio communications.
- Plan retrans capabilities, to include helicopter radio relay. Airlift retrans units onto hilltops, when possible.

PERFORM LOGISTICS AND CSS

- Use helicopter and airdrop resupply when appropriate.
- Plan for increased maintenance on vehicles and equipment due to the increased strain caused by terrain and weather.
- Plan for additional cold weather contingency items required for sustained unit operations in mountainous terrain.

PROTECT THE FORCE
- Coordinate attack helicopter or air force support for the FA battalion as the mountains may reduce the use of mutually supporting fires.
- Request MP ground reconnaissance of routes, especially at chokepoints.
- Consider the danger of flash flooding in dry river beds or flood plains.
- Consider using open column convoy techniques through mountain passes and other restrictive terrain.
- Maximize use of terrain for cover and concealment to compensate for limited hardening potential. Position units in defilade.
- Position OPs, LPs, and crew-served weapons to enhance survivability by providing early warning and defensive fires.

Appendix A

Field Artillery Support Plan

This appendix discusses the format and content of a formal FASP, written in the five-paragraph field order format as an appendix to a FS annex of a maneuver OPORD. Section I provides basic guidance on the content for the various parts and paragraphs of a FASP while Section II provides an example of a FASP. See Chapter Four for general information about the FASP.

SECTION I – FIELD ARTILLERY SUPPORT PLAN FORMAT

A-01. The FASP is the FA battalion commander's tactical plan for employing the fires of all FA assets under his span of responsibility. For a DS battalion this means the FASP must address all FA supporting the supported maneuver force. It also means that the battalion must develop the FASP as an integral supporting document to the maneuver plan, usually as an appendix to the FS annex of the maneuver OPORD. R, GSR, and GS battalions usually prepare a stand-alone FASP focused on the battalion's assets and mission execution.

A-02. The FASP explains the FA missions and tasks and provides the FA battalion commander's guidance, intent, and concept of FA operations. The FASP assigns responsibilities to subordinate and supporting elements, focusing on all tasks necessary to execute all EFATs. The FASP must address maneuver/FA commander guidance, changes to fire order standards involving how and when to attack targets, and assignment of unit responsibilities for specific HPTs and other key targets or missions. The FASP also addresses movement/positioning plans, C2 arrangements (such as sensor-to-shooter links), TA tasks, CSS information, and force protection measures.

A-03. The battalion's FASP generally does not duplicate information from the maneuver OPORD/FSP or a DS/higher FA HQ FASP, or from the battalion's TSOPs. However, it may be necessary to repeat critical information in the battalion's FASP if the higher level FSP/FASP or the battalion's TSOP are not disseminated to all of the battalion's subordinate/supporting elements.

FASP OUTLINE

A-04. The following pages provide an outline of the format for a FASP. The outline is annotated for specific information requirements or suggestions. This format is available in automated C2 systems such as AFATDS and MCS.

(Classification)

Copy no __ of __ copies
Unit preparing order
Geographical location
Date-time group (DTG) of order

APPENDIX __ (FA SUPPORT PLAN) TO ANNEX __ (FIRE SUPPORT) TO OPORD

Reference: List any maps, charts, or other documents (TSOPs, and so on) required to understand the order. Reference to a map will include the map series number (and country or geographic area, if required), sheet number (and name if required), edition, scale (if required), and the force common datum (see note below) from a GPS (specify type of GPS and datum used) or from the center of the lower margin on a map. Reference listed here should not be reprinted in tabs unless tabs are separated from the basic document.

> **Note:** Universal transverse mercator (UTM) coordinates from the same point computed on a different datum may differ as much as **900** meters.

Time Zone Used Throughout Order: The time zone applicable to the operation. Times in other zones are converted to this zone for this operation. Consistency must be maintained through all documents.

1. SITUATION. Paragraph 1 is used exclusively to provide information. It includes items of information affecting FA operations that may or may not be included in the fires paragraph of the maneuver OPORD/OPLAN or the fire support annex. It gives an overview of the general situation so subordinate commanders can understand the environment in which they will be operating. If all organic, attached, or supporting commanders do not receive complete copies of the maneuver OPORD/OPLAN and the fire support annex, then the FASP repeats those items critical to the execution of their missions.

    a. Enemy Forces. Subparagraph 1a provides enemy information vital to the FA unit. This includes enemy indirect fire capabilities that may influence FS activities, the ground threat, the air threat, counterfire threat, and any other enemy information of particular relevance to FA units. Reference may be made to an intelligence annex, an overlay, a periodic intelligence report, or to an intelligence summary (INTSUM). Consider using the intelligence annex as a tab.

(Classification)

(Classification)

APPENDIX __ (FA SUPPORT PLAN) TO ANNEX __ (FIRE SUPPORT) TO OPORD

    b. Friendly Forces. Subparagraph 1b contains the missions and commander's intent of higher HQ (two levels up) and/or that of supported maneuver elements. Missions of adjacent, supporting, and reinforcing units also may be outlined here. Information should be limited to that which subordinate commanders need to know to accomplish their missions. The supported maneuver commander's intent for fire support as well as the force FA commander's intent during GS and GSR missions are included.

    c. Attachments and Detachments. Subparagraph 1c should list units attached to and detached from the FA unit (if not included clearly in the task organization), the terms of attachment, and effective DTGs, if appropriate.

    d. Assumptions. If the FASP supports an OPLAN, assumptions may be required. If the FASP is part of an OPORD, assumptions are not included.

2. MISSION. Paragraph 2 is a clear, concise statement of the task the FA unit is to accomplish. As a minimum, it should answer the questions, who, what, when, where, and why. It includes essential tasks, EFATs/EFSTs, determined by the commander as a result of his mission analysis.

3. EXECUTION. Paragraph 3 contains the how-to information needed for mission accomplishment. The FA battalion commander's intent is expressed here. The intent should briefly address the purpose of the FA fires, the methods used by the force to reach the end state (e.g., EFSTs/EFATS that must be accomplished, guidance on movements, methods of survivability), and the end state (address criteria for success).

    a. Concept of Operations. Subparagraph 3a is a detailed statement of the FA commander's visualization of the conduct of FA support for the operation by phase to the desired end state. The concept clarifies the purpose of the operation (by phase), then how FA will support it. It is a detailed explanation of the commander's intent. It is stated in enough detail to ensure appropriate action by subordinate units in the absence of more specific instructions. This paragraph may include a summary of the maneuver concept by phase for units that do not receive the maneuver OPORD.

    b. Organization for Combat. Subparagraph 3b is a clear statement of the organization and tactical missions of the subordinate units of the FA HQ. Organization for combat normally will be done by various phases corresponding to the operation (if changes occur). Anticipated on-order changes to organization or tactical missions are included in this subparagraph.

> **Note:** Subsequent subparagraphs in paragraph 3 build on the concept of the operation and should provide the artillery organization for combat, priority of fires, priority of special munitions, positioning and movement instructions, and EFATs to be accomplished by subordinate units. This should address each step of the operation.

(Classification)

(Classification)

APPENDIX __ (FA SUPPORT PLAN) TO ANNEX __ (FIRE SUPPORT) TO OPORD

    c. * * * * * * * * * *

    d. * * * * * * * * * *

    e. * * * * * * * * * *

f. Coordinating Instructions. The last subparagraph in paragraph 3 is coordinating instructions. It includes instructions and details of coordination applicable to two or more subordinate FA units. Instructions included in the subparagraph also may be addressed in **tabs** to the FASP. If a separate tab is developed, include in the coordinating instructions subparagraph only items of general interest, with details placed in the tab. If a tab is prepared, reference it in the body of the FASP. This subparagraph should include instructions concerning the following:

- TA (includes counterfire reference grid and instructions to or about specific observers).

- Survey (includes priorities for survey, accuracy's required [if other than TSOP], timing, position requirements, future plans, spheroid, datum, ellipsoid, codes [for PADS, BUCS, AFATDS], datum codes used, time zone letter, and grid zone).

- Automated/manual fire control/fire direction instructions, especially coordination requirements with units with similar, but not identical, automated systems. MSU taskings and changes from CONOPS SOPs are identified here.

- HPTL (taken directly from maneuver OPORD/OPLAN).

- Attack guidance matrix. (This may appear as a matrix in a tab. It's taken directly from the maneuver OPORD/OPLAN. (Specific automated commander's criteria are found in the IFSAS, FDS, LTACFIRE, or AFATDS Tab).

- NBC defense (includes MOPP, operation exposure guidance [OEG], and decontamination instructions/locations).

- Met (includes source, type, and times of met messages).

- Liaison requirements.

- Fire plan (includes target list, schedules of fires and FSCMs).

- CCIR, PIR, EEFI, FFIR and other intelligence datum/information as appropriate.

- Intelligence acquisition tasks.

(Classification)

(Classification)

APPENDIX __ (FA SUPPORT PLAN) TO ANNEX __ (FIRE SUPPORT) TO OPORD

- Ammunition restrictions (includes expenditure restrictions, approval requirements, and risk limitations).

- Antifratricide measures (such as vehicle markings) that are not TSOP.

- Rehearsals.

4. SERVICE SUPPORT. Paragraph 4 includes specific service support instructions and arrangements supporting the operation. The commander's guidance regarding CSS will be here. Supply, maintenance, medical, and personnel information are included in this paragraph. As a minimum, the CSR and the CSS locations (combat trains, field trains, casualty collection points, LRP, ATP, and/or ASP) should be given. Address only those CSS aspects that apply to the operation. Address the pertinent aspects of the six tactical logistic functions of manning, arming, fueling, fixing, moving and sustaining soldiers and their systems. These functions should be addressed in turns of before, during, and after the operation.

   a. Manning - Current personnel strength (percentage), project replacements.

   b. Arming - Ammunition resupply, CSR, ATP, ASP.

   c. Fueling - Fuel points, priority of refuel.

   d. Fixing - UMCP location, allocation of recovery assets, maintenance and recovery priorities, cannibalization authority.

   e. Moving - Locations of MSR, SP, RP and checkpoints along the route, priorities of movement on MSRs.

   f. Sustaining - Medical resupply, barrier materials, restricted issue or controlled exchange items, mortuary affairs, Chaplain information, water points, locations of battalion aid station, casualty collection point, chemical casualty collection points, civil-military cooperation.

(Paragraph 4 may be amplified in a tab.)

(Classification)

FM 3-09.21 (FM 6-20-1)

(Classification)

APPENDIX __ (FA SUPPORT PLAN) TO ANNEX __ (FIRE SUPPORT) TO OPORD

5. COMMAND AND SIGNAL

    a. Command. The first paragraph should list the locations of the unit TOC and the locations of higher, supporting, and supported unit TOCs. The commander's planned location during the operation, and alternate CP can be in this paragraph. Plans should also address any alternate battalion FDC arrangements not covered in, or that are changed from, unit SOP. Other automated C2 systems used or interface requirements (such as MCS), and any particular aspects for their use also are included here. Address succession of command if other than TSOP.

    b. Signal. This subparagraph contains the index of the effective SOI to include edition in effect and courier schedule. Special instructions on the use of radios, wire, MSE, EPLRS, retransmission elements (location and priority) and signals not covered in TSOP are included here.

Acknowledge:

                                      ISSUING COMMANDER'S NAME
                                      RANK

OFFICIAL:

/Signed/

S3 NAME

Approval: The original/file copy bears the signature of the FA battalion commander. The S3 authenticates all other copies, which are disseminated to subordinate and reinforcing/reinforced FA units, any attached or supporting elements, and force FA HQ.

    Tabs: A -
                   B -
                   C -
                   D -
                   E -

Note: Tabs should be prepared for portions of the FASP that are explained better in a different format (for example, overlay or matrix), that are too extensive to be in the FASP, that are expected to change or lengthen, or that are submitted too late to be included. Often subordinate units will not receive the basic maneuver OPORD/OPLAN or fire support annex. Therefore, reprints of portions of these documents may be required and included as tabs.

(Classification)

(Classification)

APPENDIX __ (FA SUPPORT PLAN) TO ANNEX __ (FIRE SUPPORT) TO OPORD

Tabs are ordered as they are referenced in the basic OPORD or OPLAN. The TSOP may specify that some tabs will always be produced. Common tabs used at battalion level include:
- FASM - FA TOC.
- FA positioning and movement overlay - FA TOC.
- Fire plan (S3 may refer to plan names and subordinate elements, can print out target list, schedules of fires and FSCM instead of developing a separate tab) - FSE.
- Survey - FA RSO.
- TA - FA TOC.
- AFATDS, LTACFIRE, FDS, or IFSAS- FA TOC.

Other tabs used if time permits:
- Intelligence (INTSUM, overlay, annex, or PIR and IR lists) - maneuver/higher FA HQ TOC.
- Service support and CSS overlay - FA ALOC.
- Maneuver overlays - maneuver/higher FA HQ TOC.
- Met - Force FA HQ.
- Task organization (may be attached from OPORD).
- Obstacle overlay – maneuver/higher FA HQ TOC.
- Rules of engagement - maneuver/higher FA HQ TOC.
- ADA, engineer, and other supporting element plans as appropriate.
- Special distribution items (such as antifratricide prevention information).

(Classification)

SURVEY TAB TO THE FASP

A-05. The survey plan (or order) normally is incorporated into the FASP as the survey tab. The survey plan contains detailed instructions not covered by local TSOP for each survey team. It gives general information needed for the efficient accomplishment of the survey mission. The survey plan is normally written, but may be issued orally, if necessary. It generally follows the same format as the OPORD/OPLAN. Often because of the tactical situation and wide dispersal of units, part of the survey plan may be issued by radio or other communication means. The format for a survey plan is in FM 6-2.

AUTOMATION TAB TO THE FASP

A-06. The written portion of the automation tab attached to the FASP should contain changes/additions to subscriber information, and commander's criteria, geometry, units, and ammunition information that pertain to the operation (not contained in TSOP).

A-07. Since automation systems provide fire planners throughout the artillery system with instantaneous access to target files and FA schedules, the S3 no longer has to attach a fire plan tab (target list and schedules of fires) to the written portion of the plan. Instead, he can initiate, coordinate, and monitor the development of the FA schedules in accordance with the standard fire planning capabilities and procedures that apply to these systems. In the written portion of the plan, he can reference FA schedules, target lists, and FSCM by plan name and, if necessary, targets by target number. FA elements can extract detailed information as needed.

TARGET ACQUISITION TAB TO THE FASP

A-08. The TA tab is a managerial tool used by the TOC controlling FA TA assets. This tab is used to ensure that all TA assets are employed to support the overall maneuver operation. The purpose of the TA tab is as follows:
- Assigns missions to FA TA assets.
- Coordinates the FA TA efforts.
- Establishes a specific flow of target processing data.
- Assigns responsibilities not covered in unit TSOPs.

A-09. The FA Bn S2 and S3 jointly produce the TA tab with help from the targeting officer and radar section leader. For specific information on the TA order see FM 6-121.

ARTILLERY INTELLIGENCE TAB TO THE FASP

A-10. The artillery intelligence tab is not a copy or repeat of the maneuver intelligence annex but contains intelligence data that is artillery-specific. This tab includes artillery PIRs and IRs as designated by the artillery commander. The artillery intelligence tab is prepared by the S2.

ADMINISTRATION-LOGISTICS TAB TO THE FASP

A-11. The admin-logistics tab contains specific information relevant to the issuing FA HQ. Information contained in the unit TSOP should not be covered in this tab. Changes to or deviations from admin-logistics information in the TSOP must be covered in the tab. The admin-logistics tab is prepared by the S4 with assistance from the S1.

FA SUPPORT MATRIX TAB TO THE FASP

A-12. The FASM is a concise planning and execution tool that graphically depicts the FA unit's essential tasks. Like paragraph 3 of the written FASP, the matrix should answer the questions who, what, when, and where. It identifies key tasks for each element and ties accomplishment of those tasks to the requirements of the maneuver plan and the FSP.

FORMAT

A-13. The matrix is set up with the operational elements (such as firing batteries, survey sections, radar sections, and CPs) along the left side and with significant maneuver phases and/or artillery tasks along the top (for example, phase lines, events, times, groups, or programs). Maneuver phases should correspond to phases established on the maneuver execution matrix.

A-14. An example of a FASM is at Figure A-1. It also shows a way to label the FASM for easy reference. Letters identify columns, and numbers identify lines. For example, block D-4 in the following example reads "PA 12." This matrix reference system allows the S3 to easily disseminate or update matrix data by radio, MSE, or wire to all appropriate agencies.

FA SUPPORT MATRIX CONTENT

A-15. Information that may be found in the matrix include the following:
- EFATs, EFSTs, and other tasks associated with a specific time frame.
- PAs, movements, prepare to march-order (PTMO).
- Azimuth of Lay (AOL) and left/right azimuth limits.
- Priority of fires (POF) and priority of survey (POS) by phase.
- Preparations (PREP) and counterpreparations (CPREP).
- FSCMs by phase.
- Priority targets (PRI TGT) assigned to units.
- Trigger points.
- Critical targets by phase (schedules).
- Munition requirements (e.g., Copperhead (CPHD)).
- MSU information.
- Reconnaissance.
- O/o missions.
- Rearming and/or refueling.

A-16. Suggested enclosures to the support matrix tab include the FA movement overlay. The movement overlay may include the following:
- Positions and routes.
- Passage points.
- Rearm, refuel points.
- Start points, release points, and CPs.

FM 3-09.21 (FM 6-20-1)

	A	B	C	D	E	
1	PHASE / EVENT UNIT	Phase 1 AA MECH to PL BLUE	Phase 2 PL BLUE to ATK POSN	Phase 3 BREACH to OBJ CAT SECURE	Phase 4 Hasty Def	
2	6-8 FA BN TOC	AA MECH Move A-TF 2-3 PL RED Move B-TF 2-77 PL RED Move C-TF 2-66 PL RED Move TOC-TF 2-3 PL GRAY Issue mvmt order to 4-18 when C/6-8 FA SPs	PA 8--------------------------------- Move B when A set PA 11 Move C when B set PA 12 Issue mvmt order to 4-18 when A set PA 11	--------------------------------> Move A-OBJ CAT Secure Move B-A set Move C-B set Move TOC-OBJCAT Secure	PA 19 Issue mvmt order to 4-18 when C set	
3	A/6-8 FA	HIP SHOOT----------------- configuration following TF 2-3	-----> PA 11 AOL 2000 PRI TGT 2-3--------	--------------------------------> -------------------------------->	PA 20 AOL 0800 FPF 1	
4	B/6-8 FA	HIP SHOOT configuration following 2-77	PA 2 AOL 1600 PRI TGT 2-77 Move then A set PA 11	PA 12 AOL 1600 PRI TGT 2-77 Group A2C	PA 21 AOL 1600 FPF 2	
5	C/6-8 FA	HIP SHOOT configuration following 2-66 IN	PA 3 AOL 1200 PRI TGT 2-66 Move when B set PA 12	PA 13 AOL 1200 PRI TGT 2-66 Series DOG	PA 22 AOL 2400	
6	Q-36	OPCON to 4-18 FA PA 7----------------------------- 6300-1500 Adv pty w/PADS 2	-----> Move when A/4-18 set Adv pty w/PADS 2	PA 18, Search Az 1600 CFZ 1, o/o CFZ 2, o/o CFZ 3, CFFZ 1, o/o CFFZ 2	PA 23 CFZ 1, o/o CFZ 2 CFFZ 3	
7	SURVEY Priorities FA, Rdr, Mort FA-A, C, B	PADS 1 Trvl w/ A adv pty; PA 11, PA 2	Trvl w/B adv pty; PA 12	L/U w/A, B adv ptys PA 20, PA 21	Mortars	
8		PADS 2 Trvl w/C adv pty; PA7 (RDR), PA 3	L/U w/ C, RDR adv ptys PA 13, PA 18 (RDR)	L/U w/ C, RDR adv ptys PA 22, 23	Mortars	
9	FSCMs	Div CFL PL BLUE NFAs: Towns of Al-Aubin and Al-Varez	Div CFL PL Yellow Bde CFL PL GUTS -------------------------------->	Div CFL PL Yellow Bde CFL PL GUTS o/o PL BLOOD	Div CFL PL BLACK Bde CFL PL BLOOD -------------------------------->	
10	POFs	TF 2-3	TF 2-3	TF 2-3 o/o 2-66 IN	TF 2-3	
11	4-18 FA (R) BN TOC	TOC move following C/6-8 FA Counterfire HQ---------------	PA 9----------------------------- Move A when A/6-8 set Mv B, C, RDR when A set -------------------------------->	--------------------------------> -------------------------------->	PA 24 Move when C/6-8 FA set -------------------------------->	
12	A/4-18 FA	PA 4----------------------------- AOL 0900 PRI TGT 2-3--------------------	----> Move when A/6-8 set ---->	PA 15 AOL 1500 Smk for breach	Move when C/6-8 FA set PA 25 AOL 0400	
13	B/4-18 FA	PA 5----------------------------- AOL 0900 PRI TGT 2-77	----> Move when A Set ---->	PA 13 AOL 1500 GRP B1C o/o GRP B3C CPHD Pri Tgt	Move when C/6-8 FA set PA 26 AOL 1200	
14	C/4-18 FA	PA 6----------------------------- AOL 0900 PRI TGT 2-66-------------------	----> Move when A Set ---->	PA 17 AOL 1500 GRP B1C o/o GRP B3C o/o SCATMINE	Move when C/6-8 FA set PA 27 AOL 2000	
15	FSCMs	Div CFL PL BLUE NFAs: Town of Al-Aubin and Al-Varez	Div CFL PL Yellow Bde CFL PL GUTS -------------------------------->	Div CFL PL Yellow Bde CFL PL GUTS o/o PL BLOOD	Div CFL PL BLACK Bde CFL PL BLOOD -------------------------------->	
16	POFs	TF 2-3	TF 2-3	TF 2-3 o/o 2-66 IN	TF 2-3	

Figure A-1. Example FA Support Matrix

SECTION II – EXAMPLE FIELD ARTILLERY SUPPORT PLAN

A-17. An example of a battalion FASP (an appendix to the fire support annex) is shown below. Figure A-2 is an acronym and abbreviation list used in the FASP.

AAG	Army artillery group (threat)	HVT	high-value target
ACP	air control point	IAW	in accordance with
ADA	air defense artillery	ICE	individual chemical equipment
AIRCOR	air corridor	ID (M)	infantry division (mechanized)
alt	altitude	LOC	lines of communication
app	appendix	maint	maintenance
atch	attached	man	maneuver (attack guidance matrix)
avn	aviation	max	maximum
az	azimuth	mod	modification
C3	command, control and communications	MRL	multiple rocket launcher
CAA	combined arms Army (threat)	msn	mission
cat	category	N/CH	nuclear/chemical
CCCP	chemical casualty collection point	NLTPA	not later than position area
CCP	casualty collection point	PA	position area
cGy	centigray	PL	phase line
coord	coordinate	RAP	rocket-assisted projectile
COP	command observation post	REC	radio-electronic combat
Cphd	Copperhead	RSTA	reconnaissance, surveillance, and target acquisition
CRP	combat reconnaissance patrol	SIMO	simultaneous observation
CSB	common sensor boundary	SITREP	situation report
DF	direction finding	spt	support
DNE	do not engage	survl	surveillance
EA	engagement area	TBP	to be published
ENG	engineer	TD	tank division (threat)
GTD	guards tank division (threat)	TLE	target location error
HA	hide area	TVA	target value analysis
HEMTT	heavy expanded-mobility tactical truck	w	with

Figure A-2. Acronyms and Abbreviations Used in the Example FASP

FM 3-09.21 (FM 6-20-1)

FASP – BODY (EXAMPLE)

(Classification)

Copy __ of 20 copies
1st Bn, 51st FA
Opposing Force District
061200 Nov 96

APPENDIX 3 (FA SUPPORT PLAN) TO ANNEX E (FIRE SUPPORT) TO OPORD 96-2--2d Bde, 52d Inf Div (Mech).

Reference: Map, series 1501; OPFOR; sheets LJ 11-1, 11-2, 11-3, 11-5, and 11-6; edition 1982, 1:250,000.

Time Zone Used Throughout Order: LOCAL

1. SITUATION.

    a. Enemy Forces.

        (1) 16th CAA continues to defend. The bulk of the 19th CAA remains in assembly areas vicinity Deep Water Lake. Recon elements of the 19th CAA are reported moving east into the 10th (US) Corps covering force area. 19th CAA is capable of attacking with all supporting artillery and frontal air along three divisional avenues of approach. Expect the 19th CAA to attack through the 16th CAA in 12 to 36 hours. The main attack in the 52d ID (M) sector is expected in the SHALLOW Valley (19th TD and 2d GTD) approach. Initially, the primary threat to FA units is fixed-wing air, with up to 12 FROGFOOT sorties per day in the division sector. Before the main enemy ground effort, units behind the FLOT must be alert for dismounted forces and light armor air-dropped or helicopter-inserted in company or battalion strength. The enemy second-echelon division will push its artillery forward to support the main effort. Expect 12 to 15 122mm and 152mm SP battalions and 2 to 3 122mm MRL battalions to be employed in the division sector as 3 or 4 RAGs and a DAG. In addition, elements of the 19th CAA AAG may be positioned and employed in the division sector.

        (2) Intelligence estimate: See Intelligence Annex to OPORD 96-2, 2d Bde, 52d ID (M).

(Classification)

(Classification)

APPENDIX 3 (FA SUPPORT PLAN) TO ANNEX E (FIRE SUPPORT) TO OPORD 96-2--2d Bde, 52d Inf Div (Mech).

   b. Friendly Forces.

   (1) 2d Bde, 52d ID (M) moves to and occupies defensive positions from LJ234282 to LJ145185 NLT 061200 Nov 96 and defends in sector with two task forces abreast to destroy attacking enemy forces forward of PL VEGAS. TF 1-17 Armor and TF 1-81 Mech will defend in the north and south, respectively. TF 2-81 Mech will be the brigade reserve initially, then will counterattack along Axis LEE if enemy forces reach PL VEGAS.

   (2) Brigade commander's intent: The brigade will conduct a mobile defense in sector. Fires and obstacles will be used to canalize the enemy into the southern part of the brigade sector (TF 1-81). TF 1-81 will conduct a fighting withdrawal to prepared positions east of PL VEGAS, while TF 1-17 in the north holds its position in BP 3 and prepares to meet the second-echelon regiment. TF 2-81, the brigade reserve, counterattacks from positions in the north of the brigade sector into the flank of the first-echelon regiment. Artillery fires will be used to slow and confuse the enemy and attack his C2 as he comes into range at PL LANCE by concentrating Copperhead and DPICM fires in TAIs 1 and 2. COLTs will control Copperhead fires and OH-58Ds. Three OH-58Ds will be DS to the brigade. One OH-58D will be operational and in position to observe the TAIs continuously. I am concerned about the capabilities of the enemy's fire support systems ability to limit our maneuver. I want a proactive counterfire effort, using the Firefinder radar and any other available assets to locate the enemy's indirect fire systems. Plan a counterprep based on the best available intelligence to be executed on my order. Once the enemy first echelon exists TAIs 1 and 2, priority of the fire support effort shifts to EA FISH, where I want to stop the enemy and destroy his first-echelon battalions with direct and indirect fire. As TF 1-81 breaks contact and begins to move to its alternate positions, a smoke program will be fired to assist in disengagement and screen their movement. When I order the counterattack, priority of fire will shift to TF 2-81. Artillery fires will be employed ahead of the counterattack to fix the enemy and hinder his ability to shift his force to meet the attack into his flank.

   (3) 1-78 FA MLRS (GS) is positioned in the brigade sector. 52d DIVARTY will coordinate with 2d Bde FSE to clear position areas and movement routes.

   c. Attachments. Sec 2 (AN/TPQ-36), Btry A (TA), 23d FA remains attached to 1-51 FA for positioning, employment, and support.

2. MISSION. 1-51 FA provides conventional artillery fires in direct support of 2d Bde, 52d ID (M) mobile defense in sector NLT 061200Z Nov 96.

(Classification)

(Classification)

APPENDIX 3 (FA SUPPORT PLAN) TO ANNEX E (FIRE SUPPORT) TO OPORD 96-2--2d Bde, 52d Inf Div (Mech).

3. EXECUTION. FA Commander's Intent: We will provide, interdiction, close fires, and counterfires in support of 2d Brigade's defense in sector. To do this, we will initially position observers and firing units forward to provide Copperhead and DPICM fires on lead elements (first echelon), fire SCATMINE and smoke to delay and disrupt the second echelon, provide SEAD in support of CAS, mass fires on lead elements HPTs, plan a counterprep to be executed on order; and provide counterfire to protect force movements. We will be successful at the end of this operation if the enemy is unable to mass his direct and indirect fires against the brigade and we are in position to support the brigade's counterattack.

    a. Concept of Operations. FA fires will engage the enemy deep as he enters the brigade sector. COLT 2 will be located vicinity LJ1723; it will be able to observe both TAIs 1 and 2 and will be able to initiate Copperhead fires in TAI 2. An OH-58D will be operating forward vicinity LJ1526 and will be able to initiate Copperhead and other fires in both TAI 1 and TAI 2 with priority of effort in TAI 1. COLT 2 will use 1-51 FA FD 3 as a quickfire channel to C/2-636, which will provide Copperhead support. The OH-58D will call all missions directly to 1-51 FA FDC on the battalion ops/F net. Artillery will engage the first echelon of the lead division in both TAI 1 and TAI 2 to attrit the enemy and disrupt their C2 with Copperhead and DPICM fires.

A counterprep will be fired on order of the brigade commander. As the lead echelon exits TAI 2, the two planned SCATMINE targets (AB0031, AB0032) will be fired in that TAI to slow an disrupt the second echelon. CAS, supported by SEAD, will then attack the second echelon in TAI 2 under control of the OH-58D (brigade backup control). Artillery fires continue to attrit the first echelon. The main enemy attack is expected to be in TF 1-81 sector. Once Group A30B has been executed on the first echelon, the SCATMINE (AB0017) in TF 1-81 sector will be emplaced. Artillery fires will then concentrate on the first echelon as it attempts to breach the TF obstacles. When the first echelon enters EA CAT, artillery fires will concentrate on the second echelon and provide smoke or illumination to silhouette the first echelon for the maneuver forces. Three batteries will be capable of firing throughout the battle, and three batteries must be capable of ranging beyond PL LANCE to support the deep battle initially. Priority targets will initially be the targets in Group A2B, then will shift to Group A30B, and then to Target AB0015 and Group A31B. Priority of fires will then shift to the FPFs of both task forces. Priority for Copperhead fires will be C2 vehicles throughout the battle and then to engineer vehicles during breaching operations. Artillery must be prepared to support the counterattack by TF 2-81 along Axis LEE to hit the flank of the lead echelon with both DPICM and Copperhead fires as well as smoke. Be prepared to move batteries forward by echelon on order of the FSCOORD.

(Classification)

(Classification)

APPENDIX 3 (FA SUPPORT PLAN) TO ANNEX E (FIRE SUPPORT) TO OPORD 96-2--2d Bde, 52d Inf Div (Mech).

b. Organization for Combat.

1-51 FA (155, SP): DS 2d Bde
    Sec 2 (AN/TPQ-36, Btry A (TA), 23 FA: Attached 1- 51 FA
    Sec 1, 2, 3 (OH-58D), DIVARTY Spt Plt, Cmd Avn Co, 52d Cbt Avn Bde: DS 1-51 FA
2-636 FA (155, SP): R 1-51 FA

c. Priority of Fires. Priority of fires to TF 1-81, on order to TF 2-81 when committed.

d. Positioning and Movement. Initial firing battery positions are shown below. Subsequent movement and positions will be IAW Tab A. See the movement overlay for PA locations.

    (1) A/1-51 FA: PA 1 (az 5000)

    (2) B/1-51 FA: PA 15 (az 5000)

    (3) C/1-51 FA: PA 9 (az 4900)

    (4) A/2-636 FA: PA 5 (az 5100)

    (5) B/2-636 FA: PA 5 (az 5100)

    (6) C/2-636 FA: PA 2 (az 4900)

e. Coordinating Instructions.

    (1) Target Acquisition.

        (a) Counterfire Reference Grid. Lower left corner is AA at grid LJ000900.

        (b) See Tab C.

    (2) Survey.

(Classification)

FM 3-09.21 (FM 6-20-1)

———————————
(Classification)

APPENDIX 3 (FA SUPPORT PLAN) TO ANNEX E (FIRE SUPPORT) TO OPORD 96-2--2d Bde, 52d Inf Div (Mech).

  (a) Priority of survey is, in order, to firing batteries (A, C, B, 1-51 FA; A, B, C, 2-636 FA), AN/TPQ-36 radar, COLTs, OH-58D control points, and mortars.

  (b) Survey sections will establish starting control at the following survey control points:

SCP NAME	EASTING	NORTHING	ALTITUDE
MARY	525422.97	3919175.39	935.2
HELEN	531642.91	3922964.29	1054.5

  (c) Control points will be marked per TSOP. OH-58D control points will be established on prominent terrain and marked with a target cloth panel 6 feet by 6 feet with a 4-foot-diameter circle spray-painted in black and an identifying number painted in numerals 2 1/2 feet tall in the center of the circle.

  (d) See Tab D (Survey).

 (3) High-Payoff Target List.

PRIORITY	CATEGORY	DESCRIPTION OF TARGETS
1	6 (RSTA)	Recon patrol, division recon company
2	3 (MAN)	Armor heavy (company size or larger)
3	7 (REC)	Radar intercept and DF site (POLE DISH)
4	7 (REC)	Radio intercept and DF site
5	2 (FS)	RAG COP
6	2 (FS)	Battalion COP
7	2 (FS)	Sound ranging site

———————————
(Classification)

A-16

FM 3-09.21 (FM 6-20-1)

(Classification)

APPENDIX 3 (FA SUPPORT PLAN) TO ANNEX E (FIRE SUPPORT) TO OPORD 96-2--2d Bde, 52d Inf Div (Mech).

    (4) Attack Guidance Matrix.

	CAT	HPTs	WHEN	HOW/EFFECTS	REMARKS
(C3)	1		A	N/EW	Coord w EW
(FS)	2		A	N	DNE MRL > 10 min
(MAN)	3		A	N	
(ADA)	4		P	S/ALO	
(ENG)	5		P	N	
(RSTA)	6		I	N	
(REC)	7		A	D/EW	
(N/CH)	8		A	D	TLE < 200 m/TDA
(POL)	9		A	N	
(AMMO)	10		A	N	
(MAINT)	11		P	N	Not HVT/HPT
(LIFT)	12		P	N	Not HVT/HPT
(LOC)	13		P	N	Not NVT/HPT

Legend:

CAT	=	Target category from TVA.
HPT	=	Designated high-payoff target. Target numbers from TVA sheets or target description.
WHEN	=	When the target should be attacked.
	I:	Immediately, Interrupt other non-immediate attacks.
	A:	As acquired. Attack as assets are available.
	P:	Plan. Schedule to file for later attack.
HOW	=	How target is to be attacked.
	S:	Suppress
	N:	Neutralize. (10% effects)
	D:	Destroy (30% effects)
	EW:	Offensive EW.
	DNE:	Do not engage.
	ALO:	Coordinate attack with ALO.
	TLE:	Target locations error.

    (5) NBC Defense.

        (a) MOPP when 2S1s (122mm, SP) reported at PL LANCE.

(Classification)

(Classification)

APPENDIX 3 (FA SUPPORT PLAN) TO ANNEX E (FIRE SUPPORT) TO OPORD 96-2--2d Bde, 52d Inf Div (Mech).

  (b) Troop safety criteria: Negligible risk to warned, exposed personnel.

  (c) Operational exposure guidance: Do not exceed 50 cGy. Begin continuous monitoring after first use of nuclear weapons.

  (d) Decontamination. Service battery decontamination team will prepare unsupported decon site at grid LJ445094. Two battery sets of ICE packs will be prepositioned at this point to facilitate MOPP gear exchange. Firing battery decon teams will report to this site on order. Contaminated vehicles will travel Route GREEN (LJ294164 to LJ327144 to LJ373125 to LJ408114 to LJ429094 to LJ445094). Contaminated casualties will be evacuated to collection point at grid LJ438091.

  (6) Meteorology. Computer met sent by 52d Inf DIVARTY every 2 hours on battalion cmd net (voice) and ops/F net (digital).

  (7) Fire Plan. Target List, schedules of fires and FSCMs are in plan current.

  (8) CCIR, PIR, EEFI, FFIR, and other intelligence or information as appropriate.

   (a) When will the enemy attack?
    - What avenues will be used?
    - What is the 19th TD's state of readiness?
    - What are the 19th TD's objectives?

   (b) Will the 2d GTD reinforce the 19th TD? If so, will reinforcements be committed to the Shallow Valley approach? When will reinforcements be committed?

   (c) Will the enemy lead his attack with forward detachments?

   (d) What are the strength, disposition, and composition of the enemy's supporting artillery? Where are the DAG and RAGs? Where are the enemy's MRLs?

   (e) When will enemy artillery reach PL LANCE?

   (f) Where are enemy OPs located?

(Classification)

(Classification)

APPENDIX 3 (FA SUPPORT PLAN) TO ANNEX E (FIRE SUPPORT) TO OPORD 96-2--2d Bde, 52d Inf Div (Mech).

    (g) What TA assets are available to the enemy, and where are they located?

  (9) Information Requirements.

    (a) Will the enemy use NBC weapons? If so, where and to what extent? Where is persistent agent placed?

    (b) What are possible LZs and drop zones? Will the enemy conduct airmobile operations?

  (10) Intelligence Acquisition Tasks. Batteries will report as obtained.

    (a) All chemical activity and locations of enemy chemical-capable units, especially smoke operations vicinity LJ2324, LJ1820, and LJ1915.

    (b) All indirect fires. Include shelling reports and friendly battle damage assessment.

    (c) Lanes cleared through enemy controlled or emplaced obstacles.

    (d) Enemy patrols. Number, size, composition, and time observed.

    (e) All direct fire engagements, including enemy battle damage assessment when available.

    (f) Enemy rotary-wing activity.

  (11) Ammo Restrictions. Batteries will expend no more than 70% of DPICM and 50% of HC and/or WP CSR supporting the defense. Short-duration SCATMINE must be approved by the brigade commander. Illumination and HC smoke will be approved by the TF commanders.

  (12) Plan rehearsal will be conducted at the 1-51 FA CP at 061000 Nov 96. 1-51 FA XO, S3, S2, FDO, CESO, survey chief, firing battery commanders, HHB and svc battery commanders, OH-58D representative, 2-636 S3 and LO, and 2d Bde FSO and ALO will participate in person. TF FSOs, COLTs, and battery FDOs will participate via wire or FM radio.

(Classification)

FM 3-09.21 (FM 6-20-1)

_____
(Classification)

APPENDIX 3 (FA SUPPORT PLAN) TO ANNEX E (FIRE SUPPORT) TO OPORD 96-2--2d Bde, 52d Inf Div (Mech).

4. SERVICE SUPPORT.

    a. Personnel. The battalion is currently at 82% strength. 83d Medical Group reports that nine soldiers will be returned to 1-51 FA within the next 36 hours.

    b. Medical. 1-51 FA BAS is located in the combat trains (LJ363158). 1-51 will establish a CCCP for 1-51 FA and 2-636 FA. Casualty collection points are as follows:

        1-51 FA CCP   LJ304162
        1-51 FA CCCP   LJ438090
        2-636 FA CCP   LJ321155

    c. Locations.

        1-51 FA:
        Combat trains   LJ363158
        Field trains   LJ473097
        LRP   LJ306159

        2-636 FA: TBP

    d. CSR Information. CSR effective upon implementation of OPORD 96-2.

	HE	APICM	DPICM	WP	HC	ILLUM	RAP	CPHD	ADAM	RAAMS
155mm	37	3	90	6	6	3	5	5	2	7

    e. Resupply Criteria. Batteries will request resupply when CSR drops to these levels.

        HE   50%   RAAMS   10%
        DPICM   25%   ADAM   10%
        APICM   50%   M3A1   50%
        RAP   25%   M4A1   30%
        Illum   50%   M119A1   20%
        WP   25%   Viper   50%
        Smk (HC) 25%   .50 cal   30%
        5.56mm   50%   7.62mm   50%

    f. ASP Information. ASP is located at grid LJ562235. ATP will remain operational at grid LJ398128 until 062000 Nov 96, at which time it will begin to displace.

_____
(Classification)

(Classification)

APPENDIX 3 (FA SUPPORT PLAN) TO ANNEX E (FIRE SUPPORT) TO OPORD 96-2--2d Bde, 52d Inf Div (Mech).

    g. Recovery. One M578 each will be attached to Batteries A and C NLT 061000 Nov 96. One HEMTT wrecker will be available on call in the combat trains.

5. COMMAND AND CONTROL.

    a. Command.

        (1) 2d Bde TOC located grid LJ336147.

        (2) DIVARTY TOC located grid LJ588012.

        (3) 1-51 FA TOC located grid LJ366163.

        (4) 2-636 FA TOC located grid LJ412174.

        (5) 2-636 FA TOC will assume DS TOC responsibilities on order.

    b. Signal.

        (1) SOI KTV 1062, Edition BB in effect.

        (2) Retrans located at grid LJ363177. Priority of retrans will be to BDE fire support net.

        (3) Wire. Priority of work, in order, to the following external circuits.

    1-51 FA:

        (a) 1-51 FA TOC to 2d Bde TOC (MSE junction box only)

        (b) 1-51 FA TOC to Btry B, 1-51 FA.

        (c) 1-51 FA TOC to Btry A, 1-51 FA.

        (d) 1-51 FA TOC to Btry C, 1-51 FA.

    2-636 FA:

        (a) 2-636 FA TOC to 1-51 FA TOC.

(Classification)

FM 3-09.21 (FM 6-20-1)

_____
(Classification)

APPENDIX 3 (FA SUPPORT PLAN) TO ANNEX E (FIRE SUPPORT) TO OPORD 96-2--2d Bde, 52d Inf Div (Mech).

    (b) Per unit TSOP.

Wire teams will start to recover wire when the enemy's regimental CRP reaches PL LANCE.

Acknowledge:

                                        EDWARDS
                                        LTC

OFFICIAL:

/Signed/
COOPER
S3

Tabs: A - FA Support Matrix
              B - Positioning Overlay
              C - Target Acquisition
              D - Survey Plan

_____
(Classification)

EXAMPLE FIELD ARTILLERY SUPPORT MATRIX (TAB)

(Classification)

TAB A (FA SUPPORT MATRIX) TO APPENDIX 3 (FA SUPPORT PLAN) TO ANNEX E (FIRE SUPPORT) TO OPORD 96-2--2d Bde, 52d Inf Div (Mech).

Reference: Map, Series 1501; OPFOR, sheets LJ 11-1, 11-2,11-3,11-5, and 11-6; edition 1982, 1:250,000.

Time Zone Used Throughout Order: LOCAL

UNIT	FORWARD OF PL LANCE	PL LANCE-PL VEGAS	COUNTERATTACK	
1-51 CP	LJ366163			14
A/1-51	OCCUPY PA 7 AOF 5200 TF 1-81 FA POF	RECON PA 1 AB3002 (A30B) AB 3005 (A31B) PRI TGT AB0015 CPHD MSN TF 1-81 FA POF	OCCUPY PA 1 AOF 5000 o/o TF 2-81 FA POF	13
B/1-51	OCCUPY PA 4 AOF 5000 TF 1-81 FA POFO	RECON PA 10 AS3003 (A30B) AB3006 (A31B) AB0017 (SCATMINE) FPF C/1-81 TF 1-81 FA POF	OCCUPY PA 10 AOF 5200 o/o TF 2-81 FA POF	12
C/1-51	OCCUPY PA 6 AOF 5000 TF 1-81 FA POF	RECON PA 14 AB3001 (A30B) AB0018 (SCATMINE) FPF 1/1-17 TF 1-81 FA POF	OCCUPY PA 14 AOF 5300 o/o TF 2-81 FA POF	11
2-636 CP	LJ412174 MSU o/o			10
A/2-636	RECON PA 19 AB0007 (A2B) AB0004 (A1B) AB0031 (SCATMINE) TF 1-81 FA POF	OCCUPY PA 19 AOF 4600 TF 1-81 FA POF	RECON PA 5 o/o TF 2-81 FA POF	9
B/2-636	RECON PA 17 AB0008 (A2B) AB0003 (A1B) AB0032 (SCATMINE) TF 1-81 FA POF	OCCUPY PA 17 AOF 5000 TF 1-81 FA FPF	RECON PA 15 o/o TF 2-81 FA POF	8
C/2-636	RECON PA 18 AB0009 (A2B) AB0005 (A1B) CPHD MSN TF 1-81 FA POF	OCCUPY PA 18 AOF 5000 TF 1-81 FA FPF	RECON PA 9 o/o TF 2-81 FA POF	7
Q-36	RECON PA 20		OCCUPY PA 21 AZ4400	6
PADS #1 (1-51)	PAs 6, 20, 4, 17, 18	PA 12	PA 9	5
PADS #2 (1-51)	PAs 1, 5, 7, 19		PAs 5, 15	4
PADS #1 (2-636)	RADAR, COLTs		PAs 14, 21	3
PADS #2 (2-636)	PAs 2, 3, 15		PAs 1, 10	2
FSCMs	CFL PL MACE ACA JOE (o/o)	CFL o/o PL LANCE ACA BOB (o/o)	CFL o/o PL MACE	1
A	B	C	D	

ACA = airspace coordination area, AOF = azimuth of fire, RECON = reconnaissance

(Classification)

FM 3-09.21 (FM 6-20-1)

EXAMPLE POSITIONING OVERLAY (TAB)

(Classification)

TAB B (POSITIONING OVERLAY) TO APPENDIX 3 (FA SUPPORT PLAN) TO ANNEX E (FIRE SUPPORT) TO OPORD 96-2--2d Bde, 52d Inf Div.

Reference: Map, Series, 1501; OPFOR, sheets lJ 11-1, 11-2, 11-3, 11-5, and 11-6; edition 1982, 1:250,000.

Time Zone Used Throughout Order: LOCAL

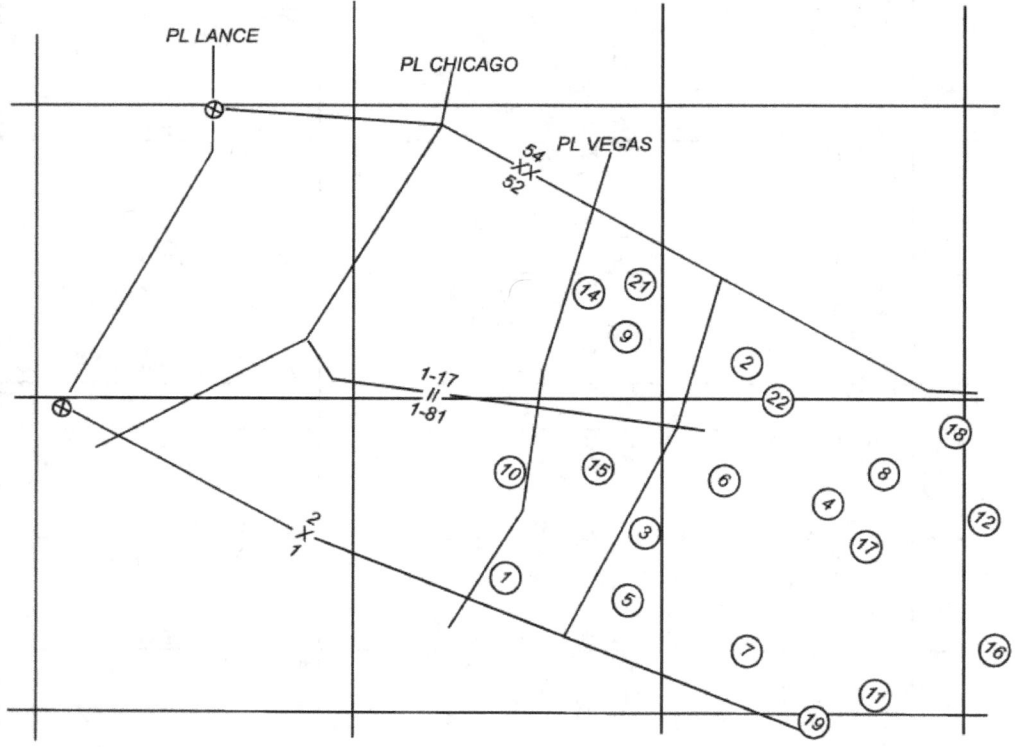

(Classification)

A-24

FM 3-09.21 (FM 6-20-1)

EXAMPLE TARGET ACQUISITION TAB

(Classification)

TAB C (TGT ACQUISITION) TO APPENDIX 3 (FA SUPPORT PLAN) TO ANNEX E (FIRE SUPPORT) TO OPORD 96-2--2d Bde, 52d Inf Div.

Reference: Map, series 1501; OPFOR; sheets LJ 11-1, 11-2, 11-3, 11-5, and 11-6; edition 1982; 1:250,000.

Time Zone Used Throughout Order: LOCAL

1. SITUATION.

    a. Enemy Forces. See App 3, paragraph 1a, and Intel Annex to OPORD 96-2--2d Bde, 52d Inf Div (Mech).

    b. Friendly Forces. 1-51 FA (155, SP) is DS to 2d Bde. 2-636 FA (155, SP) is R 1-51 FA. Sec 2 (AN/TPQ-36), Btry A (TA), 23d FA is attached to 1-51 FA. Sec 4 (AN/TPQ-37), Btry A (TA), 23d FA is operating in 2d Bde sector. 2d Bde has three COLTs. Three OH-58Ds are DS 2d Bde.

2. MISSION.

    Tgt acquisition assets (Sec 2 [AN-TPQ-36], Btry A [TA], 23d FA; Sec 1, 2, and 3 [OH-58D], DIVARTY Spt Plt, Cmd Avn Co, 52d Cbt Avn Bde; COLTs 1, 2, and 3) acquire targets, initiate fire missions, and report combat and/or targeting information commencing NLT 061200 Nov 96 in support of 2d Bde defense in sector.

3. EXECUTION.

    a. Concept of Operations. The AN/TPQ-36 will provide coverage of the 2d sector at the FLOT out to PL SPEAR. The AN/TPQ-36 will also ensure coverage of CFFZs 1 and 2 and CFZs 1, 2, and 3 (see RDO, enclosure 1). Cueing agents will be the Bde FSO, TF 1-17 FSO, TF 1-81 FSO, and 1-51 FA S2.

    b. Processing. All enemy artillery locations will be sent to the 1-51 FA TOC and the DIVARTY TOC. OH-58Ds report targets and targeting information to 1-51 FA TOC and 2d Bde FSE.

(Classification)

FM 3-09.21 (FM 6-20-1)

_____
(Classification)

TAB C (TGT ACQUISITION) TO APPENDIX 3 (FA SUPPORT PLAN) TO ANNEX E (FIRE SUPPORT) TO OPORD 96-2--2d Bde, 52d Inf Div.

    c. Visual Observation.

        (1) Ground Observation. COLTs will report location and zone of observation through the Bde FSO to 1-51 FA TOC.

        (2) Air Observation.

            (a) Sec 1, 2, and 3 (OH-58D) maintain continuous observation (at least one section on station at all times) of EA FISH. Report PIR and IR in TAIs 1 and 2.

            (b) Initiate Copperhead fires to C/2-636 FA on 1-51 FA FD 3 net when HPTs enter EA FISH.

            (c) Report lead elements of second-echelon regiments in TAI 2 (trigger point for CAS mission).

            (d) Initial position will be vicinity AIRCOR TANGO ACP 4 (LJ1626) NLT 060001 Nov 96.

            (e) Coordinate with 1-51 FA RSO for location and marking of survey update points. Contact RSO on DIVARTY survey (VHF-FM) (V) net.

    d. Radar. Sec 2 (AN/TPQ-36), Btry A (TA), 23d FA mission: Attached 1-51 FA (see RDO, enclosure 1).

    e. Coordinating Instructions.

        (1) Zones.

            (a) Critical Friendly Zones. Bde TOC, TF 1-81 (BP 6), TF 1-17 (BP 3). (See RDO, enclosure 1.)

            (b) Call-for-Fire-Zones. See RDO, enclosure 1.

            (c) Artillery Target Intelligence Zones. See RDO, enclosure 1.

        (2) Common Sensor Boundary. Grid LJ1137 to LJ1938 to LJ2736 to LJ3735.

_____
(Classification)

FM 3-09.21 (FM 6-20-1)

(Classification)

TAB C (TGT ACQUISITION) TO APPENDIX 3 (FA SUPPORT PLAN) TO ANNEX E (FIRE SUPPORT) TO OPORD 96-2--2d Bde, 52d Inf Div.

(3) Cueing Instructions. AN/TPQ-36 radiates on order of 1-51 FA S2 and designated cueing agents. Other friendly elements request radar coverage through the 1-51 FA TOC on the FA battalion command net. Radar section chief reports to 1-51 FA S2 30 minutes prior to making survivability moves due to excessive radiation time from current location. Cueing agents will request cueing only if their elements are receiving continuous or massive incoming artillery. (See RDO, enclosure 1).

(4) Survivability Moves. Radar will report to 1-51 FA S2 before initiating routine survivability moves.

(5) Survey. 1-51 FA will provide survey for Sec 2 (AN/TPQ-36), Btry A (TA), 23d FA. Radar section chief will coordinate with 1-51 FA RSO for survey as required.

(6) Visibility Diagrams. All observers will submit visibility diagrams through FSO channels to the DS FA battalion S2 NLT 061100 Nov 96.

4. SERVICE SUPPORT.

AN/TPQ-36 will coordinate Class I and III support from Btry C, 1-51 FA. All other logistic support will be provided through 1-51 FA combat trains.

5. COMMAND AND SIGNAL.

a. Command. Btry A (TA), 23d FA TOC located LJ588012.

b. Signal. SOI KTV 1062, Edition BB in effect.

Enclosure 1. Radar Deployment Order
Enclosure 2. Capabilities Overlay.

(Classification)

EXAMPLE RADAR DEPLOYMENT ORDER (ENCLOSURE TO TAB)

(Classification)

ENCLOSURE 1 (RADAR DEPLOYMENT ORDER) TO TAB C (TGT ACQUISITION) TO APPENDIX 3 (FA SUPPORT PLAN) TO ANNEX E (FIRE SUPPORT) TO OPORD 96-2--2d Bde, 52d Inf Div (Mech).

CLASSIFICATION WHEN FILLED IN

RADAR DEPLOYMENT ORDER
For use of this form, see FM 6-121. The proponent agency is TRADOC.

SECTION 2	-36	-37		MISSION ATCH 1-51 FA	
LOCATION		Primary PA 21		Alternate PA 7	
SEARCH SECTOR					
	Left Edge	Right Edge		Minimum Range	Maximum Range
Primary Azimuth 4700	-800 mils	+700 mils		.75 km meters	24 km meters
Alternate Azimuth	mils	mils		meters	meters
EW THREAT ASSESSMENT					
EW Threat (Yes or No)	Affecting Friendly Assets (Yes or No)			Type of Threat (Air or Ground)	
NOTE: Use the Firefinder survivability flowchart in FM 6-121 to determine emission limits. e					
CUEING AGENTS (CALL SIGN AND DESIGNATION) IN PRIORITY					
2 BDE FSO		1-17 FSO		1-81 FSO	
1-51 FA S2					
REPORTING CHANNELS					
FA BN CMD (V)			FA BN OPS/F (D)		
ZONE DATA					
Type and Number	Description and/or Command Priority	Grid Coordinates of Zone Corner Points			
CFZ 1	TF 1-17	273090	273122	291122	291090		
CFZ 2	TF 1-81	167111	167136	181136	18111		
CFZ 3	TF 2-81	171072	171089	193089	193072		
CFZ 4	BDE TOC	235041	235063	262063	262041		
CFFZ 1	DAG PRI 1	270280	270300	300300	300280		
CFFZ 2	RAG PRI 2	175345	175365	210365	210345		
CFFZ 3	HVY MTR - BTRY PRI 3	210240	210260	240260	240240		
ATIZ 1	RAG	221343	221359	239359	247355	247343	
ATIZ 2	AAG	265430	265460	310460	310430		

DA FORM 5957-R SEP 1990

DAG = division artillery group, PRI = priority

CLASSIFICATION WHEN FILLED IN

(Classification)

EXAMPLE CAPABILITIES OVERLAY (ENCLOSURE TO TAB)

(Classification)

ENCLOSURE 2 (CAPABILITIES OVERLAY) TO TAB C (TGT ACQUISITION) TO APPENDIX 3 (FA SUPPORT PLAN) TO ANNEX E (FIRE SUPPORT) TO OPORD 96-2--2d Bde, 52d Inf Div (Mech).

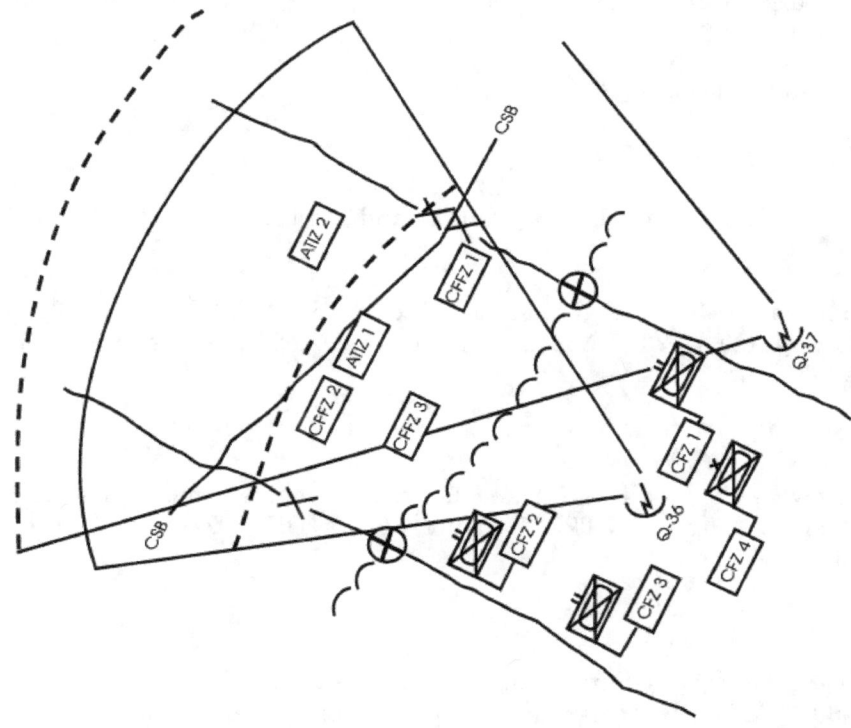

(Classification)

FM 3-09.21 (FM 6-20-1)

EXAMPLE SURVEY PLAN (TAB)

―――――――――――――――――――

_____
(Classification)

TAB D (SURVEY PLAN) TO APPENDIX 3 (FA SUPPORT PLAN) TO ANNEX E (FIRE SUPPORT) TO OPORD 96-2--2d Bde, 52d Inf Div (Mech).

Reference: Map, series 1501; OPFOR; sheets LJ 11-1, 11-2, 11-3, 11-5, and 11-6; edition 1982; 1:250,000.

Time Used Throughout Order: LOCAL

1. SITUATION.

    a. Enemy Forces. See App 3, paragraph 1a and Intel Annex to OPORD 96-2--2d Bde, 52d Inf Div (Mech).

    b. Friendly Forces. 1-51 FA (155, SP) is DS to 2d Bde. 2-636 FA (155, SP) is R 1-51 FA. Sec 2 (AN/TPQ-36), Btry A (TA), 23d FA is attached to 1-51 FA. 2d Bde has three COLTs. Three OH-58Ds are DS to 1-51 FA.

2. MISSION.

    The survey sections of 1-51 FA and 2-636 FA provide conventional and PADS survey support to 1-51 FA, 2-636 FA, AN/TPQ-36 radar, COLTs, OH-58Ds, and mortars supporting the 2d Bde in sector.

3. EXECUTION.

    a. Concept of Operations. Survey support will be a team effort by survey sections from both 1-51 FA and 2-636 FA. PADS teams will accompany firing battery recons to provide survey data for all battery primary and alternate positions. PADS teams will provide survey data for the attached AN/TPQ-36. The AN/TPQ-37 will receive PADS support upon coordinating for that support with 1-51 FA TOC when needed. Survey will be available for COLTs, OH-58Ds, and mortars.

    (1) PADS #1, 1-51 FA will provide survey to Btry C, 1-51 FA and ensure their primary and alternate positions in PA 9 have survey NLT 070001 Nov 96. PADS #1 will then accompany Btry C, 1-51 FA recon to prepare PA 6. Upon completion of PA 6, PADS #1 will survey the AN/TPQ-36 primary and alternate positions in PA 20. Then, they will provide survey to Btry B, 1-51 in PA 4. Be prepared to provide survey to Btry B, 2-636 FA and Btry C, 2-636 FA in PAs 17 and 18, respectively, and to survey PA 12 for Btry C, 1-51 FA.

_____
(Classification)

_____

FM 3-09.21 (FM 6-20-1)

(Classification)

TAB D (SURVEY PLAN) TO APPENDIX 3 (FA SUPPORT PLAN) TO ANNEX E (FIRE SUPPORT) TO OPORD 96-2--2d Bde, 52d Inf Div (Mech).

(2) PADS #1, 2-636 FA will provide survey for primary and alternate positions in PA 2 NLT 070001 Nov 96 for Btry C, 2-636 FA. PADS #1, 2-636 will then move forward to link up with the FSE, TF 1-17 to survey COLTs and mortars in the northern position of the brigade sector. Be prepared to provide survey in PA 21 for the AN/TPQ-36 and in PA 14 for Btry C, 1-51 FA. Be prepared to assist PADS #1, 1-51 FA in completing its survey requirements.

(3) PADS #2, 1-51 FA will provide survey in PA 1 for Btry A, 1-51 FA and in PA 5 for Btry A, 2-636 FA for both primary and alternate positions in both PAs NLT 070001 Nov 96. Then PADS #2 will survey PA 7 for Btry A, 1-51 FA and PA 19 for Btry A, 2-636 FA. Be prepared to provide survey in PAs 11 and 16 Batteries A and B, 1-51 FA, respectively.

(4) PADS #2, 2-636 FA will provide survey in PA 3 for Btry B, 2-636 FA and in PA 15 for Btry B, 1-51 FA for both primary and alternate positions in both PAs NLT 070001 Nov 96. PADS #2, 2-636 FA will then move forward to link up with the FSE, TF 1-81 to survey COLT positions and mortars in the southern portion of the brigade sector. Be prepared to assist PADS #2, 1-51 FA in completing its requirements. Be prepared to provide survey in PA 10 for Btry B, 1-51 FA.

(5) Conventional survey team, 1-51 FA will provide PADS updates points in the TF 1-17 sector and the northern portion of the brigade sector. It will also provide OH-58D initialization points vicinity grids LJ3817 and LJ3121. Initialization points will be marked with a 6- X 6-foot target cloth panel with a 4-foot diameter circle spray-painted in black. An identifying number with numerals 2 1/2 feet tall will be painted in the center of the circle. The team will also assist PADS #1, 1-51 FA and PADS #1, 2-636 FA in accomplishing their assigned survey tasks if necessary.

(6) Conventional survey team, 2-636 FA will provide PADS update points in the TF 1-81 sector and the southern portion of the brigade sector. It will assist PADS #2, 1-51 FA and PADS #2, 2-636 FA in accomplishing their assigned survey tasks if necessary.

(7) Survey Sec HQ, 2-636 FA will establish a SIMO station vicinity LJ366163 (1-51 FA CP). Station will be established NLT 061600 Nov 96 and will remain operational as long as weather conditions permit SIMO operations. Contact SIMO station with 2-636 RSO call sign in 2-636 FA survey net.

(Classification)

FM 3-09.21 (FM 6-20-1)

(Classification)

TAB D (SURVEY PLAN) TO APPENDIX 3 (FA SUPPORT PLAN) TO ANNEX E (FIRE SUPPORT) TO OPORD 96-2--2d Bde, 52d Inf Div (Mech).

b. Coordinating Instructions.

(1) Priority of survey is, in order, to firing battery positions (A, C, B, 1-51 FA; C, A, and B, 2-636 FA), radars, COLTs, OH-58D control points, and mortars.

(2) Survey sections will establish starting control at the following survey control points.

SCP NAME	EASTING	NORTHING	ALTITUDE
MARY	525422.97	3919175.39	935.2
HELEN	531642.91	3922964.29	1054.5

(3) All surveys will be closed. Parties will report completion of surveys to 1-51 FA TOC over ops/F (D).

4. SERVICE SUPPORT.

Service support for 1-51 FA survey section will be provided at 1-51 FA combat trains. Service support for 2-636 FA survey section will be provided at 2-636 FA combat trains. Inoperable PADS equipment will be brought immediately to the field trains.

5. COMMAND AND SIGNAL.

a. Command. 1-51 FA RSO will direct all survey operations. He will operate from the 1-51 FA CP.

b. Signal. SOI KTV 1062, Edition BB in effect.

(Classification)

Appendix B

MANUAL TARGETING AND FIRE PLANNING

One of the FA battalion CP's most critical functions is to convert raw and processed intelligence information into targets. This process may be as simple as processing a call for fire from an observer who sees a halted tank company or as complex as correlating reports from divisions, corps, and national assets, fitting the pieces of the puzzle together until an identifiable target emerges. The end product, a target that cannons, rockets, and missiles can attack with measurable results, must be the focus for artillery to provide essential support required by the force commander. In this appendix, Section I addresses manual target data processing, while Section II discusses manual fire planning.

SECTION I – MANUAL TARGET DATA PROCESSING

B-01. The amount of processing needed to develop a target varies extensively. In AFATDS/IFSAS/FDS/LTACFIRE-equipped units, target data is transmitted and processed automatically on the basis of the commander's guidance and target selection standards stored in the computer database.

B-02. Although AFATDS/IFSAS/FDS/LTACFIRE provide automated target data processing, the ability to manually process target data quickly and accurately is still a valid requirement for the FA battalion. If automated systems fail, units must still have the capability to process incoming information. This appendix explains how target data are manually managed and processed.

RECORDING TARGET INFORMATION

B-03. Targeting information (e.g., bombing and rocketing reports) reported to the CP for developing targets will be forwarded and recorded first on DA Form 2185-R (Artillery Counterfire Information) (Figure B-1). It is divided into four portions to report information by block letter to avoid confusion. It should be used as a work sheet to record information sent by voice communications and as a prompt to ensure that a complete report is received. For details on DA Form 2185-R, see FM 6-121.

ARTILLERY COUNTERFIRE INFORMATION										
(For use of this form, see FM 6-121. The proponent agency is TRADOC)										
RECEIVED BY					FROM			TIME		NUMBER
SECTION I - BOMREP, SHELREP, MORTREP, OR ROCKREP (Cross out items not applicable)										
UNIT OF ORIGIN (Current call sign address group or code name)	POSITION OF OBSERVER (Encode if HQ or important OP or if column F gives info on location)	DIRECTION (Grid bearing of FLASH, SOUND or GROOVE of SHELL [state which] in mils unless otherwise stated). (Omit for aircraft.)	TIME FROM	TIME TO	AREA BOMBED, SHELLED or MORTARED (Grid ref [in clear] or grid bearing to impact in mils and distance from observer in meters [encoded]) (dimension of the area in meters) by (the radius) or (length and width)	NUMBER AND NATURE OF GUNS (Mortars, rocket launchers, aircraft or other methods of delivery)	NATURE OF FIRE (Adjustment, fire for effect or harassing) (May be omitted for aircraft)	NUMBER, TYPE and CALIBER (State whether measured or assumed) OF SHELLS, ROCKETS or MISSILES) AND BOMBS	TIME OF FLASH-TO-BANG (Omit for aircraft)	DAMAGE (Encode if required)
A	B	C	D	E	F	G	H	I	J	K
				SECTION II - LOCATION REPORT				SECTION III - COUNTERFIRE ACTION		
REMARKS	SERIAL NUMBER (Each location that is produced by a locating unit is given a serial number)	TARGET NUMBER (If the weapon or activity has previously been given a target number, it will be entered here)	POSITION OF TARGET (The grid reference or grid bearing and distance of the located weapon or activity)	ACCURACY (The accuracy to which the weapon was located. CEP in meters and the means of location if possible)	TIME OF LOCATION (Actual time the location was made)	TARGET DESCRIPTION (Dimensions if possible): 1 - Radius of target, 2-Target length and width in meters		TIME FIRED (Against hostile target)	FIRED BY	NUMBER OF ROUNDS, TYPE OF FUZE and PROJECTILES
L	M	N	P	Q	R	S		T	U	V
DA FORM 2185-R, 1 APR 90			(Conforms with STANAG 2008)					Edition of 1 May 78 is obsolete.		

Figure B-1. DA FORM 2185-R

B-04. As soon as possible, transfer the information recorded on the artillery counterfire information form to a DA Form 4695 (Target Card) (Figure B-2). An original and one copy of each target card are prepared. The target card is used to chronologically store detailed information for quick reference in manual targeting operations. The target production/intelligence section in the TOC prepares the target cards. To disseminate targets, the original cards are circulated through all elements in the TOC before filing. Information in the header allows the cards to be referenced by target number and category.

TARGET CARD					
For use of this form, see FM 6-20-1; the proponent agency is TRADOC.					
Target No		Target (√Yes)	Category (Circle) 1 2 3 4 5 6 7 8 9 10 11 12 13		Fired (√Yes)
SOURCE	LOCATION	ACCURACY	DTG	DESCRIPTION/REMARKS	
FCE					
OPS					
OB					
DA FORM 4695					

Figure B-2. Target Card

B-05. Targeting information that comes into the TOC should be passed immediately to the intelligence section. It will be compared to target selection standards and transcribed onto a target card, if necessary. Directional information that is not associated with a grid cannot be placed on a target card and should be placed on a ray overlay. DA Form 2185-R should be retained until the ray is associated with a target.

B-06. After target cards are filled out, the original should be sent to the FDC, where it is compared to the attack guidance. If attack guidance or other target attack criteria is met, a fire mission will be processed. The target should be recorded on the master target list and, if not initiated by the force FSE, distributed as an addition to the target list. FSCM should be checked and necessary coordination made before attacking the target.

B-07. The original is then sent to the operations element to keep them informed and to aid in FS coordination. The target is then added to appropriate schedules. Ammunition status is updated, if necessary and requests for additional FS are evaluated and sent to the appropriate agency.

B-08. After all information has been added/updated by the applicable TOC sections, the cards are returned to the intelligence section and filed--one by target number and the other by target type, after data from one has been transcribed to the other.

B-09. Each TOC element (time permitting) should keep a duty journal to record major events that have occurred during their shift. Information to be recorded will be specified by the TSOP or the duty officer and will ease shift transition. Examples of types of information to be recorded should include:
- Changes in target selection standards or attack guidance.
- Changes in enemy posture, disposition or activity.
- Changes in FA missions, capabilities, or task organization.
- Changes in FSCM.
- Changes in HPTs.

RECORDING TARGETING INFORMATION (GRAPHICS)

B-10. While a detailed record of information is desirable, peak activity periods may preclude such meticulous procedures. Traditionally, in manual operations, plotting information on maps is a method of rapidly recording and displaying data. Each TOC element usually has at least one map.

TARGETS

B-11. Target information is recorded on the map by using target symbols and crater ray symbols. Do not confuse target symbols with gunnery "tick" marks. They are different in construction and information recorded on them.

B-12. A target symbol is a small cross with information pertaining to the target type and source (see Figure B-3). The upper right portion (Quadrant I) contains the target number (for example, AY2001). The lower right portion (Quadrant II) contains the source of the target and the assessed geographical accuracy (e.g., weapon-locating radar (WLR) and a 0- to 50-meter target location error). The lower left portion (Quadrant III) contains the target description. The upper left part of the symbol (Quadrant IV) is used to record the last time a transmission was picked up from that station, the last time fires were noted from the position or when the target was initially located.

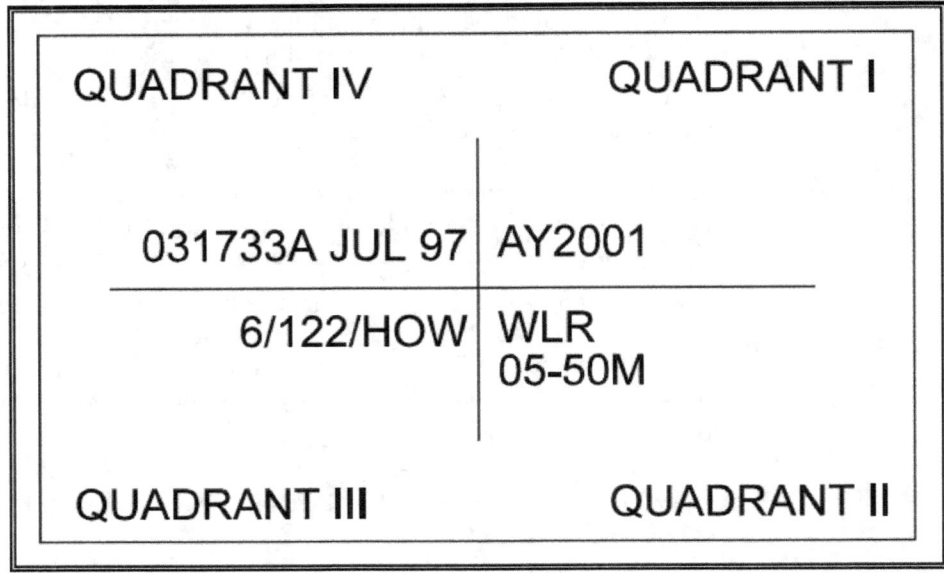

Figure B-3. Target Symbol

B-13. Not all agencies that plot targets need to record all information in the target symbol. The FDC only needs the target number and type and occasionally target location errors when such errors force a modified attack response. However, the intelligence section should plot all information to help develop and purge targets. Supervisors should establish TSOPs for required elements of targeting information plotted on maps.

SUSPECT TARGETS

B-14. Plot suspect targets using dashed lines, with everything known about the target included. Suspect targets should only be plotted by elements that are engaged in the process of developing or predicting targets. Suspect targets should not be plotted on maps used to control allocated attack means.

DIRECTIONAL INFORMATION

B-15. Directional information is a target indicator and is recorded by plotting rays on a ray overlay on the target production map. The majority of rays will be from priority target reports or target reports from Firefinder radars. While not a high-technology source of information, crater analysis is also valuable. It is the only way of confirming the caliber and, possibly, the type of weapon systems firing into the zone, short of physically seeing the weapon fire.

CRATER RAYS

B-16. Crater rays are drawn starting at the point where the rounds impacted. They are oriented in the direction reported in the shell report. The impact point is represented by a dot, around which a small circle is drawn. The ray is drawn to the scale length of the range of the weapon that was associated with the shell report. If that is not known, it should be drawn to the range of the longest shooter in the zone (Figure B-4).

Figure B-4. Sample Crater Ray

B-17. Label the ray with all information available to aid the intelligence section in developing targets. Place the description of the weapon(s) that fired on top of the ray. The description should conform to the format specified for Quadrant III of the target symbol (number, caliber, and type). Take care to ensure that a rough count of rounds, the duration of the shelling and the nature of the volley or individual gun are included in the shell report. Targeting personnel should prompt or query reporting agencies to provide such information, as it can be used to determine the number of weapons firing. In case of a large number of rounds, craters should be examined to determine the number of batteries that massed on the target.

B-18. Label the bottom right portion of the ray with the date-time groups associated with the shelling. If that is not available, record the time the shelling was reported. The number on the right is the local file number of the target information form associated with the ray. This number allows an analyst to refer back to who sent the message and to view detailed information not presented on the ray.

B-19. Color-code all rays to avoid false correlation of data and to accelerate the correlation process (Table B-1). It does not eliminate the need to review the description of the rays before converting the intersections into a target.

Table B-1. Crater Ray Color-Coding Scheme

WEAPON TYPE	CALIBER RANGE	RAY COLOR
Heavy (cannon)	161 to 210mm	Red
Medium (cannon)	121 to 160mm	Green
Light (cannon)	76 to 120mm	Blue
Multiple rocket launcher	All calibers	Orange
Mortar	All calibers	Yellow
Unknown	--------	Black

B-20. A chance for error exists if targeting personnel fail to look at the weapon description. However, the number of calibers in each type of threat weapon system precludes assigning each caliber or type a specific color.

B-21. When three intersecting crater rays are associated with a specific caliber and noted as occurring within a limited period of time, normally the result is a target. Annotate this target by placing a point in the center of the triangle formed by the intersecting rays. It is possible that the triangle could be quite large. In that case, one of the rays is probably in error and the targeteer should wait until another ray or other information pertaining to the location is received. Once a target is developed or a ray is associated with a grid coordinate, transfer the information to a target card. The ray(s) should be removed from the map and DA Forms 2185-R placed in an inactive file.

B-22. Post the ray overlay on the intelligence section map. The overlay and order of battle information aid in target prediction and situation development.

FLASH RAYS

B-23. It also is possible to record an independent flash ray (observation of a flash associated with a measured azimuth). Flash rays are difficult to relate to a weapon system (except MLRS) and usually cannot be ascribed to a caliber. They can be used in association with other crater rays and suspect targets. All information available should be placed on the rays (Figure B-5).

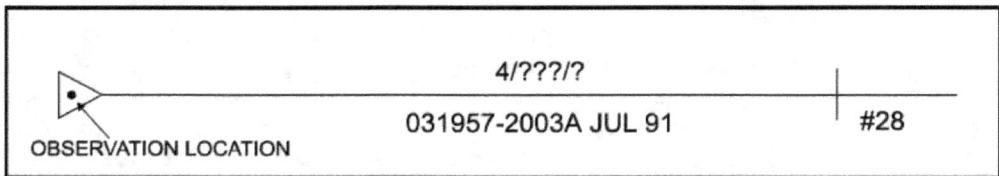

Figure B-5. Flash Ray

BATTLE DAMAGE ASSESSMENT

B-24. BDA is necessary to determine the effectiveness of attacks. In the case of critical targets, the success of the operation may hinge on determining if an attack was successful. Certain BDA will be available from organic FA TA assets. The best source of BDA is direct observation of the target, either from the air or from the ground. While it may not be possible to divert a UAV or aircraft to observe a target, critical targets may require the tasking of an acquisition asset to accomplish BDA. This requires the identification of targets requiring BDA during the planning process so that the S2 can request the necessary BDA acquisition asset. For additional details on BDA, see FM 6-20-10. Other methods of assessing BDA include the following:
- Weapons-locating radars.
- EPW interrogation.
- Refugee and agent reports.
- Stay-behind teams.
- Captured documents, reports and surveys of captured terrain.
- Signal intelligence.
- Activity analysis by intelligence personnel.

PURGING TARGETS

B-25. Purging targets is one of the most difficult aspects of targeting. It is heavily dependent on understanding opposing force tactics and having a clear picture of the tactical situation. There is no standard solution for purging targets as factors that drive purging change with the situation and terrain.

B-26. The increasing mobility of potential opponents has led to a reevaluation of movement as a survival technique for those forces. In the offense, self-propelled artillery may move as often as once every two missions for short distances (500 to 800 meters) to avoid counterfire. Command and observation posts in armored command and reconnaissance vehicles can function completely from within their vehicles. Similar vehicles are available for battery and battalion FDCs. These mobile, self-contained targets require that targeting personnel apply short dwell times to their locations.

B-27. Towed artillery and major unit HQ can be expected to remain in position for longer periods. The engineer capability to harden these targets may make them valid for longer periods than originally thought.

B-28. Always consider the rate of advance of opposing forces. Quickly purge forward CPs, command OPs, accompanying FA, and maneuver units if the rate of advance is high. Should the rate be low, purge these targets at the same rate as GS artillery, main HQ and other targets found in the division.

B-29. The dramatic increase in mobility of threat AD assets has made the concept of a SEAD program for close-in AD systems much more time sensitive than in the past. Onboard land navigation and TA systems have given short-to-medium range AD weapons the ability to set up and engage quickly.

B-30. Detailed tactics and terrain-dependent factors that determine purging criteria are provided by intelligence elements that support corps, division, and brigade. Purging guidance should be in writing and posted in the TOC. As targets are purged, the change in status must be reported to every element that maintains a target list or file.

B-31. Purging guidance should be target specific and reflect the time from acquisition to when the target is no longer valid. Delete targets from active files if the BDA indicates the target is no longer operating at that location.

SECTION II – MANUAL SCHEDULING OF FIRES

PLANNING FIRES

B-32. Fire planning is a continuous process conducted by FSCOORDs and FA TOCs at all levels to ensure that fires support the maneuver commander's OPLAN/OPORD. As part of the fire planning process, the FSCOORD, and/or FSO, nominates targets that support the commander's plan. Prearranged fires are planned to ensure responsive engagement when requested. Although some of the planned fires may apply to offensive or defensive actions only, others are appropriate to all types of operations and levels of combat. To facilitate operations as a part of a multinational force, the US has implemented STANAG 2934 (Chapter 8)/Quadripartite Standardization Agreement (QSTAG) 515. The applicable provisions have been incorporated throughout the fire planning discussions. The manual fire planning techniques for schedules of fires are described in the following paragraphs.

PREPARATION OF THE SCHEDULING WORK SHEET

B-33. The procedure for preparing a DA Form 4656-R is outlined below. A reproducible copy of DA Form 4656-R (scheduling work sheet) is at the end of this appendix.

Heading

B-34. Enter the type of schedule, the supported unit, and the OPORD for which it is being prepared.

Line Number

B-35. This is an administrative control number. Number each line sequentially. This gives all holders of the schedule a means of quick reference for finding which units have been scheduled and specific information that relates to those targets.

Organization and Caliber

B-36. Enter the organizational information, to include caliber and weapon type, for each unit for which you have planning authority.

Firing Units

B-37. Enter the site and designation of the firing unit.

Scheduling Targets

B-38. To the upper right of the Firing Units column is an untitled portion of the work sheet, referred to as the timing block. The upper portion of the block is used by the firing units to establish time to fire or lanyard pull time, so that the fires impact at the scheduled times.

B-39. Information on the lower portion of the block is based on time of impact of rounds fired. The purpose of the block is to establish the duration of a particular schedule relative to time. Schedules may start at a specific time (H-hour) or may be scheduled on call (start plotting at time 0).

B-40. Below the timing block is a block of intersecting horizontal and vertical lines, called the time matrix. It is used to assign targets to firing units. This assignment is based on the ability of the unit to adequately engage the target as shown by the target overlay. The time matrix graphically portrays time of impact and duration of fires and may refer to a specific shell-fuze combination to be used. This is done by representing the target to be engaged by either a dot (one volley) or a horizontal line (more than one volley). The interval between the vertical lines is based on the weapon system rate of fire and the number of different systems being scheduled on the same work sheet. For example, for a 155-mm howitzer, the normal interval is 60 seconds. Thus, a target being engaged by three 155-mm volleys would have a duration line three vertical lines long with impacts on each of the vertical lines. Another consideration in scheduling is the shift time of the weapon system being scheduled. Shift time is the length of time needed for the firing unit to cease firing on one target and commence firing on the next scheduled target.

Remarks

B-41. The REMARKS column is used to amplify information in the time matrix portion of the work sheet and to include information for the engagement of on-call targets. A parenthetical letter refers to the amplifying information in the REMARKS column. On-call targets are listed on the line of the firing unit assigned to engage them. Any other amplifying information is listed starting under the last firing unit line. No duration lines or dots are used for on-call targets because the duration of fire is not specified. If a unit is ordered to fire its on-call target while it is firing the schedule, it will:

- Leave the schedule.
- Fire its on-call target at the maximum rate of fire.
- Rejoin the schedule at real time.
- Report to its controlling headquarters scheduled targets that were not engaged and targets on which commander's effects were not achieved.

B-42. It is up to the controlling headquarters to notify the commander and recommend appropriate action to engage these targets.

PREPARATION

B-43. The preparation is an intense volume of fire delivered in accordance with a time schedule to support an attack. It may include a single FS means (FA only) or multiple means (mortars, FA, NSFS). Normally, fires begin before H-hour and may extend beyond it. Usually, a DS FA battalion or higher echelon plans a FA preparation. Fires may start at a prescribed time or may be held on call until needed. The duration of the preparation is influenced by the following factors:

- FS requirements of the force.
- Number of targets for attack.
- FS assets and ammunition on hand.

B-44. A preparation may be phased to allow successive attacks of certain types of targets, if time and intelligence is available to do so (Table B-2). Phase I should provide for the early attack of enemy FS means and observation capabilities including FA HQ and CPs. Such an attack degrades the enemy's ability to react with long-range indirect fires and to gain intelligence about the operation. Phase II should attack other CPs, communications facilities, assembly areas and reserves. The goal is to degrade the enemy's ability to reinforce and shift forces to counter the main effort of friendly forces. The final phase should include defensive areas in the forward portions of enemy position areas and targets that pose an immediate threat to attacking troops. The purpose of this phase is to suppress enemy direct fire systems until friendly maneuver forces have closed with them. Provisions must be made to keep hostile FS means and other critical targets neutralized throughout the preparation, time, and ammunition permitting.

Table B-2. Potential Targets in a Preparation

PHASE I	PHASE II	PHASE III
Indirect fire systems FA/mortar positions Operations and/or FA HQ	Command, control and communications facilities Reserve and logistic sites Assembly areas	Forward elements

B-45. When assigning FA systems to targets in the preparation, planners should, if possible, ensure that some fire units remain available to attack targets of opportunity. During the firing of a preparation, a target of opportunity may pose such a threat to the supported force that some FA units may have to leave the preparation to attack it. If the FA is directed to do so, the S3 assigns the units to fire on the target of opportunity.

B-46. If FA units are diverted from the preparation, they rejoin the preparation at the current point in time--not at the time they left it. For example, if a unit firing a preparation is diverted to a target of opportunity at H-5 and takes 4 minutes to attack that target, the unit would reenter the preparation at H-1. This means that some targets may not be attacked at all or may be attacked by FS assets not originally planned for the preparation. The firing unit diverted from the preparation must report to the appropriate FSE those targets that were not fired or were not fired with the scheduled amount of ammunition. This information lets the FSCOORD and the supported maneuver commander make sound decisions for the attack of those targets while ensuring the safety of the attacking force.

B-47. Units must continually update preparations to purge old targets and add new ones. The scheduler must set a time after which no other changes can be made. This cutoff time varies among units and is based on training, communications, and scheduling capabilities. The scheduler must ensure that there is enough time for changes to be sent to firing units, for technical fire direction to be performed, and for ammunition to be prepared and fired. The maneuver commander, advised by his FSCOORD, makes the final decision as to whether or not to fire a preparation. His decision is based on the following:
- Will the loss of surprise from the preparation be offset by the damage done to the enemy?
- Are there enough targets and means to warrant a preparation?
- Can the enemy recover before the preparation fires can be exploited?

B-48. The preparation must begin and end with all fire units that are used in the preparation. Gaps (for example, two or more consecutive shift times) should be avoided, if possible. Shift time is the interval between the time a FA unit can have fires impacting on one target and the time it can have rounds impacting on a new target. Shift time is affected by many variables, for example, state of training, amount of shift and type of munitions to be fired. For planning and scheduling purposes, a shift time of 1 minute is established for light and medium (105mm and 155mm) artillery. The MLRS shift time depends on launcher availability. Launchers moving to new firing points may not be ready to fire for up to 20 minutes or longer. Careful fire planning and management by MLRS battery and battalion personnel can ensure continuous launcher availability. As a rule, launchers do not engage more than one target from a single firing point. Launchers fire a second mission only in exceptional cases. Any gaps that do occur should be filled by refiring. Phase I targets or targets the maneuver commander has designated as priority targets. Units participating in the preparation should not begin firing on targets in a subsequent phase unless they have begun firing on the last target of the current phase or they have completed firing the current phase. This may not always be possible because some weapons may not have adequate range to fire at targets in all phases (Table B-3). In that case, the weapons are scheduled into the phase that is within their capabilities rather than being excluded altogether from the preparation. Fires are planned on the basis of the sustained rate of fire for each weapon system and shift time between targets (Table B-3).

Table B-3. Artillery Cannon and Rocket Characteristics

ASSET	MAXIMUM RANGE (METERS) a. WITH RAP b. WITHOUT RAP	SUSTAINED RATE OF FIRE	SHIFT TIME
SP 155mm howitzer M109A5/A6	a. 30,000 b. 22,000	1 round per minute	1 minute
SP 227mm MLRS M270	a. NA b. 30,000	1 round per 4.5 seconds	N/A
Towed 105mm howitzer M119A1	a. 19,500 (IRAP) 15,400 (RAP) b. 14,300	3 rounds per minute for first 30 minutes 1 round per minute thereafter	1 minute
Towed 105mm howitzer M102	a. 15,100 b. 11,500	3 rounds per minute	1 minute
Towed 155mm howitzer M198	a. 30,000 b. 22,400	2 rounds per minute for first 30 minutes 1 round per minute thereafter	1 minute
LEGEND: IRAP - improved rocket-assisted projectile			

COUNTERPREPARATION

B-49. Usually, a DS FA battalion or higher echelon plans a counterpreparation each time the supported force makes an extended halt. These

intensive fires are delivered just before the start of an enemy attack. They are designed to:
- Disrupt or delay the enemy's attack formations.
- Disorganize his command, control, and communications.
- Impair his TA efforts.
- Decrease the effectiveness of his fire and maneuver.
- Destroy his personnel and equipment.
- Reduce his offensive spirit.

B-50. Counterpreparations normally have two phases. Initial fires (Phase I) should provide for early and simultaneous attack of enemy forward elements, indirect fire systems, and observation posts. Phase II fires should attack the enemy's command posts, communications, and reserves while neutralization of his indirect fire systems continues. Fires from participating units should begin and end together when possible, and gaps should be avoided. When targets are scheduled in a counterpreparation, it is important that the firing begin on the last targets of one phase at the same time or before firing begins on the first targets of the succeeding phase. Shift times and sustained rates of fire discussed above for a preparation also apply for a counterpreparation.

Table B-4. Sample of Targets Phased in a Counterpreparation

PHASE I	PHASE II
Indirect fire systems	Command and control facilities
Forward elements	Logistic sites
	Reserves and assembly areas
	Communications facilities

B-51. The maneuver commander, on advice from his FSCOORD, decides when to fire the counterpreparation. Premature firing should be avoided to prevent disclosing targets for enemy counterfires. Counterpreparations are scheduled as on-call, since the firing normally depends on enemy initiative.

B-52. Fires from participating units begin and end together and as in the preparation, gaps should be avoided. When targets are scheduled in a counterpreparation, it is important that firing begin on the last targets of one phase at the same time or before firing begins on the first targets of the succeeding phase. Shift times and sustained rates of fire discussed earlier for a preparation also apply for the counterpreparations.

GROUPS, PROGRAMS and SERIES

B-53. Several fire planning techniques are useful when fire is desired on multiple targets. Groups, programs, or series of targets can be established in these situations. The manner in which each of these is graphically shown, the level at which it is established and its purpose are discussed below.

Groups

B-54. A group of targets consists of two or more targets on which simultaneous fires are desired. The fact that targets are included in a group does not preclude the attack of individual targets within the group. For FA fires, the DS battalion FDC is the lowest echelon that can form and implement a group of targets. The FSCOORD or FSO, determining the need for a group of targets, directs that the DS battalion FDC schedule the group. The planning and scheduling of groups of targets can be a time-consuming process. The groups can require considerable firing assets and limit the ability of the unit to mass fires on any single target. If the FDC does not have the assets available to fire the groups, it may pass the request to the force artillery or next higher artillery CP for planning.

B-55. Graphically display a group (Figure B-6) by circling the targets and identifying the group with a group designator. The designator consists of the two letters assigned to the block of target numbers allocated to a unit (for example, maneuver brigade, or DIVARTY TOC) with a number inserted between the two letters. For example, if a brigade is assigned the letters BC, its first group of targets is designated B1C, the second is B2C and so on.

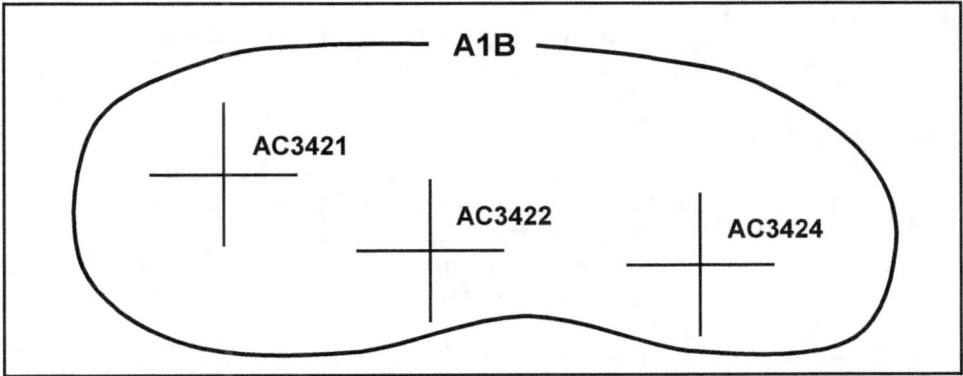

Figure B-6. Group of Targets

B-56. List groups of targets on the scheduling work sheet (See Figure B-7). Groups of targets normally are fired on call of the supported unit. Schedule groups so that initial fires strike the targets simultaneously. On the top line of the scheduling work sheet, enter the group number. Below the group number, list the targets of the group opposite the firing unit assigned the targets. Below each target number, show the number of rounds to be fired. No line or dot is drawn between the target number and the ammunition. More than one group can be scheduled on the same scheduling work sheet.

(GROUPS FOR 16 INF DIV OPORD 20)			SCHEDULING WORK SHEET For use of this form see FM 6-20-1; the proponent agency is TRADOC.														REMARKS
LINE NO	ORGANIZATION AND CALIBER	FIRING UNITS	A1Y	A2Y													
1.	3-47 FA	A	AB 4074 24 (a)	AB 4108 48 (a)													
2.	(105,T)	B	AB 4083 30 (a)	AA 3251 48 (a)													
3.		C	AZ 4123 30 (a)														(a) 50% VT

Figure B-7. Example Scheduling Work Sheet - Groups of Target

B-57. A firing unit can be scheduled for only one target in each group. More than one firing unit can be scheduled against a single target if needed.

Programs

B-58. A program of targets is a predetermined sequential attack of targets of a similar nature (Figure B-8). Targets in a particular program are normally of the same type (for example, all AD targets, all C2, or all mortar targets) and are selected and planned based on the commander's guidance. A program may be initiated on call or at a specific time or event.

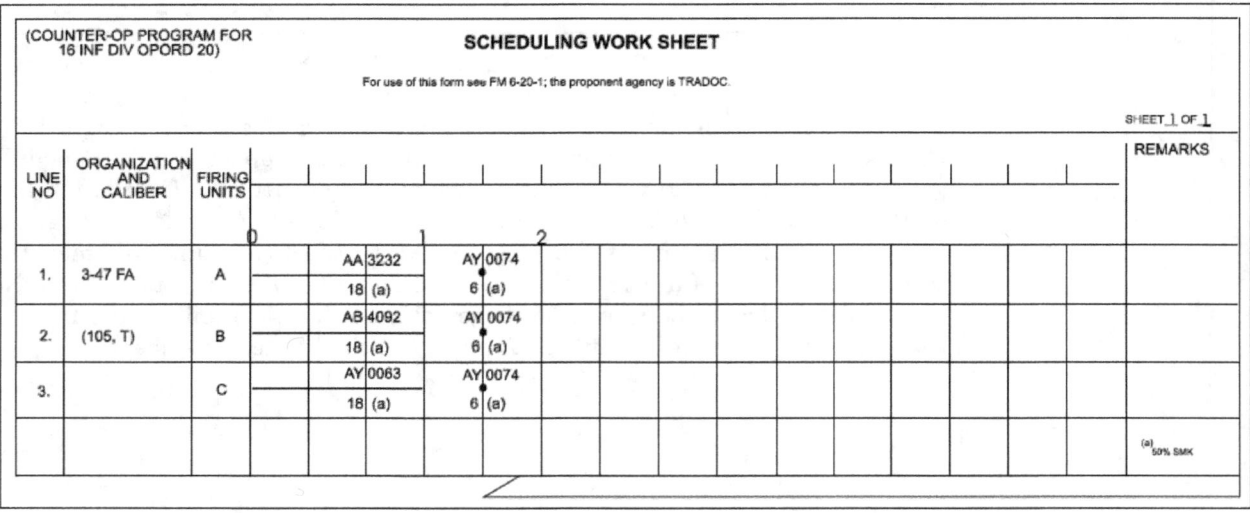

Figure B-8. Scheduling Work Sheet - Counter-Op Program

B-59. Each type of program is scheduled starting at 0 and extending as long as needed. A line indicates duration of fires. A dot indicates a single volley impacting simultaneously at a given time (e.g., the single volley may be a battery, battalion, or DIVARTY). Once a program is initiated, targets within the program are fired in a predetermined sequence as shown in the schedule. Normally, the lowest echelon that designates and plans programs of targets is the DS FA battalion. There are no special graphics associated with a program of targets. Programs appear on scheduling work sheets and schedules of fires.

Series

B-60. A series of targets consists of a number of targets and/or groups of targets planned for firing in a specific sequence to support a maneuver operation. The DS battalion FDC is the lowest echelon authorized to form and implement a series of targets. Series are planned by FSCOORDs or FSOs to support the maneuver commander's scheme of maneuver. It may be executed on call or at a specific time or event. It is scheduled to start at 0.

B-61. Once a series is begun, targets and groups within the series are fired in a predetermined time sequence. Simultaneous attack of targets in a group within a series is as requested by the initiator or as determined by the FA fire planner. Attack is based on the nature of the targets and the requirements of the force commander. Groups need not be fired as groups when fired as part of a series unless requested.

B-62. Graphically, a series is shown as individual and/or groups of targets within a prescribed area (Figure B-9). The series is assigned a code name or a nickname.

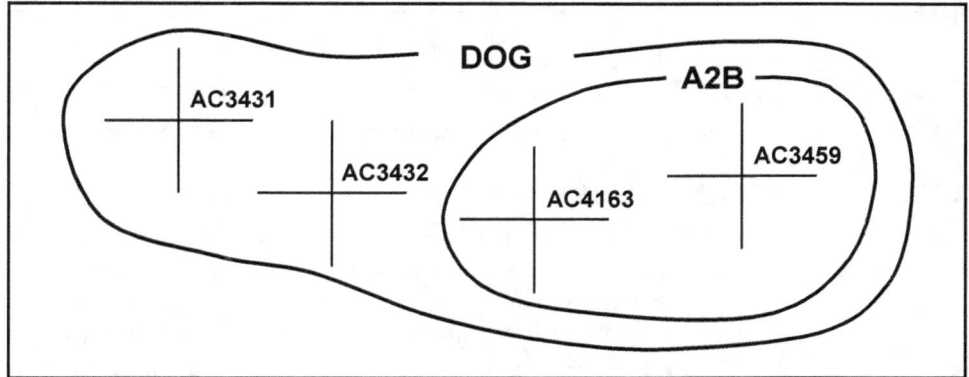

Figure B-9. Series of Targets (with a Group as part of the Series)

B-63. The fact that a series of targets has been formed does not preclude the attack of individual targets and/or groups of targets within the series. As with groups, manual planning and scheduling of series of targets can be a time-consuming process and may require fires from supporting FA units. A scheduling work sheet is prepared for each series of targets requested (Figure B-10).

LINE NO	ORGANIZATION AND CALIBER	FIRING UNITS	-4	-3	-2	-1	H									REMARKS
	(SERIES PAUL FOR 53 DIV OPORD 20)						**SCHEDULING WORK SHEET** For use of this form see FM 6-20-1; the proponent agency is TRADOC.									SHEET 1 OF 1
1.	6-10-FA	A			AA 3251 24 (a)	AA 3246 8 (b)										
2.	(155 SP)	B			AA 3251 24 (a)	AA 3246 8 (b)										
3.		C			AA 3251 24 (a)	AA 3246 8 (b)										(a) 50% VT
																(b) 50% SMK

Figure B-10. Example Scheduling Work Sheet - Series of Targets

ILLUMINATION AND SMOKE

B-64. Some targets have a specified duration of fire, but the ammunition requirements are unknown, for example, smoke and illumination targets on which expenditures are affected by wind speed and direction. Fire planners complete the illumination and/or smoke schedule as follows:

- Indicate, by a horizontal line, the time on target and duration of fire.
- Place the target above this line.
- Below the line, center a subscript keyed to a remark in the REMARKS column that shows the method of engagement (for example, two-gun illumination, lateral or range spread, first rounds WP and HC, succeeding rounds HC).
- When scheduling smoke, back off 1 minute to allow for buildup time (if using HC only and not WP for initial rounds). Buildup time is not to be used when firing on the same target. The maneuver commander must realize that because of weather, smoke fires cannot have guaranteed effects. When asking for smoke, the commander must be explicit in his intention. The FSCOORD must specifically look at alternative methods of achieving the intention if the smoke is not effective. This can be done by planning on-call HE targets to suppress selected areas (Figure B-11).

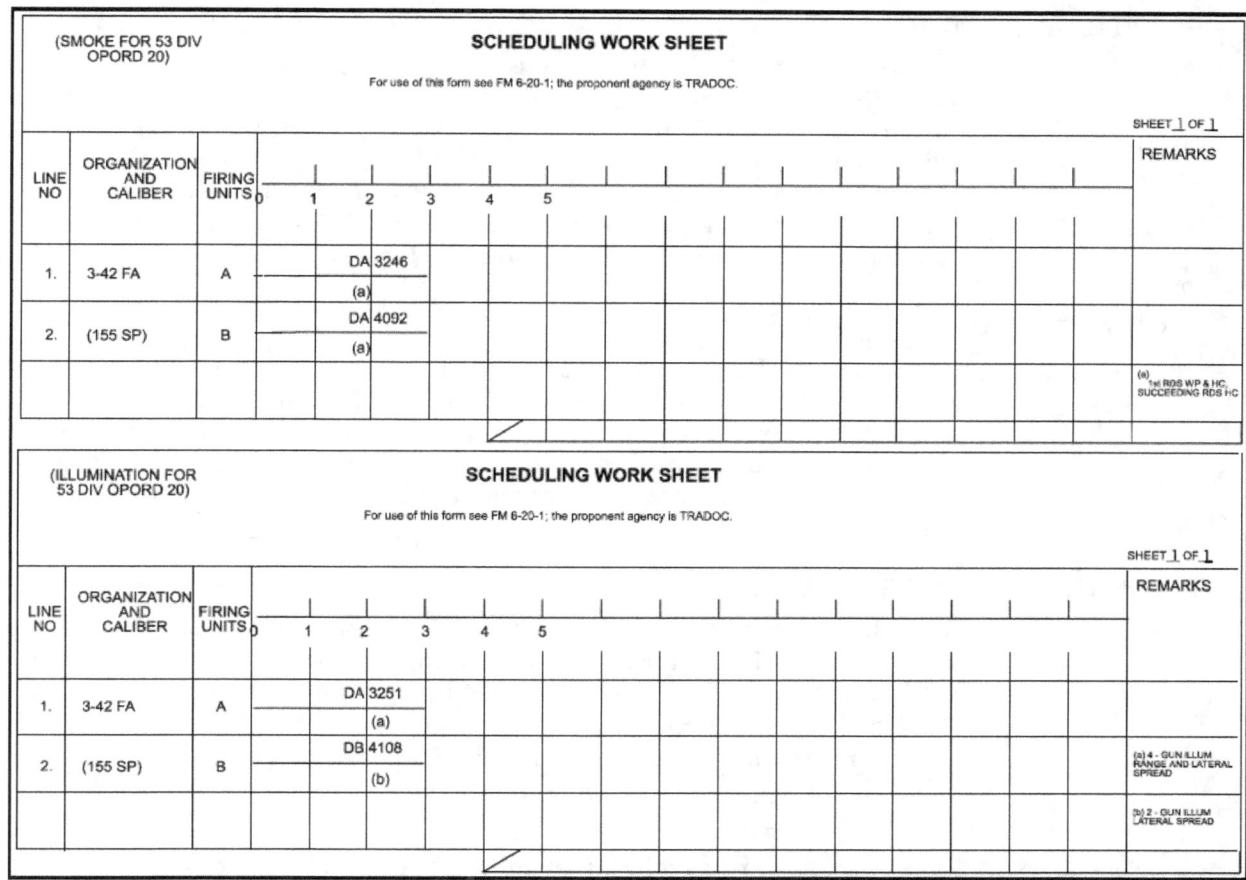

Figure B-11. Example Scheduling Work Sheet - Smoke and Illumination

FINAL PROTECTIVE FIRES

B-65. Final protective fires are immediately available fires designed to create a barrier to impede enemy movements across defensive lines or areas. They are integrated with the commander's defensive plans and are intended for use primarily against dismounted infantry. Maneuver brigade commanders allocate FPFs to maneuver battalions, which in turn allocate them to their companies. The FPFs are allocated one per FA firing unit and one per mortar section or platoon. When they are not engaged in another fire mission, weapons are laid on firing data for FPFs. This ensures immediate responses to calls for FPFs. The shape and pattern of these fires may be varied to suit the tactical situation on the basis of the supported company commander's desires. Authority to call for the FPFs is vested in the supported company commander or platoon leader in whose area they are located. On the target list work sheet, a target is designated as a FPF target by placing the letters "FPF" in the REMARKS column space for that particular target. Show FPF targets by their designated target numbers.

SCATTERABLE MINES

B-66. SCATMINE is scheduled similar to other munitions, however, it may be more difficult to properly schedule due to the lengthy times required to emplace some SCATMINE minefields. Because SCATMINE planning can complicate the scheduling process, the S3 and FDO should ensure that accurate information on the location and size of the minefield is received early in the planning process. See FM 6-40, FM 6-20-40, and FM 6-20-50 for additional details on manual SCATMINE planning procedures.

MLRS FIRE PLANNING

B-67. Since MLRS fire planning procedures deviate in some ways from the traditional fire planning methods, MLRS fire planning is discussed separately. Different procedures are required because of MLRS characteristics (its munitions, range capability, and volume of fire), and the MLRS employment doctrine (shoot-and-scoot tactics, and use of hide positions).

PLANNING AND COORDINATION

B-68. In support of force operations, MLRS uses two basic types of fire missions - scheduled (rocket fire plans) and unscheduled (all others). With DPICM, the MLRS has a high volume of fire to a range of 30 km. This makes it particularly effective against the following:
- Large or inaccurately located targets.
- Enemy artillery and ADA systems.
- C3 systems.
- Assembly areas (vehicles and/or personnel) and logistics sites.
- HPT beyond the range of cannon artillery.

B-69. Ammunition resupply is a problem for all weapon systems, but is a particularly important consideration for MLRS. FA planners must work closely with logistics planners to ensure adequate resupply of MLRS units.

B-70. MLRS ammunition consumption rates, ammunition resupply, and fire control system configuration concerns dictate that MLRS be limited mainly to the attack of HPTs. HPTs characteristics will differ from operation to operation depending on enemy and friendly force postures. Targeting priorities for the MLRS normally are:
- HPTs 15 to 30 km from the FLOT.
- HPTs 0 to 15 km from the FLOT that cannon artillery cannot effectively engage.
- Other targets 15 to 30 km from the FLOT.
- Other targets 0 to 15 km from the FLOT that cannon artillery cannot effectively engage.

CAUTION
To prevent the possibility of fratricide, MLRS should not engage targets closer than 2 km from friendly forces.

B-71. To plan MLRS fires, the fire planner must understand the response posture system used for reporting the status of the self-propelled launcher-loaders (SPLLs) of the MLRS unit. They are designated as being in a **hot, cool or cold** status by the MLRS battery FDC. Definitions and response times for the various response postures are shown below. This system helps the FDO select the MLRS launcher (or launchers) to fire a mission and helps the fire planner know the availability of MLRS fires.

B-72. The HQ performing fire planning for an MLRS unit must know how many launchers are currently in a **hot** status, how many launchers can be brought to a **hot** status, and how long it will take to bring them to a **hot** status.

B-73. When the fires of an MLRS unit are scheduled, each MLRS launcher is considered a fire unit. If all six launchers in a battery were hot, then the scheduling work sheet would have six lines for MLRS - one for each launcher. The Firing Units column of the target list work sheet is left blank for MLRS units. The MLRS battery FDC selects the launcher to fire.

B-74. When scheduling the fires of MLRS units, fire planners should never plan more targets than the total number of launchers that can be brought to a **hot** status by the time the targets must be fired, even if those targets use less than a full launcher load of rockets. Since a launcher can fire no more than 12 rockets per mission, targets requiring more than 12 rockets must be scheduled for two or more launchers. (See Table B-5.)

Table B-5. MLRS Response Postures

RESPONSE POSTURE	DEFINITION	TIME FROM RECEIPT OF MISSION TO FIRING
Hot	Fully operational, ready for a fire mission	3 minutes plus travel time from hide area to firing position[1]
Cool	Fully operational except that the stabilization reference package is turned off; requires time for the gyro to stabilize before it can fire	Hot response time plus 7 1/2 minutes[1]
Cold	Out of action	30 minutes if the launcher is mission capable
[1]This assumes a zero response time by the crew.		

B-75. Because of the difficulty in accurately determining the time required for an MLRS launcher to move from one firing position to another, each launcher normally is scheduled only once in a schedule of fires. If the schedule is long (more than 30 minutes) and the MLRS commander can give the fire planner an accurate estimate of the time it will take the launcher to move to a new firing position and be ready to fire (including time for ammunition resupply), a launcher may be scheduled to fire on more than one target. It also is possible that a launcher can fire one mission, move to another firing point, and fire again. However, this situation is not expected to occur often.

B-76. When preparing a scheduling work sheet for MLRS, do not use lines to show the duration of firing. Instead of lines, a dot is used between the target number and the number of rockets to be fired, regardless of how many rockets are fired or the duration of firing. The only exception to this rule is in the scheduling of groups, when neither dots nor lines are used. Examples of remarks that might appear on a scheduling work sheet for MLRS are shown in Figure B-12.

B-77. The preferred manner to fire MLRS in a fire plan is through the designation of a NLT TOT. This gives the MLRS unit greater flexibility and facilitates its firing of the targets on the schedule.

B-78. The time interval between rocket firings can be specified. This interval can be between 4.5 and 99.9 seconds. Even though the internal between rockets can be as long as 99.9 seconds, for reasons of survivability, the interval should be short enough that all rockets are fired within 2 minutes. If no interval is stated, the rockets will be fired at maximum rate of fire, approximately 5 seconds between rockets.

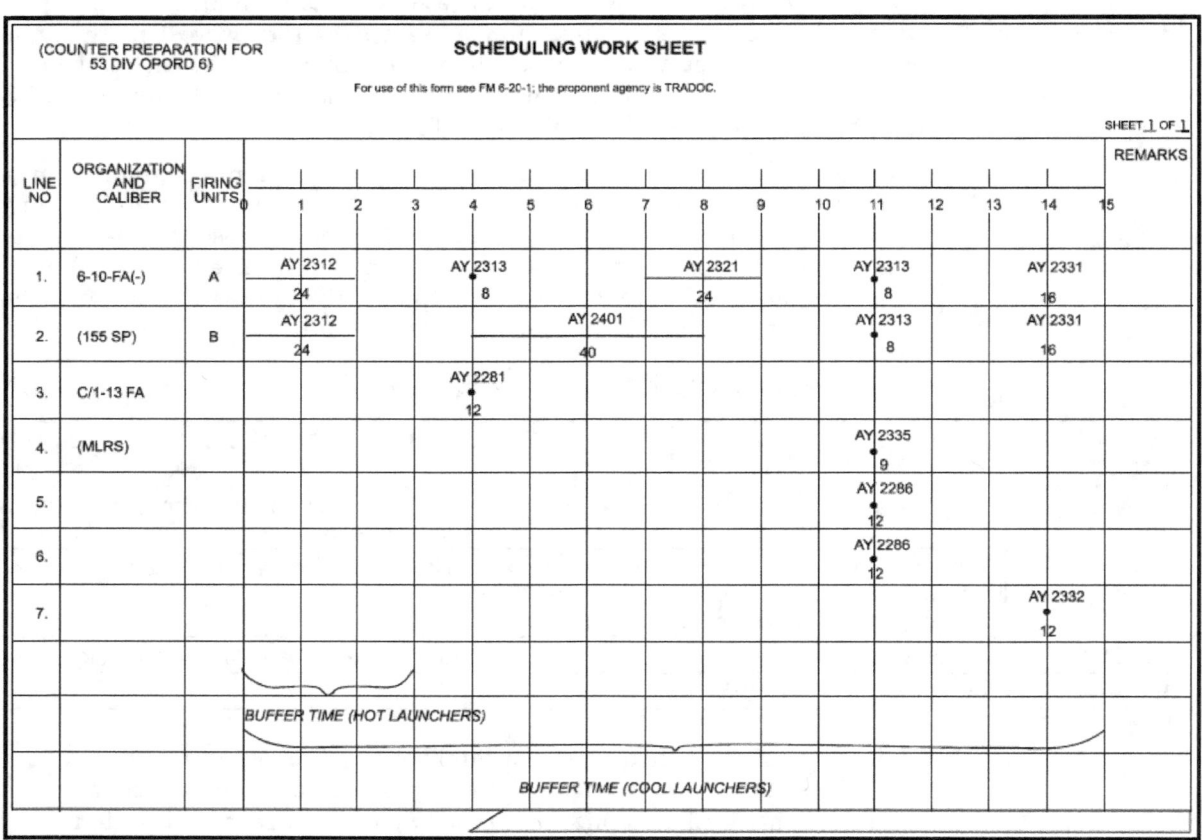

Figure B-12. Example Scheduling Work Sheet - MLRS Counterpreparation

B-79. If all available launchers fire on schedule, temporary loss of this FS asset can be expected for 20 to 45 minutes as launchers move to update points, reload, and return to hide or firing points.

COUNTERPREPARATIONS, PROGRAMS, and SERIES

B-80. These schedules are not normally fired at specific times. Instead, they are fired on call and are usually keyed to a specific event or maneuver phase. (See the counterpreparation scheduling worksheet, Figure B-12.)

B-81. When MLRS fires are planned on these schedules, a significant buffer time of 3 minutes (plus move time) is necessary for hot launchers. The buffer time for a hot launcher is needed because before a launcher can fire, it must move from its hide position to a launch position, orient itself for location, and direction and compute firing data. A 10 1/2 - minute buffer time (plus move time) is needed for cool launchers. The longer buffer time is required to bring the launcher from a cool to a hot status.

B-82. Whenever possible, the MLRS unit should be given a not-before time and not-after time to fire a target. This allows the MLRS FDC more flexibility in selecting a launcher to fire and a TOT for each target.

B-83. Because MLRS units normally fire only one target per launcher in a counterpreparation, the scheduling rules concerning gaps in the schedule and starting and ending the schedule with all units firing do not apply to MLRS. However, the rules for phasing and refiring are applied as required.

B-84. MLRS fires are usually directed at HPTs. Therefore, the MLRS may be assigned targets that must be fired at a specific point in the counterpreparation rather than in the appropriate phase. Critical targets fired by MLRS may be refired by cannon units (or in rare instances by another MLRS launcher). Normally, MLRS will not refire targets originally fired by a cannon unit.

GROUPS

B-85. Groups may at times be scheduled for fire by MLRS units (see Figure B-13). Groups must be planned with one or more launchers firing on each target. Also, MLRS and cannon units may be scheduled on targets in the same group; however, close coordination must be made between cannon and MLRS unit FDCs to ensure that the targets in the group are fired simultaneously. When given the order to fire the group, the MLRS FDC will fire the mission as a TOT or AMC mission, causing fires to fall simultaneously on all targets in the group.

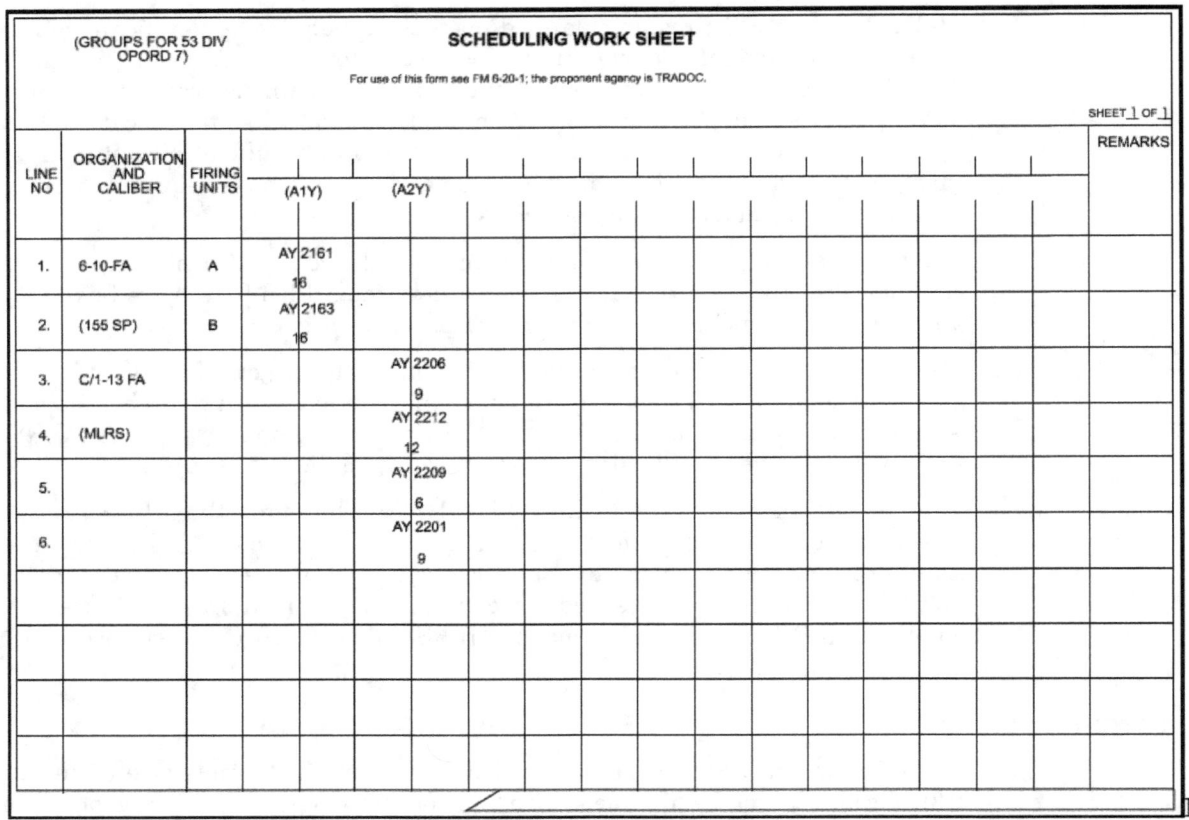

Figure B-13. Example Scheduling Work Sheet - MLRS Groups of Targets

PREPARATIONS

B-86. Because preparations are keyed to a specific H-hour, MLRS units can fire at any predesignated time during the preparation. This also applies to programs and series (See the preparation scheduling work sheet Figure B-14). Close coordination with the MLRS unit is necessary to ensure that enough launchers are in position to meet the preparation schedule.

B-87. As with counterpreparations, all scheduling rules apply except those concerning gaps and starting and ending with all units firing.

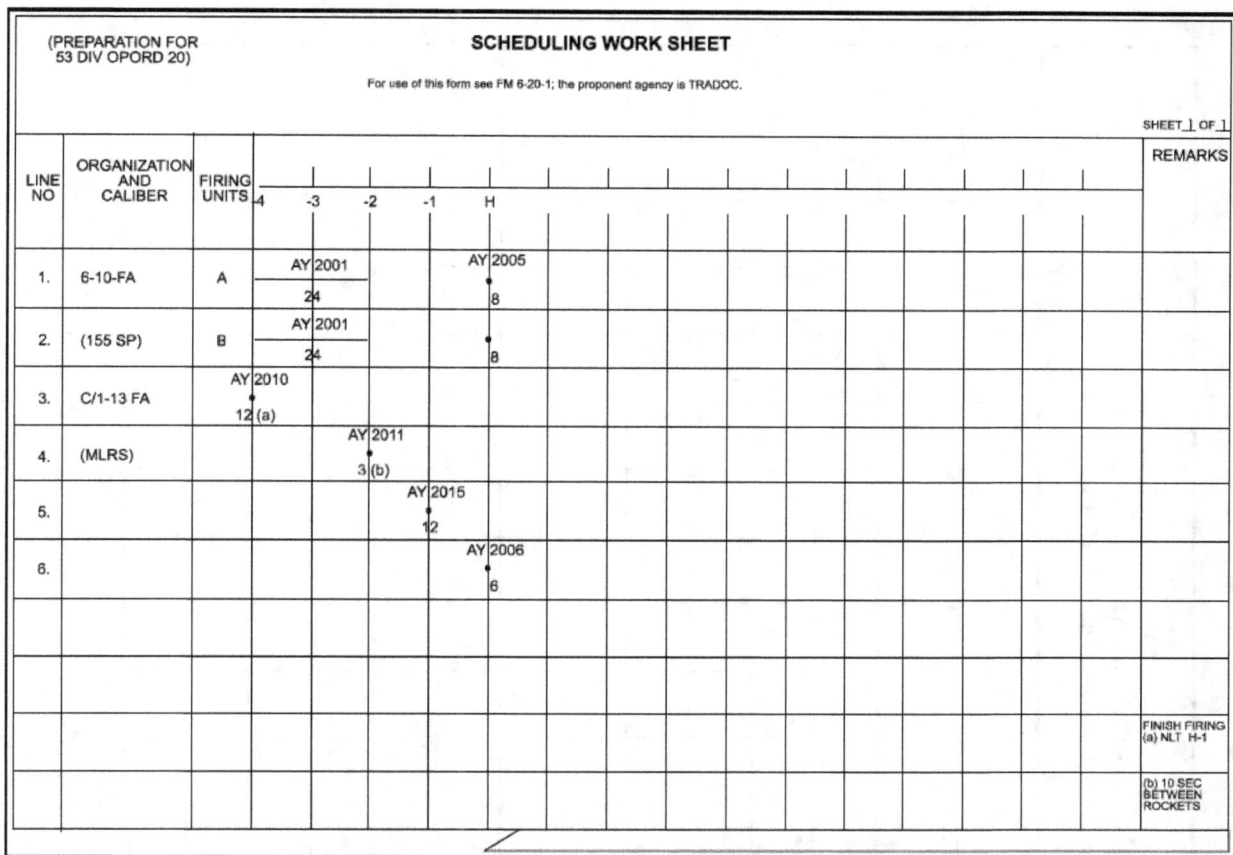

Figure B-14. Example Scheduling Work Sheet - MLRS Preparation

OTHER SCHEDULES

B-88. Programs of interdiction fires will normally be a series of TOT missions given to the MLRS battery. The not-before and not-after times discussed earlier also can be used.

B-89. MLRS normally will not be assigned a mission that would cause its involvement in a quickfire plan. The reason is its inability to operate on more than one voice net and one digital external radio net. If MLRS is included in a quickfire plan, the same techniques used to schedule a series should be used.

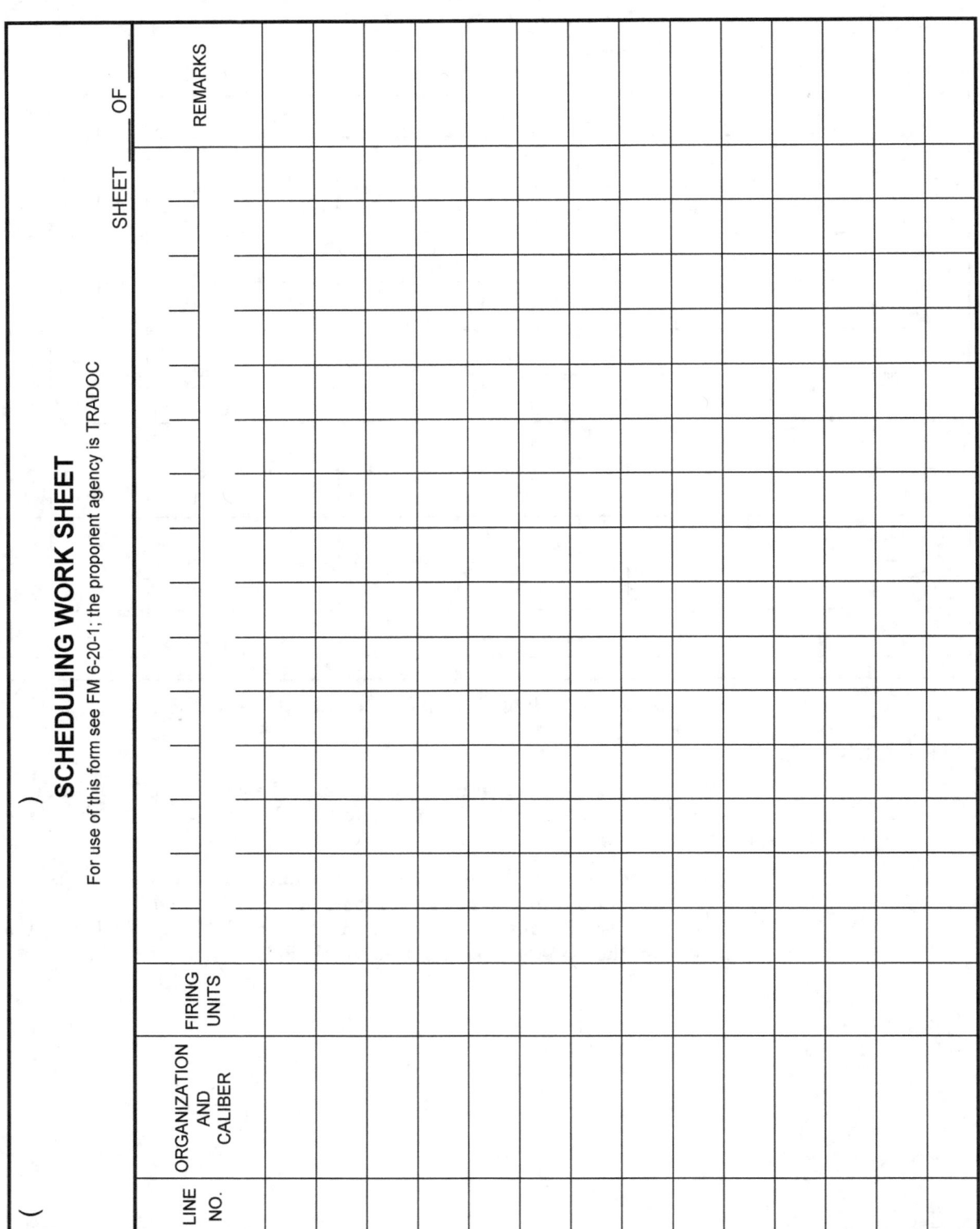

Figure B-15. Scheduling Work Sheet (Example/Reduced)

Appendix C

Environmental Awareness

All leaders and soldiers have specific duties and responsibilities concerning protection of the environment. Not all leaders are required to be environmental experts; however, they must be aware of and responsive to environmental compliance and prevention issues. Environmental stewardship is an inherent responsibility of national service for all Army personnel. This appendix provides an overview of responsibilities and duties necessary to build a foundation of basic environmental awareness. Throughout are references to material for further reading. Research these other documents to obtain a complete explanation of legal and ethical responsibilities. All training and operations must be closely coordinated with the installation's environmental office and environmental attorney to ensure compliance with all federal, state, and local requirements.

SECTION I – ARMY ENVIRONMENTAL AWARENESS

GENERAL POLICY STATEMENTS

C-01. The Army's environmental vision states: "The Army will be a national leader in environmental and natural resource stewardship for present and future generations as an integral part of our mission". To achieve this vision, the Army's environmental strategy places a high priority on sustained compliance with all environmental laws; takes into account the restoration of previously contaminated sites; focuses on pollution prevention; and accounts for the conservation and preservation of natural resources.

C-02. The Army environmental ethic calls for the chain of command to establish and support a stewardship climate which supports *compliance*, obeying the law; *prevention*, the concept of reduce, reuse, recycle; *conservation*, control and protection of natural resources; and *restoration*, the cleanup of contaminated areas. This ethic requires realistic, effective training – based on identification of the environmental realities and implementation of adequate protective measures. This ethic views our training areas as valuable multi-use resources that will lose their intrinsic training and health and welfare value unless they are properly managed and protected from excessive wear and tear.

C-03. All Army personnel should become familiar with these policy statements; they are established so that our natural environment will be available for present and future generations. Complete information regarding these polices can be obtained in Section II of *The Field Artillery Guide to Environmental Considerations*.

SECTION II – FA BATTALION ENVIRONMENTAL CONSIDERATIONS

FIELD ACTIVITIES

C-04. A FA battalion is a highly effective, lethal combat force that requires large areas of land for training. The vehicles, weapons, ammunition, materials, and types of operations required for effective training can present a threat to our environment unless they are employed prudently and in consideration of environmental preservation. This section will identify and address the various preventive measures that can be utilized in order to decrease possible environmental damage while allowing realistic training.

C-05. Key field environmental considerations include, but are not limited to, the following:

- Wheeled and tracked combat vehicles should stay on established roads, trails, firing points, and firebreaks, unless conducting specific cross-country maneuver exercises. Additionally, confine pivot turns and neutral steers to the middle of the roadway.
- Follow land contours rather than driving up and down hills or along creeks.
- In order to minimize siltation of streams; use bridges or low water crossings when crossing permanent streams. If crossing through a stream becomes necessary, then do so by the most direct route (90-degree angle).
- Establish refueling and maintenance areas away from wetlands, drainage areas, and near or over water sources.
- Federal law prohibits the removal of artifacts from federal property. Do not excavate, remove, damage, or otherwise alter or deface any archaeological resource located on a military reservation.
- Avoid and mark off-limit areas for known archaeological sites during military training exercises. Penalties can be up to $250,000 for knowingly disturbing a site.
- Be aware of and avoid nesting, bedding, and habitats of all species of birds and animals. Mark as off-limits, designated threatened or endangered species areas.
- Use camouflage netting instead of live vegetation.
- When planning training activities, conform to installation and community noise-abatement regulations. Identify and mark the off-limit boundaries.
- Open fires, such as burning of garbage, refuse, and rubbish are not allowed on range areas. For burning excess powder increments (cannon units), use only designated powder burn sites.
- Conform to field sanitation and medical standards when using soakage pits for wash water, liquid kitchen wastes, and grease traps per FM 21-10, *Field Hygiene and Sanitation*.
- Establish field satellite-accumulation site and procedures.
- Police field locations and establish field trash-collection point and procedures. Remove materials packed into training areas on departure from the training areas.

FM 3-09.21 (FM 6-20-1)

- When the training exercise is complete, repair any field damage such as ruts from vehicles, foxholes, and other emplacements.
- Conduct all training with a concern for conservation and future use of range training areas.

MUNITIONS

C-06. The point at which munitions are considered wastes is a matter of law and regulation for the area where the installation is located. The summary below is a generic review of requirements of the Resource Conservation Recovery Act (RCRA) Munitions Rule that has been adopted in many states. Since rules and guidelines vary based on location, units should consult with the local installation's environmental program and legal staff concerning possible munitions waste.

- Munitions and ordnance are not considered wastes when used for their intended purpose. Intended use includes:
  - Use in training activities, including training in the proper destruction of unused propellant bags/increments or other munitions (this includes the burning of excess propellant bags/increments that occurs during live-fire FA cannon training);
  - Use in research, development, testing, and evaluation of munitions, weapons, or weapons systems;
  - Recovery, collection, and on-range destruction of unexploded ordnance and munitions fragments during range clearance activities;
  - Unused munitions or components are being repaired, reused, recycled, reclaimed, disassembled, reconfigured, or otherwise subject to materials recovery activities.
- Unused munitions are considered waste when:
  - Abandoned by being disposed of, burned, detonated (except during intended use), incinerated, or treated prior to disposal; or
  - Removed from storage for the purpose of being disposed of, burned, or incinerated, or treated prior to disposal; or
  - Deteriorated or damage to the point it cannot be put into serviceable condition and cannot be recycled or used for other purposes; or
  - Declared a waste by authorized military personnel.
- Used or fired munitions are considered waste when:
  - Transported off range for purposes of storage, reclamation, treatment, disposal, or treatment prior to disposal; or
  - Recovered, collected, and then disposed of by burial or landfilling either on or off range; or
  - Fired off-range and not promptly rendered safe and/or retrieved.

HAZARDOUS MATERIAL AND HAZARDOUS WASTE

C-07. The RCRA is the framework for managing hazardous waste and has established standards for identifying, classifying, and storing of these wastes. RCRA regulations require those involved in managing hazardous substances to be properly trained, and the training to be properly documented. Units needing to transport hazardous substances should contact their installation environmental officer and/or DRMO to ensure compliance with the Hazardous Materials Transportation Act.

C-08. Key hazardous material and hazardous waste environmental considerations include, but are not limited to, the following items:
- Personnel dealing with hazardous materials must be trained in proper handling, containment, cleanup, and reporting procedures.
- A Material Safety Data Sheet (MSDS) must be on file, and made available to all personnel regarding hazardous material.
- Hazardous waste containers must be kept closed when not in use, free of rust and leaks, and stored separately from incompatible wastes.
- Incompatible wastes must never be transported on the same vehicle.
- Never allow the accumulation of more than 55 gallons of a hazardous waste, or 1 quart of acutely hazardous waste, at the satellite accumulation point. (A satellite accumulation area is generally the designated area or point of generation of a hazardous waste, which will store the waste until it is sent out for processing.) Process all hazardous waste in a timely manner (label the accumulation point with the date of the accumulation to ensure the time limit is not exceeded).
- Calcium hydroxide, a by-product formed from using the hydrogen generator set (AN/TMQ-3), is an environmental hazard. Conform to installation policy when storing, handling, and disposing of this waste.
- Methanol and methanol in water is used with the hydrogen generator (AN/TMQ-42); both are hazardous materials due to flammability and toxicity. Conform to installation policy when storing, handling, and disposing of this waste.
- Bore cleaner waste (cannon units). Is a chlorinated hydrocarbon product used? If so, how is the waste disposed?
- Battery electrolyte (acid) from damaged batteries should be drained and disposed of through turn-in via installation policy and maintenance TSOP. Refer to TB 43-0134, *Battery Disposition and Disposal,* for complete procedures regarding battery handling and disposal.
- Ensure all Department of Transportation (DOT) and hazardous waste transportation requirements are met prior to transporting hazardous material or hazardous waste on public highways.
- Check with local environmental office for transportation procedures within the installation boundary.
- For more information on storing and handling of hazardous materials refer to TM 38-410, *Storage and Handling of Hazardous Materials.*

MATERIAL SAFETY DATA SHEET

C-09. A MSDS is a summary of information on a given chemical identifying material, health and physical hazards, exposure limits, and precautions. A MSDS describes the hazards of a material and provides information on how the material can be safely handled, used, and stored. Insist on receiving a copy of a MSDS when receiving a hazardous chemical from supply, and retain it for when or if you turn in the material. Periodically review each MSDS pertaining to your unit. This will assure a quick response when identifying symptoms and handling emergencies.

C-10. Unfortunately, there is no specified format for a MSDS, and it doesn't contain all known data of a chemical, but there are typical components. These are outlined in 29 Code of Federal Regulations (CFR) 1910.1200. Use the following information as a guide toward what to expect on most MSDS forms.

Table C-1. Material Safety Data Sheet

SECTION/TOPIC	CONTENTS
Section 1 - General Information	Manufacturers' name and address. Trade or common name of product.
Section 2 - Hazardous Components	National Institute for Occupational Safety and Health and/or Chemical Abstract System Number. Chemical name and percentage.
Section 3 - Physical Properties	Boiling point, freezing point, water solubility. Appearance and odor under normal conditions.
Section 4 - Fire & Explosion Hazard	Fire-fighting equipment. Any unusual fire and explosion hazards.
Section 5 - Health Hazard	Routes of entry into the body. Emergency and first aid procedures.
Section 6 - Reactivity Data	Conditions to avoid. Incompatibility with other materials.
Section 8 - Control Measures	Recommended respiratory and ventilation. Personal protective equipment, if needed.
Section 9 - Special Precautions	Handling and storing precautions.
Section 10 - Transportation	Applicable regulations. Hazards class and required labeling.

MAINTENANCE

C-11. The BMO acts as the hazardous material/ hazardous waste (HM/HW) spill coordinator. He/she ensures the accountability, proper storage, and disposal of all HM/HW, and ensures that HM/HW spills are immediately contained and reported. Additionally, the BMO reports nonfunctional/inoperative treatment/collection facilities (such as oil/grease interceptors, floor drains, or catch basins) to the installation environmental office through the unit environmental compliance officer (ECO).

C-12. Key maintenance environmental considerations include, but are not limited to, the following:

- Motor maintenance areas require TSOPs and close monitoring. Maintenance operations are continuous sources of minor pollution to storm drainage systems due to the constant threat of a spill of fuel or oil. TSOPs for prevention or cleanup of spills should be posted in motor maintenance areas, and should be understood by all personnel involved in maintenance activities.
- Refueling operation TSOPs should address practices to minimize spills.
- Implement preventive maintenance on all heavy equipment to ensure petroleum products will not be released from the belly pan.
- Ensure pollutants are not discharged into storm or washrack drains or poured on the ground or along fence lines. Some common pollutants are oil, solvents, soap, diesel, gasoline, battery acid, chemicals, waste antifreeze, paint, and grease.

- Parts containing asbestos, such as brake shoes, clutch plates, and equipment insulation, should be removed, collected, and disposed according to installation policy.
- The least hazardous or preferably, non-hazardous material to perform a function should be used, unless previous research of options clearly indicates otherwise. The Defense Logistics Agency (DLA) produces a manual, *Environmental Products*, to assist in this process.
- Do not mix fuel, oil, or antifreeze together. This is considered a mixed waste.

SUPPLY

C-13. The supply sergeant is required to have a complete inventory of HM/HW generated by the unit. He/she must also know what chemicals the unit requires, where and how they are stored, how much hazardous waste is generated, and necessary spill response procedures. The supply sergeant should coordinate with the unit S3 or ECO to ensure this information is incorporated into the unit TSOP.

C-14. Key supply environmental considerations include, but are not limited to, the following items:

- Requisition only supplies needed and authorized, avoid excessive stockpiling of materials.
- Maintain an accurate inventory in unit TSOP of hazardous waste used by the generating unit. This listing should include waste by volume, type, generating process, and location.
- Use of used oil tanks for disposal of solvents, antifreeze, or other HM/HW is against regulation. Storage of hazardous material must be in clearly marked DOT-approved containers.
- Actively support a unit-recycling program.
- Ensure tires and batteries are properly turned in for recycling.
- Ensure used batteries are turned in on a one-for-one basis.

SPILL RESPONSE

C-15. Generally, only persons specifically trained to respond to a spill should handle unit spills. However, all personnel must, at a minimum, report the spill, and be aware of the following four basic steps to spill response:

- Protect yourself. Use personal protective equipment specified in the MSDS.
- Stop the flow. This may be as simple as placing the container upright or closing a valve.
- Contain the spill. Place absorbent material around the spill, and protect drains and ditches.
- Report the spill. Notify supervisor, and other key personnel. Also, notify applicable federal, state, and local environmental regulatory agencies if the amount of spilled material exceeds reportable quantities specified by the regulators.

C-16. Each unit is responsible for the cleanup of their own spills, as long as no personnel are put in danger. After the above four steps are completed, take the necessary steps to cleanup the spill. Information on cleanup procedures can be found on the MSDS, and unit TSOP. Also, the unit must contact installation environmental staff for guidance. Turn in the spilled material and absorbent to the Defense Reutilization Marketing Office (DRMO), or another designated point if a DRMO is not available. Also, ensure there are adequate spill supplies on-hand for future use.

C-17. Key spill prevention, response, and cleanup considerations include, but are not limited to, the following items:

- A spill prevention and response section must be included in the unit TSOP outlining installation spill plan requirements. Unit spill contingency procedures for spills of oil, fuel, or other hazardous materials or wastes must comply with response and reporting requirements of local, state, and federal environmental regulatory agencies.
- Each unit must maintain a spill cleanup kit near any satellite-accumulation area, or where a potential for spill exists. The kit must contain, at a minimum, absorbent material, shovel, brooms, gloves, and appropriate containers. Units that have a potential for release or spill that may impact streams must also maintain booms for containment.
- Drip pans must be used under vehicles and equipment where spills are likely to occur.
- All topsoil contaminated with oil must be removed, properly disposed, and replaced by the unit. While awaiting disposal, keep the excavated soil covered to prevent runoff in case of rain.

SECTION III – REGULATORY REQUIREMENTS

LAWS AND REGULATIONS

C-18. Military facilities are subject to federal, state, local, and host nation environmental laws. When the requirements differ, the most stringent law applies. Ignorance of environmental laws is not an excuse for non-compliance, and it will not protect commanders, soldiers, or the military services from civil and criminal liability. Figure C-1 lists the federal and military laws and regulations that are frequently encountered by Army personnel; however, it is not inclusive of all requirements.

C-19. Additionally, environmental law varies with differing countries, states, and cities. What is legal in one area may be illegal in another. Commanders and trainers should consult with their installation environmental office to ensure they are knowledgeable of local regulations and policies.

C-20. Army units outside the United States that are not subject to federal environmental regulations decreed by the Environmental Protection Agency (EPA) should comply with the final governing standards of the host nation. In areas where a host nation has minimal or no environmental laws and regulations, comply with the *Overseas Environmental Baseline Guidance Document* provided by the Department of Defense, AR 200-1, *Environmental Protection and Enhancement*, and AR 200-2, *Environmental Effects of Army Actions*.

Army Regulations	Federal Laws
AR 200-1. Environmental Protection and Enhancement	Archaeological Protection Act of 1979
AR 200-2. Environmental Effects of Army Actions	Clean Air Act of 1970
AR 200-3. Natural Resources-Land, Forest and Wildlife Management	Clean Water Act of 1972
AR 200-4. Cultural Resources Management	Comprehensive Environmental Response And Liability ACT (CERCLA) of 1980
AR 420-49. Solid and Hazardous Waste Management	Emergency Planning and Community Right-to-Know Act (EPCRA) of 1986
AR 420-76. Pest Management	Endangered Species Act of 1973
Executive Orders	Federal Facilities Compliance Act of 1992
EO 11989. Use of off-road vehicles on public land	Haz. Materials Transportation Act of 1975
EO 11990. Wetland protection	National Environmental Policy Act of 1969
EO 12114. Effects of federal actions abroad	National Historic Preservation Act of 1966
EO 12196. Occupational Safety and Health Administration compliance for federal employees	Noise Control Act of 1972
	Oil Pollution Act of 1990
EO 12580. CERCLA duties and powers	RCRA of 1976
EO 13101. Pollution prevention and recycling	Toxic Substances Control Act of 1976

Figure C-1. Environmental Laws and Regulations

REGULATORY TRAINING REQUIREMENTS

C-21. Commanders must be aware of, and comply with requirements for environmental training. This training may be at the awareness level for all personnel or at a more specialized level designed for specific personnel. The installation environmental and safety offices can best assist in determining your training requirements and who to contact for additional information. Table C-2 is provided as a reference of possible training requirements for the FA battalion.

Table C-2. Regulatory Training Requirements

NOTE: The depth or level of training will vary between target audiences. For example, K and E will need in-depth training, while A will only require broad overviews. The letters K, E, N, or A denotes target audience, and are listed below:

Knowledge	Personnel who administer, implement, or comply with contents of regulations such as program manager and technicians in the environmental field. Also includes organizations that need in-depth knowledge of the environmental laws/regulations/programs, such as staff judge advocates.
Executors	All personnel who supervise or actually handle responsibilities dealing with environmental programs, to include ECOs, technicians, and workers. Also includes unit personnel required to execute responsibilities with environmental ramifications as part of their mission.
Need to Know	Personnel who may encounter environmental issues as part of their mission. This may include personnel within the following activities: engineers; designers; emergency personnel; safety; reserve components; first-line supervisors; crew chiefs; NCO's; and various unit personnel as identified by the installation environmental office and their supervisors
Awareness	Public affairs offices, reserve components, other unit personnel.

Training Topic	Regulatory Reference	K	E	N	A
Hazardous Materials/Waste Compliance Training	29 CFR 1200; 40 CFR 262.34, 264.16, 265.16; 49 CFR 172	*	*	*	*
Hazardous Waste Operations (HAZWOPER) for Installation Restoration (IR)	29 CFR 1910.120	*	*		
HAZWOPER for Treatment Storage and Disposal Facilities	29 CFR 1910.120	*	*		
Emergency Response to Hazardous Materials Incidents/Hazardous Material Technician	29 CFR 1910.120	*	*	*	
National Environmental Policy Act (NEPA)	NEPA of 1969	*			*
National Historic Preservation Act (NHPA)	36 CFR part 800, 36 CFR part 63, NHPA of 1966	*			*
Archaeological Resources Protection Act (ARPA)	43 CFR 7.7 (4) ARPA of 1979	*			
Native American Graves Protection and Repatriation Act (NAGPRA)	NAGPRA of 1990	*			
EPCRA/Superfund Amendment Reauthorization Act (SARA)	EPCRA/SARA 1986 Title 3, Executive Order 12856	*	*	*	*
Lead Based Paint	Lead Based Paint Exposure Reduction Act of 1992, 24 CFR 35	*	*	*	*
Asbestos	40 CFR part 763, 40 CFR 61 part M	*	*	*	*
Endangered Species Act (ESA)	ESA 1973 as amended, 50 CFR par 402	*			*
Clean Water Act (CWA)	CWA S 311	*	*		*

Table C-2. Regulatory Training Requirements (Continued)

Training Topic (Continued)	Regulatory Reference	K	E	N	A
Storm Water Pollution Prevention Planning	CWA S 319	*	*	*	
Chloroflourocarbon (CFC)/Halon Refrigerants	EO 11051, 40 CFR 82.40, 40 CFR 282, 58 FR 92 (p. 28660)		*	*	*
Federal Insecticide, Fungicide, and Rodenticide Act (FIFRA)	FIFRA of 1972, 40 CFR 265.16, SARA of 1986		*		
Solid Waste Management	40 CFR 240-257/RCRA Subtitle D	*			*
Underground Storage Tanks	40 CFR part 280, RCRA Subtitle I	*			
National Pollutant Discharge Elimination System (NPDES)	CWA of 1990, 40 CFR 122-129	*	*		*
Confined Space Entry	29 CFR 1910.146	*	*	*	*
Occupational Respiratory Protection	29 CFR 1926.58, 29 CFR 1910.134	*	*		
Occupational Exposures to Bloodborne Pathogens	29 CFR 1910.1030	*	*	*	*
Storm Water Compliance	40 CFR 122-129, WPCA S 319	*	*		
Hazard Communication Standard	29 CFR 1910.1200	*	*	*	*
Department of Transportation	49 CFR172.704	*	*	*	*

ENVIRONMENTAL COMPLIANCE OFFICER RESPONSIBILITIES

C-22. It is the unit commander's duty to appoint an ECO and a Hazardous Waste Coordinator; the same person can serve in both positions, per AR 200-1. These appointments are made to ensure that environmental compliance occurs at the unit level. Appointed personnel:

- Should receive formal training and act as an advisor on environmental regulatory compliance during training, operations, and logistics functions.
- Will be the commander's eyes and ears for environmental matters, as the Safety Officer/NCO is for safety matters.
- Should function as the liaison between the unit and higher headquarters regarding environmental matters such as training requirements, equipment, or supplies that unit personnel need.
- Should inspect HM/HW accumulation sites, and ensures that soldiers handling these materials are properly trained.
- Ensure the unit's TSOP covers environmental considerations, conservation, natural resources, pollution prevention, HM/HW, and spill procedures.
- Support the Army's pollution prevention/recycling program.
- Report hazardous material and waste spills immediately.
- Conduct environmental self-assessments or internal environmental compliance assessments.
- Meet with installation environmental points of contact periodically to remain updated on any regulatory changes.

FM 3-09.21 (FM 6-20-1)

SECTION IV – ENVIRONMENTAL RISK MANAGEMENT

ENVIRONMENTAL RISK MANAGEMENT

C-23. Leaders at all levels are required to make timely and appropriate decisions regarding the environment. Failure to do so may negatively impact the training environment, which could then lead to personal liability of individuals directly involved, the chain of command, and the US Army. All leaders must properly manage, assess, and reduce environmental risks.

THE FIVE-STEP PROCESS

C-24. Risk management is a five-step process designed to provide leaders a methodology for the identification, assessment, control, and evaluation of environmental risks. The following is a summary of these steps from FM 20-400, *Military Environmental Protection,* and FM 100-14, *Risk Management.* Refer to these manuals for detailed information.

STEP 1. IDENTIFY HAZARDS

C-25. Environmental hazards include all activities that may pollute, create negative noise-related effects, degrade archeological/cultural resources, or negatively affect threatened or endangered species habitats. A listing of common environmental hazards is located in Table C-3.

Table C-3. Common Environmental Hazards

MEDIA AREA	COMMON ENVIRONMENTAL HAZARDS
Air	Equipment exhaust, convoy dust, range fires, open-air burning, pyrotechnics, smoke pots/grenades, part-washer emissions, paint emissions, air-conditioner or refrigeration CFCs, HM/HW release, pesticides, other toxic industrial chemicals or material.
Archeological and cultural	Maneuvering and digging in sensitive areas, disturbing or removing artifacts, demolition/munitions effects, HM/HW spills.
Noise	Low-flying aircraft (helicopters), demolition/munitions effects, nighttime operations, operations near post/camp boundaries and civilian populations, vehicle convoys/maneuvers, large-scale exercises.
Threatened and/or endangered species	Maneuvering in sensitive areas, demolition/munitions effects, especially during breeding seasons, disturbing habitat or individual species, HM/HW spills or releases, poor field sanitation, improper cutting of vegetation, damage to coral reefs,
Soil (terrain)	Over use of maneuver areas, demolition/munitions effects, range fires, poor field sanitation, poor maneuver-damage control, erosion, troop construction effect, refueling operations, HM/HW spills, maneuver in ecologically sensitive areas such as wetlands and tundra, industrial waste runoff, pesticide accumulation in soil, vegetation, and terrestrial organisms.
Water	Refueling operations near water sources, HM/HW spills, erosion and unchecked drainage, amphibious/water-crossing operations, troop construction effects, poor field sanitation, washing vehicles at unapproved sites.

STEP 2. ASSESS ENVIRONMENTAL HAZARDS TO DETERMINE RISK

C-26. A risk assessment is a tool used for evaluating the most pressing or most hazardous potential environmental damage. It considers two factors; probability, how often a hazard is likely to occur; and severity, the effect in degrees a hazard will have on personnel, equipment, environment, and mission. Unit leaders should conduct risk assessments before conducting any training, operations, or logistical activities that are not addressed in the TSOP, or when conditions differ significantly from the TSOP. Complete information on environmental risk assessments can be obtained from FM 20-400.

STEP 3. DEVELOP CONTROLS AND MAKE A DECISION

C-27. This step is designed to reduce the probability or severity of each hazard, which in turn lowers the overall risk. Control types fall in the categories of educational, physical, or avoidance. Table C-4 outlines examples of environmental controls.

Table C-4. Environmental-related Controls

CONTROL TYPE	ENVIRONMENTAL-RELATED EXAMPLES
Educational	• Conduct unit environmental-awareness training. • Conduct an environmental briefing before deployment. • Perform tasks to environmental standards. • Review environmental considerations in AARs. • Read unit's environmental TSOPs and policies.
Physical	• Provide spill-prevention equipment. • Establish field satellite-accumulation site and procedures. • Police field locations. • Practice good field sanitation. • Post signs and warnings for off-limit areas.
Avoidance	• Maneuver around historical/cultural sites. • Establish refueling and maintenance areas away from wetlands and drainage areas. • Cross streams at approved sites. • Prevent pollution. • Limit noise in endangered and threatened species habitats.

STEP 4. IMPLEMENT CONTROLS

C-28. Leaders must inform subordinates of risk-control measures, state how each control must be implemented, and assign responsibilities. They must also ensure these controls are in place prior to the operation. This is accomplished by using the *before, during,* and *after* checklists and the environmental risk-assessment process. Examples of checklists can be obtained from TC 5-400, *Unit Leaders' Handbook for Environmental Stewardship*, or from the Field Artillery environmental handbook referenced in Section I, in order to determine the environmental considerations that may effect battalion training and operations.

STEP 5. SUPERVISE AND EVALUATE

C-29. Leaders should monitor controls to ensure effectiveness and whether controls require modification. They should ensure the after action review process includes an evaluation of environmental-related hazards, controls, soldier performance, and leader supervision.

Glossary

ACRONYMS AND ABBREVIATIONS

1SG	first sergeant

A

AAG	army artillery group
AATF	air assault task force
ABCA	Australia, Britain, Canada, America
ABCS	Army Battle Command System
ABF	attack by fire
ACA	airspace coordination area
ACE	analysis and control element
ACP	air control point/assault command post
ACR	armored cavalry regiment
ACUS	Area Common-User System
AD	air defense
AD/LOG	Administration / Logistics
ADA	air defense artillery
ADAM	area denial artillery munition
ADAPT	adapter
ADDS	Army Data Distribution System
admin/log	administrative/logistics (net)
AFATDS	Advanced Field Artillery Tactical Data System
AG	adjutant general
AGM	attack guidance matrix
AH	attack helicopter
AIRCOR	air corridor
ALO	air liaison officer
ALOC	administration and logistic operations center
alt	altitude
AM	amplitude modulated
AMC	at my command

ammo	ammunition
AMDPCS	Air-Missile Defense Planning and Control System
ANCD	automated net control device
AO	area of operations
AOA	avenue of approach
AOF	azimuth of fire
AOI	area of interest
AOL	azimuth of lay
AP	antipersonnel
APAM	antipersonnel , antimaterial
APICM	antipersonnel improved conventional munitions
App	Appendix
AR	army regulation
ARPA	Archeological Resources Protection Act
ARTEP	Army Training and Evaluation Program
arty	artillery
ASAS	All-Source Analysis System
ASL	authorized stockage list
ASP	ammunition supply point
ASR	available supply rate
ATCCS	Army Tactical Command and Control System
atch	attached
ATHS	Airborne Target Hand-Over System
ATI	artillery target intelligence
ATIZ	artillery target intelligence zone
ATP	ammunition transfer point
AUTL	army universal task list
avn	aviation
AXO	assistant executive officer
AZ	azimuth

B

BAO	battalion ammunition officer
BAS	battalion aid station

BAT	"brilliant" anti-armor technology
BC	battery commander
BCS	battery computer system
BDA	battle damage assessment
BDAR	battlefield damage assessment and repair
Bde	brigade
BDO	battle dress overgarment
BER	bit error rate
BFACS	battlefield functional area control system
BM	battle management
BMA	battery minefield angle
BMO	battalion maintenance officer
BMT	battalion maintenance technician
BN	battalion
BOS	battlefield operating system
BP	battle position
BRAG	brigade artillery group
BSA	brigade support area
BSOC	battalion support operations center
btry	battery

C

C-E	communications-electronics
C2	command and control
C2V	command and control vehicle
C3	command, control and communications
C4I	command, control, communications, computers, and intelligence
CAA	combined arms army (threat)
CAR	combined arms rehearsal
CAS	close air support
cat	category
CATF	commander amphibious task force
Cav	cavalry
CBT	combat

CCIR	commander's critical information requirements
CCCP	chemical casualty collection point
CCL	combat-configured load
CCP	casualty collection point
CDR	commander
CDS	container delivery system
CEP	circular error probability
CERCLA	Comprehensive Environmental Response and Liability Act
CESO	communications-electronics staff officer
CF	command/fire direction (net)
CFC	chlorofluorocarbon
CFFZ	call-for-fire zone
CFL	coordinated fire line
CFR	Code of Federal Regulations
CFZ	critical friendly zone
cGy	centigray
Ch	chief
CHEMO	chemical officer
cmd	command (net)
CNR	combat net radio
CO	company
COA	course of action
COCOM	combatant command
COE	common operating environment
COLT	combat observation/lasing team
Commo	communications
COMSEC	communications security
CONOPS	continuity of operations
coord	coordinate
COP	common operational picture; command observation post
Corps Arty	corps artillery
COSCOM	corps support command
CP	command post
Cphd	Copperhead

CPREP	counter preparations
CPU	central processing unit
CROP	container roll-in/roll-out platform
CRP	combat reconnaissance patrol
CSA	corps storage area
CSB	common sensor boundary; corps support battalion
CSG	corps support group
CSM	command sergeant major
CSR	controlled supply rate
CSS	combat service support
CSSCS	Combat Service Support Control System
CWA	Clean Water Act
CZ	censor zones

D

D	data
DA	Department of Army
DAG	division artillery group
D3A	decide, detect, deliver, and assess
DAO	division ammunition officer
DF	direction finding
DISCOM	division support command
Div	division
DIVARTY	division artillery
DLA	Defense Logistics Agency
DMMC	division materiel management center
DNE	do not engage
DNL	do not load
DNVT	digital nonsecure voice telephone
DOD	Department of Defense
DODIC	Department of Defense Identification Code
DofS	days of supply
DOT	Department of Transportation
DP	dual purpose/decision point

DPICM	dual-purpose improved conventional munition
DRMO	defense reutilization marketing office
DS	direct support
DSA	division support area
DSB	division support battalion
DST	decision support template
DSVT	digital secure voice terminal
DTG	date-time group
DZ	drop zone

E

EA	engagement area
EAC	echelons above corps
EAD	enemy air defense
ECCM	electronic counter-countermeasures
ECO	environmental compliance officer
ECOA	enemy course of action
ED	emergency destruction
EEFI	essential elements of friendly information
EFAT	essential field artillery task
EFC	equivalent full charge
EFST	essential fire support task
ELINT	electronic intelligence
ENG	engineer
EOD	explosive ordnance disposal
EOL	end of the orienting line
EOM	end of mission
EPA	Environmental Protection Act
EPCRA	Emergency Planning and Community Right-to-know Act
EPE	estimated position error
EPLRS	Enhanced Position Location Reporting System
EPW	enemy prisoners of war
ESA	Endangered Species Act
EVENTEMP	event template

EW	electronic warfare
EXTAL	extra time allowance

F

F	full-time subscriber
FA	field artillery
FADAC	field artillery digital automatic computer
FAIO	field artillery intelligence officer
FASCAM	family of scatterable mines
FASM	field artillery support matrix
FASP	field artillery support plan
FATDS	field artillery tactical data systems
fax	facsimile
FBCB2	Force XXI Battle Command, Brigade and Below
FCE	fire control element
FCL	final coordination line
FCS	fire control system
FD	fire direction
FDC	fire direction center
FDO	fire direction officer
FDS	fire direction system
FEBA	forward edge of the battle area
FED	forward entry device
FFA	free-fire area
FFE	fire for effect
FFIR	friendly force information requirements
FIFRA	Federal Insecticide, Fungicide, And Rodenticide Act
FIST	fire support team
FIST-V	fire support team-vehicle
FLD	field
FLE	forward logistical element
FLOT	forward line of own troops
FM	field manual; frequency modulation
FO	forward observer

FOM	figure of merit
FOS	forward observer software
FPF	final protective fires
FRAGO	fragmentary order
FS	fire support
FSB	forward support battalion
FSCC	fire support coordination center
FSCL	fire support coordination line
FSCM	fire support coordinating measure
FSCOORD	fire support coordinator
FSE	fire support element
FSEM	fire support execution matrix
FSO	fire support officer
FSP	fire support plan
FST	fire support terminal
FU	fire unit
G	
GCCS-A	Global Command and Control System-Army
G-VLLD	ground/vehicle laser locator designator
GDU	gun display unit
GMET	graphical munitions effectiveness tables
GPS	Global Positioning System
GS	general support
GSM	ground station module
GSR	general support reinforcing
GTA	graphical training aid
GTD	guards tank division (threat)

H

HA	hide area
HARMM	**H**alt all movement. **A**void disturbing the mine(s). **R**eport the location of the mine(s). **M**ark the location. **M**ove out of the area.
HAZWOPER	hazardous waste operation
HC	smoke, hexachloroethane
HE	high explosive
HEMTT	heavy-expanded mobility tactical truck
HET	heavy equipment transporter
HF	high frequency
HHB	headquarters and headquarters battery
HHSB	headquarters, headquarters, and service battery
HI	high
HIMARS	High Mobility Artillery Rocket System
HM/HW	hazardous material / hazardous waste
HMMWV	high-mobility, multipurpose wheeled vehicle
HN	host nation
HOB	height of burst
HPT	high-payoff target
HPTL	high-payoff target list
HQ	headquarters
HTU	hand-held terminal unit
HUMINT	human intelligence
HVT	high-value target

I

IAW	in accordance with
ICE	individual chemical equipment
ICM	improved conventional munition
ICP	intelligence collection plan
ID	infantry division

ID (m)	infantry division (mechanized)
IEW	intelligence and electronic warfare
IFSAS	Initial Fire Support Automation System
ILLUM	illumination
Inf	infantry
Intel	intelligence
INTSUM	intelligence summary
IPB	intelligence preparation of the battlefield
IR	information requirements; infrared
IRAP	improved rocket-assisted projectile
ITV	intransit visibility

J

JAAT	joint air attack team
JMEM	joint munition effects manual
JP	joint publication
JSEAD	joint suppression of enemy air defense
JSTARS	Joint Surveillance and Target Attack Radar System
JTF	joint task force
JTIDS	Joint Tactical Information Distribution System
JTOC	jump tactical operations center

K

km	kilometer
kph	km per hour

L

LAN	local area network
LBE	load bearing equipment
LCU	lightweight computer unit
LD	line of departure
LDF	lightweight digital facsimile
LFC	landing force commander

LID	light infantry division
LNO	liaison officer
Lo	low
LOC	lines of communication
LOGPAC	logistics package
LP	listening post
LPB	logistics preparation of the battlefield
LRP	logistics release point
LRSU	long-range surveillance unit
LTACFIRE	Lightweight Tactical Fire Direction System
LTD	laser target designation
LZ	landing zone

M

M	medium
MAGTF	marine air ground task force
maint	maintenance
man	maneuver
max	maximum
MBA	main battle area
MCO	movement control officer
MCOO	modified combined obstacle overlay
MCS	Maneuver Control System
MDMP	military decision-making process
MDS	Meteorological Data System
met	meteorology
METT-TC	mission, enemy, terrain and weather, troops, time available, and civil considerations
MFR	mission fired report
MHE	material handling equipment
MI	military intelligence
MIBN	motorized infantry battalion
MIBR	motorized infantry brigade
MLRS	Multiple-Launch Rocket System

mm	millimeter
MMS	metrological measuring set
Mod	modification
MOPP	mission-oriented protective posture
MOS	military occupational specialty
MOUT	military operations in urban terrain
MP	military police
MRB	motorized rifle battalion
MRE	meal, ready to eat
MRL	multiple rocket launcher
MRR	motorized rifle regiment
MSB	main support battalion
MSD	minimum safe distance; medium screen display
MSDS	Material Safety Data Sheet
MSE	mobile subscriber equipment
msn	mission
MSR	main supply route
MSRT	mobile subscriber radio telephone
MST	maintenance support team
MSU	mutual support units
MTLR	moving-target-locating-radar
MTO	message to observer
MTOE	modified table of organization and equipment
MTP	mission training plan
MULE	modular universal laser equipment
mvr	maneuver

N

NA	not applicable
NAGPRA	Native American Graves Protection and Repatriation Act
NAI	named area of interest
NATO	North Atlantic Treaty Organization
NBC	nuclear, biological, and chemical
N/CH	nuclear/chemical

NCO	noncommissioned officer
NCOIC	noncommissioned officer in charge
NCS	net control station
NEPA	National Environmental Policy Act
NET	new equipment training
NFA	no fire area
NFL	no fire line
NG	National Guard
NGF	naval gunfire
NGLO	naval gunfire liaison officer
NHPA	national historic preservation act
NLT	not-later-than
NPDES	National Pollutant Discharge Elimination System
NSFS	naval surface fire support

O

O&I	operations and intelligence
o/o	on order
OB/OD	open burning / open detonation
OB	order of battle
OEBGO	Overseas Environmental Baseline Guidance Document
OEG	operation exposure guidance
OH	observation helicopter
OIC	officer in charge
OP	observation post
OPAREA	operations area
OPCOM	operational command
OPCON	operational control
OPFAC	operational facility
OPFOR	opposing forces
OPLAN	operation plan
OPORD	operation order
Ops	operations
OPSEC	operations security

ops/F	operations/fire (net)	
ops/intel	operations/intelligence (net)	
Org	organization	
OS	orienting station	
OT	observer target	
OTG	observer-target-gun	

P

P&A	personnel and administration
PA	physician's assistant; position areas
PAC	personnel and administration center
PADS	Position And Azimuth Determining System
PCC	pre-combat checks
PCI	pre-combat inspections
PD	point detonating
PEO	peace enforcement operations
PERINTREP	periodic intelligence reports
PI	probability of incapacitation
PIR	priority intelligence requirements
PKO	peacekeeping operations
PL	phase line
PLGR	precision lightweight GPS receiver
PLL	prescribed load list
PLS	Palletized Load System
PLT	platoon
PMCS	preventive maintenance checks and services
POC	platoon operations center
POD	port of debarkation
POF	priority of fires
POL	petroleum, oils, and lubricants
POR	preparation of replacements
POS	priority of survey
PREP	preparations
PRF	pulse repetition frequency

PRI	priority
PRI TGT	priority targets
PSNCO	personnel staff noncommissioned officer
PST	pass time
PTMO	prepare to march order
PX	post exchange
PZ	pickup zones

Q

QSTAG	Quadripartite Standardization Agreement

R

R	reinforcing
R&S	reconnaissance and surveillance
R3P	rearm, refuel, resupply point
R3SP	rearm, refuel, resupply, survey point
RAAMS	Remote Antiarmor Mine System
RAG	regimental artillery group
RAP	rocket-assisted projectile
RAU	radio access unit
RCRA	Resource Conservation Recovery Act
RCT	road clearance time
RDF	radio direction finding
RDO	radar deployment order
REC	radio-electronic combat
Recon	reconnaissance
ref	reference
Regt	regiment
retrans	retransmission
RF	radio frequency
RFA	restrictive fire area
RFAF	request for additional fires
RFI	request for information
RFL	restrictive fire line

ROE	rules of engagement
ROM	rate of march; refuel on the move
ROZ	restricted operating zones
RP	release point
RPV	remotely piloted vehicles
RRP	replacement receiving point
RSOP	reconnaissance, selection, and occupation of position
RSR	required supply rate
RSTA	reconnaissance, surveillance, and target acquisition
RT	receiver transmitter

S

S&S	stability and support
S&T	supply and transportation
SACC	supporting arms coordination center
SARA	Superfund Amendment Reauthorization Act
SB	service battery
SCATMINE	scatterable mines
SCP	survey control point
SD	self-destruct
SEAD	suppression of enemy air defenses
SEN	small extension node
SFC	sergeant first class
SGT	sergeant
SHELREP	shelling report
SIGINT	signal intelligence
SIGSEC	signals security
SIMO	simultaneous observation
SINCGARS	single-channel ground and airborne radio system
SITEMP	situation template
SITREP	situation report
SMK	smoke
SOI	signal operating instructions
SOP	standard operating procedure

SOSR	suppress, obscure, secure, reduce
SP	self-propelled; start point; strong points
SPC	specialist (rank)
SPCE	survey, planning, and control elements
SPL	support platoon leader
SPLL	self-propelled launcher-loader
spt	support
Sqn	squadron
SR	self-registering
SSB	single sideband
SSG	staff sergeant
STANAG	Standardization Agreement
STON	short-ton
survl	surveillance
SVC	service
Sys	system

T

T	towed
TA	target acquisition
TAB	target acquisition battery
TAC	tactical action center
TACAIR	tactical air
TACFIRE	Tactical Fire Direction System
TACON	tactical control
TACSAT	tactical satellite
TAI	targeted area of interest
TAIS	Tactical Airspace Information System
TAMMS	The Army Maintenance Management System
TAV	total asset visibility
TBD	to-be-determined
TBM	theater ballistic missiles
TBP	to be published
TC	traffic control; training circular

TCIM	tactical communications interface module
TCF	tactical combat force
TD	tank division
TDA	target damage assessment; table of distribution and allowances
TDIS	time distance
TDMA	time division multiple access
TF	task force
TFC	tactical fire control
Tgt	target
TLE	target location error
TM	technical manual
TMD	theater missile defense
TMT	total march time
TOC	tactical operations center
TOE	table of organization and equipment
TOT	time-on-target
TOW	tube-launched, optically tracked wire-guided missile
TPL	time phase line
TRADOC	Training and Doctrine Command
TRI-TAC	Tri-Services Tactical
TSA	theater storage area
TSDF	treatment storage and disposal facilities
TSM	target selection matrix
TSOP	tactical standing operating procedures
TSS	target selection standards
TTP	tactics, techniques and procedures
TVA	target value analysis

U

UAV	unmanned aerial vehicle
UBL	unit basic load
UHF	ultrahigh frequency
UK	United Kingdom
UMCP	unit maintenance collection point

UMT	unit ministry team
UNAAF	Unified Action Armed Forces
US	United States
USAF	United States Air Force
USAFAS	US Army Field Artillery School
USMC	United States Marine Corps
UTM	universal transverse mercator

V

V	voice (net)
VE	velocity error
VEH	vehicle
VFMED	variable format message entry device
VHF	very high frequency
VT	variable time

W

W	wire connection
WAN	wide area network
WARNO	warning order
WGS-84	World Geodetic System 84 (a map datum)
WLR	weapons locating radar
WP	white phosphorous
WSM	weapon system manager
WSRO	weapon system replacement operations

X

X	subscriber
XO	executive officer

Bibliography

AR 200-1. *Environmental Protection and Enhancement.* 21 February 1997.

AR 200-2. *Environmental Effects of Army Actions.* 23 December 1988.

AR 200-3. *Natural Resources-Land, Forest and Wildlife Management.* 28 February 1995

AR 200-4. *Cultural Resources Management.* 1 October 1998.

AR 310-25. *Dictionary of United States Army Terms.* 15 October 1983.

AR 310-50. *Authorized Abbreviations, Brevity Codes, and Acronyms.* 15 November 1985.

ARTEP 6-115-MTP. *Mission Training Plan for Field Artillery Cannon Battalion Command and Staff Section, Headquarters and Headquarters Battery, and Service Battery.* 1 April 2000.

ARTEP 6-037-30-MTP. *Mission Training Plan for the Consolidated Cannon Battery, M102, M119, M198, M109A5, M109A6.* 1 April 2000.

ARTEP 6-303-30-MTP. *Mission Training Plan for the Target Acquisition Battery and the Corps Target Acquisition Detachment.* 1 April 2000.

ARTEP 6-395-MTP. *Mission Training Plan for the Field Artillery Multiple Launch Rocket System Battalion. Command and Staff Section and Headquarters and Service Battery.* 1 April 2000.

ARTEP 6-397-30-MTP. *Mission Training Plan for the Multiple Launch Rocket System Battery.* 15 September 1997.

DA Form 581. *Request for Issue and Turn-in of Ammunition.* July 1999.

DA Form 1594. *Daily Staff Journal or Duty Officer's Log.* November 1962.

DA Form 2028. *Recommended Changes to Publications and Blank Forms.* 1 February 1974.

DA Form 2185R. *Artillery Counterfire Information.**

DA Form 2406. *Materiel Condition Status Report.* April 1993.

DA Form 4655-R. *Target List Work Sheet.* January 1983.

DA Form 4656-R. *Scheduling Work Sheet.* January 1983.

DA Form 4695. *Target Card.**

DA Form 5032-R. *Field Artillery Delivered Minefield Planning Sheet.* January 1982.

DA Form 5368-R. *Quick Fire Plan.* December 1984.

FM 3-09.70 (6-70). *Tactics, Techniques, and Procedures for M109A6 Howitzer (Paladin) Operations*. 1 August 2000.

FM 3-3. *Chemical and Biological Contamination Avoidance*. 16 November 1992.

FM 3-3-1. *Nuclear Contamination Avoidance*. 9 September 1994.

FM 3-50. *Smoke Operations*. 4 December 1990.

FM 3-100. *Chemical Operations Principles and Fundamentals*. 8 May 1996.

FM 5-103. *Survivability*. 10 June 1985.

FM 6-2. *Tactics, Techniques, and Procedures for Field Artillery Survey*. 23 September 1993. Change 1. 16 October 1996.

FM 6-15. *Tactics, Techniques, and Procedures for Field Artillery Meteorology*. August 1997.

FM 6-20. *Fire Support in the Airland Battle*. 17 May 1988.

FM 6-20-2. *Tactics, Techniques, and Procedures for Corps Artillery, Division Artillery, and Field Artillery Brigade Operations*. 7 January 1993.

FM 6-20-2. *Tactics, Techniques, and Procedures for Corps Artillery, Division Artillery, and Field Artillery Brigade Operations* (Approved Final Draft). 7 September 2000.*

FM 6-20-10. *Tactics, Techniques, and Procedures for The Targeting Process*. 8 May 1996.

FM 6-20-30. *Tactics, Techniques, and Procedures for Fire Support for Corps and Division Operations*. 18 October 1989.

FM 6-20-30. *Tactics, Techniques, and Procedures for Fire Support for Division Operations* (DRAG Draft). 5 November 1999.*

FM 6-20-40. *Tactics, Techniques, and Procedures for Fire Support for Brigade Operations* (Heavy). 5 January 1990.

FM 6-20-40. *Tactics, Techniques, and Procedures for Fire Support for Brigade Operations* (Initial Draft). 15 June 1999.

FM 6-20-50. *Tactics, Techniques, and Procedures for Fire Support for Brigade Operations* (Light). 5 January 1990.

FM 6-30. *Tactics, Techniques, and Procedures for Observed Fire*. 16 July 1991.

FM 6-40. *Tactics, Techniques, and Procedures for Field Artillery Manual Gunnery*. 23 April 1996.

FM 6-50. *Tactics, Techniques, and Procedures for the Field Artillery Cannon Battery*. 23 December 1996.

FM 6-60. *Tactics, Techniques, and Procedures for Multiple Launch Rocket System (MLRS) Operations*. 23 April 1996.

FM 6-71. *Tactics, Techniques, and Procedures for Fire Support for the Combined Arms Commander*. 29 September 1994.

FM 6-121. *Tactics, Techniques, and Procedures for Field Artillery Target Acquisition*. 25 September 1990.

FM 6-121. *Tactics, Techniques, and Procedures for Field Artillery Target Acquisition* (Final Draft).*

FM 7-20. *The Infantry Battalion.* 6 April 1992.

FM 7-30. *The Infantry Brigade.* 3 October 1995.

FM 9-6. *Munitions Support in Theater of Operations.* 20 March 1998.

FM 9-38. *Conventional Ammunition Unit Operations.* 2 July 1993.

FM 11-30. *MSE Communications in the Corps/Division.* 27 February 1991.

FM 11-50. *Combat Communications within the Division (Heavy and Light).* 4 April 1991.

FM 19-25. *Military Police Traffic Operations.* 30 September 1977.

FM 19-40. *Enemy Prisoners of War, Civilian Internees, and Detained Persons.* 27 February 1976.

FM 20-3. *Camouflage, Concealment, and Decoys.* 30 August 1999.

FM 21-10. *Field Hygiene and Sanitation.* 21 June 2000.

FM 21-10-1. *Unit Field Sanitation Team.* 11 October 1989.

FM 21-26. *Map Reading and Land Navigation.* 7 May 1993.

FM 21-60. *Visual Signals.* 30 September 1987.

FM 24-7. *Tactical Local Area Network (LAN) Management.* 8 October 1999.

FM 24-18. *Tactical Single-Channel Radio Communications Techniques.* 30 September 1987.

FM 25-5. *Training for Mobilization and War.* 25 January 1985.

FM 27-10. *The Law of Land Warfare.* 18 July 1956.

FM 31-70. *Basic Cold Weather Manual.* 12 April 1968.

FM 31-71. *Northern Operations.* 21 June 1971.

FM 34-8. *Combat Commander's Handbook on Intelligence.* 28 September 1992.

FM 34-8-2. *Intelligence Officer's Handbook.* 1 May 1998.

FM 34-80. *Brigade and Battalion Intelligence and Electronic Warfare Operations.* 15 April 1986.

FM 34-130. *Intelligence Preparation of the Battlefield.* 8 July 1994.

FM 55-9. *Unit Air Movement Planning.* 5 April 1993.

FM 55-10. *Movement Control.* 9 February 1999.

FM 55-15. *Transportation Reference Data.* 27 October 1997.

FM 55-30. *Army Motor Transport Units and Operations.* 27 June 1997. Change 1. 15 September 1999.

FM 63-2. *Division Support Command, Armored, Infantry, and Mechanized Infantry Division.* 20 May 1991.

FM 63-2-1. *Division Support Command, Light Infantry, Airborne, and Air Assault Division.* 16 November 1992.

FM 63-2-2. *Tactics, Techniques, and Procedures for the Division Support Command (Digitized), (Final Draft).* 30 November 1999.

FM 63-21. *Main Support Battalion.* 7 August 1990.

FM 71-2. *The Tank and Mechanized Infantry Battalion Task Force.* 27 September 1988.

FM 71-3. *The Armored and Mechanized Infantry Brigade.* 8 January 1996.

FM 71-100. *Division Operations.* 28 August 1996.

FM 71-123. *Tactics and Techniques For Combined Arms Heavy Forces: Armored Brigade, Battalion Task Force, and Company Team.* 30 September 1992.

FM 90-3. *Desert Operations.* 24 August 1993.

FM 90-4. *Air Assault Operations.* 16 March 1987.

FM 90-5. *Jungle Operations.* 16 August 1982.

FM 90-8. *Counterguerrilla Operations.* 29 August 1986.

FM 90-10. *Military Operations on Urbanized Terrain (MOUT).* 15 August 1979.

FM 90-13. *River Crossing Operations.* 26 January 1998.

FM 90-13-1. *Combined Arms Breaching Operations.* 28 February 1991.

FM 90-26. *Airborne Operations.* 18 December 1990.

FM 100-5. *Operations.* 14 June 1993.

FM 100-9. *Reconstitution.* 13 January 1992.

FM 100-10. *Combat Service Support.* 3 October 1995.

FM 100-15. *Corps Operations.* 29 October 1996.

FM 100-17. *Mobilization, Deployment, Redeployment, Demobilization.* 28 October 1992.

FM 100-17-1. *Army Pre-Positioned Afloat Operations.* 27 July 1996.

FM 100-17-2. *Army Pre-Positioned Land.* 16 February 1999.

FM 100-17-3. *Reception, Staging, Onward Movement, and Integration.* 17 March 1999.

FM 100-20. *Military Operations in Low Intensity Conflict.* 5 December 1990.

FM 100-63. *Infantry-Based Opposing Force Organization Guide.* 18 April 1996.

FM 101-5. *Staff Organizations and Operations.* 31 May 1997.

FM 101-5-1. *Operational Terms and Symbols.* 31 September 1997.

FM 101-5-2. *U.S. Army Report and Message Formats.* 29 June 1999.

FM 700-80. *Logistics.* 15 August 1985.

FM 701-58. *Planning Logistics Support for Military Operations.* 27 May 1987.

JP 0-2. *Unified Action Armed Forces (UNAAF)*. 24 November 1995.

JP 1-02. *DOD Dictionary of Military and Associated Terms*. 10 January 2000.

JP 3-0. *Doctrine for Joint Operations*. 1 February 1995.

JP 3-02. *Joint Doctrine for Amphibious Operations*. 8 October 1992.

ST 6-1-2. *Lightweight Computer Unit (LCU) for Light Tactical Fire Direction System (LTACFIRE) and Initial Fire Support Automation System (IFSAS)*. 28 June 1996.*

ST 6-3++. *Tactics, Techniques, Procedures for the Advanced Field Artillery Data System (AFATDS) in Division XXI*. 15 July 1997.*

ST 6-60-30. *Tactics, Techniques, Procedures for The Army Tactical Missile System (Army TACMS) Family of Munitions (AFOM)*. 5 January 1998.*

ST 9-38-3. *Combat-Configured Loads*. 1 December 1992.

STANAG 2014/QSTAG 243/QSTAG 506. *Operation Orders, Warning Orders, and Administrative/Logistics Orders*. 26 May 1998/27 June 1978/ 7 August 1984.

STANAG 2031/QSTAG 515. *Proforma for Artillery Fire Plan*. 26 June 1985/ 5 October 1984.

STANAG 2041/QSTAG 520. *Operation Orders, Tables and Graphs for Road Movement*.

STANAG 2082. *Relief of Combat Troops*. 24 July 1991.

STANAG 2083. *Commanders' Guide on Nuclear Radiation Exposure of Groups*. 24 June 1994.

STANAG 2099/QSTAG 531. *Fire Coordination in Support of Land Forces*. 4 November 1987/ September 1989.

STANAG 2103/QSTAG 187. *Reporting Nuclear Detonations, Biological, and Chemical Attacks, and Predicting and Warning of Associated Hazards and Hazard Areas*. 7 September 1995/21 May 1998.

STANAG 2104/QSTAG 189. *Friendly Nuclear Strike Warning*. 28 June 1995/August 1991.

STANAG 2128/QSTAG 435. *Medical and Dental Supply Procedures*. 21 November 1991/20 June 1984.

STANAG 2129/QSTAG 538. *Identification of Land Forces on the Battlefield*. 16 May 1989/15 January 1981.

STANAG 2147/QSTAG 221. *Target Numbering System*. 3 March 1987/ 15 June 1987.

STANAG 2154/QSTAG 539. *Regulations for Military Motor Vehicle Movement by Road*.

STANAG 2887/QSTAG 217. *Tactical Tasks and Responsibilities for Control of Artillery.* 15 October 1985/8 December 1981.

STANAG 2934. *Artillery Procedures.* 3 July 1996.

TB 44-46-1. *Standard Characteristics for Transportation of Military Vehicles and Other Oversize/Overweight Equipment.*

TB 55-46-1. *Standard Characteristics (Dimensions, Weight, and Cube) for Transportability of Military Vehicles and Other Outsize/Overweight Equipment.* 1 January 1998.

TM 43-0001-28. *Army Ammunition Data Sheet for Artillery Munitions: Guns, Howitzers, Mortars, Recoilless Rifles, Grenade Launchers and Artillery Fuzes.* 28 April 1994.

TRADOC PAM 350-12. *Heavy Opposing Forces (OPFOR) Organization Guide.* 15 September 1994.

TRADOC PAM 350-13. *Light Opposing Forces (OPFOR) Organization Guide.* 15 September 1994.

TRADOC PAM 350-14. *Heavy Opposing Forces (OPFOR) Operational Art Handbook.* 15 September 1994.

TRADOC PAM 350-15. *Light Opposing Forces (OPFOR) Operational Art Handbook.* 15 September 1994.

TRADOC PAM 350-16. *Heavy Opposing Forces (OPFOR) Tactical Handbook.* 15 September 1994.

XST 6-20-30. *Tactics, Techniques, Procedures for Fire Support for Digitized Division Operations.* 31 March 1999.*

XST 6-60. *Experimental Forces (EXFOR) Special Text Division Multiple Launch Rocket System (MLRS) Battalion Operations.* 29 March 1999.*

*The special texts and draft publications are not available through the US Army Adjutant General Publication Center. They can be accessed via the Internet on the Field Artillery Training Command home page:
(http://155.219.39.98/doctrine/wddfrm.htm)

Index

A

abbreviations and acronyms, Glossary
administration and logistics operations center, 2-1, 7-10
administration-logistics tab, A-8
Advanced Field Artillery Tactical Data System, 3-9
air assault operations, FA considerations, 8-25
airborne operations, FA considerations, 8-26
ammunition, 7-22
ammunition officer, 1-19
ammunition resupply, 7-26
ammunition section, 7-3
ammunition supply point, 7-23, 7-26
ammunition transfer point, 7-23, 7-26
amphibious operations, FA considerations, 8-23
antennas, 3-8
approach march, 8-10
Area Common-User System, 3-2
area defense, 8-20
area security operations, 8-35
Army Battle Command Systems, 3-9
Army Data Distribution System, 3-3
artillery intelligence tab, A-8
artillery missions, 1-3
artillery raid, 8-38
artillery target intelligence zone, 5-30
assembly areas, 6-6
assigned, 1-2
assistant S3, 1-16
attached, 1-2
attack guidance matrix, 4-24
attacks, 8-10
automation considerations, 2-14, 3-10, 5-6
automation tab, A-8

B

basic load, 7-22
battalion combat service support, 7-4
battalion commander, 1-9
battalion ammunition officer, 1-19
battalion combat service support, 7-4
battalion command element, 2-2
battalion fire direction center, 1-18, 2-7
battalion intelligence section, 1-17, 2-6
battalion logistics estimate, 7-15
battalion maintenance officer, 1-16
battalion master gunner, 1-16
battalion operations section, 1-16, 2-5
battalion support operations center, 2-1, 7-10
battalion trains, 7-6
battle damage assessment, B-6
battle position, defense of, 8-22
battery combat service support, 7-3
breaching operations, 8-38
brigade support area, 7-4

C

call-for-fire zone, 5-30
casualty reporting, 7-35, 7-38
censor zone, 5-30
chaplain, 1-15, 7-36
chemical officer, 1-17
classes of supply, 7-2, 7-20 through 7-30
climate, FA considerations, 8-48
cold weather operations, FA considerations, 8-50
combat-configured load, 7-23
combat formations, 6-16
combat net radios, 3-12
combat service support, 7-1
    organization, 7-1
    planning, 7-14
    responsibilities, 7-2
combat trains, 7-7
combined arms movement, 6-15
combined operations, 1-3, 1-7
command and control, 3-1
    systems, 3-9 through 3-11
command post,
    movement, 2-19, 2-21
    operations, 2-1
    positions, 2-19
command relationships, 1-2
command section, 1-9
command sergeant major, 1-10
commander, battalion, 1-9
commander's critical information requirements, 4-9
commander's intent, 4-11
common sensor boundary, 5-30
communications, 3-1
    nets, 3-13
    planning, 3-6
    responsibilities, 3-4 through 3-6
continuity of operations, 5-8
controlled supply rate, 7-22
copperhead, 5-20
construction materials, 7-22
counterfire, 5-24
counterfire drill, 5-33
counterpreparation, B-12, B-21

course of action,
    analysis, 4-16, 4-23
    approval, 4-18, 4-23
    comparison, 4-18
    development, 4-13, 4-22
covering force operations,
    FA considerations, 8-34
crater rays, B-4
critical friendly zone, 5-30

D

danger close, 5-22
decision support template, 4-16
dedicated battery, 1-6
defense,
    field artillery tasks, 8-16
deliberate attack, 8-12
deliver fires, 5-1
deployment, 6-29
desert operations,
    FA considerations, 8-52
direct support mission, 1-4
    nets, 3-16, 3-20
displacement, 6-18
dual trains, 7-7

E

electronic counter-countermeasures, 3-7
encircled forces,
    FA considerations, 8-31
envelopment, 8-6
environmental compliance officer, C-10
environmental considerations, C-1
environmental risk management, C-11
essential elements of friendly information, 4-9
essential field artillery task, 4-5, 4-17
essential fire support task, 4-5
executive officer, 1-10, 2-2, 4-10
exploitation,
    FA considerations, 8-12

F

field artillery,
    operations, 8-1
    organization for combat, 1-1
    support matrix, A-9, A-23
    support plan, 4-18, 4-20, A-1, A-12
    tactical data systems (FATDS), 3-9
    tactical missions, 1-3 through 1-8
    tasks, 1-1
field services, 7-33
field trains, 7-8
final protective fires, B-17
finance services, 7-36
fire direction,
    tactical, 5-4
    technical, 5-7
fire direction center, 1-18, 2-7
fire direction officer, 1-18
fire direction system, 3-10
fire mission processing, 5-1
fire missions, 5-1
fire planning,
    manual, Appendix B
    MLRS, B-18
fire support coordinator, 1-9
fire support element, 1-19
fire support officer, 1-19
fire support plan, 4-18, 4-19
flash rays, B-6
friendly forces information requirements, 4-9
frontal attack, 8-9

G

general support mission, 1-5
    nets, 3-19, 3-24
general support reinforcing mission, 1-5
    nets, 3-18, 3-23
groups, B-13, B-21
guard operations, 8-35

H

hasty attack,
    FA considerations, 8-11
hazardous material/waste, C-3
headquarters, headquarters, and service battery commander, 2-3
health services, 7-37
heavy-light forces mix, CSS, 7-16
high-payoff target list, 4-24

I

illumination, 5-11, B-16
improved conventional munitions, 5-10
infiltration, 8-9
information management, 2-12
information requirements, 4-9
inherent responsibilities of FA tactical missions, 1-4, 1-8
Initial Fire Support Automation System, 3-10
intelligence preparation of the battlefield, 4-6, 4-25 through 4-31
intelligence section, 1-17, 2-6
intelligence sergeant, 1-18

J

joint consideration, 1-3
jump TOC, 2-1, 2-20
jungle operations,
    FA considerations, 8-54

L

laundry operations, 7-34
legal services, 7-36
liaison,
    officer, 1-19
    officer checklist, 2-26
    operations, 2-23
lightweight TACFIRE, 3-10
linkup operations,
    FA considerations, 8-37
logistical support, 7-18
logistics package, 7-18

logistics,
    estimate, 7-15
    preparation of the battlefield, 7-14
linkup, FA considerations, 8-37

M

main battle area, 8-17
maintenance, 7-31
maintenance officer, 1-16
maintenance section, 7-3
maneuver, forms of, 8-6
manual fire scheduling, B-8
massed fires, 5-8
master gunner, 1-16
material safety data sheet, C-4
medical section, 7-2
medical services, 7-37
medical supplies, 7-30, 7-39
meeting engagement, 8-10
messenger systems, 3-4
meteorology, 5-39
military decision-making process, 4-1, 4-22
military operations in urban terrain,
    FA considerations, 6-9, 8-28
mission analysis, 4-3, 4-22
    briefing, 4-10
MLRS fire planning, B-18
mobile defense, 8-20
mobile subscriber equipment, 3-2
modified combined obstacle overlay, 4-26
mortuary affairs, 7-33
mountain operations,
    FA considerations, 8-56
movement, 6-12
    considerations, 6-17
    control measures, 6-19
    coordination, 6-3
    planning, 6-22
movement to contact, 8-9
    FA considerations, 8-9
mutual support unit, 2-22

multiplexers, 3-8

N

NATO considerations, 1-3, 1-7
NBC-contaminated casualties, 7-39
nets (radio), 3-13
net titles, 3-14
night operations,
    FA considerations, 8-48
nonstandard field artillery tactical missions, 1-5

O

occupation, built-up areas, 6-9
offense,
    field artillery tasks, 8-4
on-order missions, 1-6
operational control, 1-2
operations NCO, 1-16
operations section, 2-5
orders production, 4-23
organic, 1-2
organization for combat, 1-1

P

passage of lines,
    FA considerations, 8-32
penetration, 8-8
personnel and administrative services, 7-35
petroleum, oils, and lubricants, 7-21
position,
    area, 6-2
    coordination, 6-2
    occupation, 6-9
    reconnaissance, 6-10
    selection, 6-5
    types, 6-5
positioning, 6-5
positioning overlay, A-24
postal services, 7-36
preparation, B-9, B-22
priority information requirements, 4-9
prisoners of war, 7-39

programs, B-14, B-21
pursuit,
    FA considerations, 8-13

Q

quickfire channels, 5-5

R

Radar,
    cueing, 5-31
    management, 5-28
    movement, 5-30
    positioning, 5-29
    section leader, 1-21
    zone management, 5-29
radar deployment order, A-28
radio, 3-1, 3-12 through 3-23
rations, 7-21
rear area operations,
    FA support, 8-35
rearm, refuel, resupply point, 7-18, 7-20
reconnaissance, 6-10
    plan, 4-9
reconstitution, 7-41
regeneration, 7-41
rehearsals, 4-32
    FA battalion, 4-36
reinforcing mission, 1-5
    nets, 3-17, 3-22
relief in place,
    FA tasks, 8-32
remoted transmitters, 3-7
reorganization, 7-41
repair parts, 7-30
replacement operations, 7-35
required supply rate, 7-24
reserves, 8-14
responsibilities, of personnel, 1-9
restated mission, 4-10
retransmission, 3-8
retrograde,
    FA considerations, 8-21
risk assessment, 4-9

river-crossing operations,
 FA considerations, 8-33
road march, 6-12

S

S1, 1-11, 4-10
 functions, 7-35
 section, 7-2
S2, 1-12, 4-10
S3, 1-13, 4-10
S4, 1-14, 4-10
 section, 7-3
S6, 1-14, 3-5, 4-10
scatterable mines, 5-17, B-18
scheduling fires, 4-18
 manual, B-8
scheduling worksheet, B-24
search and attack, 8-9
sector, defend in, 8-22
security area, 8-16
security operations, 8-34
series, B-15, B-21
screen operations,
 FA support, 8-35
single-channel ground and
 airborne radio system, 3-12
smoke, 5-12, B-16
stability operations, 8-42
strength accounting, 7-35
strongpoint, defend a, 8-22
supply,
 classes of, 7-20 through 7-30
 methods of, 7-18 through 7-20
supply point distribution, 7-18
support operations, 8-45
suppression of enemy air
 defenses, 5-36
survey, 2-4, 6-26 through 6-28,
 plan, A-8, A-30
sustainment area, 8-17

T

tactical action center, 2-1
tactical fire direction, 5-4

tactical information,
 management, 2-12 through
 2-18
tactical operations center, 2-1, 2-2
 configurations, 2-9
 equipment, 2-11
 information management, 2-12
 jump, 2-1, 2-20
 organization, 2-5 through 2-8
target acquisition tab, A-8, A-25
target card, B-2
target information, B-1
targeting officer, 1-17
target selection standards, 4-24
tasks of the field artillery, 1-1
technical fire direction, 5-7
terrain, FA considerations, 8-48
terrain management, 6-1
theater missile defense, 5-34
trains,
 battalion, 7-6
 combat, 7-7
 command and control, 7-10
 communications, 7-11
 displacement, 7-13
 dual, 7-7
 field, 7-8
 operations, 7-13
 organization, 7-8
 positioning, 7-12
 security, 7-9
 unit, 7-6
turning movement, 8-7

U

unit distribution (supply), 7-18
unit maintenance collection point,
 7-8
unit trains, 7-6
untrained observers, 5-4

W

wargame, 4-16
wargaming, counterfire, 5-31
warning order, 4-12

weapon system replacement
 operations, 7-41
white phosphorous, 5-12

FM 3-09.21 (FM 6-20-1)
22 MARCH 2001

By Order of the Secretary of the Army:

ERIC K. SHINSEKI
General, United States Army
Chief of Staff

Official:

JOEL B. HUDSON
Administrative Assistant to the
Secretary of the Army
0116202

DISTRIBUTION:

Active Army, Army National Guard, and U. S. Army Reserve: To be distributed in accordance with the initial distribution number 114392, requirements for FM 3-09.21.

www.ingramcontent.com/pod-product-compliance
Lightning Source LLC
Chambersburg PA
CBHW080241290526
45790CB00005B/1664